Praise for *Passing Strange*

"*Passing Strange* tells an astounding true story that would beggar most novelists' imaginations. It exposes the bizarre secret life of a well-known historical figure, but that secret is its least sensational aspect. The secret was hidden in plain sight until Martha A. Sandweiss, the deductive historian who pieced together this narrative, happened to notice it. Her great accomplishment is to have explored not only how the nineteenth-century explorer and scientist Clarence King reinvented himself but also why that reinvention was so singularly American. Best of all are Ms. Sandweiss's insights into what King's deception and its consequences really mean. . . . Ms. Sandweiss offers a fine, mesmerizing account of how one extremely secretive man, 'acting from a complicated mix of loyalty and self-interest, reckless desire and social conservatism,' could encapsulate his country's shifting ideas about race in the course of one family's anything but black-and-white history." —Janet Maslin, *The New York Times*

"Martha A. Sandweiss explores [King's secret life] with great sensitivity, insight and painstaking research. . . . An immensely fascinating work."
 —Annette Gordon-Reed, *The Washington Post*

"A staggeringly researched, absorbing, and page-turning account of a stunning deception carried out by a complex man." —*The Ottawa Citizen*

"Sandweiss serves a delicious brew of public accomplishment and domestic intrigue in this dual biography of the geologist-explorer Clarence King (1842–1901) and Ada Copeland (c. 1861–1964). . . . A remarkable feat of research and reporting that covers the long century from Civil War to Civil Rights, *Passing Strange* tells a uniquely American story of self- invention, love, deception and race." —*Publishers Weekly* (starred review)

"*Passing Strange* is one of those books with precisely the right title. It is indeed a story about passing, in every sense of the term, and historian Martha Sandweiss tells it with a scholar's rigor and a storyteller's verve. . . . *Passing Strange* is not only a lesson in the intricacies of class, race, and gender relations. It also demonstrates how to write a particular kind of history—how, that is, to reconstruct lives in the absence of historical records." —*Columbia Journalism Review*

"Remarkable . . . The fact that King/Todd did all of this long before there was any hint of radical change coming in America makes what he did even more astonishing and Sandweiss's work in uncovering it more noteworthy."
 —*BookPage*

"An intriguing look at long-held secrets, Jim Crow, bad faith—and also, as Sandweiss observes, love and longing that transcends the historical bounds of time and place." —*Kirkus Reviews*

"Balancing scholarly exploration with readability . . . Sandweiss demonstrates just how racial identity and inequality circumscribes behavior, adding both general background and individual perspectives on the conundrum of race in America. Her literary references add to a historical narrative that should catch the attention of both specialists and the reading public. A welcome choice for both academic and public libraries."   —*Library Journal*

"Sandweiss relies on letters, newspaper accounts, and interviews to chronicle the extraordinary story of an influential blue-eyed white man who passed for black at a time when passing generally went the other way. An engaging portrait of a man who defied social conventions but could not face up to the potential ruin of an interracial marriage."   —*Booklist*

"Although *Passing Strange* reads like a suspenseful novel, it introduces us to a real American hero who lived a fascinating life on both sides of the color line. Sandweiss gives us a great lesson in American history that spans three generations."   —Lawrence Otis Graham, author of *Our Kind of People*

"*Passing Strange* combines remarkable detective work, riveting storytelling, and the enduring question of race to fashion a most unusual but very American family saga about a famous white man and a heretofore unknown black woman. This book is a stunning achievement and example of just how deeply race is woven into our history, our imaginations, and our lives. Ada Copeland, who became a Todd and then a King, rescued from obscurity by a talented historian, steals the show."   —David W. Blight, Class of 1954 Professor of American History, Yale University, and author of *A Slave No More*

"*Passing Strange* is a masterful work of scholarship and a deeply moving human story well told. Here is a riveting new narrative about a hidden history of American race relations, one filled with love, deception, and utmost tragedy on both sides of the color line."
          —Neil Henry, dean, Graduate School of Journalism, University of California at Berkeley, and author of *Pearl's Secret*

"*Passing Strange* is an irresistible story of love and deception beautifully told. But it is also a major contribution to our understanding of race, class, and gender. This biography of a secret interracial marriage also tells more about the social experience of big-city life—New York in this case—than a shelf full of urban histories."   —Thomas Bender, University Professor of the Humanities, New York University, and author of *The Unfinished City*

"This is a wonderfully intelligent and haunting book about love and race and secrets and revelations. The secrets were personal and closely guarded. In showing how and why they remained secret, Martha Sandweiss reveals much about the American past and the American present."
          —Richard White, Margaret Byrne Professor of American History, Stanford University, and author of *The Middle Ground*

PENGUIN BOOKS

PASSING STRANGE

Martha A. Sandweiss is professor of history at Princeton University. She began her career as a museum curator and taught for twenty years at Amherst College. She is the author of numerous works on western American history and the history of photography, including *Print the Legend: Photography and the American West*, winner of the Organization of American Historians' Ray Allen Billington Prize, and *Laura Gilpin: An Enduring Grace* and is coeditor of *The Oxford History of the American West*.

Passing Strange

A

GILDED AGE TALE

.... *of* ....

LOVE AND DECEPTION

ACROSS THE COLOR LINE

Martha A. Sandweiss

PENGUIN BOOKS

PENGUIN BOOKS

Published by the Penguin Group
Penguin Group (USA) Inc., 375 Hudson Street, New York, New York 10014, U.S.A.
Penguin Group (Canada), 90 Eglinton Avenue East, Suite 700, Toronto,
Ontario, Canada M4P 2Y3 (a division of Pearson Penguin Canada Inc.)
Penguin Books Ltd, 80 Strand, London WC2R 0RL, England
Penguin Ireland, 25 St Stephen's Green, Dublin 2, Ireland (a division of Penguin Books Ltd)
Penguin Group (Australia), 250 Camberwell Road, Camberwell,
Victoria 3124, Australia (a division of Pearson Australia Group Pty Ltd)
Penguin Books India Pvt Ltd, 11 Community Centre, Panchsheel Park, New Delhi – 110 017, India
Penguin Group (NZ), 67 Apollo Drive, Rosedale, North Shore 0632,
New Zealand (a division of Pearson New Zealand Ltd)
Penguin Books (South Africa) (Pty) Ltd, 24 Sturdee Avenue,
Rosebank, Johannesburg 2196, South Africa

Penguin Books Ltd, Registered Offices:
80 Strand, London WC2R 0RL, England

First published in the United States of America by The Penguin Press,
a member of Penguin Group (USA) Inc. 2009
Published in Penguin Books 2010

1   3   5   7   9   10   8   6   4   2

THE LIBRARY OF CONGRESS HAS CATALOGED THE HARDCOVER EDITION AS FOLLOWS:
Sandweiss, Martha A.
Passing strange : a Gilded Age tale of love and deception across the color line / Martha A. Sandweiss.
p.   cm.
Includes bibliographical references and index.
ISBN 978-1-59420-200-1 (hc.)
ISBN 978-0-14-311686-8 (pbk.)
1. African Americans—Race identity—Case studies.   2. Passing (Identity)—United States—
Case Studies.   3. Married people—United States—Case Studies.   4. Deception—United States—
Case studies.   5. King, Clarence, 1842–1901.   6. King, Ada, 1860–1964.   7. King, Clarence,
1842–1901—Marriage.   8. United States—Race relations—History—19th century.   9. African
American women—Biography.   10. New York (N.Y.)—Biography.   I. Title.
E185.625.S255 2009
305.896'073—dc22
2008034886

Printed in the United States of America
Designed by Stephanie Huntwork

FOR MY PARENTS

Was he merely being another American and, in the great frontier tradition, accepting the democratic invitation to throw your origins overboard if to do so contributes to the pursuit of happiness? Or was it more than that? Or was it less?

—Philip Roth, *The Human Stain*

Contents

Passing Strange

An Invented Life

EDWARD V. BROWN, THE CENSUS TAKER, MOVED SLOWLY DOWN
North Prince Street, knocking on each and every door in this Flushing
neighborhood of Queens, New York. It was June 5, 1900, a mild and
sunny day in the first spring of a new century. And as federal census agents
had done once a decade for more than a hundred years, he was counting
Americans, compiling a mosaic portrait of the nation. Who lives here, he
asked at each residence, and what is the occupants' "color of skin," their sex,
their marital status, their age? For each of the inhabitants he recorded a
birthplace, as well as the birthplaces of their parents, and for the foreign-
born he noted when they had emigrated and whether they were citizens of
the United States. He wrote down everyone's occupation, asked whether he
or she could read and write, and separated the renters and boarders from
the home owners. In his careful, neat hand, Brown dutifully recorded
the data on the preprinted census sheets that would eventually find their
way to Washington, D.C., and become part of the official twelfth census
of the United States. Queens, that census would show, was much like
the more densely settled community of Brooklyn, just to the west: it was
overwhelmingly white, about 98 percent, with close to a quarter of those
white residents foreign born.[1]

As Brown made his way down North Prince Street, he encountered immigrants from Germany, England, Ireland, and Poland, families supported by
men who worked as policemen, machinists, and clerks. At number 50, he

met Mary Chase, a sixty-year-old widow from Rhode Island who ran a small boardinghouse, and took note of her black housekeeper, the widowed Deborah Peterson. He had counted seventy-two white residents on the street thus far, and Peterson, who descended from an African American family long resident in New York, was the first black person he had encountered. But then he walked next door and knocked at the large and comfortable home at 48 North Prince Street. Two black servants lived here. Phoebe Martin was a thirty-three-year-old widow, and Clarine Eldridge, just fourteen, was scarcely older than the children she had been hired to watch. It was afternoon, and Grace, age nine; Ada, age eight; and Sidney, age six, were home from school, perhaps playing with their three-year-old brother, Wallace. Whoever answered the door probably invited the census taker into the parlor; neither the servants nor the children could have answered his long list of personal questions about the family. And so Edward Brown entered the home to talk to Ada Todd, the lady of the house. Her husband, James, was away, she said, so she would answer the census agent's long list of questions herself.

Brown hardly needed to ask her race. With a glance at her dark complexion and wavy black hair, he noted her "color of skin" as "black." Mrs. Todd reported that her parents came from Georgia, and she told Brown that she could read and write. She said that she had been born in Georgia in December 1862. If Brown remembered his history, he might have wondered if Ada Todd had been born a slave. That question was not on his list, though, and he would not have asked.

Mrs. Todd then told Brown about her husband, James. She said that she had married him eighteen years earlier, in 1882. He was a black man, some twenty years her senior. Born in the West Indies, he had come to the United States in 1870, she said. Now a naturalized citizen, he had a job as a traveling steelworker. Perhaps Brown noted that the house seemed proof that Mr. Todd had done pretty well for himself, even if his work often kept him away from his home and his children. Mrs. Todd explained that there had been five: the four still at home and a fifth who had died as a toddler.

Edward Brown took pride in the accuracy of his records, in the neat way in which he filled in the 1,350 blank boxes on each of his census sheets, recording into being a portrait of the polyglot neighborhood springing up in the sparsely settled borough of Queens. And so, he would have been stunned to learn that almost nothing Mrs. Todd told him was true.

To begin with, she had knocked two years off her age, a gesture of vanity, perhaps. And she and her husband had been married for twelve years, not eighteen, a fact of which Mrs. Todd was surely aware, and a lie that seems hard to fathom, since the children's ages raised no questions about their legitimacy. But the other untruths were more stunning. Her husband was not black. He was not from the West Indies. He was not a steelworker. Even his name, James Todd, was a lie. Ada Todd was in fact married to Clarence King, an acclaimed public figure and the person Secretary of State John Hay once called "the best and brightest man of his generation."[2]

King was a larger-than-life character: an explorer of the American West, a geologist, an accomplished writer and storyteller. He hobnobbed with presidents and congressmen and counted some of the nation's most distinguished writers and artists among his closest friends. His physical agility and bravery, combined with his keen intellect and wit, commanded near reverence from those who knew him best. With King, the historian Henry Adams wrote, "men worshiped not so much their friend, as the ideal American they all wanted to be."[3] But of all this, of her husband's true identity and even his real name, Ada had not a clue.

Not until he lay dying of tuberculosis in Phoenix in late 1901, his last desperate hope of a desert cure gone, did James Todd write a letter to his wife telling her who he really was.[4]

KING SUSTAINED HIS DOUBLE life for thirteen years. He lived as the celebrated Clarence King—a man who traced his English ancestry back to signers of the Magna Carta—in his workplaces, in the homes of his friends, in his Manhattan clubs. But he was James Todd, the black workingman, when he went home to his wife and children in Brooklyn and later in Queens. His well-to-do friends in New York and his family back in Newport, Rhode Island, thought him a bachelor; they never knew about Ada.

And she knew nothing of them. Secrecy bounded his separate worlds. An attentive watchfulness governed his every move. No wonder King found married life fraught and complicated.

Ada, however, found nothing particularly clandestine about her domestic life. She might sometimes find it hard to understand why she never met her husband's family or friends, or difficult to explain to neighbors why he was so often away. But her life as Ada Todd gave her a foothold in a middle-class world she could scarcely have dreamed of as a girl in Civil War and Reconstruction Georgia. She embraced the world her marriage gave her and took pleasure in being Mrs. Todd. When she became a widow, she claimed the name of Ada King and did everything she could to assure that the peculiar circumstances of her married life would not remain a secret or become a source of shame to her children.

James and Ada Todd thus understood their life together in different ways. We know the story they told the world. Ada's report to the census taker conveys the public tale, or at least one of them. But precisely what they said to each other or, indeed, to themselves lies beyond all knowing. Clarence King took care to make sure that scant record of his secret life would survive. No pictures of the two of them together exist. No piece of paper bears both his signature (either one) and hers. The wedding ring he gave to her had no inscription inside the gold band.

OF CLARENCE KING, WE know much; of Ada Copeland, very little.

We can trace King's early life through family genealogies and the writings of various relatives, his own boyhood letters, and the memories of his friends. We can follow his professional career through his books and essays, the correspondence of his associates, and the records of the various government agencies for which he worked as a geologist, an explorer, and an administrator. His race and his social status, his education and his professional career, all let us know far more about King than about most Americans born in 1842. Even so, he left behind no stories to explain his secret marriage or account for his deceptions, no detailed accounts to lay bare the daily rituals that enabled him to pursue his extraordinary double life as an eminent white scientist and a black workingman. The surviving excerpts from his now-lost letters to his wife, however, reveal a man deeply in love. For that love, it seems, King risked all.

Of Ada Copeland's early life, virtually nothing is known. By virtue of *her* race and social status, she lived the first two and a half decades of her life beyond the reach of the civil officials who might have inscribed her into the historical record. It seems unlikely her immediate family members could even read and write; certainly, no letters from them survive. And because Clarence King was so wary of having any documents that might identify him as James Todd, he destroyed whatever letters Ada wrote to him. What little we know of Ada's childhood comes from indirection, from what we can know about the place where she lived or how other African American people born around the same time recalled their own childhoods in Georgia's cotton country. Our understanding of her experience as a married woman comes largely through spare public records, through the few stories she told many decades later, and through the inferences we can draw from our knowledge of the events that transpired around her. We cannot know, for example, what she thought on a particular day, but we can know that the air on her street hung heavy with the odors of a nearby slaughterhouse, or that her apartment would have felt cold and dark after a blizzard felled the utility lines. What she believed about her husband we can infer only from the slightest of evidence. Her public stories about her marriage—those tales she told the census taker—are more easily known than the private assurances she gave herself.

KING AND COPELAND CAME from different worlds. Because of that, and because King was almost nineteen years older, they experienced the same historical events in different ways. The Civil War, for example, directly shaped every aspect of Ada's earliest years. It drew the local white farmers off to war, produced shortages of clothing and food, and led indirectly to ever more ruthless and restrictive slave codes. For King, the conflict unfolded as a more distant event that attracted friends and relatives to military duty. But he did not want to fight and he went west, in part, to avoid the killing fields of war. The Civil War thus disrupted their separate lives but created opportunities for the two of them in vastly different ways. The war's end meant emancipation for Ada's family and the start of their new life as freedpeople. For King, it meant an era of renewed government funding for science that made possible his career as a geologist-explorer. Postwar industrialization opened up yet more work opportunities for King as a mining consultant but offered Copeland few new economic opportunities in rural Georgia, where her options remained restricted by race and gender.

Race, more than anything else, played out differently for Ada Copeland and Clarence King. Copeland's dark complexion circumscribed where she could work, how she could travel, how safe she could feel. King professed a lifelong fascination with dark-complected peoples. Their skin tone seemed to him exotic and fascinating, precisely because it hinted of worlds so different from the convention-bound society of Newport in which he was raised. Like many white Americans, he understood race as something that belonged to other people, and he romanticized dark skin color as the mark of a more natural and sensual life. Ada, however, knew race to be more than an abstract cultural idea. For her it had very real social and economic consequences.

Even the city of New York, where they made their home, meant different things to King and Copeland. Clarence saw it as a nexus of economic power and social prestige, a place where he could live on his good name and past achievements and have access to the moneymen who might bankroll his mining ventures. He could live as a celebrity in New York—people would acknowledge him there as the famed leader of the U.S. Geological Exploration of the Fortieth Parallel, the man who mapped the West. They would know him as the "King of Diamonds" who exposed a fraudulent gem mine; recognize him as the first director of the United States Geological Survey; laud him as the author of a popular book on mountaineering and as one of the most charming dinner guests to be found in all Manhattan. Ada, however, embraced New York less as a place that acknowledged her past than as the place that let her leave it behind. In New York no one need know about her girlhood in slavery, the soul-crushing poverty of her rural life, the limited options available to a black girl of ambition in western Georgia. The city offered her a stage upon which she could reinvent herself.

Eventually, King would reinvent himself there, too. Racial passing itself was not rare. Many Americans with an African American ancestor passed as white, seeking the greater freedom of movement and choice accorded white Americans in the late nineteenth century. They might cross over the color line for good, never looking back. Or they might cross it every day, living in a black world and working in a white one. Their passing might be an act of careful calculation or, for a lighter-skinned person, it could be inadvertent: an onlooker, not detecting any hint of African heritage in someone's light-colored skin, might simply begin to treat him or her as white.

The practice of passing generally involves adopting a particular identity to move *toward* greater legal and social privilege. It might mean taking on a different gender, or ethnic or national identity, but it most often involves the assumption of a different racial identity. And since, in the United States, social privilege has been associated with lighter-colored skin, passing usually entails concealing one's African American heritage to assume a white identity. The entire practice hinges on a peculiar idea. Since one's race could be determined by heritage as well as appearance, very light-colored skin did not necessarily make one a "white" person. In the aftermath of emancipation, a host of laws sprang up throughout the Deep South clarifying just what defined a person as "black" or "Negro," almost always for the purpose of restricting his rights. In 1896 the Supreme Court of the United States upheld these laws in the case of *Plessy v. Ferguson*, which affirmed that people with one "black" great-grandparent could, for all intents and purposes, be considered black themselves, no matter what they looked like. This peculiarly American idea came to be known as "hypodescent." "One drop of black blood" trumped seven drops of "white."

Clarence King took advantage of these distinctive American ideas about race to pass the other way across the color line, claiming African ancestry when he had none at all. Grasping that appearance alone did not determine his racial identity, the fair-haired, blue-eyed King presented himself as a "black" man named James Todd. Rather than moving *toward* legal and social privilege, he moved *away* from it. He glimpsed something he sought in Ada Copeland and her African American world, and he acted to seize the promise of that rich emotional life.

Other Americans have crossed the color line from white to black—to join a family, to evade antimiscegenation laws, to claim some other sort of political or economic advantage. But Clarence King stands out because of his prominence as a public figure. This was a white man who dined at the White House, belonged to Manhattan's most elite clubs, and parlayed his privileged upbringing and Ivy League education into a career as an eminent scientist, writer, and government official. American history holds no comparable tale of a high-profile white man crossing the color line. In an era in which the insidious "one drop of blood" rules consigned many phenotypically "white" Americans to live on the wrong side of the Jim Crow laws, King harnessed Americans' most deeply held beliefs about race to pass voluntarily—if only part-time—as a "black" man.

How, one must ask, did he pull it off? And what might we make of it?

At one level, the story of the Todds' marriage is simply a love story about two people from opposite ends of the American social spectrum who met and married and raised a family. But it also illuminates larger stories about race and class and identity in late-nineteenth-century America, stories that lie at the very core of national thinking about the new social order emerging in the wake of emancipation. That King would *want* to pass in the first place—despite his position of prominence and power—reveals not just his love for Copeland but his awareness that a true interracial marriage would upset both his white world and his wife's black one. And that he *could* pass across the color line—despite his own visual appearance—illuminates the extraordinary arbitrariness of racial categorization at the end of the nineteenth century. At the very moment that laws sought to make racial categories fixed and unchanging, King showed just how fluid they could be. The laws that pinned racial identities on ancestry rather than appearance paradoxically made it possible for a light-skinned American like King to claim a black identity.

King and Copeland married at a moment when many Americans could not abide a public marriage between a prominent white government scientist and a black woman born into slavery. King's secrecy speaks to his desire to preserve his reputation. But it speaks also to the very real constraints of public opinion. American society offered no way for Clarence King to maintain both his public career and a life lived in the open with an African American wife and their mixed-race children. Even someone with his education, political savvy, and social cachet could not rise above the powerful racial stereotyping that permeated every aspect of American life. King bought into some of those stereotypes himself, even as he struggled to transcend them and fashion a life unbound by the racial assumptions of the day.

Though American society was far less tolerant of interracial marriage in the Gilded Age than it is now, it nonetheless afforded its citizens more privacy in the conduct of their personal lives. News and information circulated in different ways. King and Copeland married in an era when telegraphs were common but residential telephones were rare; radio and television did not exist; and daily newspapers were plentiful but seldom illustrated. They could carve out for themselves a zone of privacy that seems almost unimaginable today, especially for a public figure like King. The particular structure of New York City also helped them to protect the secrecy of their shared life. Then, as now, New York was a collection of neighborhoods, many defined by the residents' class or race or national origin. Horse-drawn trolleys and elevated trains let New Yorkers move about from place to place, but in this presubway era, many city residents lived largely within the bounds of their immediate neighborhoods, rarely venturing into worlds where their social class or physical appearance might make them conspicuous. King lived his secret life for thirteen years, and no one, it seems, ever found him out.

MUCH ABOUT THIS STORY remains unknown and even unknowable. What, for example, did Ada really believe about her husband's identity? How did Clarence justify to himself deceiving his wife and children? The paucity of historical evidence makes it difficult to track their separate lives and even harder to reconstruct the world they built together or glimpse their innermost thoughts. But most families in late-nineteenth-century New York left behind some traces in the historical records, and this family was no exception. With a careful reading of the surviving evidence and an informed historical imagination, we can at last tell the long-silenced story of Clarence King and Ada Copeland and the world they built together as James and Ada Todd.

PART ONE

Clarence King

and

Ada Copeland

Becoming Clarence King

EQUALLY AT HOME IN A REMOTE DESERT FIELD CAMP AND AN elite Manhattan club, Clarence King could plot revolution with a Cuban peasant or deliver a learned lecture at Yale. He cherished his New England heritage but felt drawn to the "silken Latin and meridional temperament."[1] He clung to social niceties but loved to flout convention. "King loved paradox," Henry Adams wrote; "he started them like rabbits, and cared for them no longer, when caught or lost."[2]

Raised in a New England household of bookish women, King became the very model of a hardy western man. He headed west with a Bible, returned east "saturated with the sunshine of the Sierras."[3] He inspired confidence with his intellect and commanded obedience with his energy. "No one ever saw him lounge or loll or doze—except expressly," wrote a friend. "His movements were rapid; his step was quick.... He was alertness incarnate."[4] Over drinks in New York drawing rooms, King loved to embellish the stories of his frontier bravery: the tale of the buffalo stampede, the Indian attack, the encounter with a grizzly bear. But this western man in Manhattan delighted in playing the eastern man in Nevada: in the rudest western field camps, he dressed for supper in formal attire. And for all his wandering, he clung to sentimental notions of home. "Repose and calmness are the avenues that lead to Heaven," he wrote a fellow field geologist in 1873. "The stability of character which comes of settled citizenship should be yours and mine, the humanity and Christianity which ought to be the fruitage of our careers, needs the influence of home and stability."[5]

"Paradox...enjoyed the hegemony of his mental states," the critic William Crary Brownell wrote of King. "He had an undoubted predilection for its undoubted stimulus."[6]

KING'S CONTRADICTIONS RAN DEEP. He was a young man of intense faith and poetic yearnings who devoted his life to science; a public figure with democratic instincts who harbored aristocratic aspirations; an openhanded friend who struggled under crushing debt. With a pocket never more than "indifferently lined," one friend observed, "his was ever the generosity and often the munificence of a prince."[7] Intense bursts of manic energy alternated with bouts of paralyzing melancholia and ill health. And although he could be the most public of men, sometimes he would just disappear. "We seldom met when he had not just come from a distant region or was departing for some other point as far," a friend recalled. "In the wise, I could not free myself from the illusion that he was a kind of visitor, of a texture differing from that of ordinary Earthdwellers."[8]

The novelist William Dean Howells attributed King's baffling doubleness to the pull between his scientific and literary interests, as if an artistic temperament could excuse quixotic behavior. "There was doubtless something in the exactness of science which formed a pull on his poetic nature strong enough to draw him to the performance from which the vagueness of aesthetic motives and impulses relaxed him." King acted quickly enough in the scientific realm, Howells thought, but in the rest of his life "he was much controlled by what we may call the literary side of him."[9]

That literary side manifested itself in King's mesmerizing conversation, "iridescent with the imagination of the born romancer."[10] "Was there ever so good a talker?" asked William Crary Brownell.[11] A fellow member of New York's elite Century Association, the journalist Edward Cary, proclaimed King's talk incomparable. "It was impossible to foresee at what point his tangential fancy would change its course. From the true rhythm of Creole gumbo to the verse of Theocritus, from the origin of the latest *mot* to the age of the globe, from the soar or slump of the day's market to the method of Lippo Lippi...."[12] King never expected his talk to lead to anything, another friend explained. "It was its art that attracted him. He enjoyed 'travel, not arriving.' "[13]

King's dazzling talk was part mental exercise, part jest, and all performance. As his close friend the diplomat John Hay recalled, "It was hard to remember that this polished trifler, this exquisite wit, who diffused over every conversation in which he was engaged an iridescent mist of epigram and persiflage, was one of the greatest savants of his time." He seemed "so deliciously agreeable" it could be hard to take him seriously.[14] Like an actor, King calculated how to enthrall his listeners. "One fancied him tingling with consciousness, so thoroughly aware of himself and what he was doing, how he was appearing, as to produce the happiest possible effect," one friend recalled.[15] And sometimes he even enchanted himself. His own stories could hold him "quite enthralled within an almost hypnotic control."[16]

King deployed his verbal charm to entertain, impress, disarm. "It is but a suggestion of his rare equipment," Edward Cary wrote of King, "to say that in his talk, as in his work, his imagination was his dominant, at moments his dominating, quality."[17] But the talents that let King wear his learning lightly as he rose through the ranks of American science and letters also allowed him to conceal his secret world. Feinting and dodging with words, he could deflect probing queries, brush off uncomfortable speculation, invent plausible explanations for his sometimes inexplicable behavior. With words he wove the stories that allowed him to live not just a life of contradictions, but a truly double life.

CLARENCE KING WAS BORN in Newport, Rhode Island, on January 6, 1842, to parents of old American stock. His father's family emigrated from England to the Massachusetts Bay Colony in 1637. Clarence's great-great-grandfather Benjamin King later settled in Newport and reportedly assisted Benjamin Franklin with his early electrical experiments.

Benjamin's son, Samuel, became a notable portrait painter and an instructor of the artist Washington Allston. And Samuel's son, Samuel Vernon
King—Clarence's grandfather—became a merchant. By 1803 Samuel Vernon King was a partner in the China trading firm of King and Talbot (later
to become Olyphant, King and Company), and four of his sons followed
him into the business, including Clarence's father, James Rivers King.[18]
Samuel Vernon King suffered some sort of mental collapse in 1809, and his
sons later acquired a reputation for being "a little queer," less for any emotional instability than for their principled opposition to the opium trade.[19]
Clarence himself inherited none of the family's business sense. But from his
father and uncles he acquired an expansive view of the world and a particular sense of how families worked: while men ventured far afield to earn their
livings, women stayed home to raise the children.

KING'S MOTHER, CAROLINE FLORENCE LITTLE KING, also came from
a distinguished family and could trace her ancestry back to Alfred the Great
and three signers of the Magna Carta. Florence, as she was known, grew up
in a devout Moravian household that emphasized education and public service. Her maternal grandfather, Asher Robbins, represented Rhode Island
in the United States Senate from 1825 to 1839 and helped shape the direction of the new Smithsonian Institution. Some lawmakers had called for
James Smithson's bequest to support an observatory or an improved system
of common schools. But Robbins articulated a broader view of government-
sponsored science, much as his great-grandson would later do, arguing
that the "increase and diffusion of knowledge among men" would be better
achieved through the establishment of a "scientific and literary institution,"
along the lines of a research university.[20] Florence's father, William Little
Jr., a talented linguist and orator, died young. But her formidable mother,
Sophia Robbins Little, a social reformer and writer, lived to be ninety-four.
An acquaintance of Frederick Douglass, an outspoken abolitionist, and
the benefactor of prisoners and homeless girls, Mrs. Little shaped young
Clarence's view of the world with her strong antislavery views and religious

pacifism. She also bequeathed to him, family members thought, her "rapid diction."[21]

Florence Little married James Rivers King on September 5, 1840, the month she turned fifteen. James was six years older. He had been working in the New York office of the family's China trading firm. But his personal interests tended more to natural science, and he gave his young bride a geology book by the British scientist and divine William Buckland, whose writings about the physical evidence for a great flood gave religious conservatives a way to reconcile the Bible with the new science of geology. He wanted "to awaken my mind to the subject," Florence later recalled.[22] But there proved scant time for philosophical conversations. Within a year of their marriage, James sailed for China to fill in for his older brother, Charles, who had become too ill to return to Canton to handle the family affairs. When sixteen-year-old Florence King gave birth to her first child, Clarence Rivers King, her husband lived half a world away. She hired domestic help to assist with the baby. King's "nurse was a colored woman," a close friend wrote many years later, "an old family servant, for whom he ever after cherished a life-long regard and affectionate sympathy."[23]

Clarence was more than three and a half years old before he ever met his father. James returned from Canton in the fall of 1845, hoping to find work at home, now that his brother Charles had returned to China. But Charles died at sea that very fall, and in the spring of 1847 James felt compelled to return to China, despite his lack of interest in the family business. Clarence was just five. Florence, still mourning the recent death of a baby girl named Florence, was pregnant again. And she was again alone, without her husband, when in late 1847 she delivered her daughter Grace. It would take months for James to receive news of his daughter's birth; perhaps he never did. For in 1848, as a family friend put it, came "the shock of tragedy, the pall of bereavement and the manifold burdens of a sweeping family disaster."[24] In September of that year, on her twenty-third birthday, as she mourned the recent death of baby Grace, Florence opened a letter and learned that James had died in Amoy in June.[25]

She turned, for comfort, to her six-year-old son, their already tight bond now intensified by shared grief. As a friend later recalled, she became at "the outset, as she remained always, his sympathetic and competent intellectual companion."[26] They were "then and always a devoted pair," recalled another.[27] Florence herself thought Clarence not just "a devoted child, but the closest and tenderest *friend*. . . . He came to me so early in life that I can say like Goethe's mother, 'We were young together.' "[28]

Clarence King retained faint memory of the father with whom he lived for only a year and a half, and seldom spoke of him. But the loss haunted him. In the back of a journal he kept as a seventeen-year-old he wrote his father's name out next to his mother's and his own in his clear neat hand.[29] He held on to his father's Chinese phrase book and treasured the Chinese antiques in his aunt Catherine King's house.[30] Later, as an adult, he collected Chinese textiles and antiquities himself—"kakemonos, screens, porcelains, remarkable palace and sanctuary embroideries"—and kept them locked away in a storage room, faint echoes of that secret world of his father's out on the Pacific and in the hongs of Canton.[31]

KING THUS GREW UP an only child in a world of women. His widowed grandmother, Sophia Little, looked outward to the world and never rested, as a friend recalled, "till such of the needy as she was able to help had been provided for, and such of the suffering as she could reach had been consoled."[32] But his widowed mother, Florence, left nervous and melancholic by the loss of two children and a husband before she was twenty-three, became "completely centred in her son."[33] She held up before him the example of her own scholarly father and grandfather.[34] And she threw herself into his education, "learning with an inherited facility both classical and modern languages that she might teach them in turn to him."[35]

In 1848 Florence took her six-year-old son to Pomfret, Connecticut, sixty miles northwest of Newport, to enroll him in Christ Church Hall, an academy run by the Reverend Dr. Roswell Park. A former professor of natural philosophy at the University of Pennsylvania, Park held liberal views about the relationship between science and religion and had a keen interest in geology, already a favorite subject of the young King.[36] Florence kept close watch over her son's education. To save the expense of keeping house, she lived with him in a crowded Pomfret boardinghouse, packed with native-born students and Irish-born laborers.[37] Later she recalled the bitter winter day Clarence took her on a mile-long walk through the snow to examine a fossil he had found. Unable to answer his questions, she sent away for a copy of Edward Hitchcock's *Geology*. And from that time on, she said, their rooms "became a veritable museum where all kinds of specimens were studied with enthusiasm."[38] As King's secretary later noted, Florence's single-minded devotion to her son's interests meant that "almost from his very childhood every step of his studies was a tangential advance upon a certain goal."[39]

Florence's ambitions for her son kept them on the move. Sometime around 1852, she took Clarence to study at a Latin School near Boston, with the intention of preparing him for Harvard.[40] But they soon moved on to New Haven, where her younger brother, Robbins Little, taught Greek at Yale. As a youth, Little suffered from a vague nervous malady, and he had sailed to Hong Kong on one of the King company's clipper ships in search of a cure. He returned healthy, graduated from Yale in 1851, and stayed on to teach. Later he became a lawyer and then superintendent and trustee of New York's Astor Library, the forerunner of the city's great public library that would be founded in 1895.[41] Florence rented rooms on Church Street, opposite the house of the university president, and there, in the shadow of Yale, she resumed her devoted instruction of her son.[42] "He was absolutely obedient to her," one friend wrote, "and she governed him with a firm will and a gentle hand. I never saw a mother with a keener sense of [the] quality and characteristics of a boy or with greater wisdom or power to develop the best possible."[43] Daniel Coit Gilman, later the Yale University librarian and president of Johns Hopkins University, remembered that the young Clarence "had the same bright face, winning smile, agile movement, that we knew in later life."[44]

In the fall of 1855, Florence moved again, now taking her thirteen-year-old son to enroll in the "Classical Division" of Hartford High School, one of New England's best public schools. They boarded together in other people's homes as Clarence studied Latin, Greek, and English, along with mathematics and both ancient and modern history.[45] But in Hartford, King finally stepped outside his mother's orbit to form his first deep friendships with other boys. He and his fellow students Daniel Dewey and James Terry Gardiner became an inseparable trio.[46] They took long tramps out across the Connecticut countryside, and as Dan later recalled, "talked as boys seldom do." "Truly," he wrote to Clarence, "we have had a strangely happy boyhood together."[47]

The three friends addressed one another as "brother," and King wrote that they "resolved never to lose our confidence in each other and never get the bashfulness of saying 'love.'"[48] Like other adolescent boys of the mid-nineteenth century, they embraced intense same-sex friendships as a matter of course, and they exchanged long, self-absorbed letters whenever they were apart. They pondered the state of their souls, worried about their futures, speculated about the mysteries of women. King, however, also worried about money.

In December 1856 mobs rose up against the foreign-owned warehouses and factories in Canton. The family firm of King and Company, in which James had invested his assets, lost nearly everything, and the company collapsed completely the following year when a steamer sent with money to Shanghai to cover the firm's obligations disappeared without a trace.[49] These far-off events halfway around the globe left Florence King and her son with scant financial resources. In April 1859 seventeen-year-old Clarence withdrew from school without a diploma because of an "illness," unspecified in the records, but perhaps an early manifestation of the depression that would stalk him later in life.[50] The future "looks very dark," confessed "Clare" to James Gardiner in 1859. "My only comfort is that God who over-rules all, will be the father of the fatherless, and trusting to that promise I pray for patience and real humility." He hesitated to confide even in the "kind and sympathizing" Dan, "for fear of making him sad."[51]

But King did join Gardiner and Dewey that summer for a camping trip in the Green Mountains of Vermont and in the outdoor life found the balm for his low spirits and wavering self-confidence. As he would write many years later, "Nature is the greatest medicine for my soul."[52] Already, King had a keen eye for observation. "If any question arose as to any object seen during the day, whether we had particularly noted it or not," Gardiner later wrote, "King could always describe it from memory with great minuteness. He seemed to photograph everything that passed before his eyes."[53]

And yet, even as he lived in the present, King had an ability to think beyond his immediate surroundings and to imagine how personal experience might play out as part of a more dramatic tale. In his small pocket journal, he plotted how to tell the *story* of his long mountain walks, jotting down shorthand notes to expand later into literary vignettes.[54] The teenage King "wrote beautifully," Gardiner recalled, "being trained to it by his mother who is gifted with wonderful power of expression and power to inspire enthusiasm for literature." Indeed, as far as Gardiner could tell, all of King's "literary and artistic tastes and his critical perceptions seemed the natural outgrowth of his mother's mind and training."[55]

At summer's end, Gardiner moved back to his hometown of Troy, New York, to enroll in the Rensselaer Polytechnic Institute, and Dewey returned to Hartford to finish high school.[56] But without any educational plans of his own for the fall, King felt unmoored. He moved to Brooklyn in late 1859 and found work with the flour merchants William Brown and Company. He chose to believe he secured the job on his own, but more likely he had help from George S. Howland, a widowed Brooklyn businessman and philanthropist then courting Florence King. Howland served as secretary of the board of the Brooklyn White Lead Company, which prospered, as the local newspaper explained, "due to his intelligence in all the chemical, mechanical and productive departments of the business."[57] Five years older than Florence, he had lost a wife and child in an 1854 shipwreck and buried two of his other children.[58] His surviving son, John Snowden Howland—"Snoddy"—had a physical disability that, as Florence put it, left his body "like an exquisite vessel of cracked glass which a rough touch might shiver in atoms."[59] Howland likely saw in Florence a potential mate young enough to bear more children; in him, she probably spied financial salvation. They married in July 1860, and Florence inherited a nine-year-old stepson. But nothing could shake her devotion to Clarence. Her eighteen-year-old son would remain her intellectual companion and confidant, and Clarence would find it difficult ever to escape the grip of that maternal embrace.[60]

KING REVELED IN NEW YORK'S cultural attractions. He attended the opera and purchased a season's pass to the National Academy of Design, where he particularly admired Albert Bierstadt's grand *Base of the Rocky Mountains, Laramie Peak,* the first of the painter's monumental Rocky Mountain landscapes to be exhibited in the city.[61] But New York also struck him as a sinful place. "It was all very nice to talk about moral purity in a little city," he wrote to Gardiner, "but Great Jones! Jim there are more than one seductive, wicked, beautiful, fascinating, jolly, voluptuous, apparently modest artful woman to one poor chicken here; they show you their necks and bosoms without intending to and all sorts of abominable wiles they practice on a fellow that are mighty inflaming."[62] He felt compelled to fight back against the dangerous lures of city life and went to church in an effort to fend off his melancholy and vague urban unease.[63] After a few months, he proudly told Gardiner, "I have succeeded with Heavenly aid in eradicating melancholy from my heart and now that I am free from its bands my soul is much more free to look at all the world's realities in a healthy light."[64]

This new perspective made him more keenly aware of his own advantages in life, more thankful than ever for his mother's devotion. "Now almost daily," he told Gardiner, "I see some poor unfortunate little girl or boy with scarce food to keep them out of the grave and clothes to cover them, young and with a heavy weight of *deep deep* sorrow in every furrow of their little old hard faces.... Oh my God why were my young days cloudless and why did I have a kind devoted Mother, why was I permitted to live in ease while those whom thou lovest as well are going down to premature death from famine and degradation." This first glimpse of the urban poor sparked his empathy and drove away his "sorrow and all discontent."[65]

. . .

NOT EVEN AN INWARD-LOOKING eighteen-year-old could find shelter from the stiff winds of politics that winter and spring of 1860. Talk of slavery, states' rights, and the impending possibility of civil war dominated the papers and the talk on the street. "I am more than ever a Wendell Phillips man," King wrote to Gardiner that March, "heart and soul with the philanthropic 'radicals' " allied with Phillips's strong antislavery views. But he explained that his "mental" allegiance lay with the Illinois senator Stephen Douglas, who believed that the residents of the western territories should decide for themselves whether to allow slavery within their boundaries.[66] The radical abolitionists had the right end in mind, but King favored a more tempered means of ending America's peculiar institution.

King grew up an "enthusiastic abolitionist," Gardiner recalled, receiving from his mother "an ardent hatred of slavery, and a clear foresight of the impending 'irrepressible conflict' of the Civil War."[67] But both Florence and Clarence took their lead from King's grandmother, Sophia Little, with whom they lived while in Newport.[68] "During the 1850s," King later wrote, "she ate no sugar but free soil maple and refused southern oranges as they were to her mind 'full of the blood of slaves.' "[69]

Little's impeccable antislavery credentials extended back to at least 1835, when she attended the famous Boston meeting that ended when an angry mob seized abolitionist leader William Lloyd Garrison and dragged him through the streets with a rope tied around his neck.[70] Later, during King's boyhood, she helped lead the Rhode Island Anti-Slavery Society and earned local notoriety for shunning the neighbors unsympathetic to her criticism of the proslavery church.[71] Mrs. Little "has suffered, and counted it joy to suffer for the enslaved," pronounced her admirer Frederick Douglass.[72]

Little wielded her pen as a weapon. Her antislavery letters and poems appeared in Garrison's abolitionist weekly, *The Liberator*, beginning in 1837.[73] After Congress passed the Fugitive Slave Act in 1850, however, an enraged Little sought a broader reading audience and turned to the more popular genre of the novel, in the hope that her "feelings, concerning that law, should reach the ears of the people." She completed her book *Thrice through the Furnace* months before Harriet Beecher Stowe finished *Uncle Tom's Cabin*. But through "circumstances over which the Author had not control," it appeared a few months after the March 1852 publication of Stowe's novel. Mrs. Little deferred to her literary better: "While my little bark lay hindered in port, God had launched forth a noble vessel on the chafed waters of the public mind."[74]

In her story of a slave family's escape to freedom, Little lashed out at the institution of human bondage, insisting that "the dreadful truth exceeds anything my pen has here portrayed!" She wrote like the nineteenth-century religious poet she was, but even her sentimental prose did not mask her political sting. A reviewer for Frederick Douglass's Rochester, New York, newspaper pronounced the novel a "thrilling" story and admirable testimony against the Fugitive Slave Act.[75]

Just ten when his grandmother's book came out, Clarence left no account of his response. But Florence paid indirect homage to the novel in 1862 by naming the daughter born to her and George Howland "Marian," after the saintly quadroon heroine of Little's story. Her gesture suggests the place of the book in the family's life. Clarence probably knew the novel well, and one imagines Florence referring to it whenever Marian asked about her name.

Like other readers, Florence seemed to understand the novel as a tribute to the common humanity of all peoples, whatever their race or creed. But Little's radicalism had its limits. Although she soundly denounced slavery, her liberal views about race fractured—as so many abolitionists' did—over the issue of intermarriage. The aristocratic white protagonist of her book, lured by Marian's primitive charms, frees her as his uncle's slave. "I never saw a white lady that had any heart; they fritter it all away by false education," he tells her. "Your greatest charm for me, is the sensibility I have vainly sought for among my own race."[76] Little dismissed such racial romanticism, however, arguing that there could be no true love across the lines of color or class. An educated white man's love for an untutored black woman would corrupt them both. So she wrapped up her complicated plot with a cluster of marriages that wed white to white, black to black, mulatto to mulatto. One can only wonder whether the adult Clarence King ever looked back on his grandmother's novel with ironic appreciation for its uncanny anticipation of his own life.

FLORENCE KING'S MARRIAGE TO George Howland in the summer of 1860 freed Clarence from his day-to-day worry about his mother's financial situation and let him imagine his way out of his job in Brooklyn. In the fall, he accepted Howland's offer to bankroll his education and enrolled in the three-year course of study in chemistry at the Yale Scientific School (to be renamed the Sheffield Scientific School the following year). The school offered the best scientific training in America, and King sped through the program in just two years. As Daniel Gilman later wrote, he had "that token of genius which is said to be 'the art of lighting one's own fires.'"[77]

The Scientific School offered a stark alternative to the classical curriculum of Yale College, with a focus on chemistry, engineering, and independent work in its newly equipped labs. The "Sheffs" studied and lived apart from the other undergraduates who roomed together in the "college yard." "They do not mingle," wrote one student who arrived a few years after King, "and few acquaintances are formed."[78] The Yale Scientific School had developed slowly from the School of Applied Chemistry that formed in 1847, and it was still evolving when King arrived in the fall of 1860. The new building that opened that year allowed chemistry and engineering to be taught under the same roof for the first time and provided students with state-of-the-art laboratories for analytical chemistry and metallurgy.[79] James Dwight Dana, veteran of the celebrated U.S. Exploring Expedition (1838–42) under Charles Wilkes and a pioneer in the scientific study of the Pacific, presided over the school as a kind of éminence grise and lectured on geology. The philologist William Dwight Whitney instructed the young scientists in French and German. Benjamin Silliman Jr. lectured on chemistry. George J. Brush, "the life of the school," helped students do research with his superb private collection of minerals. Others taught crystallography, astronomy, and natural philosophy.[80] Charles Darwin's revolutionary *On the Origin of Species* (1859) had not yet affected the course of instruction; during the 1860–61 school year, the third-year curriculum still included classes in theology and "Paley's evidences of Christianity."[81] But King's fellow student Othniel Marsh had already uncovered some extraordinary fossils that would fuel the impending debate about evolution and help earn him a reputation as one of the nation's foremost paleontologists.[82]

"I am happy in my studies," King wrote to Gardiner. "I don't love the practical minutiae of lower details of science although I work at these for discipline, but the lofty laws of creation, the connection of the material with the human the aesthetic and the eternal, the cosmical relation of God's earthly planes."[83] Time would later temper King's faith. But for now he sought a unified explanation of the world. "Nature the key to Art and Science, God the Key to Nature," he scribbled in a notebook. "You Clarence King never dare to look at a peak of nature save with respect and the admiration you are capable of. Nature is a solemn force a glorious reality which ought to move us to high thought and true nobility."[84]

The mining engineer James Duncan Hague, who first met King during his New Haven years, remembered him as "an active, sprightly youth, quick to observe and apprehend, full of joyous animation and lively energy" and not above engaging in midnight pranks that involved swapping the front gates of the stately Yale buildings along Hillhouse Avenue.[85] A muscular five feet six inches tall, King excelled at athletics.[86] He skated, played cricket, captained the baseball team, and rowed stroke on a racing crew. He also excelled in the classroom, mastering mandatory classes in mathematics, physics, chemistry, mineralogy, crystallography, geology, and German.[87] In quieter moments, however, he still struggled with matters of the soul. "I find myself alone and I draw nearer to God, Mother and you," he wrote to Gardiner.[88] None of his new Yale friendships had muted the intensity of their old bond. "My heart is taken up with you," Clarence wrote to Jim, "... my love for you grows always and is a most absorbing passion."[89]

Campus talk that fall of 1860 revolved around politics: the impending presidential election, Abraham Lincoln's victory, the likelihood of war. In a community of soldier-aged young men, the abstract issues soon became concrete. With the secession of the southern states and then the outbreak of war in April 1861, most of the school's southerners, never more than a small minority, headed home. In a first flush of enthusiasm, at least thirteen undergraduates left school to join the military in the early months of war. Many more enlisted as soon as they received their degrees; from King's small class at "Sheff," three students eventually joined the Union side. But the reality of war soon intruded on the students' youthful idealism. The College boys watched somberly in June 1861 as Theodore Winthrop, one of the first Union officers killed in battle—an abolitionist, a Yale man, a local boy of impeccable Puritan lineage—was laid to rest in the Grove Street Cemetery, across the street from the Sheffield Scientific School.[90] Clarence's own uncle, his father's younger brother David, died in West Virginia during the war's first year.[91]

Dan Dewey wrote King that his own Trinity College was "all in a military furor just now. A company is being organized, and everybody expects to join. . . . I am getting more and more anxious to go to the war." He anticipated a long struggle and felt "thoroughly convinced that it is my duty to be amongst the defenders of our national principles."[92] Gardiner, too, felt swept up in the fervor of the moment, drilling two hours a day with his fellow students at Rensselaer Polytechnic Instititute.[93]

King abhorred slavery. But he struggled over how to fight it while remaining true to the religious pacifism he had inherited from his grandmother. During the summer of 1861, he went up to Vermont to hike with Dan Dewey and to visit his mother and her family. He was teaching his stepbrother Snowden "to fish and be manly," King wrote to Gardiner. But the issue of military service raised questions about his own manliness. He had just endured "another battle with my inclinations about going to war," King told Gardiner. "Bitter and many were the blows it cost me but now see clearly my duty to keep myself for the future."[94] He wavered, then wavered again. In March 1862 he confessed to Gardiner, "When I said I wanted to 'push a bayonet' I was wrong. God knows that for my country I *would* 'push a bayonet' and that I would not quail before death for my land but the act would crucify in me so many of my noblest impulses. It is like tearing my soul in sunder." King worried that Gardiner would misread his ambivalence as moral weakness. "I do want to lead men," he insisted. "It will be my life's object. Why can I not. Don't think that because I show you my tender side my weak one if you will, that I have no fire, no firmness, no mental power." He boasted that at Yale he already led men in his "own humble way"; people thought him a man of some consequence.[95]

In July 1862, as soon as he received his Ph.B. "with honor" from the Sheffield Scientific School, King headed not south but north.[96] For months he had plotted how to ship a Yale boat to Lake Champlain for a rowing expedition from upstate New York into Canada, with Gardiner and Dewey, and two Yale classmates, Samuel Parsons and William Stone. They set off right after commencement. But not even on the open water could the young men escape the widening ripples of war. On August 8 the secretary of war forbade all men of draft age from leaving the Union as long as military quotas remained unfilled.[97] As the boys rowed toward Canada, unaware of this recent order, a U.S. Customs inspector stopped them as suspected draft dodgers. They talked themselves out of trouble and continued on, holding tight to the inspector's official letter that declared they were "not leaving the United States to avoid any military draft."[98] If the incident stirred up any old doubts, King just shrugged them off. Dewey, though, took it as a call to duty, and when he returned home in September he enlisted in the Twenty-fifth Connecticut Volunteers.[99]

KING DID NOT VOLUNTEER for military service. Nor, after Congress passed draft legislation in March 1863, did he register for possible duty, despite the fact that he could have purchased a substitute with $300 of his stepfather's money.[100] Antiwar feelings ran strong on his father's side of the family as well as his mother's. His paternal aunt, Charlotte King, the widow of his father's brother Charles, refused to let a tombstone acknowledge the military service of her son, William Vernon King, an officer in an all-black regiment, who defied her will to reenlist and died at Petersburg in 1864.[101]

The novelist Henry James, cousin to Charlotte King, thought that military service gave young Vernon a valuable independence, calling forth "some exhibition of a young character too long pressed and impressed, too long prescribed to and too much expected of it, and all under too firm a will."[102] But Clarence never saw military service as a way to build character, at least not his. He avoided any situation that might call public attention to his disinclination to fight. In May 1863, when local enrollment officers went door to door recording the names of men to be called up later in a military draft, King was nowhere to be found.[103] He was already heading west.

King later described his decision to go west as a kind of epiphany. Back in New Haven in October 1862 to row in a regatta, King stopped by the home of his former professor George J. Brush and listened as Brush read aloud a long letter from his old friend William H. Brewer. Brewer was in California, assisting Josiah D. Whitney (the older brother of King's German professor) on the California State Geological Survey. His letter recounted his recent ascent of Mount Shasta, the "sublimely desolate" peak he thought the highest in the state, and emphasized not just the scientific features of the volcanic mountain but the tremendous rigors of the high-altitude climb and the awe-inspiring views.[104] King later told Brewer, "That settled it."[105] He would go west himself.

That the news from the battlefields might have pushed him west remained unsaid. Just weeks before King sat in that New Haven drawing [room] to hear stories of Mount Shasta, more than 4,800 Union and Confederate troops had died on the bloody battleground of Antietam, with 18,500 [more] left wounded and maimed. King's decision to go west stemmed, in [part] from his decision not to pursue the commercial life that his father and [grandf]ather had followed.[106] But it also reflected a deliberate choice not to go [west] with a gun.

[In] January 1863 King wrote Brush to say that he had been reading geol[ogy a]nd "pretty much made up my mind to be a geologist if I can get any [start] in that direction."[107] That winter, he went to Cambridge to study gla[ciolog]y for a brief time with the eminent Harvard scientist Louis Agas[siz, t]hen moved to New York to continue reading on his own. He shared lodgings in Manhattan with Jim Gardiner, who was now studying the law, and together with a handful of other disciples of the English critic John Ruskin, they formed a group called the Society for the Advancement of Truth in Art—the "American Pre-Raphaelites," one journalist called them. King had been pondering the interconnections between science, art, and religion, and he found validation for his nascent ideas in the society's motto: "Truth to Nature."[108] By that, its members meant not slavish realism but art grounded in honest observation of the natural world and imbued with spiritual feeling: "The greatest Art includes the widest range, recording, with equal fidelity, the aspirations of the human soul, and the humblest facts of physical nature."[109]

King felt restless in New York. He drifted up to the Howlands' new house in Irvington, along the Hudson River about an hour north of Manhattan, to spend time with his mother and visit with his new half sister, Marian.[110] When Gardiner's health broke down—from overexertion at his legal studies, he claimed—King seized the moment to propose a western trip. Gardiner later thought the invitation proof of his friend's great prescience about the future of the American nation. "It must have been a sense of the coming development of this continent," he wrote, "and a desire to be a part of it that led him to plan, when we were twenty-one, our trip to the West across the Plains."[111] In truth, King likely felt less concerned with his historical legacy than with his immediate future and how he would avoid the inevitable questions about military service. When he headed west, a Union victory seemed far from certain.

But if the Civil War provided the backdrop to King's decision, he nonetheless went west with a genuine scientific curiosity about the region whose complex geological structure remained so little known. Brewer's letter had fired his imagination, and *John Brent*, a frontier novel by Theodore Winthrop, Yale's own Civil War martyr, stoked the flames.[112] King secured letters of introduction to the scientists working on the California State Geological Survey. And then, with a friend named William Hyde, whose father owned a foundry in Gold Hill, Nevada Territory, King and Gardiner prepared to travel by rail to St. Joseph, Missouri. There they would outfit themselves for the overland journey on horseback.

On April 14, 1863, as the boys prepared for their trip, Dan Dewey fell in battle at Irish Bend, Louisiana, a fatal bullet to his head.[113] "He died a hero," a comrade wrote to his mother; "the best could do no more."[114]

Mrs. Howland assured Mrs. Dewey of her son's deep affection for Dan, "to whom his soul was knit as David unto Jonathan," and reminded her that the two boys "were one in their keen intellectual zest for the highest mental enjoyment, and one in their fervent desire to become Christlike in heart and life."[115] Months later, on a frosty Sunday morning in the Sierra, King settled into a "sweet sabbath mood," and thought back to the Sundays he spent with his "brother" Dan in the Green Mountains of Vermont.[116] Their separate fates made him feel reflective, stirred him to imagine the far West as a proving ground, akin to what Dan had found on a Civil War killing field. Some years later, in 1877, when he returned to Yale to address the boys of Sheff, King likened a field geologist's travails to military service, expressing hope "that year by year men might stand here, fresh from the battle-field of life, out of the very heat of the strife, to tell us of their struggles, and hang the shield they have won along the walls of this temple of science."[117] In the West, King became a risk taker; in part for the thrill, in part to prove his manliness. "The possible danger of the trip," a colleague in the field later wrote, "was an additional temptation to him."[118]

KING'S FIRST TRIP WEST provided him with stories he would dine out on for years. In St. Joseph, he and his friends joined up with a St. Louis mule trader named T. M. Speers and his family, agreeing to help with the animals in exchange for board on their overland trek. On May 1 they started west along the Oregon Trail, driving the horses and mules alongside four wagons packed high with supplies. Less than twenty miles out, on the rain-soaked Missouri River bottomlands near Troy, Kansas, King and his friends got hauled into court by a sheriff's posse and accused of "kidnapping some negroes." The summer before, on Lake Champlain, King had convinced a federal agent that he was no draft dodger. Now Speers had to testify that the boys were not smuggling free blacks from Kansas into the slave state of Missouri. He won their release, and the travelers hurried on into Nebraska, following the muddy ruts of the overland trails along the Platte River, sometimes passing small bands of Potawatomi, sometimes glimpsing great herds of buffalo stampeding across the plains.[119] And always, passing more emigrants. Some 3,600 Mormons traveled west across the trails to Salt Lake City in this season of 1863. Another 16,000 gold-seekers and prospective settlers—some drawn west by the free land promised by the Homestead Act of 1862, some fleeing the chaos of war—walked and rode to California, Oregon, the territories of Nevada and Idaho, and the future territory of Montana. Still more traveled across Nebraska Territory en route to the goldfields of Colorado.[120]

Gardiner wrote to his mother about quieter moments on the trail: the unnerving sight of a blanket-wrapped corpse on a windswept Indian burial platform and the "vast loneliness of those deserts" that every day helped him feel stronger and healthier.[121] King, too, found his spirits improved as he moved farther and farther from his family and the social conventions of his New England world. "In that journey," Gardiner later wrote, "he showed his wonderful power of entering into the lives and sympathies of every human being on the train, from the half breed Indian hunter to the gaunt and bigoted Southwestern Missouri emigrant. With everyone he made friends."[122]

As they neared Fort Kearney, about two hundred miles into their trip, King determined to go on a buffalo hunt. It was sport, not necessity, a boyish act of bravado that distinguished King from the more sober pioneers moving across the prairies that spring. He hired a guide, traded his pony for an experienced horse, and galloped off with his revolver. Later, he described "with thrilling effect" how he spied a large herd of animals—ten thousand, he guessed—and pursued a large bull for two miles before firing as they descended into a shallow depression on the prairie. The wounded bull turned and charged King's horse, which in turn fell on top of King. And then, "in mortal fear of being trampled to death by the flying herd, King remained conscious while, as he said, a mile and a half of solid buffalo galloped past."[123] King's adventure became the stuff of hunting lore. Years later, Theodore Roosevelt speculated that King saw a herd "nearly seventy miles by thirty in extent" and offered it as evidence of the bygone days when "seething myriads of shaggy-maned cattle" roamed the American prairies.[124] His taste for thrill-seeking indulged, King caught the overland stage to meet up with his traveling companions, dragging his sore leg like a badge of honor.[125]

The Speers wagon train traveled through South Pass, past Fort Bridger, and across the Wasatch range into Salt Lake City. They camped there on the public square, and the Mormon leader, Brigham Young, came out to greet them and warned them to leave his people alone. Fearful that the emigrants might turn the Indians farther west against his settlements, he urged them to greet the Great Basin tribes with "a biscuit instead of a bullet."[126]

Next came the most difficult part of the overland trip. Traveling at night to avoid the punishing heat, the travelers walked and rode for more than a month across the hot sagebrush plains of Nevada Territory. It would have been weeks before they heard news of the costly Union victory at Gettysburg in the early days of July or learned about the bloody New York City draft riots two weeks later. In the streets of Manhattan, in neighborhoods that would have been familiar to King and Gardiner, working-class white men—angered that they could not buy their way out of the draft—rose up in ugly violence against local blacks who seemed an easy target for their political and economic frustrations. On August 6 the Speers party finally reached Carson City, at the eastern base of the Sierra Nevada, and here, in a town linked to the world by the recently completed transcontinental telegraph, they likely got word of the world they had left behind.

King, Gardiner, and Hyde left the Speers party in Carson City and continued on their own to Gold Hill, where Hyde's father owned a foundry. In this boomtown set on top of the great Comstock Lode, King hoped to see firsthand how abstract geological and mineralogical knowledge could be put to practical use.[127] But disaster struck their first night in town, when a windswept fire burned through Hyde's foundry, where the boys had bunked for the evening. They escaped with their lives but lost everything else, including their clothes, guns, money, and the letters of introduction King had to William Brewer of the California State Geological Survey.[128]

When Hyde decided to stay behind to help his injured father, King and Gardiner resolved to continue west on their own. They worked in town just long enough to earn some money, sold their horses, and started walking to California. A teamster picked them up and gave them a ride to the gold-mining town of Placerville. From there they made their way to Sacramento, where they boarded a steamboat downriver to San Francisco. On the boat, quite by happenstance, they bumped into the man they had come all this way to meet.

Men from the mines packed the steamboat, Gardiner wrote to his mother, "many rough, sunburned men in flannel shirts, high boots, belts and revolvers." But one man looked more "intellectual" than the rest, despite his old felt hat, heavy revolver belt, and weatherworn face. "Clare walked up to the man, the roughest dressed person on the boat, and delib-erately asked him if he was Professor Brewer. He was; and Clare introduced himself as a student from Yale Scientific School and was warmly received." King introduced Gardiner, the three spent the evening together, and when they reached San Francisco, Brewer took them to his hotel. The next day, after the boys spent their last money for "decent clothes," Brewer took them to the headquarters of the California State Geological Survey and intro-duced them to his boss, Josiah Whitney. Gardiner soon found work as res-ident engineer in charge of mapping and designing the defense batteries on Angel Island in San Francisco Harbor. And within just three days of arriving in the city, Clarence King was assistant geologist, without pay, for the very surveyors whose exploits had first flamed his imagination of the West.[129]

THE CALIFORNIA STATE GEOLOGICAL SURVEY heralded a new era in western exploration. Most government surveys of the antebellum period had a more military focus, stressing the topographical knowledge necessary for the construction of transportation routes that could facilitate the flow of people and supplies across the sparsely settled West. But the California survey, authorized by the state legislature in April 1860 and patterned after several similar state-sponsored projects in the East, aspired to a more disinterested scientific description of the state's "rocks, fossils, soils, and minerals, and of its botanical and zoological productions." It sought to address fundamental questions about the formation of mountains, the effects of glaciers, and the age of mineral-bearing strata. As the survey's director, Josiah Whitney, later told the legislators, "it was not the business of a geological surveying corps to act to any considerable extent as a prospecting party."[130]

Whitney's associates found him quick-tempered and stubborn, "troublesome" as a subordinate but a "just and generous superior." After graduating from Yale in 1839, he had studied chemistry in Europe, conducted fieldwork in the Midwest, and won additional respect as a serious scientist with his 1854 treatise, *The Metallic Wealth of the United States*.[131] His assistant, William Brewer, was likewise a Yale man who had done postgraduate work in Europe. After a short tenure as a chemistry professor at Washington College, in Pennsylvania, he had come to California to regroup after the recent loss of his young wife and child.[132]

Brewer thought King a young man of "light and ardent nature," who seemed even younger than his twenty-one years.[133] "Of course, he was not so thoroughly informed or so deeply interested in geological problems as he afterwards became," Brewer later explained. King's knowledge came from books, not experience, and Brewer found him "saturated chiefly with Ruskin and Tyndall. The remarks of the latter on the glaciers of the Alps were constantly upon his lips."[134]

King had embraced Ruskin's aesthetic theories about the "truth of earth" in an abstract way before, and in California he intended to see whether the contemplation of mountains really would elevate his mind to higher aesthetic truths. Ruskin believed that the earth's nobility would reveal itself to those who could look beyond the disguise of vegetation to see "the facts and forms of the bare ground." And who better than a geologist, especially one standing atop a mountain, to perceive the essential truths of the natural world or the titanic drama of the earth's creation? "Mountains are, to the rest of the body of the earth," Ruskin wrote in 1843, "what violent muscular action is to the body of man. The muscles and tendons of its anatomy are, in the mountain, brought out with fierce and convulsive energy, full of expression, passion and strength; the plains and lower hills are the repose and effortless motion of the frame."[135] To the perceptive geologist, natural formations could not only narrate some great cosmic drama but speak to the fundamental truths of life. "What would Ruskin have said, if he had seen *this*!" King exclaimed from the summit of Lassen Peak in September 1863.[136]

After a period of intense scientific work, King always found it a relief to stop "analyzing" and just expose himself to nature, like "a sensitized photographic plate." "No tongue can tell the relief to simply withdraw scientific observation," he wrote, "and let Nature impress you in the dear old way with all her mystery and glory, with those vague indescribable emotions which tremble between wonder and sympathy."[137] King's fascination with the geological sublime struck some of his survey colleagues as decidedly unscientific. The paleontologist William More Gabb grumbled that King "had rather sit on a peak all day and stare at those snow-mountains, than find a fossil in the metamorphic Sierra."[138] But Brewer accepted King's dreamy introspection as the complement to his remarkable physical vigor. "King is enthusiastic," he wrote, "is wonderfully tough, has the greatest endurance I have ever seen, and is withal very muscular."[139]

The work of the Irish scientist John Tyndall appealed to this more active aspect of King's character. An expert on glaciers and a seasoned alpine explorer, Tyndall cared less about looking at mountains than climbing them, and his writings balanced scientific observation with narrative adventure. King kept the two ideals in balance: Ruskin's reverential contemplation and Tyndall's active mountaineering. From the top of Lassen Peak, King might dream of Ruskin, but Tyndall guided his descent. When King pronounced his intent to slide down the snowslopes on the side of the peak, Brewer objected. "But he had read Tyndall; and what was a mountain climb without a *glissade*? So he had his way, and came out of the adventure with only a few unimportant bruises."[140]

. . .

KING'S SURVEYING CAREER BEGAN just two days after his arrival in San Francisco, when he headed north with Brewer for the lava fields of Lassen Peak, an active volcano in the southern part of the Cascade range. They passed through Sacramento and the old gold rush country where huge hydraulic operations had replaced the original placer mines, pausing along the way to examine copper deposits and gather fossils. After their ascent of Lassen Peak, where King broke out in his Ruskinian "rhapsodies of admiration," they explored the east side of Mount Shasta, a place to which King would later return to test his theories about glaciers.[141] Their investigations took them north to the Klamath River and then west toward the Pacific, in search of information about mineral deposits that they could incorporate into a comprehensive geologic map of the region. By early November, when King arrived back in San Francisco, he had completed an intense two-month course in geology no Yale classroom could match.

King's field journals, however, focused less on science than on spiritual matters. Geology required a particular set of technical skills, a knowledge of mineral structure, and an ability to read in the physical landscape a record of deep historical change. But it remained a science intimately connected to more profound questions about the structure and age of the earth and the very nature of life itself. Geologists argued over whether the earth had been shaped through *uniformitarian* forces, the slow, gradual effects of glaciers, erosion, and wind, or through *catastrophic* changes, more sudden and violent upheavals that might explain the uplift, tilting, fracturing, and faulting so easily observed in the mountains of the American West. And as Darwin's ideas about evolution gained currency, scientists also turned to geology for evidence to prove or disprove the new biological theories. The age of rocks held clues to challenge biblical theories of the earth's creation, and the fossil record could be used to support Darwin's theories about the slow, gradual evolutionary changes in the biological realm. Some California clergymen thought Whitney's state survey nothing less than blasphemy.[142]

King himself struggled with the tensions between science and religion, wondering how to reconcile the laws of nature with the laws of God. The biblical book of Revelation prophesied a new heavenly kingdom. But if earthly life was transitory, pondered King, "why study so hard into all the intricate sources of fact which will be swept away and known no more. I have looked for lessons. I have believed that God created all with design that with all was a lesson, that lessons were taught in nature which were not elsewhere."[143] He and Brewer "sat up long and talked about morals."[144] And when King returned to San Francisco after his first trip into the Sierra, he seemed newly serious and intent. When he posed that winter for a group portrait with the other members of the survey, he wore his one dress suit and adopted the formal, sober gaze of his older colleagues. Gardiner wrote to his mother about his old friend: "Out in the wilderness away from all outside Christian influences, God is bringing him into the closest communion with the things that are unseen and eternal. He is being cleansed for some great work."[145]

Although King recorded his personal struggles with faith in his private journals, much of his writing seems self-consciously literary, as if he imagined a more public audience for his words. "The air has changed," he wrote late in the season; "a slight frostiness creeps down from the north and the stars as I wake up mornings have a sort of cold brilliancy and frosty sparkle. The little pleiades no longer look down through a soft warm night. They gleam like a setting of cold gems."[146] King seemed to live on a kind of double track. Even as he lived in the present, he liked to step outside of his life to imagine it as a story.

King rested only briefly in San Francisco. He was still there, though, on November 19, 1863, when President Lincoln dedicated the memorial on the battlefield at Gettysburg and delivered the memorable address that recast the war. A war once imagined as a fight to preserve the Union became an epic battle to forge "a new birth of freedom" for all Americans, black and white. There was now a higher cause at stake, but this was still not King's fight. On November 24 he headed east to survey the famed Mariposa Estate. Once the property of the explorer John C. Frémont, it was now superintended by Frederick Law Olmsted, designer of Manhattan's Central

Park and an old friend of King's from his Hartford days. The mine stood at the southern end of the gold belt that stretched along the Sierra foothills, and in the surrounding countryside King made one of the survey's key scientific discoveries. With fossils gathered from rocks that contained veins of gold, he conclusively dated California's gold-bearing slate to the Jurassic period and showed that the auriferous placer deposits had formed during the Pliocene. King's find would prove useful to geologists and mining engineers alike.[147]

During the winter and spring of 1864, King made several more short trips for the survey. He saw Yosemite for the first time and went on to Lake Tahoe to take the barometric readings that would establish its altitude. He met up with Whitney in Virginia City, in the Virginia range east of the Sierra, and at his request conducted a trial survey as far east as the Humboldt range, to test the possibility of extending the California survey out across the Great Basin. Later, as the weather improved in late spring, the survey team plotted a return to the high mountains.

When Gardiner quit his job in the spring of 1864 rather than obey orders to work on the sabbath, King recommended him to Whitney as an additional member of the survey crew.[148] In May Gardiner joined on as a volunteer assistant topographer, unpaid like King. The two friends anticipated high adventure as they headed out to explore the southern part of the Sierra where, as Gardiner wrote to his mother, there stood "an immense tract...as yet unexplored."[149] King had seen the distant peaks of the High Sierra a few months earlier and hypothesized, with a nod to Tyndall, that these would be America's "new Alps."[150]

King posed again for a formal photographic portrait with Gardiner and two of the other members of his field party. The young man so intent upon demonstrating his seriousness in the picture made just a few months before now wore his field clothes to play the part of a swaggering frontiersman. With a mercury barometer slung across his back like a rifle and a geologist's hammer in his hand, he no longer seeks to disguise his youth. Instead, he revels in it.

King's field party of five set out from San Francisco in late May, in the midst of a brutal drought. Across desolate dirt trails, through dust storms that obscured their vision, they rode east into the San Joaquin Valley and headed south across land littered with the carcasses of dead cattle. With Brewer, King, and Gardiner rode the topographer Charles Hoffmann and the drover and packer Richard Cotter, whom Gardiner and King had met while crossing the continent the year before. Climbing into the foothills of the Sierra, near the town of Visalia, the exploring party came upon an impressive stand of giant sequoias. They received credit for "discovering" them, but, as King later confessed, a group of Indians directed them there.[151] They lingered for some days among the enormous trees, then continued up the divide between the Kings and Kaweah rivers. From the peak of a mountain that they promptly named for the Yale professor Benjamin Silliman Jr., they spotted a ridge that seemed to contain the highest mountains of this vast terrain. With their barometers they measured altitude, and with transit, sextant, and compass they slowly mapped this uncharted part of the High Sierra, using a method of triangulation that let them establish the location of new landmarks by taking sightings from two already known locations. As they rode deeper and deeper into the Sierra, King took note of the "purely Gothic" form of the mountains, resorting to Ruskinian language to describe the scene: "Whole mountains shaped themselves like the ruins of cathedrals,—sharp roof-ridges, pinnacled and statued; buttresses more spired and ornamented than Milan's...with here and there a single cruciform peak, its frozen roof and granite spires so strikingly Gothic I cannot doubt that the Alps furnished the models for early cathedrals of that order."[152] The Gothic spires of the Sierra allowed him to imagine that America could stake claim to a tradition as noble as Europe's.

The range that from the west seemed to be the "highest land" soon revealed itself to be lower than a range farther east, across the "terribleness and grandeur" of a deep canyon. King had long dreamed of getting to the "top of California," and he now asked Cotter to head east with him, up the highest peak they could spy. "I felt that Cotter was the one comrade I would choose to face death with," King later wrote, "for I believed there was in his manhood no room for fear or shirk." Brewer at first said no to the plan, feeling "a certain fatherly responsibility." But eventually he gave in.[153]

Some years later, in 1871, King wrote the story of his epic adventure, mingling a dramatic account of physical trials with descriptions of the geological sublime.[154] Scrambling to the top of the westernmost range of the Sierra, beneath the shadow of the peak the surveyors named Mount Brewer, King contemplated the "gigantic mountain-wall" that lay to the east, a "noble pile of Gothic-finished granite and enamel-like snow." He later wrote, "I looked at it as one contemplating the purpose of his life; and for just one moment I would have rather liked to dodge that purpose, or to have waited, or have found some excellent reason why I might not go; but all this quickly vanished, leaving a cheerful resolve to go ahead."[155] Leaving their comrades behind, Cotter and King walked east, traversing steep granite slopes, debris fields, and bleak stretches of frozen snow. They spent their first night on a small granite ledge near a frozen lake, huddled together under a blanket for warmth. They rose the next morning in "cold, ghastly dimness" and trekked on across the snowfields with their heavy packs, "animated by a faith that the mountains could not defy us." Later climbers accused King of overly dramatizing a not very difficult climb. But with scant equipment and no maps, King and Cotter had to rely on trial and error. They improvised, using their ropes to toss a lasso around the granite blocks that lay above them, pulling themselves up sheer cliffs, hand over hand; and they again used their ropes to descend, first one then the other, down rock crevices from ledge to ledge. "Our blood was up," King recalled, "and danger added only an extra thrill to the nerves." On the third day, they cut steps into a spire of ice that rose toward their long-sought summit, and when the ice spire became too thin and precarious, they wrapped their bodies around it and climbed it like a tree trunk. At last, they stood on the mountain's peak. But "to our surprise," King said with muted understatement, they could now see an even higher peak about six miles away to the south. Later they would name it Mount Whitney, in honor of the survey chief. For now, though, they would celebrate their conquest as if their triumph had been complete. At exactly twelve noon, King wrote, "I rang my hammer upon the topmost rock; we grasped hands, and I reverently named the grand peak MOUNT TYNDALL."[156]

The exuberant act celebrated their heroic sense of self. By the end of the survey season, there would be not just a Mount Tyndall, a Mount Whitney, and a Mount Brewer, but a Mount Clarence King (carefully named to avoid confusion with other Kings), a Mount Gardiner, and a Mount Cotter.[157] Earlier European explorers had marked their new American world with names that honored kings and queens and patron saints. But the men of the California State Geological Survey named their new world after their scientist-mentors, their political patrons, and themselves.

King's descent from Mount Tyndall proved as difficult as his climb. Later, he recounted Cotter's painful barefoot hike, their improvised rope climbs, their night in "weird Dantesque surroundings" with a voice that scarcely concealed his manly pride in their triumph over danger. Five days after leaving their companions, King and Cotter walked back into camp. As King later wrote, "Brewer said to me, 'King, you have relieved me of a dreadful task. For the last three days I have been composing a letter to your family, but somehow I did not get beyond 'It becomes my painful duty to inform you.'"[158] King held on to that anecdote like a badge of courage. And in his telling of the tale he minimized all that their small survey crew had accomplished that summer, unable perhaps to shake his disappointment over a failed attempt to scale Mount Whitney later in the season. Their expedition had added to the map of California an area "as large as Massachusetts and as high as Switzerland."[159] And the explorers had proved themselves, in the historian William Goetzmann's phrase, "Ruskins on a grand scale."[160]

King and Gardiner returned to San Francisco in September, but within a week set out for the Yosemite Valley. The United States Congress had set the land aside as a state park just a few months earlier, in June 1864 (it would become part of a larger national park in 1906). Now, as temporary employees of a special commission headed by Frederick Law Olmsted, King and Gardiner had less than three months to survey the park's boundaries and gather mapmaking data before the state legislature reconvened in

December. King found Yosemite a kind of open book, the marks left by glaciers "restoring in imagination pictures of the past." By the time early winter storms cut their work short, King could see that much more work would be needed to understand the titanic forces that had shaped the deep valley and the granite peaks of the surrounding cliffs.[161]

Between the weather and Whitney's perennial funding problems, the winter months promised little work. Whitney had already gone home to Boston for the season and Brewer had returned east to accept a professorship at Yale. So King and Gardiner returned to San Francisco "wet and exhausted," gave copies of their notes to Olmsted, and caught a steamer for Nicaragua, the first leg of a long trip home that would require them to cross the isthmus by land, then catch another northbound boat. Twelve days after leaving San Francisco, King found himself beneath a palm tree in Nicaragua, watching "a bewitching black-and-tan sister thrumming her guitar while the chocolate for our breakfast boiled." It made for a sharp contrast to the high windswept mountains of the Sierra. "Warmth, repose, the verdure of eternal spring, the poetical whisper of palms, the heavy odor of the tropical blooms, banished the cold fury of the Sierra, which had left a permanent chill in our bones," King wrote.[162] The Nicaraguan interlude left a permanent impression. For the rest of his life, King would associate tropical warmth with relief, with rest, and with exotic dark-skinned women.

KING BROUGHT AT LEAST one souvenir from Central America back east with him in January 1865. He spent weeks bedridden at his mother's house in Irvington, ill with malaria that he blamed on the Nicaraguan swamps. It would become his "usual August illness" anticipated "with the regularity of an astronomical phenomenon."[163] However glad she felt to see him, though, Mrs. Howland had little time for the son she had not seen in nearly two years. She gave birth to a baby boy, named George Snowden after his father, on February 12.[164] Clarence slipped out of this awkward situation as soon as he felt well enough—this half brother was twenty-three years younger than he, young enough to be *his* son—and went to New Haven to catch up with old friends and sit in on an astronomy course. In late February he and Gardiner went up to Boston to tell Whitney they wanted to stick with the survey for a while longer. Through the spring and summer he worked on his California maps. His mother and stepfather were ill that summer, King told Brewer, and their difficulties felt oppressive. "I long for the old Sierras this housed half smothered existence is damaging alike to mind morals and temper." When he posed for a formal portrait in October, he dressed the part of the gentleman-scholar in his fashionable muttonchop whiskers, with a dark suit, a gold watch chain, and an open book in his lap. But he fancied himself an adventurer. In November he and Gardiner caught a steamship for California.[165]

King's time back east coincided with the truce at Appomattox, the assassination of Lincoln, and the wrenching events of the immediate postwar era that marked the nation's first tentative efforts at political reconstruction. The end of the Civil War would eventually trigger renewed public interest in the far West: Civil War veterans would head west to fight Indians, mining investors would look westward with renewed interest, the government would help subsidize the construction of a vast infrastructure of roads and rail lines. But in the fall of 1865, the federal government had not yet resumed its support of the sort of western exploration that had marked the antebellum years, and the financial picture for exploration in California remained bleak. Whitney had insufficient funds for his hoped-for survey of the California deserts, so to keep King and Gardiner busy over the winter he sent them to Arizona to help General Irvin McDowell survey the territory for possible military roads. King and Gardiner found the work frustrating, difficult, and dangerous, and when the enlistments of their military escorts expired, they gave it up.

But King took away a story. On a road near Prescott, as they rode out ahead of their cavalry escort, King and Gardiner were ambushed by a group of Hualapai Indians armed with bows and arrows (they became Apache in King's later telling of the tale). They ordered the two surveyors to disrobe and lit a fire, giving every indication they intended to burn their captives. King stalled for time, using Spanish and sign language to explain that his cistern barometer, in its long cylindrical case, was actually a long-range gun. At the last moment the cavalry appeared, quickly perceived the situation, and charged the gathered crowd. "There is no doubt that King's presence of mind, coolness and ingenuity saved the lives of his friend and himself," explained a colleague.[166] This account of King's heroism came straight from the hero himself.

From Arizona, King headed back to California. He hesitated, at first, to rejoin the state survey. Whitney sensed why, writing to Brewer that "King wants to get more glory by doing something on his own hook."[167] But King eventually accepted the position of assistant geologist and he spent most of that summer of 1866 surveying in Yosemite and the surrounding high country of the central Sierra, working with Gardiner to perfect a new method of topographical mapping that would let them chart mountainous terrain with greater facility. This marked the end of their apprenticeship. The two young friends, still in their early twenties, chafed under someone else's command. They had ambitions of their own.

Sitting on a Sierra peak, looking eastward into Nevada, King and Gardiner hatched the plan that would shape American exploration of the West for the next decade. As Gardiner later recalled, their walk across the continent and their subsequent work in Arizona had persuaded them that "the survey of California and the problems to be solved there were but a part, and possibly a minor part, of the great problems of the structure, topographical and geological, of the whole mountain-system of western America from the plains to the Pacific." They thus conceived of a great national survey that would proceed along the Fortieth Parallel, examining a continental cross-section of the western United States. The idea was an outgrowth of their experience, wrote Gardiner, "coupled with King's great aggressive energy and consciousness of power to persuade men to do the thing he thought ought to be done."[168]

Returning to San Francisco after his summer in the mountains, King received an urgent telegram from his mother. Her husband, George S. Howland, had died of brain fever on September 21.[169] At age forty-one, Florence King Howland was a widow for the second time, now with a year-old son, a four-year-old daughter, and an adolescent stepson with severe physi-cal disabilities. King resigned his commission with the California survey, wrangled support from Whitney for his idea to mount an expedition along the Fortieth Parallel, and headed for home. "Family trouble and misfortune cannot be anticipated or prevented," he later wrote; "it comes like a shadow and darkens one's days most painfully."[170]

IN THE FALL OF 1866, no other American of King's generation combined such rigorous scientific training and experience with such sheer brainpower and physical energy. A brilliant future seemed within his grasp, and when King went to Washington a few months later to press his plan for a Fortieth Parallel survey, "senators, representatives and government officials of every grade became at once his admiring friends."[171]

But as King stood at the brink of the most creative and ambitious period of his professional life, he felt the painful tug of duty. Returning east, he discovered that his stepfather had died insolvent—his estate mysteriously disappeared—without making any arrangements for his wife or children.[172] And at the age of twenty-four, as he later wrote, King suddenly found him-self with "eleven people dependent on me alone," including his maternal grandmother and his mother's servants.[173] He borrowed money from Jim Gardiner to help his family through the crisis at hand.[174] But his days of glo-rious freedom were at an end. A few years later he looked back and recalled his years of mountaineering in California as "the pass which divides youth from manhood." He had traversed it, he wrote, "and the serious service of science must hereafter claim me."[175]

2

King of the West

KING BURST ON THE WASHINGTON SCENE IN JANUARY 1867, a boy wonder, scarcely twenty-five. "Small in size," a colleague called him, "compact, agile, active—all alive."[1] Somehow he had steadied his mother's household, and now he sought to press his plan to map the West. He wanted the federal government to give him command of an expedition to survey the land and resources along the Fortieth Parallel, some 450 miles from the Sierra to the western slope of the Rockies. Sensing what it would take to win federal support, he proposed to include "sufficient expansion north and south" to embrace the proposed route of the transcontinental railroad.[2] The rails would soon open for development vast stretches of the country that many Americans imagined to be a wasteland. But King, like other contemporary geologists, knew the region contained valuable minerals and other natural resources. "All that is needed," he said, "is to explore and declare the nature of the national domain."[3] He promised science with a practical payoff, detailed knowledge that would enable the federal government to promote the economic development of the far West and weave the region ever tighter into the fabric of the nation. "In these days, when the West is covered by a network of railways," one colleague later wrote, "it is difficult to conceive the obstacles that had to be encountered at that time in carrying out so ambitious and, as some then thought, so chimerical a plan."[4]

With letters from some of the nation's leading scientists and what even friends called "supreme audacity," King pitched his plan to Secretary of

War Edwin Stanton.[5] He had a "gift of winning men's feelings," Gardiner said. King quickly enlisted Stanton's support and then won the endorsement of Brigadier General Andrew Atkinson Humphreys, chief of the Army Corps of Engineers.[6] For backing from Congress, King turned to California's junior senator, John Conness (for whom King had fortuitously named a peak in the Sierra). Conness introduced legislation authorizing the secretary of war "to direct a geological and topographical exploration of the territory between the Rocky Mountains and the Sierra Nevada," and the bill authorizing three seasons of fieldwork—later to be renewed—passed on March 2, 1867.[7] When Stanton handed King his letter of appointment as U.S. Geologist-in-Charge of the U.S. Geological Exploration of the Fortieth Parallel, he reportedly said, "Now, Mr. King, the sooner you get out of Washington, the better—you are too young a man to be seen about town with this appointment in your pocket—there are four major-generals who want your place."[8] The young geologist who less than four years earlier had walked across the continent rather than enlist in the military now found himself a salaried employee of the War Department.

Technically, the survey would be a military operation. But in the field King's only connection to the army would be with military supply depots and the armed escorts accompanying his crew through Indian country. Humphreys let him write his own orders and select his own staff, and King chose all civilian scientists, mostly young men like himself who had come through Harvard and Yale rather than the topographical engineering program at West Point. He appointed his best friend, Jim Gardiner, as principal topographer, and as geologists hired the Boston-bred brothers James Duncan Hague and Arnold Hague, graduates of the scientific schools at Harvard and Yale, respectively. At Arnold Hague's suggestion he also took on the geologist Samuel Franklin "Frank" Emmons, a Harvard graduate who—like the Hagues—had studied in Europe. He handpicked a botanist, an ornithologist, and a photographer, the Irish-born Timothy O'Sullivan, whose work during the Civil War had taught him a thing or two about making pictures under difficult field conditions.[9] All told, with the camp men and the military escort, the team numbered thirty-five.[10] King's scientific crew remained remarkably stable through an eventual six seasons of fieldwork, a key factor in the survey's success and a tribute to his considerable talents as a leader.[11]

THE RELATIVE EASE WITH which King secured funding for his survey reflected not just his own infectious passion for his work but the concurrent ambitions and disorganization of the federal government with regard to western exploration. Clearly, the nation needed more information about the topography and natural resources of its vast western lands. But who should gather it? Federal exploration of the West during the 1860s and '70s reflected the triumph of ambition over planning, as two military expeditions and two civilian surveys took to the field with competing and sometimes conflicting agendas. Ferdinand Vandeveer Hayden, a geologist, medical doctor, and veteran of several military exploring expeditions of the late 1850s, went west again in 1867, leading the Geological Survey of Nebraska for the General Land Office. In 1869 his project expanded to become the more ambitious U.S. Geological Survey of the Territories under the Department of the Interior. In 1870, the Interior Department also funded John Wesley Powell's continued exploration of the southwest plateau country, establishing the Geological and Topographical Survey of the Colorado River of the West, a project that encompassed the ethnographic study of local Indian groups and sounded a little-heeded warning about the limits of expansion in an arid climate. In 1872 the War Department (already underwriting King) funded First Lieutenant George Montague Wheeler's U.S. Geographical Surveys of the Territory West of the One Hundredth Meridian, under the auspices of the Army Corps of Engineers, to focus on Nevada, Arizona, and the plateau country of southern Utah and western Colorado.[12] Inevitably, Hayden, Powell, and Wheeler clashed and sparred for congressional support; King, who twice received multiyear funding for his survey, largely stood apart from the annual scramble for funds. The conflict over funding and turf resolved only in 1879, when the separate surveys were discontinued under the legislation that established the United States Geological Survey, with King as its first director. But singly and collectively, the surveys represented American ambitions for the West writ large. And King's efficient field organization, emphasis on the practical uses of basic science, and new, more rigorous methods of topographic mapping provided a model and standard for the rest.[13] The data he and his fellow survey leaders gathered aided economic development in the post–Civil War West, and the scientific reports, maps, popular literature, and stunning photographic views that flowed forth year after year built broad public support for western exploration as a valuable national enterprise.

At a moment when most Americans conceived of the nation as a country divided between North and South, King broadened the geographical scope of the debate. He not only brought the West firmly within the realm of American science but also helped suggest that in the West lay the future of a newly unified nation.

NONETHELESS, SURVEY WORK POSED a personal dilemma for King. In his own peculiar way, he was now a family man, with a large household to support. The survey would keep him out west for the better part of three years, and his government paycheck of $250 a month could not compete with the potential, if uncertain, remuneration to be had in the private sector as a mining consultant. The very day Congress authorized the survey, Jim Gardiner reported to his mother that Mrs. Howland was "very, very sad." Her children were ill and her mind was in "such a condition that it is only with the greatest effort that she can write a letter.... She seems perfectly crushed."[14]

Family obligations had called King home. But they proved insufficient to keep him there. His mother's needs and the relatively modest income of a government explorer notwithstanding, he had a calling. He would go west. Following a grand farewell dinner at Yale, most of the Fortieth Parallel party sailed from New York on May 1, 1867. King, recovering from one of his frequent bouts of illness, followed ten days later.[15]

The trip to California required an eleven-day passage to Panama via steamship, a railroad trip across the isthmus, and a steamer up the Pacific coast to San Francisco, a speedy voyage in comparison to King's first trip west across the continent. King "hypnotized" his shipmates, wrote one of the younger survey members on the ship. "We were really listening to one of the great raconteurs of the world."[16] The social reformer Charles Loring Brace, traveling west with his wife in search of improved health, found his shipmate King a "truly American phenomenon," a young man of just twenty-five who had "already proved himself one of the most daring of living explorers" and now had command of "the most important American scientific survey of this generation."[17] Brace thought King an exemplary figure, the living proof of "what a field of manly training and scientific work there is now on the Pacific slope for our *jeunesse dorée,* who have no taste for business or the professions. The civilized man comes down and gathers up the best qualities of the barbarian—quickness of hand and eye, firm nerve, contempt of cold, hunger, and privation, power to use his body to the best advantage, and the ability to front coolly danger and death—and with them he combines all which training and culture have given, to gain new conquests over Nature and to advance the frontiers of knowledge."[18] King seemed an intoxicating blend of manly vigor and cultural refinement, a new sort of frontiersman who could stand up against the debilitating corruptions of urban life.

King reached California in early June and joined his crew at their camp near Sacramento, where they prepared for survey work while waiting for the mountain snows to melt. While King stayed in camp to wait for the government's shipment of gold coin—the currency of preference in the West—most of his crew headed east to set up a work camp in Truckee Meadows, near present-day Reno.[19] By the time King rejoined them in mid-July, they had hired a Jamaican-born cook named Jim Marryatt, who had approached the crew in search of work. Marryatt had run away from home at the age of seven and spent many years at sea before ending up in California. He was "a mulatto-like young man," James D. Hague wrote, "large, strong, well-built and pleasing in look and manner."[20] And in little time he became not just a valued cook but King's personal valet, a peculiar job for a camp man on a survey crew. But King was a dandy. And now, in command of his own survey rather than a volunteer geologist in another's, he dressed the part. Rossiter W. Raymond, a mining commissioner who encountered King later at a field camp in Salt Lake Valley, expressed surprise to find the famous explorer he knew by reputation attired in "immaculate linen, silk stockings, low shoes, and clothing without a wrinkle." Roughing it might be fine for the man who spent only a few weeks in the field, King explained. "But I, who have been for years constantly in the field, would have lost my good habits altogether if I had not taken every possible opportunity to practice them."[21]

King called Marryatt a "servant" in the expense report he filed with the federal government. But a government disbursing agent refused to reimburse King for a purely personal expense, insisting that "the kind of service should be stated so as to show its proper connection with a *public* duty."[22] King figured a way around the regulations, and Marryatt eventually outlasted all the other camp men, remaining through all six seasons of fieldwork and at least once accompanying King back east as "personal servant and office-man."[23] It became "almost invariably his custom," Raymond later wrote of King, "to have with him a personal attendant, who looked after his clothing, etc."[24] And almost invariably, these servants were black.

Marryatt grew close to his employer in ways that elude easy categorization, much as King's subsequent African American valet, Alexander Lancaster, would in the 1880s and '90s. He was at once friend and servant, confidant and social inferior, a man who surely knew much about King's personal affairs but kept his counsel close. He appears in plain sight on the peripheries of the survey records—King's companion on the trail, the dark figure standing in the photographs with the survey crew. But he enjoyed privileged access to King, sharing a house with him one winter and spring in Washington, D.C., while the rest of the survey crew bunked elsewhere, an indication of King's deep trust, if not a friendship between equals.[25] After the conclusion of the survey's fieldwork in 1872, Marryatt moved to San Francisco, where he lived with his Maryland-born wife, Adaline, and, for a time, continued to go back and forth to Nevada, working for other seasonal survey parties.[26] What he thought of King and the world to which the geologist introduced him remains unknown. But when his first child was born in 1878, he gave her the same name as King's mother—Florence.[27]

. . .

DURING THEIR FIRST SEASON in the field, King's men surveyed roughly twelve thousand square miles in a rectangular block of land that stretched across Nevada and gathered more than three thousand specimens of rocks, minerals, and fossils. In 1867, as King later wrote, "science ceased to be dragged in the dust of rapid exploration and took a commanding position in the professional work of the country."[28] Nonetheless, the fieldwork often proved difficult and dispiriting, "not over encouraging," as Frank Emmons recalled. Emmons suffered from the recurrent malarial fevers that affected so many nineteenth-century westerners, and he "fully made up my mind before the close of the campaign that once completed I would not undertake another year's work in such a region." But at season's end King provided "comfortable quarters and good food" for everyone at the winter quarters in Virginia City, Nevada. By March they felt ready to soldier on, taking up their survey work in waist-high snows. King's "enthusiasm was so contagious," Emmons wrote, "that however we might doubt the possibility of accomplishing a given project, we were always willing to try it after a talk with him. And the very most difficult things he generally undertook to do himself. So that in all his corps every one felt the impulse to make his best efforts if only to please King."[29]

King took pride in himself as a leader. "If I succeeded in anything," he later insisted with a tone of self-reassurance, "it was in personally impressing the whole corps and making it uniformly harmonious and patient; and I think I did that as much as anything else by a sort of natural spirit of command and personal sympathy with all hands and conditions, from geologists to mules." King thought it notable that he should succeed at such a young age, but "that . . . was not done without some rough and tumble work." And for the rest of his life, he regaled friends with carefully honed stories of his adventures. He liked to recount how he "forever reduced the soldiers and the working men of the survey to obedience" through his fearless pursuit of a deserter from his military escort: "I captured him in a hand to hand struggle in which I nearly lost my life and only saved myself by dodging his

shot and cramming my pistol in his ear in the nick of time." And he told
and retold the story of how he crawled into a cave in pursuit of a grizzly
bear and, as soon as his eyes adjusted to darkness, "put a ball into his brain."
With the bravado of a man who felt his place as a scientist firmly secured,
King urged James Hague to highlight these incidents in a brief biographical
sketch because "I care very little about my reputation as a geologist, but a
good deal as being a fellow not easily scared."[30]

KING LED HIS MEN into their winter quarters at Virginia City on a cold,
wet Christmas Day in 1867. Gardiner later wrote his mother that a fierce
snowstorm blew in that night and "I slept in Clare's arms on luxurious
mattresses and between snowy sheets; instead of rolling a blanket on the
ground."[31] Such close physical contact seemed to him normal, nothing at
all to hide from his mother. Physical intimacy (as distinguished from sexual intimacy) was a normal part of the intense friendships formed between
adolescent and young adult men, along with the exchange of confidences
about faith or work or women. These close relationships did not preclude
marriage, they simply preceded it.[32] And indeed, "Jamie" and "Clare" often
talked late into the night about their romantic prospects. Gardiner hinted
to his mother that he and his old friend sometimes lamented the personal
sacrifices they made in the name of science. "Professionally the year is a success. I wish I felt so sure of my heart work as that of the brain.... Man must
give himself time for loving thoughts and not crowd them out or stifle them
by too intense devotion to scientific subjects."[33] Soon enough, though, in
Virginia City, both men found time for "loving thoughts."

Sprawling up the steep slopes of Mount Davidson, Virginia City sat atop
the silver-rich Comstock Lode, isolated and remote from other cities but
bustling with boomtown energy and vitality. Mark Twain, a correspondent
for the city's *Daily Territorial Enterprise* from 1862 to 1864, joked that his
newspaper was little more than "a ghastly factory of slaughter, mutilation and
general destruction."[34] But amid the manufactured accounts of disaster, the
paper conveyed a portrait of a lively town "crowded with quartz and lumber

teams, freight teams loaded with merchandise, drays, job and express wagons, carriages, buggies, hacks and coaches—not to speak of donkeys, dogs and other small cattle."[35] Jews celebrated their holy days in a local Masonic lodge; Chinese and Mexican workers staged holiday parades through the steep blue clay streets; Irish laborers danced late into the night at gatherings organized by their own fraternal organizations.[36] Blacks had their own saloon and a separate, parallel social world. After King's cook and valet, Jim Marryatt, witnessed a shooting at a "'darkies' ball" in Carson City on New Year's Day 1868, he pronounced it the last "nigger ball" he would ever attend.[37]

In this crowded urban outpost in a remote part of Nevada, King fell in love.

King and Gardiner settled into the Ophir House, the well-appointed home of a mining superintendent, and plunged into the city's social whirl.[38] "Clare and I are having a lovely time together in our little house," Gardiner wrote to his mother.[39] During the days, they snowshoed under the bright winter sun. And in the evenings, King decked himself out in tight doeskin trousers, a vest and coat, pastel-shaded gloves, and a white tie and stepped out with Gardiner into a whirl of dinner parties and social calls, musical entertainments and dancing lessons.[40] Soon King took a liking to Ellen Dean, a "school marm" known as "Deany," and Gardiner began courting her friend Josephine Rogers, a young schoolteacher from Illinois. Frank Emmons, who shared living quarters with King and Gardiner that winter, noted that they often spent their evenings "out calling."[41]

On April 12, 1868, King returned to Virginia City from a trip to San Francisco and announced his engagement to Dean. "Gardner's expected," Emmons wrote, in anticipation of a similar decision from his other friend.[42] That spring, as the weather improved and the surveying parties took to the field, Gardiner and King spent little time in town. But King seemed in ebullient spirits, boasting to William Brewer of his administrative "boldness" in cutting through government red tape and joking that Virginia City so agreed with him that his weight had increased to 153 pounds.[43] He sounded confident, if curiously unspecific, about his matrimonial plans. From a field camp in late August, he wrote a cryptic note to Brewer to offer congratulations on the news of his impending marriage. "I can bid you Godspeed in this move with more thankfulness and more hearty good will than I once could, for one of the best of God's own girls has promised bye and bye to crown my life with the same blessing yours is about to receive."[44]

But something went awry. On September 7 Jim Gardiner and Josie Rogers wed in Virginia City in a small ceremony at the home of her father, a mining engineer.[45] King was nowhere near. He was away in Bone Valley, in the northeastern part of Nevada, hundreds of miles from Virginia City and the man he called his "brother."[46] When the survey season ended later that fall, Gardiner brought his wife back to Washington to work on the season's reports with King. On December 4 Frank Emmons went to call on the Gardiners in their Washington lodgings and from there he went to see King. He wrote in his diary: "At room find King very despondent."[47] Concern over the future of the survey seemed just part of it.

Scant clues document the collapse of King's marriage plans. In a small pocket journal filled with stray notes for the stories he would never write, King penciled in on March 1, 1869, "Novel note—after the breaking of the engagement he dreams he sees her drown and only her hands above water and her cry then wakes on the gray hills."[48] A few months later he scrawled, "The idea of mother and God triumphs over passion."[49] Gardiner had told his mother of King's impending marriage but now informed her it was off. "Please say nothing to anyone about Clare's engagement unless to Mrs. Howland," Gardiner instructed his mother in July 1869. "She feels terribly at its being broken for she admired and loved Ellen's noble qualities."[50] King must have brought Dean home to Newport and everything fell to pieces. He backed out of his commitment. "I would never marry a woman anyhow, *just because I said I would*," King later told James Hague. "That is the poorest possible reason men or women can ever have for marrying each other. People who marry without any better reason than that must surely come to grief."[51]

Florence Howland had firm ideas about marriage and about daughters-in-law. She offered unsolicited advice to the recently wed "Jamie" Gardiner, urging him to foster a warm relationship between his new wife and his family: "Because of their love for her husband...they should be endeared to her."[52]

Whatever words passed between her and her own son remain unknown, but she seemed to expect Clarence's new family to have plenty of room for her.

The twice-widowed Mrs. Howland had reason to fear the presence of another woman in her son's life; she could ill afford to lose Clarence's emotional and economic help. In 1869 she was back in Newport, struggling to support her sixty-nine-year-old mother, her eighteen-year-old stepson, her own young children, just seven and four, and two live-in servants, one white, one black.[53] Her make-do living arrangements seemed too "uselessly slip shod" for guests, and she confessed to Jim Gardiner in April 1869 that she no longer had "the strength to supplement the very insufficient service of this improvised establishment."[54] King resigned himself to going to Newport that spring, shuttling back and forth between the chaos of his mother's house and the more peaceful repose of his aunt Caroline King's.[55] "Only a sense of duty keeps me here," he wrote a colleague. "I have nothing to do but yield gracefully....I shall stay here until I go West."[56] King felt loath to disappoint his mother but tired of always doing the proper thing. He scribbled a note in his pocket journal that spring about "the intense yearning I feel to get through my analytical study of nature and drink in the sympathetic side."[57] Some years later, he remarked to a friend that he had lost the only woman he had ever wanted to marry through "too much attention to duty. Duty has stood between me and almost every good thing."[58]

KING HEADED BACK WEST in the spring of 1869, arriving in Salt Lake City on May 15, just days after the golden-spike ceremony at nearby Promontory Point marked the completion of the transcontinental railroad. In this third season of survey work, King and his men mapped the area around the Great Salt Lake and surveyed the coal deposits on either side of the Uinta Mountains, along the route of the Union Pacific. Then King stayed on, beyond his colleagues, to finish up his work on the Comstock Lode. The three seasons of fieldwork for which he had secured appropriations then complete, he speeded back to Washington on an eastbound train.

King took Jim Marryatt east with him that winter. And amid a busy social schedule that involved receptions at the White House, meetings at the Smithsonian, and long horseback rides with friends, King helped his men work to bring to conclusion the formal reports summarizing the findings of the survey. *Mining Industry* (1870), James Hague's massive volume, with three reports by King, bore the designation "Volume III," but King pushed to have it appear first, correctly anticipating that it would assuage congressional concerns about the utility of the survey.[59] The botany volume soon followed, and King looked forward to having concentrated time to review the survey's findings and to work on his own geological text. On June 1, 1870, he moved with Marryatt to New Haven, to be closer to the laboratories at Yale, where he could analyze the rock and mineral samples he had brought back east. But almost immediately thereafter he learned from General Humphreys that more funds had been allocated for additional fieldwork. Though King hoped to stay on in New Haven, Humphreys ordered him west in July. Leaving Gardiner behind to supervise the writing of the reports, King headed west with a scaled-back crew to explore the dormant volcanoes of the Pacific coast.[60]

A short and unanticipated survey season yielded what King characterized for Humphreys as a "somewhat startling discovery."[61] Climbing Mount Shasta from a new approach, King discovered an active glacier, the first to be found in the continental United States. Whitney, Dana, and Agassiz had all declared no such thing could exist. But ever since he observed what looked like a glacial stream on his first visit to Mount Shasta in 1863, King had suspected a glacial ice field might lie concealed high up in the mountain. Now proven right, he named Whitney Glacier in honor of his doubting chief. When Arnold Hague and Frank Emmons soon afterward discovered more glaciers on Mount Hood and Mount Rainier, King asked Humphreys to keep the news quiet until he could return east to announce it himself.[62]

The glacier stories brought King a new popular acclaim: invitations for public talks, requests for magazine articles, and even an invitation to the Parker House in Boston, where he rubbed shoulders with the likes of Emerson and Longfellow.[63] King had grown up surrounded by writers—

his grandmother Sophia Little and his mother, Florence, a sometime-poet herself.[64] Now, besieged by requests for stories of his adventures, he tried his own hand at writing. He gave a piece about Shoshone Falls to his old friend Bret Harte, editor of *Overland Monthly*, who published it in October 1870. Then he agreed to give James T. Fields, of the *Atlantic Monthly*, a series of essays recounting his western adventures and promised publisher James R. Osgood that he could later issue these essays in book form.[65] Osgood thought the word "geological" would "be too heavy ballast for my sketches," King recalled, so he chose a lighter title: "Mountaineering in the Sierra Nevada."[66] And even as he returned to his field journals, gathering ideas for his essays, he dashed off an elaborate little Christmas gift for his half sister Marian and two of her young friends, a slender leather-bound volume with printed pages and twelve mounted photographs, *The Three Lakes: Marian, Lall, Jan, and How They Were Named.* In two brief letters, he described for the girls his climbs to the high mountain lakes he named in their honor, and in the two accompanying poems spun a haze of gentle fantasy about the alpine world, animating the lakes with the spirit of a "kindly Snow Giant" and the legacy of a terrible "ice dragon."[67]

King wrote quickly that winter and spring of 1871, racing to have five essays done by April so he could look at proofs before he headed back west for another season of work for which he now had funding to extend the survey eastward to the eastern edge of the Front range. When the first of the essays appeared in the *Atlantic Monthly* in May 1871, a wide reading audience discovered what King's intimates had long known: he was a born storyteller. And if some readers found it difficult to distinguish literal fact from a more exaggerated version of King's mountaineering adventures, the long descriptions of the scenery and the underlying topography of the country gave it all the ring of glorious, exciting truth.

Now survey leader, scientist, and popular writer, too, King became increasingly peripatetic, his travel enabled by the railroads that shuttled him in mere days between East and West. In June and July 1871 he supervised his survey crews in Wyoming and stole time away to climb Mount Whitney in ill-fated pursuit of his long-held ambition to be the first white man to stand on the highest point in the United States.[68] He returned east in July to help shepherd through work on the contour maps for his geologic atlas, raced up to Newport to see his mother, and was back in Colorado in early August.

And there, in Estes Park, King met the man whose words would later keep his name and memory alive long after the stories of the West's exploration faded from public memory. In his own day, King won acclaim as a geologist and an explorer, a writer and an administrator. But he would live on in popular memory chiefly as a spectacular friend.

RIDING THROUGH THE PARK in search of his crew, King had paused for the night in a cabin with "a room and one bed for guests" when a small, frail, mustached Harvard history professor rode into camp on a mule, lost after a day of fishing. It was Henry Adams. "As with most friendships," Adams later wrote, "it was never a matter of growth or doubt.... They shared the room and the bed, and talked till far towards dawn."[69]

The grandson of one president and great-grandson of another, Adams had gone west that summer at the suggestion of his boyhood friend Frank Emmons, in search of adventure in the "land of the future" and a temporary respite from the weighty world of Brahmin Boston. "The West was still fresh," Adams wrote, "and the Union Pacific was young. Beyond the Missouri River, one felt the atmosphere of Indians and buffaloes."[70] He brimmed with abstract admiration for the hearty western field scientists who "felt the future in their hands," and in Clarence King he met his ideal. "A new friend is always a miracle," Adams reflected, "but at thirty-three years old, such a bird of paradise rising in the sage-brush was an avatar."[71]

Years later, in his memoir *The Education of Henry Adams* (1907), Adams wrote of King in his own peculiar, third-person narrative voice. But neither literary style nor the passage of years could mute the intensity of the author's attraction to the man who seemed everything he was not. "The one, coming from the west, saturated with the sunshine of the Sierras, met the other, drifting from the east, drenched in the fogs of London." In King's vibrant presence, Adams felt small and diminished. How could he compete with King's unrivaled charm? "Adams was never guilty of a witticism, unless by accident."[72] But the professor found himself entranced. "King had everything to interest and delight Adams. He knew more than Adams did of art and poetry; he knew America, especially west of the hundredth meridian, better than any one; he knew the professor by heart, and he knew the Congressman better than he did the professor. He even knew women; even the American woman; even the New York woman, which is saying much."[73]

Trained in one world, Adams felt adrift in another, where technology and biology challenged old truisms, and a classical education no longer assured success. King, by comparison, seemed exquisitely poised to seize the moment. "King had moulded and directed his life logically, scientifically, as Adams thought American life should be directed. He had given himself education all of a piece, yet broad." Adams wrote with hindsight, years after King's death and with a keen sense that his own could not be far off. But he could still capture his young man's sense of wonder at King's extraordinary talent. "Whatever prize he wanted lay ready for him—scientific, social, literary, political—and he knew how to take them in turn. With ordinary luck he would die at eighty the richest and most many-sided genius of his day."[74]

Adams and King talked "till the frost became sharp in the mountains"; then Adams headed back to Cambridge to "take up again the humble tasks of schoolmaster and editor" and King continued on, triangulating his way across the West.[75]

THE SEASON'S WORK AND travel left King worn. After leaving Adams he headed to Cheyenne to invest in a ranching operation. Nothing about his employment with the survey prohibited a little speculation of his own, and the ranching, ironically, proved a much sounder investment than any of King's later mining ventures.[76] He worked in the Uinta and Escalante ranges in late 1871, then retreated to San Francisco for the winter, ill and exhausted. Across the bay in Oakland, Jim Gardiner's wife, Josie, died of tuberculosis that January, and Gardiner soon left to take his young daughter back east to be raised by his mother.[77] A dispirited King requested a brief leave of his own from survey duty, and in early February set sail with Arnold Hague for several weeks in the Hawaiian Islands. The "old-gold girls that tumble down waterfalls" entranced; the warm tropical air and swaying palms seduced. King garlanded himself in flowers to attend "a merry Kalakauan fête" and rode the "breasting breakers on a Hawaiian beach, himself daring and swift in the water as the lithest brown maid." King and Hague investigated some volcanoes, but in memory, at least, the physics of lava flows proved less engaging than the real or imagined pleasures of Hawaiian women. "I came perilously near falling in love with the Princess," King joked.[78]

He liked to jest this way, suggesting an idea so preposterous his listeners could only smile. But his remark contained more than a kernel of truth. As Henry Adams often observed, "it was not the modern woman that interested him; it was the archaic female, with instincts and without intellect."[79]

WHEN *MOUNTAINEERING IN THE SIERRA NEVADA* first appeared in February 1872, King was en route to Hawaii, far beyond reach of the first reviews that heralded him as a remarkable, fresh literary voice. "A more varied or entertaining book than this of Mr. King's we have not met for a long time," wrote a critic for the *New York Times*.[80] A quick commercial success, *Mountaineering* went through nine printings in its first two years, with an expanded edition released in 1874. King had aimed for a broad audience— once telling Emmons that he wrote *Mountaineering* "as an experiment to see if a piece of writing description of scenery could be made popular literature"—and he found it.[81] Emmons recalled hiking in 1874 "to a little inn in a remote valley of the Austrian Tyrol, and finding the only other guest a very cultivated Englishman, whose first question as soon as he learned I was an American was 'Do you know Clarence King?'"[82]

Part popular science, part cultural commentary, the collected essays narrate King's adventures in California and position him as a virile young hero of this new American place. But the book also provides a window into King's interior life. King keeps a light touch, builds narrative suspense, splashes the world with a colorful wash of descriptive prose. Yet beneath the surface gloss one senses a divided man—tempted by risk and attracted to the exotic but fearful of losing the social prerogatives that defined his place in the world.

King counted among the explorer's greatest pleasures "the frequent passages he makes between city life and home; by that I mean his true home, where the flames of his bivouac fire light up trunks of sheltering pine and make an island of light in the silent darkness of the primeval forest. The crushing juggernaut-car of modern life and the smothering struggles of civilization are so far off that the wail of suffering comes not, nor the din and dust of it all."[83] The explorer could find true repose only in the wilds, and yet there he could never remain for long. Duty compelled him to return to the "heat and pressure" and "huddled complexity" of town, leaving behind the liberating freedom of the out-of-doors. "As often as one makes this transit between civilization and the wilds," King wrote, "one prizes most the pure, simple strengthening joy of nature."[84]

Even in the field, however, King could never quite surrender his social privileges or abandon the idea that he had a particularly superior appreciation of nature. He was no tourist; he was a pathfinder. He thus had scant regard for those western travelers " 'doing America,' " who with hired guides would "cause themselves to be honorably dragged up and down our Sierras, with perennial yellow gaiter, and ostentation of bath-tub."[85] He conceived of himself as different, nothing like those other visitors to Yosemite's Inspiration Point whom he disparaged as "that army of literary travellers who have here planted themselves and burst into rhetoric."[86]

Much as he thought himself superior to the average tourist, he also considered himself a notch or two above the average frontiersman. King wrote elsewhere of his admiration for those Americans who showed "a determination to grapple with the continental *terra incognita*, to wrest it from barbarism, to dare its solitudes, to search in the great vacant spaces between the eastern fringe of civilization and the far Pacific for whatever of goodly land or other lure lay therein."[87] But King had in mind pioneers like himself, men of refinement who could find spiritual renewal in nature's wilds. For the less savory frontiersmen he described in *Mountaineering*, the wilderness represented not spiritual touchstone but social disintegration.

Looking around at the West's recent immigrants, King saw the very worst of human nature. The brave spirit of "Westward Ho!" might inspire an explorer like himself, "but when, instead of urging on to wresting from new lands something better than old can give, it degenerates into mere weak-minded restlessness, killing the power of growth, the ideal of home, the faculty of repose, it results in that race of perpetual emigrants who roam as dreary waifs over the West, losing possessions, love of life, love of God, slowly dragging from valley to valley till they fall by the wayside."[88] It was the classic dilemma of the American frontier: did it call forth the very best in the pioneers by compelling them to develop a new sense of hearty self-reliance, or did it destroy the very moral underpinnings of American life?

In a family he dubbed the "Newtys of Pike," King found proof of a common western story that never failed to startle him "with its horrible lesson of social disintegration, of human retrograde."[89] The popular interpretation of Darwin presumed a steady improvement of the human race, but King wondered whether the laws of evolution might also countenance social decline: "Are not these chronic emigrants whose broken-down wagons and weary faces greet you along the dusty highways of the far West melancholy examples of beings who have forever lost the conservatism of home and the power of improvement?"[90] He doubted whether a vibrant American culture could ever thrive in the West. Californians might have a cheerfulness, physical vigor, and "glorious audacity" King found lacking in the East. But he counseled that "we must admit the facts. California people are not living in a tranquil, healthy, social *régime*....Aspirations for wealth and ease rise conspicuously above any thirst for intellectual culture and moral peace."[91]

Despite his scorn for the West's new American immigrants, King found the region's Hispanic and Indian inhabitants curiously alluring, their poverty less a sign of social decline than picturesque appeal. "The American residents of Lone Pine outskirts live in a homeless fashion; sullen, almost arrogant neglect stares out from the open doors," he wrote. "There is no attempt at grace, no memory of comfort, no suggested hope for improvement. Not so the Spanish homes; their low, adobe, wide-roofed cabins neatly enclosed with even basket-work fence, and lining hedge of blooming hollyhock."[92] Likewise, while the disorderly American ranches "send a stab of horror through one," the Indian rancheros had a "quaint indolence and picturesque neglect" that conveyed "a sort of aesthetic satisfaction."[93]

Women presented similar aesthetic distinctions. The "heavy ample" Spanish "donna" [sic] offered "a study of order and true womanly repose."[94] An Anglo-American woman, by contrast, seemed "a bony sister, in the yellow, shrunken, of sharp visage, in which were prominent two cold eyes and a positively poisonous mouth; her hair, the color of faded hay, tangled in a jungle around her head."[95] She had a "hard, thin nature, all angles and stings."[96] King preferred more voluptuous types. As Henry Adams observed, "King had no faith in the American woman; he loved types more robust."[97]

He loved types more dark-complected, too. For King, the Chinese workers' "fresh white clothes and bright olive-buff skin made a contrast of color which was always chief among my yearning for the Nile."[98] And no sallow-complected immigrant from Missouri could compare to the middle-aged Spanish woman of whom King observed that "in her smile, in her large soft eyes, and that tinge of Castilian blood which shone red-warm through olive cheek, I saw the signs of a race blessed with sturdier health than ours."[99]

Few contemporary readers saw in *Mountaineering in the Sierra Nevada* a guide to the author's social thought. Most read it as an adventure book—the thrilling tale of King's ascent of Mount Tyndall, his flight from some Mexican banditos, his exploration of the Yosemite Valley—a bit of vicarious excitement to be enjoyed from the comfort of home. "Those whose circumstances compel the enjoyment of adventure at second hand, and those whose temperament makes them prefer to contemplate the grand and terrible in nature without risking their necks or breaking their backs with violent exercise, will find a delightful guide in Clarence King," proclaimed *Scribner's Monthly*.[100] "In vividness of picturesque description no Alpine writer excels it," wrote a reviewer in *Appletons' Journal of Literature, Science and Art*.[101] With time, how-ever, the book would come to seem more valuable as the vivid record of a particular historical moment. It will remain King's "monument," the novel-ist William Dean Howells wrote in 1904. "He has brilliantly fixed forever a phase of the Great West already vanished from reality."[102] The "prime Rus-kinian document of the age," the historian William Goetzmann later called *Mountaineering*. Others classed it with works by Bret Harte and Mark Twain, John Burroughs and Francis Parkman, crediting King with a place as founder of a California school of literature.[103]

Curiously, King's new friend Henry Adams weighed in with the rare negative review. "King is a kind of young hero of the American type," Adams conceded in an essay in the *North American Review*. But to grasp King's true genius, one ought to read his amusing book in tandem with the great scientific reports still to come from the Fortieth Parallel survey. "Artistically speaking," Adams wrote, "Mr. King's book errs perhaps in car-rying sensationalism too far for effect...the wonder always is that a day passes without accident. If he is not dragging or riding a mule up or down a perpendicular precipice, he is shooting at bears, getting struck by lightning, or catching rattlesnakes by the tail." The book displayed only "the superfi-cial qualities of a lively *raconteur*."[104]

Adams thought the book an incomplete portrait of his complicated friend. He knew the boyish adventurer to be a sober-minded scientist and the man of intuitive thought and action a person of calculating intellect. In *Mountaineering*, King resolved the old pull between Ruskin's poetic "myth-making" and Tyndall's more narrative and hard-edged style. He drew suc-cessfully from both literary styles. But the deeper conflicting impulses that emerged from his encounters with the natural world seemed harder to reconcile. King felt ineluctably drawn to the immediacy, sensuality, and aesthetic picturesqueness of western frontier life, exemplified particularly by the region's Spanish and Indian inhabitants. "Among the many serious losses man has suffered in passing from a life of nature to one artificial," he wrote, "is to be numbered the fatal blunting of all the senses."[105] But New-port and Yale, the expectations of his mother, and the conventions of his time held him tight. King felt torn. He could acknowledge the attractions of another, more "natural" life but felt compelled to dismiss them as the humorous musings of a literary man.

THE FORTIETH PARALLEL CREWS spread out across the West during the summer of 1872, their last season of fieldwork, to gather the final bits of topographical and geological data they would need for their comprehensive reports. King elected to keep the survey's offices in San Francisco, where he could focus on a study of the ancient glaciers in the High Sierra for his grand synthesis of the region's geology. But the highlight of the season came from unexpected quarters. By autumn, the nation had proclaimed Clarence King its hero, a dazzling "King of Diamonds" who had saved the country from economic collapse.

San Francisco buzzed with rumors that summer, vague stories of diamond fields richer than the Comstock Lode or any California gold mine, in Arizona perhaps or maybe Nevada. Speculation reached a peak in July when banker William Ralston incorporated a mining company capitalized with $10 million. His board of directors included a former California governor and two Civil War generals. Expectations ran high, fueled by a report from the eminent mining expert Henry Janin, who had reportedly studied the secret gemstone fields and pronounced they would yield "gems worth at least a million dollars a month." Investors poured money into competing companies, all in search of the fabled fields of riches.[106]

King had fieldwork to attend to. He spent most of September in the Sierra, much of it in the company of the painter Albert Bierstadt. But the diamond story rankled. If by chance the gemstone deposits lay within the territory covered by the Fortieth Parallel survey, their discovery by private parties would cast into doubt the work of the government scientists who had found no trace of such riches. Quite by chance, Emmons and Gardiner found themselves on a westbound train with Janin and several mysterious diamond prospectors as they returned to San Francisco at the conclusion of their survey work in October. They shared with King the intelligence they had gleaned, and the men decided to undertake their own secret investigation of the rumors, not even informing General Humphreys back in Washington of their change of plans. Various clues suggested that the mystery field lay in the mountains of Browns Park in northwestern Colorado, right within the scope of the survey. Traveling with utmost secrecy, speaking in code in case they should be overheard, King and Emmons headed by train to Fort Bridger, Wyoming, with survey topographer Allen David Wilson, then rode some 150 miles to the south. Their intuition proved correct. On a high sandstone mesa they found the gems. In a nearby stream gulch fluttered a note from Henry Janin claiming water rights.

The first afternoon of exploration made the men believers. Rubies, diamonds, garnets, and sapphires abounded for the taking. But a more sober examination the next day revealed the field to be a colossal fraud. The gemstones, in unnatural mineralogical and stratigraphical associations, lay only in places where the earth had been disturbed; in untrampled ground there lay nothing at all.

King raced back to San Francisco to lay his evidence before Janin and Ralston. When a shaken Ralston sought one more opinion, King volunteered to lead his men back to the site. This time, even Janin could see how he had been duped by the unscrupulous swindlers who had salted the field. The expedition returned to San Francisco in late November and presented its findings to Ralston's board, which immediately voted to publish King's report. Instantly, King became a hero, the public servant who had saved prospective investors countless sums of money and helped the nation avoid a disastrous economic bubble. "We have escaped, thanks to God and Clarence King, a great financial calamity," pronounced the *San Francisco Chronicle*.[107]

Humphreys grumbled that the whole affair represented an improper use of King's time. But in fact the episode demonstrated the real value of government science. As the *Nation* observed, "This single exposure, the work of a few days in appearance, the result of several years in reality, has more than paid for the cost of the [entire] survey."[108] Coming as it did at the very end of the survey's six years of fieldwork, the diamond affair gave the entire Fortieth Parallel survey the glittering aura of triumphant success.

Much of the hard intellectual work of the survey still lay ahead: King would not finish his grand synthetic volume, *Systematic Geology*, until 1878. But with the fieldwork complete, a phase of his life seemed finished. Since 1863, when he walked across the West, King had spent long periods every year in remote mountain and desert field camps, exploring, mapping, and doing the basic science that would help him to develop a comprehensive understanding of the region's deep geologic structure. Now, weary as he felt, he looked back on those ten years with a deep sense of loss for the freedom, excitement, and clear sense of purpose of the survey years. He was no longer a boy wonder. He turned thirty the year of the diamond hoax; his receding hairline and stout carriage lent him a solid, even portly look.

During the winter of 1872–73, King elected to stay in San Francisco to work on his survey maps, hoping that the mild climate would prove a good antidote for his general exhaustion and rheumatic aches and pains. But there was no escaping the complications of life here, even for a man whose scientific derring-do had made him an American celebrity. He moved his mother and her three children to California for the winter. His stepbrother Snowden was "still in status quo requiring endless care and attention and showing little hope of ultimate recovery," King wrote to Emmons in late January. "My Mother is extremely delicate and altogether the family gives me pretty constant anxiety."[109] He requested a two-month leave of absence from government service in February and March, apologizing to Emmons for leaving his crew on their own. "I have sought to do my duty and hope I have saved my Mother from a decline but the sense of being absent from my post has galled me from morning to night."[110]

Life besieged him from all sides. Jim Gardiner wrote to say that with the Fortieth Parallel fieldwork complete, he intended to go to work for King's rival, Ferdinand V. Hayden, who was now leading a civilian survey team in the Rockies. "I am shaken to the heart and well nigh crushed," King wrote his "dear brother." He thought Hayden "a selfish and Christless man," and of course he felt betrayed, especially since Gardiner had not yet completed his work for the folio atlas of King's survey. But mostly, now at a turning point in his own life, King found it hard to fathom that his dearest friend did not see the world as he did. Fieldwork is for *"young* men," King told Gardiner; "we have already done *more* than our share." With an uncharacteristic tone of regret, he now wrote of science's "relentless chill," which made it all but impossible to find the spiritual calm "which may *alas* only come of a settled mode of life." "We give ourself to the *Juggernaut* of the intellect," King wrote his friend. "And in such a life as we have lived and as you propose, the veritable demands are *too* much for the large, sweet, beautiful perfection of the soul." Nonetheless, he reassured his brother, whatever his final decision, *"our* love will outlive time and circumstance."[111]

King could make light of his new worries. To Emmons, who had already headed back east, he wrote, "Now you have only to write me that there are numerous eligible girls to make me feel more keenly my loneliness here."[112] But in addition to his anxieties about his mother and his friend, on top of the adjustment from fieldwork to office work, he worried about money. A close friend of his stepfather's, taking pity on the widowed Mrs. Howland, had put some securities in trust in 1871, directing that the interest be turned over to King to manage for his mother's benefit.[113] But that scarcely met the family's needs. That winter King accepted a job as an expert witness for a California mining company at a fee of $5,000.[114] No regulations prohibited government scientists from accepting outside work. But for the King of Diamonds, who had just made his name by showing how government scientists could put the public good above private gain, the work always made him feel just a bit defensive, even as he won a reputation for incorruptible honesty.

Thus, when King moved back east in late 1873, to set up offices for the survey's laboratory and related work in New York, he felt a man divided: between public duty and private profit, the intellectual challenges of science and the repose of a simpler life, the pleasures of his true celebrity and the worries of his private world. Looking back at his long years in the West, he could already sense that life would never quite be the same. "My years in the Sierras and the plains of California, Oregon and Nevada," he told a friend in 1875, "were the happiest I have ever known or ever expect to know."[115]

Becoming Ada Copeland

ADA COPELAND TOLD FOLKS SHE CAME FROM WEST POINT, Georgia.[1] The small market town along the Chattahoochee River, at the western edge of the state, provided a reference point for residents of the tiny farming hamlets tucked in and around the surrounding pine-covered hills. If you came from Shiloh or Pine Mountain, Long Cane or Milner's Cross Roads, you might claim to be from West Point; it was big enough to find on a map. In the years just before the Civil War, when it was a thriving cotton town, you could bring your cotton there to put in a warehouse or ship out on the railroads and then stay to shop on two downtown blocks crowded with stores, hotels, and pharmacies.[2] If you lived out in the country, you might consider this the center of your world.

The Chattahoochee River (from the Creek words for "colored stones") cuts diagonally through northern Georgia to reach its westernmost point at West Point, then bends to the south to form the undulating border between Georgia and Alabama. As it bisects West Point, however, it provides no neat border at all. The town of West Point, Georgia, straddles the river, and the state boundary lies on solid ground, a few blocks west of the downtown on the river's western shore. It's "a mere imaginary line," said a local resident in 1871.[3] Since the metropolitan community also straddled several county lines, one's precise loyalties could be hard to pin down. A West Point resident might technically reside in either Troup or Harris County, Georgia, or live in Chambers County, Alabama. Ada, however, always told the same tale: she was from West Point, Georgia; if not from the town itself, then from one of the outlying rural communities on the Georgia side of the river.

For her birth date, she told a less consistent story, occasionally shifting the year, though always celebrating the day on December 23. The preponderance of evidence points to a birth date in 1860. No legal records exist to confirm it, but as a young adult, before vanity or forgetfulness altered her story, she repeatedly provided that date to medical authorities. And that date, coupled with her place of birth and the evident complexion of her skin, opens a window onto the world of her childhood. Ada Copeland was born a slave.

IN THE SUMMER OF 1860, a few months before Ada's birth, federal census takers found fewer than eight-tenths of 1 percent of the Negroes living in Georgia to be free people.[4] In Troup and Harris counties, home to 17,738 slaves and just fifty-eight free blacks, the percentage was even lower. The average slaveholder in these counties owned fewer than twenty slaves, but the average slave lived on one of the larger farms run by "planters," who owned twenty or more human beings.[5] In the absence of any historical documentation, then, we can imagine Ada's being born into slavery, most likely on a cotton plantation that her parents had helped carve out of the tree-covered hills and valleys of west Georgia. Her earliest memories would be of cotton and work. And, of course, the sound of her name. She later said that "Ada Copeland" was her maiden name, but she would not have been called that at birth. Few slaves had a surname; their owners would not wish to acknowledge the bonds of family ties. She would have been just "Ada."

The winter of 1860–61 was a time of increasing racial tensions in Georgia, exacerbated by white fears of a slave uprising and anxiety over the recent election of Abraham Lincoln.[6] Only a few weeks before Ada's birth, a group of local white men interested in "making one more effort to preserve the honor and rights of the South" met in the town of Hamilton, in Harris County, not far from West Point, to organize a military militia.[7] In January

1861, after a contested and divided vote of its secession convention, Georgia withdrew from the Union.

THE HANDFUL OF ELDERLY ex-slaves from the surrounding west Georgia counties interviewed for the Federal Writers' Project during the 1930s recalled their early lives for their white interlocutors in relatively benign terms, their memories shaped by the limited perspective of childhood and burnished by age, nostalgia, and a certain wariness about contemporary race relations.[8] "Mammy Dink" Walton described the easy familiarity that prevailed between white children and "their little Negro playmates, satellites, bodyguards, 'gangs,' and servants" up until the age of ten or twelve, when whites and blacks alike would be schooled in the racial hierarchies of the slave system. She recalled being well fed as a child, even if forced to eat from wooden troughs. The ex-slave Easter Jackson had a similar memory: "A big bucket o' milk would be brung and po'd in little troughs and de'd lay down on dey little stommacks, and eat jest lak pigs!" Both women recalled the exceptional days more readily than the routine ones, summoning up memories of the special treats received to mark a holiday or the birth of a new baby. Rias Body, an ex-slave from Harris County, likewise recalled the Christmastime treats, but he also recalled seeing slaves "driven to Columbus in droves—like cattle" to be sold at the old slave market, where "prospective buyers would feel of, thump, and examine the 'Nigger' to see if sound."[9]

No anecdotal stories from Ada's own childhood survive. We can imagine it only through the lives and memories of others.

Ada told people her parents were from Georgia, and that her mother's name was Mildred.[10] Such facts might let one track a white girl through the historical records, but they do not help one recover Ada's girlhood. No sure trace of her as a small child in Georgia survives. Because she was a slave, she had no formal birth certificate, and because she was born in December 1860, she does not appear on the slave census that federal agents compiled when they passed through Georgia earlier that summer. The census takers likely counted her pregnant mother, Mildred. But they did not list her by name. Slaves had no names on the census sheets. They appeared, specified only by age, sex, and "color," under the names of their owners. A twenty-three-year-old black woman, for example, would be recorded simply as "23, F, B." The age and sex would help identify individuals and hint at their monetary value; a strong young man would be worth more than an elderly woman. But the racial categorization seems peculiar, and a statement of the obvious. Presumably, the census takers intended their careful distinctions between "blacks" and mixed-race "mulattos" to provide additional information, useful in identifying a runaway, for example. But the racial designations offer unintended insight into the complicated world of southern race relations, implicitly documenting the South's long history of interracial sex and emphasizing the primacy of African American descent in determining one's legal status.

The namelessness of the enslaved people listed on the federal census sheets underscored their status as property. Ada's mother, Mildred, had a name, of course. She might be "Mildred" on the plantation where she lived and "Mr. Smith's Mildred" if she needed to be distinguished from others. But the census records denied her even that bit of individuality. As anyone doing African American genealogy quickly learns, matching the cryptic record of a slave census to the full name of a newly emancipated freedman can be difficult work.

After the Civil War, former slaves took family surnames as an assertion of their new legal status. Sometimes they adopted the name of a former master, sometimes a symbolic name such as "Freeman," sometimes a name whose very serendipity celebrated their newfound autonomy. One Troup County story, for example, tells of three brothers, recently freed from slavery, who pondered a new family name as they sat by the side of a river and, looking at the ground around them, chose "Banks."[11] Whether a mundane evocation of a place or a sentimental assertion of deep friendship, a surname powerfully denoted a freedman's new standing in the post-emancipation world.

In the west Georgia counties around West Point, "Copeland" became a common African American surname in the years following the Civil War.

Most of the freedmen selecting this name likely had a connection to William "Billie" Copeland, a Virginia-born planter who lived in a two-story, five-bay house with a long covered porch across the front, set out among the fields in the Pine Mountain Valley area of Harris County. The frame house did not advertise its owner's wealth, as some of the nearby plantation homes did, but Copeland was among the district's largest slaveholders. In 1850 he owned thirty-six slaves.[12] When he died in 1859, he willed to his wife a "negro named Cicero" and the use of three other slaves: "Green a man, Caroline a woman and Rich a boy." To his married daughter, Martha Copeland Mullins, he gave "a negro girl named Adaline." The balance of his property he divided into six shares to be distributed among his surviving children and the offspring of his deceased daughters and son.[13] His extended family owned a large number of slaves. In 1860 Billie's son and namesake, William, oversaw a plantation in Harris County with seventy-four slaves, only some of whom were inherited from his father.[14] In early 1862 he filed a notice declaring his intention to sell the "undivided negro property" included in his father's estate.[15]

At war's end, when the Copeland family slaves became freedpeople, many apparently took their former masters' surname as their own. The gesture asserted their individual or group identity more than any sort of filial respect. "Mr. Copeland's Jack" might choose to become Jack Copeland, for example, to legalize the name by which he had always been known. Or unrelated people who lived together on a Copeland farm might all decide to become "Copelands" because they considered themselves kin. The 1870 and 1880 censuses document many black Copeland families living in close proximity to William Copeland Jr. and his family in Harris County. Listed as farm laborers, they were sharecroppers or bound-contract laborers, legally free but still working the land they once farmed as slaves.[16]

Ada was likely a part of this extended family of Copelands. But even after emancipation, she does not appear in the records where we would expect to find her. The federal census of 1870 recorded for the first time the name, age, birthplace, and family members of people who had been born into slavery. But no black Ada Copeland of the right age appears in the census records in west Georgia in 1870, or anywhere else for that matter. And though several Adeline or Adaline Copelands surface, none of them lives with a mother named Mildred.

A FEW POSSIBILITIES PRESENT themselves. There is, first of all, the "negro girl named Adaline" that Billie Copeland bequeathed to his married daughter Martha in 1859. In the inventory compiled after his death in April 1859, "Adaline" had an assigned value of $1,250, a price that made her Billie Copeland's most valuable female slave, worth almost as much as his most valued men.[17] Very young slave children had relatively low appraisal values, though, largely because prospective buyers feared that the high mortality rate might deprive them of the benefits of their investment.[18] In all likelihood, then, Copeland's "Adaline" was a woman of childbearing age, far too old to be the Ada we seek (even if Ada was born in, say, 1858 rather than 1860).[19]

A second possibility emerges in the 1870 census records, which document a twelve-year-old "black" girl named Adaline Copeland living about twenty-three miles from West Point, in the vicinity of Hamilton, in Harris County, Georgia, near William Copeland Jr. and the families of the former Copeland slaves. Her 1858 or 1859 birth date puts her very close in age to the Ada Copeland who later moved north to New York. But young Adaline does not have a mother named Mildred. She lives with ten siblings, ranging in age from one to eighteen, and her parents, Abbie and Harry. Abbie is a forty-year-old black farmworker born in Georgia; Harry, a black Virginia-born farm laborer about sixty years of age.[20] By the next census, in 1880, Adaline is gone; married, perhaps, for under her childhood name she does not appear again in the census records in Georgia or elsewhere.

A third possibility appears in the Harris County census records of 1880, which document an Adeline Copeland living with her husband, Scott Copeland, and their three young children in the district around Valley Plains, not far to the east of Hamilton.[21] She had been born a Trammell, a member of a local family whose name, like "Copeland," had become as popular in these parts among ex-slaves as among their former owners.[22] Both her married name and her place of residence make her a figure of interest. Moreover, her mother's name was Milley Trammell and her mother-in-law's, Millie Copeland, both names diminutive forms of Mildred.[23] Nonetheless, even given the notoriously inaccurate birth dates recorded for people born into slavery, she seems too old to be the Ada Copeland for whom we search. The census taker recorded her birth date as 1851.

Still, one wonders. Adeline Trammell Copeland disappears from the historical records. Her husband, Scott Copeland, remarries in 1887, suggesting that Adeline had either moved or died.[24] The timing of her disappearance coincides, more or less, with Ada Copeland's arrival in New York, a connection at once tantalizing and tenuous.

Tracking people born into slavery can be difficult and frustrating. The absence of legal birth or christening records, the initial absence of surnames, and then the adoption of surnames that mask familial connections all make it difficult to trace people who stayed out of trouble with the law (and hence out of court records), kept their names out of the newspapers, moved away from home, or became disinclined in later years to pass family stories down to their children. In the end, however, we can feel reasonably confident of this: Ada Copeland was born a slave, just months before the Confederate guns fired on Fort Sumter and war turned life in rural Georgia upside down.

ADA WOULD HAVE LIVED her first years in a world regulated by the rigid rules that enforced the power of white masters over black slaves. Georgia's slave codes dictated that no slave could carry a gun, own property, travel without a pass, or learn to read and write. Slave marriages had no legal status. Even religious gatherings among slaves were prohibited without the presence of a white person. Slaveholders in this part of Georgia operated with defiance in the face of civil war. Reporting on the high prices obtained at a slave auction staged in front of the Harris County courthouse in January 1862, the local paper noted, "The prices do not indicate that our people are very much frightened at the prospect of emancipation, notwithstanding Mr. Lincoln had announced that to be his intention towards the seceded States."[25]

But war upset the fragile balance of the slaveholders' world as well as the slaves'. Inflation soared, clothing and food became scarce, blacks and whites alike faced a shortage of basic resources. "Across the entire spectrum of slave life," writes one Georgia historian, "the meager fruits of selectively bestowed paternalistic indulgence withered and died in the arid soil of economic self-interest and racial exploitation."[26] Slaveholders became increasingly reliant on slave labor as white farmers disappeared into the Confederate army, but anxiety over possible slave rebellions contributed to ever harsher and more punitive regulation of blacks. Increasingly, local slaves sought to escape, to join the Union army or to hide out in anticipation of the war's end. And many of those who could not flee from home tested the bounds of self-expression in a world newly reconfigured by the absence of so many white men. In a world of women overseers, few patrollers, and a shortage of white men who knew how to farm, slaves might exercise a new sort of resistance to the old rules of work.[27]

Even without knowing precisely where Ada spent her earliest years, we can imagine them marked by physical hardship and uncertainty. President Lincoln's Emancipation Proclamation of January 1, 1863, declaring free all slaves held in the rebellious states of the Confederacy, mattered little in western Georgia, where local papers recorded the continuing trade in slaves throughout the war.[28] And the Civil War lasted longer here than elsewhere. Word of the April 9, 1865, surrender at Appomattox traveled slowly to this part of the state, where severed telegraph lines made communication with the outside world slow and difficult. On Easter Sunday, April 16, a full week after the official end of hostilities, Union troops led by Colonel Oscar LaGrange attacked Fort Tyler, the small earthwork fort constructed to defend West Point. They wrecked the two bridges across the Chatta-hoochee that linked West Point's commercial center on the west bank with the farms and markets to the east, destroyed the rail tracks, and ruined 340 railcars. From inside the fort, General Robert Taylor fought back with a small ragtag group of Confederate defenders, mostly young boys and the elderly and infirm left behind when the able-bodied men went off to war. At day's end, seven Union and nineteen Confederate soldiers lay dead, as

Fort Tyler became the last Confederate fort to fall.[29] Soon thereafter, the news arrived: The war was over here in Georgia. The slaves were free.

Around West Point, slave owners and freedpeople alike struggled to come to terms with the new order. The newspapers in Columbus and in La Grange, about sixteen miles from West Point, reported rumors of incipient insurrection among the freedpeople of Harris County. The evidence came from a cache of hidden firearms and from a general disinclination among the freedpeople to sign long-term work contracts.[30] Such independence on the part of former slaves stirred anxiety among the former planter class. As much as local white farmers feared life *with* the former slaves, they feared life *without* them. The *La Grange Reporter* noted with anxiety the reports that disgruntled freedpeople might leave their former owners to seek work elsewhere. "It would be a *burning disgrace* for any Southern man to take the advantage of a negro in a pecuniary transaction... the *truest* and *finest* friends of the freedmen are their former masters."[31] The former slaveholders' avowed affection for their former workers, however, would be sorely tested as black men and women claimed the right to negotiate contracts on their own terms.

West Point is "a village of cheap frame houses," wrote the New York journalist Whitelaw Reid, who passed through town shortly after the war. Reid, later to become a close friend of King's, observed the "gangs of negroes" outside of town, clearing land for cotton with primitive tools, and acknowledged that their crude cultivation methods seemed to produce fair crops.[32] But another northern reporter, who passed through the area in 1867, saw only poor, overworked land and a people stuck in a deep rural poverty. In a dispatch filed with the *New York Times* he wrote that "when you look at the ragged and slovenly agriculture, the washed hillsides seamed by gullies in every direction, the plains covered with pools of stagnant water, the un-drained bogs, the tumble-down stables and barns, the rude and unpainted houses, the endless snake fences in every stage of decay and hideousness, and learn that the lands are becoming less and less productive... the wonder is, not that they do not produce more, but that they produce so much; not that the people are not more comfortable, but that they are not less so."[33]

For the ex-slaves of west Georgia, the early years of freedom brought not just crushing poverty but brutal and unpredictable violence. In May 1867, in Troup County, John Copeland, a member of the extended clan of white Copelands, assaulted a freedman named Andrew Boozier with a gun.[34] In September 1867, according to the official records of the Georgia Freedmen's Bureau, whites killed two black men in Harris County in unprovoked attacks and shot and severely whipped another. The civil authorities took no action. Nor did they act in Troup County, where that same month a white assailant killed a black man for being a "radical" and an unknown attacker stabbed another black man.[35] C. S. Cherry, a white schoolteacher and a Republican who lived in Chambers County, Alabama, just across the state line from West Point, Georgia, testified in June 1871 before the congressional committee set up to investigate Klan violence in the South that violence escalated yet further just before the election of 1870. Passions ran high, he explained, as Klan members sought to intimidate Republican voters, reinforce white supremacy, and disrupt the Reconstruction programs designed to move blacks into the public sphere. "I know quite a number of prominent colored men who did not sleep in their houses there for more than a month after the election; I do not know that they all sleep in their houses yet," Cherry testified. Some, he thought, still lived in the woods. Angry threats slipped easily into violent acts. A week or two before the election, about twelve miles from West Point, eight white men broke into the home of a well-respected, elderly black preacher named America Trammell, who provided room and board to a Mrs. Randall, the white schoolteacher from West Point who ran a local school for the freedmen, after no white family would house her. The youthful terrorists murdered Trammell in his bed and shot and wounded his son; the teacher escaped into the woods in her nightclothes. The attackers operated without masks or disguise; they escaped without ever being brought to justice.[36]

Even as vigilante violence exploded, however, the freedmen's schools managed to survive. And somehow, in the harsh and violent world of post-emancipation Georgia, Ada Copeland learned to read and write. The first evidence of her literacy comes from the period after her marriage, and it remains possible that she learned to read and write from a sympathetic friend or employer in New York. But it seems more likely she learned as a girl in the Reconstruction or post-Reconstruction South.

During the antebellum period, black literacy posed an incipient threat to slavery and the South's repressive social order. Georgia's original slave code of 1755 prohibited teaching slaves to read and write, and a law of 1829 extended the restriction to free people of color. "If a man had a slave and taught him to read," a former slave from Columbus, Georgia, recalled, "he was sent to the penitentiary, and consequently the door of literature was barred against us."[37]

When Ada was born circa 1860, fewer than 5 percent of black adults in the state could read and write.[38] An African American minister writing a history of "Negro education in Georgia" in the late nineteenth century reported that outside of Savannah, Augusta, and Columbus during the antebellum days there were "not a dozen colored people able to read and write, and in the country places, perhaps not one."[39] Ada's parents, then, were unlikely to be her teachers. Like so many other freedpeople, they were probably illiterate and vulnerable to exploitation by unscrupulous employers in their new post-emancipation world. "Well the older ones are ignorant," admitted a black clergyman in 1883, "and you can impose on them.... But you can't do that with one of these live men that have had the advantages of education."[40] A black schoolteacher in Opelika, Alabama, about fifteen miles from West Point, told a government agent in 1883 that he had "three married ladies" in his school, the eldest of whom was around forty-eight. "What is their object in learning to read at their age?" asked the agent. The teacher replied, "Well, their object is just to learn to read and write, so that they can act for themselves."[41] Blacks of all ages understood that literacy could provide a path to the economic as well as political independence that could give real meaning to their new legal freedom. Still, as late as 1890, almost two-thirds of the black men and just over 70 percent of the black women in Georgia remained illiterate; the older you were, the slimmer the chance you could read and write.[42]

If Ada learned to read and write in Georgia, she might have acquired her skills at one of the freedmen's schools set up by private missionary societies and later supported, in part, by the Freedmen's Bureau, the federal agency established in 1865 to help oversee Reconstruction programs in the Deep South. Only 5 percent of Georgia's school-aged black population attended elementary school in any one year during Reconstruction, 1865–70 (a figure that would grow to more than a third by 1877 and 43 percent in 1880), and few of them could attend on a regular basis.[43]

School attendance in the rural districts around places like West Point mirrored the seasonal rhythms of cotton farming. Few families could spare their children's labor when harvesttime came around. And indeed, as a new system of public schools emerged to replace the Freedmen's Bureau schools as Reconstruction waned after 1870, many of the country schools for African American children operated only during the summer months, using teachers on vacation from their regular jobs in the town schools. One African American trained in the Freedmen's Bureau or so-called Yankee schools, became a teacher himself in 1872, and worked in the Harris County schools. "I find that the people in the country care but little for public school," he observed, and send their children only about thirty days out of three months. "Along about July, when they lay by the crops, then they have a little spare time and they send their children to school, but when it is fodder pulling time they take them out of school again. Then, before school closes, the cotton time opens and then the children are off for good."[44]

And yet, in one of the schools scattered around West Point, in Troup or Harris County—in a simple frame structure, probably borrowed from a church—Ada seemingly learned to read and write.

Learning could be difficult in these ill-equipped schools, especially in the climate of violence that gripped postbellum Georgia. In 1866 there were seventy-nine schools with 7,792 pupils, 3,000 of whom had learned to read in just the past six months.[45] But in 1865–66 "white incendiaries" torched seven black school buildings. In 1866 in La Grange, the Reverend J. H. Caldwell and his wife opened day, night, and Sunday schools affiliated with the Methodist Episcopal Church that enrolled more than six hundred black children.

"The whites manifest great indignation," Caldwell wrote, "and make severe threats. A large mob surrounded my church one night recently for the purpose of intimidating me and my pupils, and gave us much annoyance by firing pistols and guns in the air." Other teachers had their lives threatened, their homes burned.[46] And no one had enough money. At the smaller Baptist school in La Grange, fewer than half of the sixty-five students could pay the dollar-a-month tuition.[47] Daniel McGee, a teacher at McGee's Chapel School in Troup County, wrote letter after letter pleading for money and in September 1868 filed his final report: "McGee's Chapel and school house was burned to the ground Saturday night, 19th Sept."[48] In West Point itself, a teacher at a school connected to the Methodist Episcopal Church reported in December 1869 that public sentiment toward the "colored schools" was "bitter."[49] But there were at least two freedmen's schools in West Point that winter that Ada turned eight, and together they enrolled some 120 students.[50] By 1871, 3,563 black children attended classes in the small schools spread out across rural Troup County.[51] The conditions were basic, surely no better than those James Weldon Johnson encountered when he taught in a rural Georgia school for African American children in the early 1890s—no desk, no blackboard, nothing but hard, backless benches for the children.[52] One minister recalled he had attended school in an abandoned boxcar near Atlanta. Others, he said, attended school in old fodder houses or simply sat outdoors under the trees.[53]

Such was the world Ada Copeland would leave behind. Even during the postwar years, the West Point area offered little to a young black woman of ambition and imagination, particularly one who understood, as one unschooled freedman put it, "that a man that is educated is going to get ahead of a man that aint."[54] The new textile mills that opened up along the Chattahoochee during Ada's girlhood offered employment to poor whites displaced from the land but confined blacks to menial jobs. "All mill operatives having to do with the process of cotton manufacturing involving quick perception and manipulation are white," testified a Columbus cotton mill owner in 1883. But "where it is only a question of muscle, and where intelligence is not a necessity" a "coloured laborer" would do.[55] The African American principal of a "public colored school" in west Georgia explained to a Senate committee investigating local labor conditions in 1883 that his ambitious students might aspire to careers as teachers or preachers. But he added, "It is no use to educate ourselves for anything else; there is no other work for us to do. We cannot get employment in the higher branches of art or mechanics; we cannot be civil engineers or anything of that sort, we cannot even be operatives in factories." A senator interjected, "You are as badly off as the women." The principal replied, "Well, very nearly."[56]

As Klan violence supplanted the terrors of the slave codes and sharecropping replaced slavery, many ex-slaves in the rural cotton country of west Georgia found their lives as economically uncertain as ever. By 1880 more than two-thirds of the farmers in Troup County were tenant farmers.[57] For most blacks, land ownership remained an unrealizable dream. The southern historian Ulrich B. Phillips, born in the Troup County seat of La Grange in 1877, when Ada was a teenager, recalled his boyhood there in rosy terms. "In happy childhood," he recalled, "I played hide-and-seek among the cotton bales with sable companions."[58] But such romantic memories of racial harmony most often took root among those southerners, like Phillips, whose white skin left them immune to the everyday indignities imposed upon black people in the post-Reconstruction South. A young African American girl like Ada most likely understood her own rural childhood in a very different way: perhaps recalling the tense relations between landowners and tenant farmers, the capricious violence directed at poor blacks, or the natural disasters like droughts or tornadoes—or even illness—that could turn months of hard, backbreaking work to naught.[59] Whether pushed from west Georgia by violence or poverty, or lured by ambition and opportunity, Ada buried deep the memories of her early life, never passing down to her family stories of her childhood.[60] When she left the familiar landscape of her girlhood, trading the piney hills and cotton fields of west Georgia for the bustling urban streets of Manhattan, she demonstrated a desire for the new more powerful than any sentimental attachment to the old.

. . .

ADA LIKELY LEFT GEORGIA in the mid-1880s. But she left behind no stories about her flight north, by foot or horse, train or boat, in the company of friends or relatives or on her own. Like many rural southern migrants in the late nineteenth century she perhaps moved first to a southern city, testing the possibilities of urban life, before moving north. Her age made her a typical migrant. The southern blacks who migrated to New York in the 1880s were overwhelmingly single and young, most moving between the ages of fifteen and twenty-eight.[61] Born free or raised in freedom, they felt less rooted than their parents, less willing to endure the daily humiliations that blacks faced in the harsh racial climate of the post-Reconstruction South. The older generation's deep memories of slavery might inure them to the social and economic discrimination that flourished in a later era of greater political and personal freedoms. But younger people, without their own memories of chattel slavery as a reference point, would see the South of the 1880s differently, less as a place of expanded opportunities than one of harshly limited possibilities, especially when measured against the failed promise of Reconstruction. For all that had changed in local race relations, much remained the same. "Well, it is just like as it was in time of slavery," a black carpenter from Columbus said in 1883. His fellow freedmen were afraid to speak up; "they want to say things, but are afraid of the white people."[62] Ada, no doubt, had grown up with similar fears. Her move north powerfully suggested, however, that she wanted more in her young life.

If Ada's age made her a typical migrant, she remained in other ways unusual. Relatively few blacks emigrated north before 1900 from Georgia and Alabama, Mississippi and Louisiana, despite the harsh Jim Crow laws that governed life across the Deep South. Most African Americans moving north during the late nineteenth century came from the upper South and border states, and those heading to New York City came largely from areas near the Atlantic seaboard, where they could catch a steamboat headed up the coast.[63] In the 1880 census, for example, 5,350 black and mulatto residents of Manhattan and Brooklyn listed their birthplace as Virginia; only 460 claimed to be from Georgia.[64]

In the years following the war, the local Democratic newspapers of west Georgia did their best to persuade African Americans (or at least those who could read) to sign labor contracts and stay put as a labor force by pointing out that work conditions elsewhere might be worse. In 1869 Troup County's largest paper, the *La Grange Reporter*, claimed that "the poor, over-worked needle-women of the North, who are struggling in the cold sweat of life and death, not knowing whether they will have bread to eat to-morrow, would consider the condition of the negro woman of the South far better than their own."[65] But the winds of discontent inevitably swept across the cotton fields, where even the poorest black sharecroppers now understood their lives differently than they had before. And these winds of change swept young Ada north.

From the lower Mississippi Valley in the late 1870s and early 1880s, many thousands of rural blacks moved north and west into Kansas in search of farmland and the political and economic freedoms that, with the collapse of Reconstruction, seemed so hard to secure in the Deep South. Fewer migrants from the southeastern states joined the great movement of the "Exodusters," but in the summer of 1879 crowds of freedpeople gathered in eastern Alabama and western Georgia to listen to speakers extol the economic virtues of Kansas, and recruitment agents spread out across the farms of western Troup County. "The emigration idea prevails more largely in this section of Georgia than many suppose," the *La Grange Reporter* noted in August. "There are many negroes who would quickly leave for Kansas if they could see their way clear. They have an idea that they would have more privileges, social, political and commercial, in the West and North than they have here."[66] Possibly, Ada and her family heard talk of the opportunity to be found far from the rolling red clay hills that marked the boundaries of their known world. Eventually, however, Ada's interests focused not on the farmlands of Kansas but on New York City, where her life would be governed by something other than the cyclical rhythms of the growing seasons. No records document when she left home. Her son believed she arrived in

New York around 1884. It seems at best an approximate date, confirming that Ada came north not as a small child but as a young woman—not as the result of someone else's decision but as a consequence of her own.[67]

Traveling north, Ada would have been reminded of the harsh racial logic of the South at every step of her journey. Writing about travel conditions in Georgia in the late 1880s, a local reporter remarked upon the strict segregation that governed train travel: "Dirty and half-clad white men and women may ride in these first-class coaches, but never mind how neatly dressed colored persons may be, they are not permitted to enter if it is known that they have a drop of colored blood in their veins."[68] Required to pay first-class prices, African Americans could not ride in the first-class cars.[69] Throughout the South, segregation prevailed on all forms of public conveyance.[70] However Ada traveled, she could not help but observe that her color, as well as her gender, determined where she could ride, or eat, or sleep, where she would be safe and where she would not.

But finally, from the deck of a boat or through the dirty glass of a train window, she spied New York, a polyglot city of crowded streets and densely packed blocks of multistory tenements where people moved about amid the anonymity of strangers, a place that could scarcely be more different from the rural cotton-farming country of Troup or Harris County, Georgia. Alexander Walters, a Kentucky-born bishop of the African Methodist Episcopal Church, who first visited the city in 1884, recalled the wondrous sight of an elevated railroad that transported half a million people a day and explained that in New York he felt "amazed at its inhabitants, astonished at the enterprise and aggressiveness of its business men and delighted at its beautiful and immense park."[71] But to the Tennessee-born Henry Hugh Proctor, who first saw New York in the late 1880s, the city seemed almost overwhelming. "What high buildings, what throngs on Broadway, what a crush at Brooklyn Bridge, where everybody seemed to get up and rush for the entrance at the same time!" Almost immediately, he learned a painful lesson from a porter and cabdriver who cheated him as he disembarked at the dock.[72]

"To the provincial coming to New York for the first time," the African

American novelist Paul Laurence Dunbar wrote in 1902, "ignorant and unknown, the city presents a notable mingling of the qualities of cheeriness and gloom. If he have any eye at all for the beautiful, he cannot help experiencing a thrill as he crosses the ferry over the river filled with plying craft and catches the first sight of the spires and buildings of New York." The new immigrant might feel bewildered and lonely. But "after he has passed through the first pangs of strangeness and homesickness, yes, even after he has got beyond the stranger's enthusiasm for the metropolis, the real fever of love for the place will begin to take hold upon him. The subtle, insidious wine of New York will begin to intoxicate him."[73] So much would seem new to a rural southerner like Ada: the sheer number of horses and trolleys and pedestrians that clogged the streets, the tall buildings and elevated train lines, the possibility of walking through town anonymous and unknown. Along with fear and loneliness, she likely experienced a sense of wonder and astonishment, a rush of joyousness at being so far from the crushing racial order of the South.

No records document Ada's early months, or even years, in New York. But many years later, she revealed that she had at least one connection there. Her widowed aunt, Anne, or "Annie," Purnell, was in the city as early as 1882, living first downtown on Minetta Lane, in a largely African American neighborhood, and then, beginning in 1883 or 1884, in a tenement at 149 West Twenty-fourth Street.[74] During the 1870s and '80s, many of the city's blacks had migrated uptown to this so-called Tenderloin district that extended from the west twenties to the west fifties, leaving to newly arriving Italian immigrants the packed downtown neighborhood in Greenwich Village where Clarence King had once strolled at night. In Annie Purnell's crowded apartment building lived waiters and hotel porters, widowed washerwomen and homemakers, all—according to a zealously attentive census taker in 1880—not exactly "Black," but with the "perceptible trace of African blood" that marked them as "Mulatto."[75]

Purnell worked out of her own home, laundering other people's clothes.[76] In January 1886 she or one of her neighbors placed a short ad in the *New York Times:* "Washing.—By respectable colored laundress; will do washing and ironing from 75 cents per dozen; good city references. Call at 149 West 24th St., third floor, back."[77]

Perhaps Purnell wrote or sent word to Ada back in Georgia, encouraging her to come try city life, or maybe she simply offered refuge when unknown events drove Ada from her childhood home. In any case, no matter how small and cramped her own quarters might be, Annie Purnell perhaps took her niece in until she could find a job, showed her how to navigate the city, lent her money until she could stand on her own two feet. If so, that familial connection would make Ada more fortunate than many of her contemporaries. Relatively few of the Georgia-born blacks living in Manhattan in 1880 lived with members of their immediate family, a consequence of a migration dominated by young, single southerners.[78] "Chain migrations," with one relative paving the way for another, would become more common several decades later, with the "Great Migration" of southern blacks to northern cities that began during World War I. Young African American migrants like Ada often found themselves alone in mid-1880s Manhattan.[79]

In addition to providing Ada with lodging, Purnell might have instructed her in how to find a job. On March 1, 1886, less than two months after the washerwoman's ad appeared, another ad appeared in the "Situations Wanted" section of the *New York Times:* "NURSE—BY A COMPETENT YOUNG WOMAN as a nurse to growing children; good city reference. Address A. C. Box 260 Time Up-town Office, 1,269 Broadway."[80] The timing is right, even if it remains impossible to prove whether "A. C." might be Ada Copeland, who we know became a nursemaid. The language of the ad remains coyly quiet on the issue of the job seeker's race or ethnicity. Other ads placed by would-be nursemaids referred to the applicants as "Scotch Protestant," "Canadian," "Protestant," or "Scotchwoman"—all discreet ways of suggesting the job seekers were white. One referred to a "respectable young colored girl." But many provided no clue as to the applicant's race or ethnicity. "A. C." implied she had held one other job in New York, offering one "good city reference" rather than multiple testimonies to her reliability or skill. And unlike many, though not all, of her fellow job seekers, she did not give her own home address as the place where a prospective employer might find her. There could be many reasons for this. Perhaps she did not want a current employer to know she sought a new job, or maybe she shared tight and crowded living quarters that she feared would not convey a good impression to a new employer. A rented mailbox at the newspaper office offered a more private venue for employer and employee to contact one another. The uptown office of the *New York Times,* on Broadway at West Thirty-second Street, was less than three-quarters of a mile from the Purnell apartment on West Twenty-fourth Street.

Whether Ada Copeland was the anonymous "A. C." of the ad, or whether she sought work through friends or one of the city's domestic employment agencies, she eventually found a job as a nursemaid with a family in lower Manhattan.[81] Her precise whereabouts in the city during the mid-1880s remain unknown. Federal census takers did take note of servants, carefully recording the names of domestic workers who boarded with their employers, lived with their own families, or maintained rooms in lodging houses. But they compiled their snapshots of the city's population just once a decade. In the intervening years, domestic workers like Ada remained largely unseen, going about their work unobserved by the officials who noted the heads of households for commercial city directories or kept track of property owners for the municipal tax records. Annie Purnell, Ada's aunt, appeared in the city directories only because she was a widowed head of household; had she lived with her husband she, too, would have remained unnoted. King's biographer Thurman Wilkins later surmised that Ada worked for a friend of King's, but none of King's close associates mention in their personal papers a young household servant recently arrived from Georgia.[82] Anonymity might have been hard to find in a small Georgia farming community, but in New York Ada slipped into the city's silent army of invisible domestics, and anonymity became a defining feature of her life. No one would know where she came from, who her people were, what her life had been like before she landed in Manhattan and became a working girl.

. . .

HOWEVER SMITTEN ADA COPELAND might have felt at her first sight of the city, however eager to leave behind her memories of the violence and poverty of rural life, her race and sex circumscribed her world. And although her new job might seem singularly new and strange to her, it in fact made her a typical worker. Roughly 90 percent of young African American women in late-nineteenth-century New York held a job in "domestic and personal service." Some toiled in hotels or restaurants, but most worked in private homes, where they often received room and board.[83] Bending the curves of their lives to fit the needs of someone else's household, they set their own rhythms of sleep and work to match the tempos set by others. Jessie Fauset, a leading writer of the Harlem Renaissance and an assistant editor of the NAACP's journal *The Crisis*, never did domestic service herself, but she knew many women who did. In her 1929 novel *Plum Bun: A Novel without a Moral*, she described a young woman who "had known what it meant to rise at five o'clock, start the laundry work for a patronizingly indifferent family of people who spoke of her in her hearing as 'the girl' or remarked of her in a slightly lower but still audible tone as being rather better than the usual run of niggers.... For this family she had prepared breakfast, gone back to her washing, served lunch, had taken down the clothes, sprinkled and folded them, had gone upstairs and made three beds, not including her own and then had returned to the kitchen to make dinner." At night Fauset's fictional character would be too tired to undress before collapsing into her own unmade bed. No wonder she longed for marriage and a new life in which she could "enjoy the satisfaction of having a home in which she had full sway instead of being at the beck and call of others."[84] Ada, too, must have dreamed of such freedom.

A study of African American domestic workers in Philadelphia in the late 1890s found that nearly two-thirds of unmarried women boarded with their employers. Since there was a negligible difference in pay for those living in and those going home in the evenings, it made good economic sense.[85]

A nursemaid's salary of $3 to $3.50 a week might seem grand in comparison to the $3 a month a young woman like Ada could make as a house servant in Georgia or the $40 to $50 a year she might make as a Georgia field hand, but it would not go very far in an urban center, especially if she sent money home to her family.[86] In New York City, even the rudest room in a dark tenement rented for a minimum of $6 to $10 a month.[87] So forgoing privacy, flexibility, or any real home life of her own, Ada most likely lived with the family that employed her, free like most nursemaids to go out into the city to test the boundaries of her new life just one afternoon a week, with an additional afternoon or evening every other Sunday.[88] Marriage might seem a possible escape. But it would be difficult to meet men with so little free time of her own; doubly difficult because black women in New York so outnumbered black men. In 1890 there were roughly five black females in the city for every four black men.[89]

Nursemaids like Ada would devote long hours of work to the "washing, dressing and feeding of children" as well as the "general care of [their] health and well-being," acquiring the skills and experience they would later put to good use with their own families. Almost 70 percent of nursemaids worked ten- to twelve-hour days, and nearly a quarter worked even longer hours, more time than was demanded from any other sort of domestic servant. But child care carried little social status. The women with "skilled" domestic positions as cooks, seamstresses, and laundresses earned more and worked less.[90]

Confinement and inflexibility likely ordered Copeland's working life. Unable to entertain friends at home, control her own working hours, or hope to advance to a better-paying position, she possibly never felt free of the overbearing sense of being a menial and dependent employee in her own house. Whether she had her own room or shared it with one or more other young women, she likely had a dark and poorly ventilated living space. It might be shut off by walls from the more spacious rooms occupied by her employer's family, but even a room of her own would not necessarily assure privacy. Her employers might enter her room at any time to ask for help or demand assistance. Domestic workers complained frequently about the monotony of their work and the brutally low pay. But "probably the chief objection of colored city domestics against service," wrote the social worker Isabel Eaton in 1899, "is the social stigma which rightly or wrongly attaches to it. It savors to them of the degradation of their slavery days." Those who leave domestic employment, she continued, leave "to escape social degradation first, from the desire for greater personal freedom next, and finally from the hope of higher remuneration."[91]

Even the unmarried African American workingwomen who did not live with their employers faced the social stigma of domestic service. And their privacy would come not just at the expense of their pocketbook, but with a loss of comfort or even safety, in the crowded tenement boardinghouses where they could find rooms. Their domestic work began early, the sociologist Mary White Ovington wrote in 1911, "seven at the latest and lasts until the dinner is cleared away, at half-past eight or nine. Released then from further tasks, the young girl goes to her tiny inner tenement room, dons a fresh dress, and then, as chance or her training determines, walks the street, goes to the theatre, or attends the class meeting at her church."[92]

The church played a critical role in the life of young African American women like Ada, providing not just a place of worship but a social gathering spot where they could relax with others who also felt displaced from the familiar rituals of their southern homes.[93] The African American church provided northern blacks with a kind of family structure, the sociologist W. E. B. DuBois wrote in 1899. "Its family functions are shown by the fact that the church is a centre of social life and intercourse; acts as newspaper and intelligence bureau, is the centre of amusements."[94] As James Weldon Johnson would later write, "a Negro Church is for its members much more besides a place of worship. It is a social centre, it is a club, it is an arena for the exercise of one's capabilities and powers, a world in which one may achieve self-realization and preferment." A church might mean something similar to other people, he conceded, "but with the Negro all these attributes are magnified because of the fact that they are so curtailed for him in the world at large."[95]

Ada Copeland turned for her own social and spiritual support to the

Union American Methodist Episcopal Church, a small but lively congregation in Manhattan. This "invisible" sect of African American Methodism, based in Wilmington, Delaware, was minuscule in comparison to the much better known African Methodist Episcopal Church.[96] It began in 1865 as a splinter group of the Union Church of Africans, itself formed in 1813 in protest against the racial policies of the nation's mainstream Methodist Episcopal churches.[97] By the late 1880s, the sect had only about 2,200 members, some 170 affiliated with Ada's church, the Reverend James H. Cook's congregation in New York.[98]

The church offered worship services, classes, musical evenings, and summer excursions on chartered boats to a park outside the city that offered working congregants a rare respite from their daily labor. For 50 cents, a young woman like Ada could enjoy the boat ride, try her hand at fishing along the shore, and watch the young men of the church play baseball or cricket (a suggestion that some of the church members came from the West Indies).[99]

Ada almost certainly discovered the Union American Methodist Episcopal Church after she arrived in Manhattan; it had scant presence in the South. Growing up near West Point, Ada perhaps attended local prayer meetings, such as those that Easter Jackson, a former slave from Troup County, later recalled: "de prayer meetin's, once a week, first on one plantation den a nother; when all the niggers would meet and worshup singin praises unto the Lord."[100] As a small child Ada likely attended the segregated black worship services held in the white Baptist or Methodist churches around West Point, and later, as a young woman, she might have gone to one of the new black churches sprouting up in Reconstruction Georgia.[101]

The Union American Methodist Episcopal Church in New York began in a building downtown, on West Fifteenth Street, not far, perhaps, from Ada's place of employment. Maybe her aunt or some friends led her there. Or perhaps she stepped in on her own and soon found herself embraced by the community. "Each church forms its own social circle," W. E. B. DuBois wrote of the black churches in Philadelphia in the late nineteenth century, "and not many stray beyond its bounds. Introductions into that circle come through the church, and thus the stranger becomes known."[102] The confidence and dynamism of the church leader, the Reverend James Cook—a man the *New York Times* later eulogized as "one of the most prominent negro ministers in this part of the United States"—likely felt comforting to a young woman alone in the city.[103] His church might not be large or prosperous, but with a liberal doctrine that emphasized lay involvement, admitted women to the ministry, and decried racism, it would feel welcoming.[104]

In February 1888 the African American journalist and activist Ida B. Wells penned an essay on the model woman for New York's black newspaper, the *New York Freeman* (later the *New York Age*). In it she wrote, "The typical girl's only wealth, in most cases, is her character, and her first consideration is to preserve that character in spotless purity.... She regards all honest toil as noble, because it is ordained of God that man should earn his bread by the sweat of his brow. She does not think a girl has anything of which to be proud in not knowing how to work, and esteems it among her best accomplishments that she can cook, wash, iron, sew and 'keep house' thoroughly and well." A Negro girl like this, Wells wrote, might be rare, but she provided the pattern others should copy.[105] In hard work, a black woman should find nothing but pride.

We know little about Ada Copeland's day-to-day life in the years before she met Clarence King, nor can we know with any certainty what moral values she learned as a child. Later family stories depict Ada as a "queen," a woman with regal good manners, a penchant for proper dress, and a deep sense of propriety that included Sunday morning church and formal Sunday dinners.[106] We can only speculate as to whether Ada read New York's black press. But like Wells's exemplar of true womanhood, she worked hard, went to church, and aspired to a better life. Born to slavery, she could, in New York, dare to imagine her way into an independent working-class world, perhaps even a middle-class life, even if she could not yet see how to get there. On the eve of her first encounter with King, Ada had weathered the transition from slavery to freedom, from girlhood to adulthood, from rural southern life to life in the nation's largest metropolis. She had made the shift from farmwork to domestic work, from an extended-family world to a more solitary and independent life, from the rhythms of the agricultural world to the rattle of the urban elevated trains. Behind her lay the restraints of the Jim Crow South, which limited where she could eat, how she could travel, what sort of work she could do, and even what kind of identity she could embrace. In place of these restrictions, she lived within those of the world of a live-in domestic, with limited free time or social independence. In all likelihood, she worked for white people. But even in New York, through her aunt and through her church, she remained tied to a black community. Her widowed aunt's independence likely suggested to Ada that with hard work she, too, could make it in the city. And through her church, she surely knew African Americans who likewise had made a successful place for themselves in this bustling urban world. Still, even in New York, Ada's race continued to shape how she could earn her keep, where she could live, and—in all probability—how she imagined she would spend the rest of her life.[107]

4

King of the City

WHEN KING MOVED TO NEW YORK IN LATE 1873, HIS SURVEY'S fieldwork complete, he was a celebrity. The widely acclaimed author of *Mountaineering* and tough-minded hero of the diamond hoax seemed the vigorous archetype of a new American man. "He could do so easily what I could not do at all," remarked the historian Hubert Howe Bancroft; "he was so young, with such an elastic athletic brain, trained to do his most ambitious bidding, with such a well-employed past, a proud present and a brilliant future, and withal such a modest bearing and genial kind-heartedness, that I could not but envy him."[1] Henry Adams sensed that same sort of worshipful admiration among King's friends, but thought King too perfect to envy. "So little egoistic he was that none of his friends felt envy of his extraordinary superiority, but rather groveled before it, so that women were jealous of the power he had over men; but women were many and Kings were one."[2]

King's ebullient, self-confident presence nonetheless masked a more conflicted sense of self. King still worried about the tension between duty and desire, science and money, the pleasures of his social station and the unfading allure of other, less rarefied worlds. And for the next fifteen years, in New York and Washington, in London and Paris, while he moved among the social and political elite looking for ways to live up to his promise, he secretly tested and indulged his desire to be someone free of all the obligations that came with being a model son of Newport (and of Florence King Howland) and one of the most admired scientists in America.

King had never much liked New York. But it made sense to base the survey offices there for the next few years while he and his men finished up their reports. The city put him within reach of the resources he needed to complete his own geological volume and the investors who seemed key to his business ambitions. It stood convenient enough (though not too close) to Newport, where he resettled his mother and her children. And although the city stood far from the site of his own fieldwork, it nonetheless put King within the orbit of a larger world of science. He raked in the honors: membership in the American Philosophical Society, the Geological Society of London, and, in 1876, the National Academy of Sciences, the youngest living person ever elected.[3]

Science occupied King's days. He hired a secretary named Edgar Beecher Bronson—fresh from his duties as a court reporter in the trial of Henry Ward Beecher—to take down the words of his growing treatise on geology. But talk occupied his evenings. Dinners at the Knickerbocker Club, the Round Table Club, or the fabled Century Association, which he joined in 1874, drew King into a social world of artists like John La Farge, Eastman Johnson, and Quincy Ward and literary men such as the novelist Bret Harte and Whitelaw Reid, editor of the *Tribune.* The geologist who had passed the better part of a decade dining in simple field camps (albeit in fancy dress) now spent his evenings in rarefied company with the likes of the architect Frederick Law Olmsted; E. L. Godkin, the editor of the *Nation;* and Congressman Abram S. Hewitt, later to be a crucial political ally and the mayor of New York.[4] King's talk dazzled. "The trouble with King," one Centurion wrote, "is that his description of a sunset spoils the original."[5]

None of his burgeoning New York friendships proved so important to King as his new connection with John Hay, a writer and public servant as precocious in his own field as King had been in his. A recent graduate of Brown, Hay went to the White House in 1861 as the twenty-two-year-old assistant secretary to Abraham Lincoln and a part of the extended household at 1600 Pennsylvania Avenue. While King walked across the continent and mapped the California peaks, Hay stood by Lincoln's side through the long, dark days of war, and he was there at his bedside as the president drew his last breath. For five years following Lincoln's assassination, Hay lived mainly overseas, in a series of diplomatic posts in Paris, Vienna, and Madrid. At some point, though, his path crossed King's.[6] In 1870 he resigned to return to the United States, and by the time he and King struck up their friendship again in the mid-1870s, Hay had reinvented himself as a man of letters: hardworking journalist for Reid at the *Tribune* and author of a series of comic ballads and of *Castilian Days* (1871), a book of essays based on his time in Madrid.[7] As an investor in the diamond bubble of 1872 who was saved from loss by King's brilliant exposé, Hay no doubt felt indebted to his new friend.[8]

King and Hay struck up a conversation in New York—about art and politics, life and women—that would be rekindled a few years later in Washington and continue unabated until King's death. If it lacked the adolescent physicality of King's friendship with Gardiner and the easy intimacy born of a shared boyhood, it had the tempered steadiness of a deep friendship between two men already tested in the forge of life. Through shifts in fortune and family circumstances, personal tragedy and professional triumphs, the two would remain devoted confidants. They kept in touch by letters during their long periods apart, arranged weekend rendezvous, fell into impromptu get-togethers whenever they unexpectedly found themselves in the same locale. They shared an interest in Republican politics, Spanish culture, public duty, and fine things (an interest easier for Hay to indulge since he married a wealthy heiress in 1874). King admired Hay's stolid respectability; Hay felt drawn to King's "astonishing power of diffusing happiness wherever he went."[9] Both, it turns out, kept secrets from the other. But till the very end, their mutual devotion endured. And, as the world would later learn, Hay's devotion to King continued on long after King's death.

KING'S WORK ON HIS survey report proceeded slowly, in part because he dealt with a complex subject, in part because he occasionally fled west to deal with his various mining and ranching ventures. The scientific world thus looked forward with anticipation to his commencement address at

Yale's Sheffield Scientific School in June 1877, expecting that the talk on "Catastrophism and Evolution" would offer a preview of his long-awaited summary of his geological tome.

King did not disappoint. Tackling the ongoing debate about the rate of change in the environment, he took a bold swipe at the uniformitarians, who posited a slow, gradual rate of geological change, projecting present-day conditions back into the past. The uniformitarians held sway in the American scientific community, and their ideas seemed to find support in Darwin's theories about the gradual rate of change in the biological record. But King argued that they failed to take into account the geological record, which revealed breaks more dramatic than could be found in the fossil record alone. "A mere Malthusian struggle was not the author and finisher of Evolution," King proclaimed; "he who brought to bear that mysterious energy we call life upon primeval matter bestowed at the same time a power of development by change, arranging that the interaction of energy and matter which make up the environment should, from time to time, burst in upon the current of life and sweep it onward and upward to ever higher and better manifestations. Moments of great catastrophe, thus translated into the language of life, become moments of creation, when out of plastic organisms something newer and nobler is called into being."[10] King offered up a theory of modified catastrophism, admitting of sudden but not all-destructive change, to explain what he read as the evidence of great volcanic eruptions and cataclysmic glacial floods in the geology of the American West. He believed in Darwin's theories but thought the fossil record would show that the *rate* of biological adaptation, rather than always proceeding at a uniform pace, could occur with greater rapidity in response to abrupt climatological change.[11]

King's great synthesis of western geology appeared in 1878, the penultimate volume in the Fortieth Parallel survey's series of scholarly final reports. In the pages of King's *Systematic Geology*, the Great Basin fully entered the realm of American science. King told his story chronologically, beginning with the Archean or Precambrian period and working toward the present, carefully explaining the great climatic forces that shaped the creation and movement of the earth's geologic layers. The 815-page book never found a fraction of the readers of King's popular *Mountaineering in the Sierra Nevada,* but it became an instant classic in the field of historical geology. King laid out the age and composition of the sedimentary rock sequences and traced their structural dislocations, mapped out the location and composition of the igneous rocks, documented the effects of glaciation, and put it all together to tell the deep history of a vast stretch of the American continent. "It was," writes the historian William Goetzmann, "a story only a trifle less dramatic than Genesis."[12]

The completion of his scientific magnum opus and the official end of the survey left King poised to make what he considered "the most important contribution I ever made to science." "That act," he later wrote a colleague, "was the crushing of the old system of personal survey."[13]

FERDINAND V. HAYDEN, GEORGE WHEELER, and John Wesley Powell had competed for years for government funding of their western surveys, while King enjoyed the luxury of multiyear appropriations. First in the field, and now first to finish, King could step back to assess the efficiency of the system knowing he had nothing to lose. In March 1878, as part of a broader effort to stimulate the economy, reduce federal expenditures, and improve the civil service system, Congress requested through the secretaries of the interior and war that Hayden, Wheeler, and Powell outline their accomplishments and detail any duplication between the surveys. And at King's suggestion, New York congressman Abram Hewitt (whose own holdings in the steel and iron industries made him a particularly interested party) arranged in June for Congress to direct the National Academy of Sciences to examine the federal survey system. King positioned himself as an adviser to the academy's study group and helped shape its final recommendation to replace the current surveys with two larger agencies: a Coast and Interior Survey responsible for the geodetic, topographic, and land-parceling surveys of the public domain, and a Geological Survey to study the geological structure and natural resources of the public lands. In line with a growing concern about the integrity of civil servants, the advisory committee also recommended that the director and members of the Geological Survey have no personal interests in the land or resources of the region under study and make no investigations on behalf of private parties or corporations.[14]

Congress took some of the recommendations to heart, but in the end decided to create only one new agency to deal with the public lands. On March 3, 1879, legislators passed an act establishing the United States Geological Survey within the Department of the Interior for the "classification of the public lands and the examination of the geological structure, mineral resources, and products of the national domain."[15] And less than three weeks later, thanks to some serious political maneuvering by his friends and support from his fellow survey leader John Wesley Powell, King defeated his rival, Ferdinand V. Hayden, to secure President Rutherford B. Hayes's nomination to become the agency's first director. There had been a bit of whispering against King "on the grounds that while in Government employ, formerly, he performed service for one or more corporations and exacted large fees from them." But supporters testified to the excellence of his work and explained that under his contract it "was entirely legitimate" for him to take on outside jobs.[16] King, who had helped to write the legislation's ethics clauses, prevailed. He intended to stay at the helm of the bureau "only long enough to appoint its staff, organize its work and guide the forces into full activity."[17] He had personal business interests he wanted to pursue. But for now, no other position could give him such an extraordinary opportunity to shape the future of American science. He prepared to move to Washington and leave New York behind.

FEW OF KING'S FRIENDS or associates knew it, but King's New York was a complicated place that extended far beyond the cozy reading rooms of the Century Association or the familiar blocks of his workaday world. For late at night—his day's work complete, his social obligations discharged—Clarence King liked to go slumming, setting out into the darkened streets of lower Manhattan, an anonymous denizen of the night.

"Often of a night," King's secretary, Edgar Beecher Bronson, recalled,

King would order him to grab a "stout stick" and follow him out from the survey headquarters at 23 Fifth Avenue where they lived and worked into the dark. "And then down through Washington Square we would go, plunging thence into the wildest jungles of 'Africa,' as the Thompson-Sullivan Street region was then known, there wandering, not infrequently, throughout the livelong night, in Quixotic search of adventure."[18] The African American writer James Weldon Johnson visited the neighborhood in 1884 and recalled it as little more than a succession of "stuffy rooms" in which he sat while his grandmother talked about "old times" with her elderly friends.[19] But in search of adventure, King and Bronson never noticed that domestic world.

The term "slumming" entered the English language in the mid-1880s to describe the practice of visiting the crowded neighborhoods of the urban poor "for charitable or philanthropic purposes, or out of curiosity, especially as a fashionable pursuit."[20] But neither philanthropy nor fashion motivated King's late-night strolls. He ventured out into the neighborhoods of the poor to recapture that sense of heightened sensual excitement he had experienced among the Spanish ranchos of California or the simple huts on a Hawaiian beach. "With a learning so comprehensive and profound as to have maintained him among the foremost *savants* of his generation," Bronson wrote of King, "the hours dearest to him were spent in absolute or semi-savagery." Bronson recalled how King treasured the hours spent sitting by an Indian fireside, watching the games of a Paiute village, competing in a bronco-riding contest, hiking the Sierra: "silent in a negro cabin, listening to the croonings of a turbaned black grandmother, hungry for some sort of voodoo mysteries—such were the hours he loved best."[21] And so, during the day and into the evening they labored over the survey reports, but at night they went out walking.

King's friends later recorded the stories of his similar expeditions into the slums of London, where the practice seemed charming, evidence of his insatiable curiosity and vast sympathy for all mankind. But of these New York rambles they knew nothing.

In his brief account of their nighttime strolls, Bronson never suggests whether he and King ever sought sexual adventures. He preserves only a tale of pugilistic glory. One morning before dawn, in a dark and silent alley off Sullivan Street, the two happened upon a policeman "needlessly clubbing a drunken sailor." Without hesitation, King handed Bronson his stick, "pitched into the policeman with his good bare hands, and pounded him to a pulp; and then, before the policeman could recover sufficiently to summon aid, we legged it back north for our diggings." King loved the "fair chance of a good hard scrap, when the incentive was the righting or avenging of a wrong." Indeed, Bronson added, "he used to hunt such chances."[22]

In secret, then, King claimed the Manhattan night as his new frontier, a place to test himself in a world governed by rules and values so different from those of his comfortable professional life. The dim and flickering gas lamps, not to be replaced by electric lights until the late 1880s, cast an otherworldly glow on the downtown streets, making the urban night a ghostly shadow of the busy sunlit city.[23] In Manhattan, King might not have the opportunity to chase down deserters or show his stuff in a buffalo stampede, but after a day at his desk he could still test his manhood on a midnight stroll through the darkened streets.[24] Like the "white Negroes" or "hipsters" that Norman Mailer would write about after World War II, King drifted out after dark into the city's African American communities, "a frontiersman in the Wild West of American night life."[25]

The Senate confirmed King's appointment as director of the United States Geological Survey (USGS) on April 3, 1879, and on May 24 (after returning to Washington from a hurried trip west to tend to his cattle interests) King took the oath of office. He moved quickly to establish a clear mission-oriented program of research, much as he had done with the Fortieth Parallel survey, emphasizing investigations of the nation's mineral resources that would not only yield results of practical value to industry but also help answer more basic questions about earth science. The attorney general's interpretation of "national domain" restricted the agency's focus to land in the public domain, a deep frustration for King, who saw the need for a more comprehensive survey of the nation's mineral resources. So he forged an informal alliance with the Census Office to conduct a fuller investigation of resources east of the Mississippi and on the West's private lands. In the public-land states west of the Mississippi, King moved decisively to set up regional headquarters to oversee the USGS's fieldwork, mindful of how much time he had lost shuttling between East and West. He also sought to reform the existing system for distribution of the public lands, proposing new methods that would, among other things, take into account John Wesley Powell's prescient warning that the older systems of land distribution developed in the East were ill suited for the arid West. These land-reform plans came to naught, but King's ambitious first year of operations (his men visited more than two thousand mines) made a lasting impact on government science and set the tenor of USGS operations for many decades to come. King showed the importance of employing highly skilled scientists to do the agency's work and clearly demonstrated that research intended to yield immediately useful results could also contribute toward the advance of basic science.[26]

King spent scant time in Washington during his twenty-two months as director of the USGS. As so often seemed to be the case, his life was a balancing act: politicking in Washington conflicted with the work to be done in the far West, and the obligations of a public servant made it hard to pursue his own private business ventures. But during his rare months in Washington, King fell into an enchanted circle of friendship, one he would long cherish but could never re-create.

When John Hay moved to Washington in November 1879 to become assistant secretary of state, he took rooms at the very hotel where King resided, and the two quickly resumed their friendship. Hay's wife, Clara Stone Hay, daughter of a wealthy Cleveland industrialist, had stayed behind in Cleveland with their young children, and in her absence King and Hay became inseparable dinner partners, bonding even more over their shared antipathy to the political posturing of the Washington social scene. They later rented a house together, where their collective lack of domestic skills made entertaining all but impossible. But in the fall of 1880, Henry Adams returned to Washington from a year abroad with his brilliant, if fragile, wife, Clover. Adams had given up his teaching position at Harvard and his editorship of the *North American Review* to become a historian, and he was now at work on a history of the United States under the Jefferson and Madison administrations. He and Clover rented a house on Lafayette Square, across from the White House. King and Hay began to come to tea almost every day, and when Clara Hay came to Washington that winter she joined the group.

Soon the teatimes stretched into dinner, and the dinners into long evenings of talk. The five took an intense delight in one another's company, and their exclusivity (one got invited to dinner only if sufficiently amusing) reinforced the sense that they were a rarefied crew. Henry James transformed Clover into a character in his short story "Pandora," casting her as a lady of "infinite mirth" whose salon "left out, on the whole, more than it took in."[27] The group soon dubbed themselves the "Five of Hearts," an echo of King's nickname, the King of Diamonds, and poet Henry Wadsworth Longfellow's old social club known as the "Five of Clubs."[28] They celebrated their little joke with specially printed stationery that sported a small image of a playing card (the five of hearts, of course), and King later gave the Adamses a Five of Hearts tea service, with heart-shaped teacups and a china tray printed with a clock fixed forever at the time for five o'clock tea.[29]

The Adamses and Hays thought King their favorite Heart: a creature whose energy and wit brought him success in everything he tried—as explorer, writer, scientist, even bureaucrat. Adams later used him as the model for the geologist George Strong in his pseudonymous novel *Esther* (1884): "an intelligent man, with a figure made for action, an eye that hated rest, and a manner naturally sympathetic."[30] John Hay joked about King to Clover Adams, "There ought to be more like him—but I suppose the Almighty could not afford it, at the price."[31] King returned this devoted admiration, envying the Hays and Adamses their cozy domesticity. In Clover Adams, an avid reader and frustrated intellectual, he saw a woman of extraordinary wit and charm. In the more domestic Clara Hay, who preferred ladies' lunches to long books, he found an admirable quality of solid placid stability.

The deep friendships laid down that winter between the three men endured long after King and the Hays left Washington in the spring of 1881, as James Garfield replaced President Rutherford B. Hayes. In time, Clover Adams's suicide would send her husband into a deep and enduring depression, John Hay would ascend to the very top of the nation's diplomatic corps, and Clarence King would enter into a secret double life. But in that winter of 1880–81, their talk sealed the bonds of friendship and devotion that would last their lifetimes.

EVEN AS A PUBLIC servant, King found it impossible to resist the siren song of money. After becoming director of the USGS he took an interest in the flooded Minas Prietas, a lode of gold and silver in the mountains of Sonora, Mexico (technically outside the scope of the agency's work in the United States and thus not a legal conflict of interest), and persuaded a group of friends to buy it. He agreed to manage the mine in exchange for a share of the stock. In early 1880 he talked some of his investor friends into purchasing a silver mine in southern Arizona. Since this mine lay within the jurisdiction of the USGS, King flirted with the ethics rules here, and he asked Gardiner to hold his mining shares along with his own. Later in the spring, he brought his pool of investors in on the Yedras mine, a flooded silver mine in the Mexican state of Sinaloa, taking a quarter of the shares of the Yedras Mining Company for himself, largely with money loaned to him by Gardiner and Hay. Then in late 1880, after dashing down to Mexico to look into a problem at the Yedras mine, King set off on horseback to search for treasure in the Sierra Madre, home to the fabled silver mines of Spanish Mexico. And there he found the Sombrerete mine, with a vein the great German explorer Alexander von Humboldt once hailed as the richest in two hemispheres. Dormant for years, the mine had yielded fantastic riches in the late seventeenth and late eighteenth centuries. Its prospects, King thought, seemed hard to exaggerate.[32]

With an eye toward the fortunes to be found in private enterprise, he decided to step down from government service. On March 11, 1881, King wrote to President Garfield. "Finding that the administration of my office leaves me no time for more personal geological labors, and believing that I can render more important service to science as an investigator than as the head of an executive bureau, I have the honour herewith to offer my resignation as Director of the Geological Survey."[33] King never again held a government job. Two months after leaving the USGS, he was president of the newly formed Sombrerete Mining Company, one more corporation financed largely by his eastern friends.[34]

King was playing for high stakes, but the year brought a cascade of ill health and the sorts of engineering difficulties that always make mining a speculative venture. The Minas Prietas proved disappointing, King lost $25,000 in another venture in Chihuahua, and the Yedras investors grew impatient and asked King to negotiate the sale of the company.[35] King seemed "as full as a juggler would be with four knives in the air," Hay wrote to Clover Adams that fall.[36]

King fantasized about finding buyers in Europe for the mine. But he had money troubles on the home front, too. Before he could leave for Europe he had to go to court to help his mother.

The legal case in January 1882 revolved around the will of John H. Prentice, a real estate partner of George S. Howland, King's long-deceased stepfather. When Howland's business affairs "became embarrassed," he defaulted on his portion of their payments and forfeited his share of their profits. But after Howland died insolvent in 1866, Prentice felt "moved by [his] sympathy" for the widowed Mrs. Howland and her children. In 1871 he delivered some securities in trust to his friend Joshua Van Cott, directing him to collect the interest and turn it over to Clarence King for Mrs. Howland's benefit. For ten years, Mrs. Howland had enjoyed this secret stream of revenue. But Prentice's death in 1880 threatened the arrangement. Since Mrs. Howland's financial calamity would be her son's as well, it behooved him to come to her aid.

After Prentice died, his executors denied any obligation to continue fulfilling his gift. But Van Cott went to court on Mrs. Howland's behalf, suing for the principal that Prentice had promised before his death, bonds worth about $60,000 (more than $1.25 million today).[37] King testified for his mother in January 1882, but when he sailed for Europe that spring the outcome remained far from certain. Indeed, not until 1887 would the case be resolved, with Mrs. Howland receiving something, but less than she felt her due.[38] The proceedings foreshadowed, with uncanny similarity, the legal situation King's own children would face half a century later, when they went to court to secure a mysterious and long-promised trust fund. King might have taken away a valuable lesson about estate planning, but his mother's difficulties taught him nothing.

KING SAILED FOR EUROPE on May 6, 1882. He had been maddeningly vague with his friends about his plans, leaving the Hays with the impression that he would sail with them in July and even suggesting that his mother might come. But as she clarified for the Hays, with a familiar tone of self-sacrifice, although she longed to share her "first impressions of the old World" with her son, she "believed that my child's rest of mind would be more complete if he knew I held the family helm."[39] Indeed, Mrs. Howland's peculiar ideas about travel—"Even a too great and too rapid succession of impressions are bad for the brain"—ill suited her for the sorts of adventures King had in mind.[40]

King's first trip to Europe promised a break from his mining woes, a respite from his mother, a glorious escape from routine and social expectations as liberating as that first tramp across America almost two decades before. The poet Edmund Clarence Stedman, who knew King only by reputation, met him for the first time on the transatlantic steamer and found him a grave and dignified dinner partner: there was nothing "in this thorough-bred, travel-dressed, cosmopolitan to suggest that he had not spent repeated seasons upon the hemisphere to which we were bound." But the next morning, King appeared on deck transformed. "He broke out into a thousand pranks and paradoxes," Stedman recalled. "Freedom was what we both needed, and my own reserve was at an end the moment I saw him changed from the dignitary to a veritable Prince Florizel with the tray of tarts, offering lollipops right and left." King felt gloriously rich. He showed Stedman a single draft for a thousand pounds, pronouncing it "a very sacred special fund, which was to be piously expended for some one work of art... the most beauteous and essential thing he might come upon in this tour." His "frolic" was contagious.[41] Once the effete easterner roughing it in the Sierra, he now intended to play the robust American in a more staid European world.

AN IMAGINED TRIP OF two or three months stretched into a stay of more than two years. A quick stop in London, followed by a week in Paris, let King make contact with a few promoters who promised to help him find some mining investors.[42] Then he set off to Spain to play. King had long been enamored of Spanish culture, at least as he understood it from Cervantes or his own travels through California and Mexico. And though he visited a few mines, he treated this side trip as a grand jest. He raced about Spain in a special costume of his own devising: a green velvet suit, snugly fit across his waist, with tightly fitting knickers, light-colored stockings, and a jaunty tam that hid his receding hairline. The costume seemed just right for his quixotic mission to find "Mambrino's golden helmet," the barber's basin that Don Quixote wore on his head. King later wrote up the story of his search for the basin's intended recipient, his old San Francisco friend Don Horacio Cutter.[43] It was a lighthearted wisp of an essay, but King's friends forever after cited it as evidence of his all-too-little-exercised literary talent.

Everywhere he went, King bought art, with what Hay called "unerring judgment and unflinching extravagance."[44] He got laces in Spain, Fortuny watercolors in Paris. He swept up antiques from the Far East wherever he could find them and prowled the picture shops of London buying Italian genre paintings and Dutch landscapes. The highlight of his search came when he got into a discussion of aesthetics with a man in a London dealer's shop. After a spirited conversation, King learned he was speaking to John Ruskin himself. The great man invited King to his home and offered him a choice of his two greatest watercolors by Turner. "One good Turner deserves another," King replied, and he took them both.[45]

. . .

IF KING'S FORAYS INTO the world of working-class Manhattan remained a secret from most of his friends, everyone seemed to know what he was up to in London. John Hay ran into his old friend in both Paris and London and made light of King's rambles across the cities' class divides. "He was 'the delight of the nobility and gentry' and not of them only, but he made friends also in Whitechapel and Soho, and even to some in the submerged fraction, the most wretched derelicts of civilization, he brought the ineffable light of his keen comprehension and generous sympathy."[46] King charmed the Baron Ferdinand James de Rothschild, one of England's wealthiest men; dined in Scotland with Sir William Thomson, later Lord Kelvin, whose scientific paper on the age of the earth had stimulated his own interest in geophysics; and finally met his old hero, the alpinist John Tyndall. He passed his time in London with a continual round of dinner parties with the resident American literary set—William Dean Howells, Bret Harte, and Henry James, a distant relative by marriage whom King now met through their mutual friend John Hay—and endless gatherings of minor British nobility.[47] But as in New York, King had another world. Sometimes alone, sometimes in the company of a friend, he liked to slip out into the streets of London's poorest neighborhoods to explore.

The "prince of paradox" delighted in the extremes of London society.[48] He told Howells how the city fascinated him, "in the mirky purlieus of the poorest, where you could buy for a penny a slice of wonderful pie which included the courses of a whole dinner in its stratification, not less than in the circles of the Prince of Wales set, where the young archworldlings went ingenuously about showing their vaccinations to one another, and exchanging boyish congratulations and condolences."[49] These rambles through the slums of London evoked pleasurable memories of King's time in the far West. The English seemed amusing, King told Howells, for "their novelty of type and natural frankness, in the same degree if not the same kind as the wild or wilding children of the Pacific Slope and of the intervening alkaline regions."[50] In London he sought the freedom of the West.

. . .

Slumming was all the rage in the London of the early 1880s: a "fashionable amusement," the *Saturday Evening Post* declared in 1884.[51] And it provoked parody as readily as social debate. The British satire magazine *Punch* published a cartoon in December 1883 depicting a group of upper-class women garbed in raincoats rushing away from a social gathering: "Lord Archibald is going to take us to dear little slum he's found out near the Minories."[52] Benevolence mixed uneasily with voyeurism, altruistic compassion with self-serving pride. It might be easy for the slummers to be "*amused* and affected, as in the same degree they would have been amused and affected at a theatre in witnessing a pathetic drama of Life in a London Slum," wrote one critic in 1884. But it would be all but impossible for these urban voyeurs to truly grasp the horrors of poverty in London's most desperate neighborhoods.[53]

King moved easily between one world and the other. One day King would be out buying extravagant antique fabrics, wrote Henry James, "selling silver mines to the Banque de Paris or philandering with Ferdinand de Rothschild, who appears to be unable to live without him." But then he could turn away to dine with "publicans, barmaids and other sinners."[54]

James warily accompanied King on some of his urban adventures, and King joked that whenever the novelist was more than one cab fare from Piccadilly, "there is a nervous, almost nostalgic, cutting and running for the better quarters of the town." King confided to Hay that James so worried about being caught in "these gruesome and out-of-the-way parts of the town, he actually gathers up a few unmistakably good invitations and buttons them in his inner pocket, so that there should be no mistaking the social position of the corpse if violence befell him." James felt compelled to hold on to markings of his social station. But for King the whole point of rambling was the opportunity to try on a new self and slip the bounds of convention.[55]

Years later, "veiling with a transparent whimsical humor of narration his earnest feeling," King told his old mining friend Rossiter Raymond of Sunday-afternoon trips to talk with the girls who worked in Cross and

Blackwell's pickle factory. King boasted that he spoke to them in a fashion "not quite orthodox, perhaps, but then, again, not so awfully heterodox either!"[56] Why and about what, he gives no clue. Perhaps he felt drawn to them by their speech or their dress, their reddened laborer's hands, the strong vinegar smell that hung about their hair and clothes. In the polyglot world of late-nineteenth-century New York, King found the antidote to the smothering weight of civilization among the black and European immigrant neighborhoods of lower Manhattan. But in the more ethnically homogeneous, if economically stratified, world of Victorian London, he found the balm for his social discomfort among these white factory workers.

It remains hard to know whether the Yale-educated geologist revealed his real identity to the girls, used his own name, or perhaps disguised his background by adopting a working-class accent designed to set them at ease. He possessed a "remarkable ease in acquiring a colloquial command of languages," Hay noted.[57] And, as another friend remarked, King took a particular interest in all the variations of English, recording "reams of notes on dialects whole fathoms below the strata touched by Dickens in *Oliver Twist*."[58] But at some point, whether he revealed his identity to the girls or not, he slipped back into character and organized for the women "by unlimited use of his aristocratic acquaintances" an excursion via special train to an afternoon tea on the lawn in Windsor Park. Queen Victoria herself stepped out of the palace and joined them for tea.[59]

Such class-crossing excursions seemed to intrigue King, providing a kind of inverse of his own experience as a man of substance drawn to a working-class world. On one occasion, he introduced himself to the Honourable Maude Stanley, "founder of the first Working-Girls' Club" in London, and announced that he wished to provide her charges with a memorable day. King "arranged every detail," Stanley recalled. He took one hundred girls by train from Waterloo to Windsor, where each spent half the day on a carriage ride around the park and the other half out on a river launch. At midday they all joined together for an elaborate multicourse dinner in the Town Hall, "in a splendid room hung round with pictures of kings and queens," where King gave each girl a specially printed menu to take home as a souvenir.[60] Lady Stanley, a friend of Hay's noted, became "quite as charmed with Frascuelo [King] as the barmaids."[61]

KING FELT ATTRACTED TO the girls and curious about their lives, but by playing the host he reaffirmed the vast class difference between his world and theirs. In his frequent nighttime visits to London's bars and pubs, however, he often concealed his background in order to grasp a more immediate experience of working-class life. Bronson recalled King's stories of "chaffing bar maids with Bret Harte," and Henry James drily noted after King's departure, "The British barmaid mourns his absence."[62] To justify himself to his friends, King announced he intended to write a book with ten stories about women from the depths of London life. But most perceived what he was up to. "Think of it Hay," one friend wrote to King's old confidant. "He goes down to the lowest dive at Seven Dials, chirps to the pretty barmaid of a thieves' gin mill, gives her a guinea for a glass of 'bittah,' [and] gets the frail, simple clean thing gone on him. Then [he] whips out his notebook and with a smile that would charm a duchess asks her to tell her story. Naturally she is pleased and fires away in dialect that never saw print, which the wily geologist nails on the spot. Of course, she is a poor, pitiful wronged thing who would have been an angel if she had been kindly treated and taken to Sunday School when she was a child—they are all so, you know."[63]

"Let us *hope*," concluded Hay's correspondent, "that King is walking through all these narrow slippery places upright and unstained as an archangel."[64]

King joked with Raymond about his afternoons with the working girls. But perhaps sensing King's true attraction to the women and his deep ambivalence about the privileges of class, Raymond imagined "something dearer and deeper in it than its sparkling surface."[65]

BUSINESS AFFAIRS OCCUPIED LITTLE of King's time in Europe. In the late summer of 1883, more than a year after his arrival, he finally sealed a

THE PHOTOGRAPHIC RECORD PROVIDES NO DIRECT EVIDENCE OF THE MARRIAGE between Clarence King and Ada Copeland. King enjoyed posing for the camera, and his early professional career is amply documented, but scant visual records exist for his later years, and no images depict him with his wife and children. Conversely, no photographs of the young Ada Copeland exist. The earliest surviving likeness of her dates from 1933, more than three decades after her husband's death.

A youthful Clarence King dressed as a woman on the photographic calling cards he made up to distribute to friends.

COURTESY OF THE HUNTINGTON LIBRARY, SAN MARINO, CALIFORNIA (09954)

Just back from his first expedition into the field, King stands in the back at *right* in this formal portrait of the men of the California State Geological Survey in December 1863. Josiah Whitney stands at *center;* William Brewer sits at *far right*.

With a mercury barometer slung across his back and a geologist's hammer in his hand, King dressed the part of a swaggering explorer when he posed with the field party of the California State Geological Survey in the spring of 1864. *From left to right:* James Gardiner, Richard Cotter, William Brewer, King.

The twenty-three-year-old King visited a Boston-area photography studio in October 1865, while on a trip back east before his final season of work with the California State Geological Survey.

A formally attired King, *center*, with James Gardiner, *left*, and Richard Cotter in a field camp of the Fortieth Parallel survey outside Sacramento in the summer of 1867.

At a Fortieth Parallel campsite near Salt Lake City, in October 1868, King sits at *left* while his valet, James Marryatt, stands at *far right*.

Never shy about promoting his mountaineering feats, King posed as if pausing in a rope descent of a rock face, c. 1869. He used the image to illustrate a gift book prepared for his half sister, Marian.

King posed in field dress for this photograph by Timothy O'Sullivan made at Uinta Lake, Utah, c. 1869.

King as director of the United States Geological Survey, 1879.

King reportedly wore this green velvet suit as he raced around Spain in 1882, searching for a barber's basin like the one Don Quixote had worn. He purchased the basin for a friend and wrote an account of his search in "The Helmet of Mambrino," an essay republished by his friends in the memorial volume issued after his death.

FROM *CLARENCE KING MEMOIRS* (1904)

In this undated photograph, King reads in the library of his friend John Hay.

FROM *CLARENCE KING MEMOIRS* (1904)

King's gray beard in this undated photograph suggests that it may be the only image known from the period after his marriage to Ada Copeland in 1888.

DETAIL FROM *CLARENCE KING MEMOIRS* (1904)

Ada King leaves the courtroom, escorted by her son Wallace, during the November 1933 trial to recover the trust fund she believed her husband had left her.

COURTESY OF THE *NEW YORK DAILY NEWS*

A formal studio portrait of the younger Ada King, Clarence and Ada's daughter, offers visual evidence of the light complexion that enabled her to marry as a white woman in 1913.

COURTESY OF PATRICIA CHACON

IN MYSTERY SHOOTING.—Unidentified man ran up to car in which John Ancona, auto dealer of Corona, Queens, sat with Ada King (above), at Bayside, Queens, early yesterday, and shot Ancona in stomach. Victim died later —*Story on page 8.*

The younger Ada King, daughter of Ada and Clarence, appeared on the front page of the *New York Daily News* on November 15, 1929, after the drive-by shooting of her companion, John Ancona.

COURTESY OF THE *NEW YORK DAILY NEWS*

Ada King, age ninety-one, poses
in her Kalmia Avenue home with
her granddaughter, Thelma, at
a party in honor of Thelma's
wedding in 1952.

Wallace King, Ada and Clarence's
son, *right*, in the family's Kalmia
Avenue home in the 1950s. After
his niece, Thelma, *left*, married a
white man and moved to an
all-white neighborhood on Long
Island, Wallace visited from time
to time. His darker-complected
mother, however, remained at home.

Thelma Burns Thomas, Ada and Clarence King's
only grandchild by blood, with her granddaughter
Tricia, c. 1990.

deal with a group of British investors for the purchase of the Yedras mine and told friends he would be sailing home in December. But the newly capitalized Anglo-Mexican Mining Company ran into financial difficulties of its own, leading King's American investors to worry. King delayed his return.[66]

Writing from London in the summer of 1884, after two years abroad, King adopted the bemused stance of an expatriate. "All the phenomena of a sudden, unfinished civilization such as yours," he wrote to James Hague, "will afford me the greatest amusement and keenest study." He meant to provoke a smile. But he sounded anxious about returning home to resume his expected social station and hinted that he intended to hold himself apart as an observer, a kind of tourist in his own country. If he could stand on the outside looking in, perhaps he could avoid the suffocating crush of his old social world. "I do feel very much like an early Briton," he told Hague, "and approach the idea of America with intense curiosity." He joked that having become accustomed to "our well regulated and orderly methods of politics, I shall take a great interest in observing the passionate activity, and the frank corruption of your system." And he confessed to a certain curiosity about the American social scene. "I am anxious to see what your Broadway and Fifth Avenue look like," he wrote, "and whether the vaunted beauty of the American girl approaches that of her calmer and heavier sister over here."[67]

King's friend Henry James had immortalized the "American girl" in his 1878 novella *Daisy Miller*. She was pretty and fresh, audacious and charming, more high-spirited and frank than her Old World counterpart.[68] From Europe, King could imagine her allure. But in America, her imagined attractions faded.

King sailed for home with his crates of treasures in September 1884.[69] Once there, he quickly lost the hopeful optimism of a tourist who finds the charm in every unfamiliar scene. New York felt oppressively familiar. "The rush and whirl of New York life," King wrote to his old Yale acquaintance Daniel Gilman, "the detestable social pressure of the place are so thoroughly antagonistic.... But for the crime of forsaking one's own country, I should live in London without hesitation."[70]

King lived out of a trunk. He stored most of the art collection he had amassed in Europe in a dark room in the old Studio Building on West Tenth Street and lent some pieces out to friends. "It pleased him to have others enjoy what he had not the time and the place for," John La Farge recalled.[71] From time to time, King dazzled his friends with a Millet or a Turner pulled out of a chest, but most of his European treasures remained hidden away, along with the paintings acquired from friends like Albert Bierstadt, La Farge, and R. Swain Gifford.[72] King fantasized about an "abiding home" for his collection. There would be a decorative frieze of scenes from Dante's *Divine Comedy* wrapping around a grand room, high up above the doors and windows, and light would pour in through stained-glass windows to illuminate the space like a jewel.[73]

But it was all idle talk. There would be no grand homes for Clarence King, only a series of furnished hotel suites and the secret homes in Brooklyn and Queens of which his closest friends would know nothing.

KING SEEMED AT HOME everywhere, thought Henry Adams, ever admiring of his friend's chameleon-like ability to blend in when he traveled. "Where was he ever a stranger?"[74] But where, one might also ask, was he ever at home? King could settle with ease into Clover Adams's Washington drawing room or chat for hours with the British barmaids, but he seemed unable to create a home of his own. He professed to envy his friends' settled domesticity. "If I were married, how I should delight in buying the house you are now living in and remaking it a little to suit my need," he wrote to Adams soon after his return to the United States. "But I am human and could not bear the exasperating spectacle of your and Hay's domestic happiness."[75]

At the start, when he returned to New York in the mid-1870s to finish his survey reports, King tried to maintain his own lodgings, renting rooms and employing a succession of male and female servants as befit a man of his standing.[76] But he later came to prefer residential hotels. And these institutions, as much as the city's segregated housing patterns and the anonymity of the crowded urban streets, helped make possible his double life.

When King moved back to New York in the spring of 1881, after leaving his job in Washington as director of the United States Geological Survey, he took up residence at the Brevoort Hotel, on the corner of Fifth Avenue and Eighth Street, about a block from his old survey headquarters on lower Fifth Avenue. The Brevoort boasted a reputation as one of the city's "most elegant hotels" with "a fine view of the *beau monde*."[77] As one guidebook explained, the hotel's "quiet and refined" surroundings coupled with "the superior excellence of the cuisine department" helped it attract a "cultivated class of patrons."[78] A decade earlier, when an African American senator from Texas and his wife tried to obtain a room by requesting reservations in advance and announcing their race, the Brevoort turned them away.[79] It sought a different clientele. King shared the hotel that spring of 1881 with a stylish set: the Danish chargé d'affaires from Washington; the secretary of the French Legation; the painter John La Farge, his old friend; and the Duke of Sutherland, who delighted the royalty-conscious Americans by "chatting" with them in the reading room.[80]

The Brevoort and New York's other residential hotels filled an important niche in the urban housing market by accommodating both short-term guests and long-term residents. Members of the middle and upper classes could find in hotel living a kind of instant social prestige, a domestic simplicity free of the burdens of housekeeping or the supervision of servants, and—as King would discover—an anonymity that made it possible to live a private life far from the gaze of neighbors or family. One might embrace the convivial social life of the lobby, the reading room, or the dining rooms and count on a casual exchange with the maids, a friendly wave to the desk clerk, or a brief chat with the doorman. But especially as the hotels embraced the new European style of pricing that allowed guests to take their meals elsewhere—leaving the older, all-inclusive American meal plans for "persons of regular life, who can command their time"—one could keep one's own hours without attracting the notice of the other residents.[81] No one would notice whether you ate dinner at the hotel or what time you came home at night. An absence of days or even weeks might go unobserved by any but the paid staff: neither darkened windows nor uncollected packages would attract the attention of curious passersby. For someone like King, who would eventually direct his friends to write to him at his gentlemen's clubs, there would not even be a growing stack of mail to signal his whereabouts. He could just shut up his hotel suite if he needed to go off to Newport to visit his mother, head west to check out a mining prospect, or go down to Washington to visit with friends. When he left for Europe in May 1882, he could simply put his few personal belongings in storage or lend them out to friends, turn in his hotel key, and leave.

When King returned from Europe in the fall of 1884, he again made his residence in a hotel. He took rooms at the Brunswick, a seven-story brick building at the corner of Fifth Avenue and Twenty-sixth Street, whose top two floors, arranged in "retreating stories, turned back to catch the sun," evoked the "picturesque" mansard roofs of Paris.[82] Its "beautifully frescoed" dining room rivaled the celebrated restaurant Delmonico's, which stood across the street. Together, the two establishments anchored this stretch of Fifth Avenue, dubbed "the Belgravia of the American metropolis, the center of its fashion and splendor, the home of its merchant-princes."[83] The Brunswick, too, operated on the European plan, so King had no obligation to take his meals in the hotel's formal dining room. If he did not wish to find refreshment in the hotel café or bar—a gathering spot for the "*jeunesse dorée* who are interested in sport"—he could just walk out to the street and head elsewhere.[84]

Like the Brevoort, the Brunswick housed a mix of long- and short-term guests. For about $2 per night guests could have a single room with "gas, service towels, etc.," but long-term residents paid as much as $40 per night for the suite of rooms and "extra privileges" that made hotel living a comfortable substitute for domestic life.[85] The New York City directory for 1890 listed a host of business types as residents of the hotel: the architect George Edward Harding, soon to win attention for his design of the new Postal Telegraph-Cable Company building; Thomas Bullock, president of the Prescott and Arizona Central Railroad; and theater impresario Edward

"Ned" G. Gilmore, the manager of Niblo's Garden, a venue for amusements ranging from highbrow ballets to "dangerous theatrical feats" performed by children.[86]

The Brunswick offered King a steady flow of social diversions. As the urban headquarters for "coaching," a "favorite diversion of the wealthy people of the city," it served as the departure point every morning during the late-spring season for an old-fashioned English coach that carried paying passengers north through Central Park and Harlem to Pelham Bridge and returned them in the late afternoon in time for drinks. On sunny spring afternoons, members of the city's fashionable coaching club could be seen driving their own four-in-hands out in front of the hotel, dodging the other horse-drawn carriages and delivery wagons along Fifth Avenue. (Prankster Ned Gilmore once slipped a mule-drawn coach into the procession.)[87] And on Coaching Day, the last Saturday in May, they would all gather in front of the Brunswick with their brilliantly decorated coaches—"their boxes filled with richly dressed women flashing in silks and jewels"—to move out in parade formation up Fifth Avenue and through Central Park before returning to the Brunswick for their annual banquet.[88]

A broad swath of the city's social and business elite passed through the Brunswick meeting rooms and banquet halls: the Lost Cause sympathizers of the New York Southern Society; the Goethe Society; the Rockaway Hunting Club; and the National Electric Association, whose work, claimed King's old friend, now mayor, Abram Hewitt, would "revolutionize the world and regenerate society."[89] King lived on the periphery of this social world. His life at the Brunswick was intensely private. If anyone ever called on him upstairs in his private rooms, he left no record.

King's social life took place, instead, at his clubs, and he collected memberships like calling cards. New York boasted more "first class clubs with mansions of their own" than London, a reporter noted in January 1887, and they struggled to maintain their distinctive character in the face of pressure to admit the "business element" that could support those luxurious clubhouses.[90] Within a few years of returning to New York from Europe, King belonged to at least seven groups. He moved among the "gilded youth" of the Knickerbocker, and the "men of great wealth" at the Metropolitan. He found the artsy set at the Century, the elite literary enclave founded in 1847, and chatted about the outdoor life with the hunters and fishermen at the exclusive Tuxedo. King could count on finding like-minded Republicans at the Union League Club; old college friends at the Yale Club; fellow adventurers at the American Geographical Society, the only one of his clubs to admit women. King's membership fees totaled at least $455 a year, an expensive way to keep up social appearances.[91] But the clubhouses were an extension of his living quarters at the residential hotels; they became his library and living room, his dining room and study.

King received and entertained friends at his clubs, dealt with his mail there (the postal service even added a late-night delivery to accommodate the clubmen), and used the club rooms to tend to the business arrangements that would keep him flitting from one mining venture to the next during the 1880s and '90s.[92] His public life in the clubs, the illusion that his entire life transpired there, helped ensure that what happened elsewhere unfolded beyond the notice of friends or neighbors, colleagues or associates. By switching his primary base of operations from club to club—he might ask friends to direct his mail to the Century Association or the Knickerbocker, might greet friends at either the Century or the Union League—King could keep even his closest associates wondering where he really was.[93]

The clubs enabled King's peripatetic life. But as Edith Wharton wrote in *The Age of Innocence* (1920), her novel of manners about 1870s New York, "the New York of literary clubs and exotic restaurants, though a first shake made it seem more of a kaleidoscope, turned out, in the end, to be a smaller box, with a more monotonous pattern, than the assembled atoms of Fifth Avenue."[94] Even the club life came to seem confining to King.

KING COULD BE MADDENINGLY elusive, and not simply because he was often away from New York, chasing down problems at the Sombrerete mine or dashing off to Texas and California in search of equipment and financing.[95] Even in the city he seemed hard to find. His friend James Hague noted that King's many friends often called him to account "for neglected letters, unkept engagements, broken promises and similar offences," though five minutes of his presence seemed to assure complete forgiveness. "Many of his promises and engagements remained unperformed because it was a physical impossibility to keep them," wrote Hague. "In his friendly and obliging way he recklessly made many conflicting and interfering appointments, which, without the gift of ubiquity, he could not possibly keep."[96] Family duties, unpaid bills, uncertain business prospects, and chronic illnesses all made it difficult for King to meet his obligations.

At some point, he began to imagine a different life.

The late-nineteenth-century American city offered a stage for social reinvention: a place where freedpeople could reimagine their lives without the shackles of slavery; European immigrants could refashion themselves as Americans; small-town migrants could embrace all the new possibilities of urban life. "Play the old role, the role that is great or small according as one makes it!" enjoined the New York poet Walt Whitman.[97] One could be one person at home; another on the streets or in the workplace. A fair-skinned person of mixed race might live with her black family at night and pass as a white worker during the day. A dutiful wage earner might live with his wife and children but pursue secret homosexual assignations after dark. The immigrant youth might speak her native tongue at home but use English to fit in at school. In New York such double lives were enabled by the sheer numbers of people on the streets, the ways in which one could travel about on public transportation, the distinctive character of different neighborhoods, the continual influx and outflow of residents. One could shed one's personal history like a snake sheds its skin, to emerge new, unmarked— with a different name, an invented past, an imagined story—ready to glide into a future of endless possibilities. "In a great city," the memoirist "Earl Lind" wrote at the close of the century, "the temptation to a double life is exceptional."[98] "Far stronger," he said, "than in a village."[99]

It is not entirely clear just how Clarence King's double life began. Missing the thrill of an explorer's life, emboldened by the privacy afforded him by his residential hotels and gentlemen's clubs, perhaps he resumed his nighttime rambles when he returned to New York from Europe. Slumming had become increasingly popular on that side of the Atlantic, too. Within a few years, guidebooks would respond to the new demand with carefully plotted "nocturnal rambles" for those interested in Manhattan's lowlife thrills. "If you are in search of evil in order to take part in it," teased one guidebook writer, "don't look here for guidance. This book merely proposes to give some hints as how the dark, crowded, hard-working, and sometimes criminal portions of the city look at night." The guidebook directed the enterprising tourist to the Bleecker Street station at the intersection with South Fifth Avenue, not far from where King had once begun his own nighttime rambles with his secretary, Edgar Beecher Bronson. Keep your eyes open, the writer cautioned. This neighborhood "is largely inhabited by negroes, mainly of a very low class, becoming still more low and vicious as you go down Sullivan and Thompson Sts., below Bleecker; and a large proportion of the white residents, American, Italian, French, and Irish, are fond of shady places and shady ways."[100]

No stories survive to tell of King's nocturnal rambles through the streets of New York during the mid- and late 1880s, the years he moved in and out of the Brunswick Hotel. But years later, it would become evident that he was spending time far from the attentive gaze of friends or the watchful eyes of servants.

Perhaps he found one neighborhood to frequent, watching carefully how its inhabitants moved through the streets, went about their work, tended to their families. Perhaps the idea crept up on him slowly, or maybe it hit him with all the suddenness of a Sierra storm. But at some point, he began to imagine that he could slip the bounds of upper-class respectability to live as someone else, not just on his nighttimes rambles but in a deeper, more sustained way. He would not only flee his past—he would invent a different one.

KING HAD BECOME USED to being the eligible man at New York dinner parties, though his closest friends had given up on finding him a mate. John Hay tried once in 1879 when they bunked together in Washington,

D.C. Having heard that a particularly attractive young woman named Emily Beale was interested in King, Hay asked his friend his opinion. King replied, "To see her walk across a room, you would think someone had tilted up a coffin on end and propelled the corpse spasmodically forward."[101] So much for that.

King wrote about women, though, especially to Hay, and sometimes joked about his search for the "sixth heart."[102] "I dragged myself out to dinner," King wrote him in the spring of 1885, and sat between "two girls of this favored land. They were in fine form...and screamed scraps of subjects at me in their macaw voices till they left my slow faculties in a state of irritated daze." The New York woman seemed to have a mind that was a "mere crazy quilt of bright odds and ends, snips of polite error patched in with remnants of truth which don't show the whole pattern, little rags of scandal &c &c all deftly sewed together in a pretty chromatic chaos well calculated to please a congenital dude but fatiguing to a lover of natural women, such as I am."[103]

But King seemed unable to find his "natural women" in New York, at least among his society set. As the coaching season wound down in late June 1886, King complained to Hay that the society world contained just two types of women, "those who have got their gowns and fled and those who are fretting and fuming and being fitted."[104] To another friend, he sneered, "New York society reminds me of nothing so much as a simian circus."[105] He fled for Lake George, to spend time with his half siblings, George and Marian. But the women there seemed equally inane, their attempts at conversation as absurd as the city women's obsessions with fashion. King reported to Hay that he actually tried to speak to a woman he met, but "it is as if she had picked up an education at Macy's when they were selling off for below cost, a world of snips of unseasonable information. She has something quite apropos but utterly mistaken about everything." It fatigued him to correct her, as if she were "a very bad proof."[106]

King searched farther afield for his natural woman. And so, in the summer of 1887, once again ensconced at the Brunswick after a trip to Mexico, Texas, and California to tend to his Mexican mining interests, King shared with Hay the story of Luciana. Ever the buoyant storyteller, he used charm and wit to put a gloss on a story that hinted at real and deeper desires.

KING HAD BECOME ENGROSSED that spring in Helen Hunt Jackson's recent novel *Ramona*, the romantic love story of a young mixed-race woman raised among the Californio elite and her Indian husband. Jackson hoped her book would do for the Indian what Stowe's *Uncle Tom's Cabin* had done for the slave, inspiring her readers to take action on behalf of the oppressed. King thought her story about the injustices visited upon the Mission Indians to be the "gospel truth." But like most readers he focused less on the politics than on the romance, and he wished for "a few more jets of melted lava in the love passages."[107] In the summer of 1887, when he met Luciana, King was actually staying at Camulos, the California ranch reputed to be the setting for Jackson's story. Immersed in the aura of Jackson's romance and drawing on her story for imaginative resonance, King made his escapades seem more fictive than real, an amusing story that would vaporize into ethereal anecdotes in the hot, humid air of a New York summer.

"Man in the process of transit from his Archaic state to his very best forms of culture tires me," King wrote to Hay. "I like him at the start and at the finish. Woman, I am ashamed to say, I like best in the primitive state. Paradise, for me, is still a garden and a primaeval woman." Had he been in Eden, he wrote, he would never have eaten the forbidden fruit. He would have picked up his sword to defend his garden paradise. And in California he had come close enough. Luciana, he told Hay, "is herself as near Eve as can be."[108]

"I escaped from her by a miracle of self-control," he wrote. "I had cock fights in the most classic style of the art and I rode with Luciana alone in the mountains among the straying families of cattle. The world was all flowers and Luciana's face the most tender and grave image of Indian womanhood within human conception. I had an almost overpowering attack of—well, Locksley Hall."[109] King could count on Hay to know that Tennyson poem about the man who dreams of fleeing the industrialized world for a tropical paradise: "There the passions cramp'd no longer shall have scope and breathing-space;/I will take some savage woman, she shall rear my dusky race."[110]

In California, King's fantasy seemed within reach. He and Luciana "came upon a spring high up in the mountains," he wrote to Hay, "where the oaks were dewy with sea fog and the orange poppies all aflame in the grass; and there we dismounted and looked out on the silver sea, and I came as near it as I ever shall."[111]

Years before, in a little pocket journal he carried west, King mused about the relations between the sexes. He sketched a little diagram: his ideal partnership of mutual trust, respect, and strength rested on a woman's patience and repose, and a man's action and support. "Man's is the larger nature," he wrote, "woman's the most perceptive." Men were "analytical," women "deductive." But he thought the sexes could be "equally logical, [equally] critical, equally appreciative and equally creative." He fantasized about a woman capable enough to sometimes take care of him. "It is a failing," he wrote, "to suppose woman all tender and man all strength."[112] His ideal mate would not be as dependent as his ever-needy mother.

Indeed, King seemed most attracted to those women whose race and class and educational background rendered them most unlike the devoted Florence Howland. In King's own peculiar brand of romantic racialism, people of color possessed innate qualities that marked them as different from Anglo-Saxons like himself. But these differences did not, as in the minds of scientific racists, consign them to a lower rung on a hierarchical ladder of racial superiority. King's "primaeval" archetypes—whom he almost always imagined as women—possessed attractive qualities that his Anglo-Saxon peers lacked: a powerful intuitive side, an emotional openness, a calm and accepting nature that stood in stark contrast to the frenzied worry and competitive striving of the men and women he knew in New York. "Whoever has strolled at dusk where palm groves lean to the shore," King wrote in a book review some years earlier, "and watched the Indian women sauntering in the cool of evening with a gait in which a ripple of grace undulates—whoever has seen their soft, dark eyes, and read the expression of tenderness and pathos which is habitual on their faces, can but feel that here simple nature has done all she can for woman."[113] King idealized those women who operated with feeling rather than intellect. For all his education, all his accomplishments as a geologist and an explorer, King sometimes yearned to be a person of action rather than thought, passion rather than calculus.

Basking in the glow of his romance with Luciana, King likely gave little thought to the ending of Jackson's novel about interracial love, letting feeling prevail over literary analysis. But a closer look at the book might have given him pause. The saintly Ramona, a kind of Indian counterpart to the tragic mulatto figure of so many nineteenth-century novels about African Americans, is herself of mixed European and Indian blood. Grief-stricken after the racially motivated murder of her Indian husband, she can find no peace in California. The once orderly Spanish paradise has become fatally American, overrun by selfish, violent, and money-grubbing settlers. She decides to flee this place of racial intolerance for Mexico, a dimly imagined racial Eden, where "she would spare her daughter the burden she had gladly, heroically borne herself, in the bond of race." And at the novel's conclusion, with her new pure-blood Spanish husband, she sails south to begin her new life. "It was indeed a new world," writes Jackson. "Ramona might well doubt her own identity."[114] King might not want to embrace the novel's message about American racial intolerance any more than he wished to take to heart the moral of his grandmother's Underground Railroad novel: in neither book did interracial marriage have any real future in the United States.[115]

King returned from California to New York via New Orleans, where he "found a lodgment in the heart of several middle aged females, who consecrate hours to gumboes for me."[116] And while there, he wrote a friend, he "had a woman thrust on me whose character and history form one of those strange, dark lines of Southern history which every friend of southern men in ante bellum days knows all about." The woman was an "old quadroon" linked by birth or marriage, he hinted mysteriously, to a distinguished white political figure. An old associate of King's had been her legal adviser but was now in failing health, and it fell to King to find someone to help her with her legal affairs. He sought someone who had "outgrown idle curiosity" about interracial affairs of the heart, some "fine old character among the French Creole lawyers," perhaps. The complications of interracial sex were not solely the stuff of novels.[117]

Back alone in New York he felt "unfit" and began to think that he might rent a house in Washington with his mother, sister, and ailing grandmother so that he might be closer to his friends Hay and Adams.[118] The Hays and Adamses had purchased land together in Washington in 1883 and commissioned the eminent architect H. H. Richardson to build adjacent houses for them on their lots on H and Sixteenth streets, on Lafayette Square, opposite the White House. But they had barely moved in when, in December 1885, Clover Adams swallowed a fatal dose of potassium cyanide. A long bout of mental depression, made worse by her father's recent death, had driven her to suicide. Her death diminished the Hearts by one, and gradually the others dropped all references to their quintet. Henry Adams stayed on alone in his big empty house, piecing together a new life, destroying the diaries that documented his old one. And John Hay, now absorbed in the writing of a monumental biography of Lincoln with his colleague John Nicolay, remained next door with his wife, Clara, and his children, including a young son named Clarence, after his childless friend.[119]

King dreamed of having his friends nearby. He went up to New Hampshire later that summer to look at some property on Lake Sunapee he contemplated buying with Hay. But Luciana haunted him. The women of his own social set seemed repellent. He explained to Hay, "You know the type—caramels, matinees, and E. P. Rice's novels, the last slang, a good dress and a bad hat—fine eyes and unDarwinized mouth." And then there was "Sarah," a local woman who greeted him with a kiss. "It was a revelation," King wrote to Hay, "so thin and cold, so dreary and colorless." He would walk up to the "cannon's mouth," he wrote, "but I refuse to ever again march up to the mouth of a New Hampshire woman." At least, he continued, "till I forget the goodbye of Luciana with its oceanic fullness of blood and warmth." His fantasies about Luciana refused to stay put. "I have tried and prayed," he explained, "to adjust [her] into a mere literary figure, a lay woman draped with rich emotions and posed as a model for my book, but she will not down." So he tried to turn his misery into a joke and cautioned Hay not to worry. "Business troubles I am told have a way of grinding off the fairest pictures from the soul, and I have always enough of them on hand to erode the bloom off any thing."[120]

King fancied himself a peculiar sort of realist. He did not much like the new contemporary fiction of "the detective camera period, the day of little snap-shots and instantaneous pictures of the petty realities of common social life."[121] He valued a different sort of literary realist, "not . . . one who is contented with the visible actualities of men and nature, but who has imagination and poetic vision enough to truthfully discern those equally active motives and tendencies which constitute the whole hidden framework of society."[122] Likewise, he told Hay, when it came to art he preferred the classical statue of the Venus de Milo "to that plaster knee of the little french slut we saw in a studio with all the droll realism of the gooseflesh and the adhering hairs." In an armless marble statue of a half-clad Greek goddess, King found his unattainable ideal. "You can learn as much about woman from the Milo as you can from all the distorted creatures who crowd the pages and canvases of modern art put together."[123]

KING'S DREAMS OF HOUSES in Washington or New Hampshire came to naught. Back in New York, haunted by fantasies of Luciana and scornful of the women in his own social circles, King plunged back into the streets. And somewhere in the city, in late 1887 or early 1888, he met an African American nursemaid who caught his eye. For all his adventuresomeness, he remained a creature of what Edith Wharton called "the old New York way . . . the way of people who dreaded scandal more than disease, who placed decency above courage."[124] And so King did not reveal his true identity to Ada Copeland. His name, he told her, was "James Todd."[125]

PART TWO

James
and
Ada Todd

New Beginnings

CLARENCE KING AND ADA COPELAND MET SOMEWHERE IN Manhattan in 1887 or early 1888. No documents survive, however, to tell us precisely where the geologist met the nursemaid, how they struck up a conversation, what they talked about.

They could have met in a public space. Strolling out from his rooms at the Brunswick Hotel in search of evening amusement, perhaps King spied Copeland as she walked with friends or sat on a stoop to relax after work. He might have struck up a conversation or sat down to talk. Or perhaps he caught up with her on a sidewalk one afternoon as he strode through midtown or sat beside her on a public trolley. The conventions of race and gender would dictate that he, not she, initiate any conversation. He might offer to carry a package, guide her across the street, help her find an unfamiliar address.

Or, if not on the street, maybe they met in a restaurant or place of amusement, such as the so-called Black and Tan clubs in the emerging "black Bohemia" of the Tenderloin district on Manhattan's West Side, where Ada's aunt Annie Purnell lived. "Satan's Circus," some clergymen called the neighborhood, where gambling houses and bordellos stood alongside more legitimate music clubs and the homes of working-class African Americans.[1] "Almost every night one or two parties of white people, men and women, who were out sight-seeing, or slumming" would come to the black clubs, James Weldon Johnson later wrote. "They generally came in cabs; some of them would stay only for a few minutes, while others sometimes stayed until morning."[2] King's own musical tastes ran from Beethoven to the latest ragtime, so he might have dropped by the clubs to hear some music or catch a variety act.[3] But Ada likely had neither the time nor the money, and she would probably feel wary of these clubs. Urban reformers targeted them as sites of vice, where interracial socializing inevitably led to illicit, interracial sex.[4] For a churchgoing, working girl like Ada, the clubs might threaten the sort of respectable urban life she sought to create for herself.

We might thus consider whether they met at the home where Ada worked. If she worked for one of King's acquaintances, the house would be the one domestic space where King and Copeland might plausibly find themselves together. But a home seems an improbable stage for King's masquerade. He would enter the house as Clarence King, a dapper friend of the family, and even from the nursery, where she might remain with the children, Ada would know he had come in through the front door—an invited guest, not a service worker. She might hear him called "Clare" or, affectionately, "King." He might step into the back of the house to chat with the servants, but he could not pretend to be someone else there, in his friends' home. His deceptions would need more anonymous spaces in which to unfold.

If by chance Clarence glimpsed Ada at the home before she ever saw him, he could have returned another day to find her alone, or waited outside to catch her on the street while she walked with the children. Wherever he met her, he laid the foundation for his alternative identity from the start. With an accent or an expression, a familiarity with southern culture or a knowing wink at the foibles of Ada's employers, he could imply that he was a workingman, maybe a fellow southerner. Such playful and seductive banter would feel familiar to him, akin to the verbal games he had played with women in Hawaii or London or California. But this time there would be no walking away from the persona he invented with his charming words and beguiling smile. On a street or in a bar, in a kitchen or on a trolley, King told Ada the story of his life. He was from Baltimore. He was a Pullman porter. And his name, he said, was "James Todd."[5] From the circumstances of his life, if not through a clear declaration or the obvious physical appearance of his skin, he let Ada believe he was black.

Psychologists say that to be a successful liar, one needs three attributes: the ability to plan ahead, a talent for managing one's own emotions, and the capacity to read the needs of other people.[6] Whether King invented the actual *details* of his alternative identity with careful forethought, the very concept of it suggested advance planning, triggered by his awareness that a public relationship with a black, working-class woman could destroy the web of friendships, familial connections, and business relations that sustained his world. King was a risk taker. But in many respects he remained fundamentally conservative—a dutiful son, loyal friend, and responsible mining expert, reliant on his good name for his livelihood as well as his fundamental sense of self. Quite literally, he could not afford scandal. In concealing his true identity from Ada, he signaled his intention to keep his social world as invisible to her as she would remain to it.

King's celebrated talent and bravado as a storyteller served him well in this masquerade. He could spin a convincing story for Ada, then turn around and conceal his activities from his friends behind the bluff posturing of a skilled performer. He could displace real emotions as humorous stories, transform painful experiences into entertaining anecdotes. His charm belied his deception. And while that deception served his own need for self-protection, it also suggested a capacity for empathy. Early on, King seemed to intuit what Ada wanted: not just the emotional intimacy of marriage or the financial freedom that might come from a relationship with a working-man, but the relative simplicity of a same-race relationship. Marriage to a very light-skinned person of African American descent would seem to Ada, in her color-conscious world, a step up the social ladder. Marriage to a white man might feel more like trouble.

King had told dissembling stories before, but the false name, coupled with Ada's presence in his own backyard, made this feint more complicated than his previous cross-class flirtations in London or rural California. There, King could just say good-bye and flee for the familiar, if confining, comforts of home. But as much as he lived anywhere, King now lived in Manhattan, where residential living patterns kept people apart even as work brought them together. Wealth did not insulate one from the poor. Someone like King would have relied on domestic servants and low-wage workers to do his laundry, clean his rooms, cook his food. In the most private of domestic spaces as on the most public of city streets, the well-to-do crossed paths with the working poor. So King would have to be very careful. Once he lied to Ada about his identity, he could not risk seeing her again in the presence of her employers or any of his friends who knew him by his true name. Should they call him "Clarence" or "Clare" instead of "James" or "Jim," Ada might suspect his deceit. By the same token, if Ada called him "James" or "Mr. Todd" within earshot of his friends, Clarence King would have some serious explaining to do.

SOMEHOW CLARENCE, AS JAMES, courted Ada, taking advantage of the anonymity of city life to talk in public spaces or to slip off to more private ones where he would not be recognized. King joked to his friends about women, but he remained silent about Ada. Nothing in his surviving correspondence or in the letters of his friends comments on this new woman who had sparked his interest. Somehow, though, the playful banter of a first encounter turned more serious, and the excitement of an initial conversation developed into a pattern of carefully plotted rendezvous. At some point, whether he recognized it or not, King crossed a line. An identity invented to facilitate an evening's conversation or a series of afternoon walks became more fixed.

Ada's work gave her little flexibility. But since Clarence King controlled his own time, he could rearrange his schedule, give excuses to friends, travel to a different part of town. Perhaps he ducked out of the Brunswick in the evenings, telling anyone who noticed that it was, as one contemporary memoirist wrote of his own illicit nighttime adventures, "a perambulation to obviate insomnia."[7] Since he kept no regular office hours, King could also step out between prearranged meetings at his clubs to meet Ada during the days, shedding one identity and assuming another. Ada could meet

James in public places during her time off, or perhaps slip out the back door in the evenings to visit when her workday ended.

Like secret lovers in any large city, they might paradoxically find the most privacy in the busiest of public spaces. There they could feign ignorance of each other or disappear into the crowd if they spied a familiar face. In 1888 people of African descent made up less than 2 percent of the population of New York County.[8] But in a dense metropolitan area, even one with ethnically segregated neighborhoods, people of all different backgrounds would be found together on the sidewalks, in the markets and the parks, on the trolleys and the elevated trains that whisked New Yorkers up and down Manhattan's streets. Clarence and Ada could hide together in plain sight. That they should hide at all, of course, would have been King's idea. Ada had no reason to doubt that James Todd was not the man he claimed to be. Why worry about being seen with James, the fair-complected Pullman porter? She might have invited him to visit with her at her aunt's house or in the home of another friend. But King would have worried. He probably insisted on meeting Ada far from the neighborhood where she worked, lest gossip get back to her employers or King see people he knew, and far from his residence at the Brunswick Hotel, where Ada's appearance would attract attention and he might be addressed by his real name. The clubs where he conducted most of his social transactions were out of the question as rendezvous sites. Even wives were not welcomed there. In King's everyday world of upscale residential hotels and elite clubs, most black women were servants.

For a domestic servant like Ada, the meetings with James might seem to be a pleasurable break from a life defined by the tedium of work, providing a few hours a week in which to live beyond the watchful eyes of her employers and imagine a different world, even fantasize about a home of her own. Returning to her workplace after visiting with James Todd, she might tell her fellow servants all about her new gentleman friend or take the children out so that she could gossip with the other nursemaids in the neighborhood. James Todd was nearly twenty years older than she, and he likely struck her as a stable man. After all, he was a Pullman porter, a job that put him among the elite of the black working class, with the possibility of grasping a middle-class life. In Manhattan, where her own employment possibilities seemed so limited, James Todd had made quite a success of himself.

James Todd likely found the meetings a bit more fraught, even dangerous. It was not just the anxiety of running into an acquaintance or surprising a close friend. He also had to worry about Ada's learning of his deceit. Even the simplest conversation with her would carry its hazards of disclosure, causing Ada to wonder just who he truly was. As James Todd, King would have to conceal his worldliness, account for his past without mentioning his family, dissemble about his friends, his politics, his cultural tastes. Merely accounting for his daily whereabouts would require a constant exercise of the imagination. He would have to lie about his day at work, lie about where he ate, finesse the truth about what he had seen, whom he had talked to, where he had been since Ada saw him last. The little lies would build on one another, the untruths slowly taking on a recognizable shape of their own.

Having a secret can be fundamental to a healthy sense of self, a way to distinguish oneself from others while crafting an independent identity.[9] King's secrets, however, went well beyond the run-of-the-mill sort that might protect a friend or conceal an embarrassment. They went to the very core of who he was. While Ada might have raced home to talk to her girlfriends, he probably returned to his clubs in silence, burying deep the pleasures of the intimate emotional world he and Ada were building together. Psychologists describe the type of person best equipped to pull off a double life as an intelligent, highly personable high achiever: a person much like Clarence King. Skilled in the psychological tools of "repression," such a person can block out the demands and complications of one life while pursuing another.[10] Certainly, as King moved with increasing frequency between his two different worlds, he had to police and enforce the rigid boundaries that separated one life from the other. His friends might shrug off his fling with an Indian woman in the high meadows of California as a kind of romantic lark. But his relationship with Ada would seem more unsettling because of her race, her class, and her residence in New York.

A segmented life is not inherently disruptive or destabilizing. The ability to juggle different roles at home and work, for example, generally signals a healthy adaptation to the demands of distinctive social environments. But a *secret* double life is different. Ralph W. Tyler, a U.S. Navy auditor and self-described mulatto, wrote in 1909 about the anxiety that shaped the lives of the "colored" people he knew who passed as white. "At all times fear,—the fear of detection, haunts one. No thief hugging his ill-gotten gains; no murderer, fleeing from city to city, like a deer chased by the hounds, passing night after night in but fitful slumbers, ever was haunted more by fear of discovery, or lived in greater suspense."[11] When the disclosure of one facet of a person's identity threatens to destroy another—when, for example, the discovery of an ethnic or racial heritage endangers one's family, livelihood, or personal safety—the creative satisfaction and thrill of a double life can be tempered by fear.

KING'S INVENTED IDENTITY AS James Todd, the black Pullman porter, hinged not just on one lie but on a cluster of related, duplicitous assertions. First, a name. Pseudonyms seemed to run in the family. King's grandmother Sophia Little published her earliest poetry as "Rowena"; his mother later disguised her name and gender by publishing poems as "Ellery Boyd."[12] And King had been in on the secret that the "Frances Snow Compton" who wrote the novel *Esther* (1884) was really his dear friend Henry Adams.[13] He understood that names could mask the connections between public and private selves.

It is difficult to know, however, whether King selected his pseudonym in the excited rush of the moment as he approached Ada Copeland, or whether he had used it before, when out slumming in the urban night. "James" might spring to mind as his father's name, and a sly way to honor his parent while shedding his surname. It would also pay secret tribute to some of his closest companions: his boyhood friend James Gardiner, his colleague James Hague, and James Marryatt, his Jamaican-born servant of the survey years. The names "James" and "Jim" would feel familiar to him. And because a good number of Todds lived in New York, the first and last names would together seem unremarkable, unlikely to attract special scrutiny or unwanted attention.[14]

And yet the name bespeaks a certain calculation, or perhaps an unconscious choice, to preserve a link to his real identity. Because for all the James Todds King never met, there was one he likely knew.

In 1888, when Clarence King became "James Todd," Professor James Edward Todd was teaching natural history at Tabor College in Iowa and working for the United States Geological Survey during the summers as a seasonal field employee. A graduate of Oberlin College with a keen interest in the relationship between science and religion, Todd had studied at King's alma mater, Yale's Sheffield Scientific School, in 1870–71. There Todd likely got an earful about the architect of the Fortieth Parallel survey. Less than a decade out of school himself, King was already among the school's most distinguished alumni, the very model of the scientist the students hoped to be.[15]

By 1888, King surely knew of Todd as well, through conversations with his former Yale professors or less directly through the twenty articles Todd had published in leading scientific journals such as the *American Naturalist* and the *Proceedings of the American Association for the Advancement of Science*. King's old Washington colleagues had probably mentioned Todd, too; the young geologist had worked for the USGS for seven years, doing summer fieldwork chiefly in the Dakotas, virtually from the moment King left the agency.[16]

In calling himself James Todd, King seemingly borrowed the identity of a junior colleague whose career, from earnest student to ambitious government geologist, shadowed his own.[17] King might feel exhilarated by the possibility of self-reinvention, but for his new identity he took the name of someone whose past he knew well enough to wear like a comfortable old coat.

A NEW NAME ALONE, though, would not constitute a new identity. King's masquerade required more than a simple pseudonym. A Yale-educated government geologist could not slip easily into Ada Copeland's world, and James Todd would need to account for his work, his background, his class: all the little details and stories and habits of character that add up to the picture of a full human life. Some years later, in "South of the Slot" (1909), the writer Jack London tried to imagine how a University of California sociologist could pass as a worker in the "great labour-ghetto" of San Francisco in order to gather information for a book. It could be "monstrously difficult to get along among the working people," he thought. His protagonist "was not used to their ways, and they certainly were not used to his. They were suspicious. He had no antecedents. He could talk of no previous jobs. His hands were soft. His extraordinary politeness was ominous." To account for his presence, London's character offers himself up as a man who has seen better days.[18]

Clarence King knew something about physical labor, especially mining, and probably had the roughened hands to prove it. But a mining career could not explain James Todd's presence in New York City. And unlike London's protagonist, Todd could not afford to be a man so down on his luck. Much as he wished to fit into Ada Copeland's working-class world, he would want to impress her with his prospects. So he told her he was a Pullman porter.

The fiction would account for his knowledge of distant places, his relative financial well-being, his familiarity with fine things, and his frequent absences from Ada's life. After all, a Pullman porter's livelihood depended upon constant movement. As one porter joked, the railroad "makes it possible to have a sleigh ride with your second wife in the City of the 'Saints' on Sunday and pick flowers and eat oranges with your first wife in the City of the 'Angels' on Tuesday."[19] Since the job literally required one to disappear from home, it offered endless possibilities for deception.

In King's case, it even let him be deceptive about his race. By claiming to be a Pullman porter, King implicitly affirmed that he was black, whatever the apparent complexion of his skin. For as everyone knew, only black men could work as porters in Mr. Pullman's sleeping cars.

Anticipating a new market for train travel after the Civil War, George Pullman had established the Chicago-based Pullman Palace Car Company in 1867 to manufacture furnished sleeping and dining cars that he could then rent, fully staffed, to the railroads. And, from the start, he hired only African American men to work as sleeping car porters. Pullman drew many of his employees from among the southern freedmen, whom he thought to be inexpensive, pliant, and eager for work, and he counted on their dark complexions to underscore their subservience to his white passengers. By the late nineteenth century, he probably had more black employees than any other American company, and well into the twentieth century, the job of Pullman porter remained a black man's job. As Justice Felix Frankfurter wrote in 1941 in *Railroad Commission of Texas v. Pullman Co.*, a case that tested the ability of state agencies to impose discriminatory laws based on race, "As is well known, porters on Pullmans are colored."[20]

A porter's jobs could be physically and emotionally demanding. One had to behave obsequiously toward white passengers, especially in the South's segregated railcars, and cope with long absences from home. "Out of twenty-four hours we get about four hours sleep," one porter complained in 1885. "We are not allowed a voice in any cases of conductors vs. porters; neither are we allowed to leave the sleeper at eating stations for a warm meal."[21] But for most, the work seemed preferable to their parents' slave labor or to the repetitive jobs performed by family and friends in fields or factories. The job provided a steady income, an opportunity to travel, and a way to observe a broad spectrum of American life. To Ada's relatives, left behind in the fields and mills of west Georgia, the job of a Pullman porter would likely seem a ticket to fortune.

King probably settled on the Pullman porter story because it accounted for his frequent absences and affirmed his black heritage. But the romance and adventure of a porter's life also echoed the excitement of his own earlier days in the West. Nat Love, an ex-slave and former cowboy who found city life "stale and uninteresting," thought the variety and adventure of his job as a Pullman porter akin to "the excitement and continual action of the range." Once he "learned the knack of pleasing the greater number of my passengers" and thus increased his earnings, he never looked back. James Todd might make $15 a month as a new porter (not much more than Ada's salary as a nursemaid), perhaps as much as $40 as a porter in charge of his own car—not even enough to pay Clarence King's annual club dues.[22] But his job let him seem to be a responsible sort of adventurer, someone poised to climb into a black middle class. As a litigant testified more than half a century later, in the 1941 case that challenged the racially driven rules that circumscribed their work, Pullman porters were "pretty high-classed colored men."[23]

James Todd would not need to spell out his racial heritage for Ada Copeland. By calling himself a Pullman porter, he signaled his African American ancestry, whether or not he claimed as much in words. But it was a risky move. Pullman put the lightest-skinned African Americans to work as dining car waiters, permitting only those with the darkest skin to work as sleeping car porters.[24] King must have presumed that Copeland knew about the racial identity of the porters and had some sense of their social status. But likewise, he seemed to gamble that by virtue of her southern upbringing, dark complexion, and limited financial resources, she had never been in a Pullman sleeping car herself. If she had, she would know that her friend was too light-complected for the job.

King's white friends read his complexion one way: King's "blondness was affirmed rather by his blithe blue eyes and fresh tint than by the light hair which was cropped close on the head where it early grew sparser and sparser," the writer William Dean Howells recalled.[25] But Ada likely read his color differently. She probably knew people of African American descent who passed as white in New York and understood that a fair complexion could conceal a mixed racial heritage. One 1921 study estimated that during the 1890s about twenty-five thousand people a year once identified as black or mulatto passed into the white world.[26] A 1909 story in New York's black press reported that Washington, D.C., had "at least one thousand Negroes who pass for white at all times," with another two thousand passing occasionally.[27] Ada's own dark complexion gave her no flexibility about crossing back and forth across the color line herself. But she would be acquainted with all manner of African Americans and know that their skin could shade in color from very dark to very light.

Thus, if he put on a Pullman porter's coat—found or purchased on one of his many cross-country trips—King might persuade Copeland he *was* a Pullman porter. And if he was a Pullman porter, he had to be black.

. . .

IN LATE-NINETEENTH-CENTURY AMERICA, skin color did not necessarily determine the way in which others perceived one's racial heritage. Race could also be inferred by language and behavior, by dress and subtle mannerisms. Because the perception of racial heritage depended on social circumstances as well as visual cues, King might behave in ways that suggested an African American heritage, just as fair-skinned persons of African descent might somehow behave "white." In September 1888, as King played out his own racial masquerade, the *New York Times* reported the tragicomic tale of the white woman in Brooklyn who had "Married a Negro Instead of a Cuban." After five happy months of marriage to a "swarthy-visaged" Cuban, the young woman found in her husband's coat "a tintype picture of a full-blooded negro concealed in the lining. Although of a much older man, it bore a strong resemblance to [her husband], and this discovery called to her mind the hitherto unnoticed way in which her husband often defended and upheld the colored race and some peculiarly negro expressions that he often used." She confronted her husband, who confessed to his "true" race, and "nearly crazed with grief" she now sought a divorce.[28] The news story suggested how unstable racial categories could be, how unnerving that race could not be determined by physical appearance alone. The dissembling Cuban *looked* white, but he betrayed his "true" race through particular "expressions."

Mark Twain satirized this American anxiety about the fluidity of racial boundaries in *Pudd'nhead Wilson,* his 1894 novel about a slave mother who swaps her own infant with her white master's son. While the slave boy becomes a dandy and studies at Yale, the boy born to privilege grows up a slave. When the deception is revealed, the white boy finds himself "rich and free, but in a most embarrassing situation.... His gait, his attitudes, his gesture, his bearing, his laugh—all were vulgar and uncouth; his manners were the manners of a slave." His behavior trumped his skin color. Treated like a slave, he behaved like one, and in effect became "black." "Training is everything," notes Pudd'nhead Wilson, the novel's wry commentator. "The peach was once a bitter almond; cauliflower is nothing but cabbage with a college education."[29] The idea that social context—rather than heritage—might shape the perception of one's race upset the biological determinism that lay at the core of American racial thought.

"Any white person—including the lightest blond—can, if he wishes, pass for colored," the sociologists St. Clair Drake and Horace Cayton wrote in their study of black Chicago in 1945. Working at a moment when American social scientists took particular interest in the issue of racial mixing, they cited the white social worker in the "Black Belt" whose clients simply assumed she must be black if she worked there, and noted that the sociologist Robert Park twice passed "for a Negro in order to obtain a room in a Negro hotel."[30] Another scholar researching interracial couples in Chicago in the 1930s documented white partners in mixed marriages who concealed their racial heritage in order to live in the black world.[31] Blackness could thus be inferred through circumstance, where one worked or lived, for example, or through hearsay about one's parents or grandparents. "To cross the caste line from the white side would be a relatively easy matter," wrote the sociologist Gunnar Myrdal in 1944, "since in America a Negro is not necessarily supposed to have any Negro features at all."[32] As Walter White, a graduate of the historically black Atlanta University and for a quarter century the executive secretary of the National Association for the Advancement of Colored People (NAACP), wrote in his 1948 memoir *A Man Called White:* "I am a Negro. My skin is white, my eyes are blue, my hair is blond. The traits of my race are nowhere visible upon me."[33]

THESE LATER TWENTIETH-CENTURY STUDIES affirmed what had been true in King's day as well. In the absence of any *visible* evidence of African American heritage, the *knowledge* (or the very suspicion of knowledge) that one had an African American ancestor—however remote—could relegate one to a public identity as a black person; likewise, it could be a turn of phrase, or even a porter's uniform. In Jim Crow America, where the so-called one drop of black blood, whether visible or not, could consign one to live on the far side of the color line, everyone had a heightened and attenuated awareness of race. In Ada Copeland's home state of Georgia, the law was clear: a single black great-grandparent made someone a "colored" person in the eyes of the law; the visible color of his or her skin mattered not at all.[34]

In New York City in 1888, Clarence King's fair complexion might, paradoxically, have been almost as persuasive an argument for his African American heritage as a Pullman porter's coat or a made-up story about his family's past. Even in the North, where racial divisions remained less sharply etched than in the increasingly rigid racial world of the late-nineteenth-century South, why would anyone that light skinned claim to be a Negro unless he or she truly was? In terms of political rights or social freedoms or economic opportunities, an African American heritage conferred no privileges or advantages at all. King, though, had more private reasons for passing across the color line.

THE SUCCESSFUL DOUBLE LIFE, almost by definition, leaves no trail of visible evidence. It depends on secrecy. Hence the value of a book by King's contemporary, the pseudonymous Earl Lind (known also as Ralph Werther or Jennie June), whose remarkable memoir details his own double life in New York during the 1890s. By day, Lind was a respectable college student and office worker; by night, a female impersonator who sought sexual partners in New York's roughest neighborhoods. He wrote to persuade physicians that homosexuals deserved their empathy and understanding. But he inadvertently provides a rare kind of how-to manual that explains just how a man of means might disappear into the streets of New York, cross the bounds of class and social expectations, and emerge, temporarily, as someone new. "Passing," in the fluid urban world of late-nineteenth-century America, took many forms. In its most conventional meaning it implied disguising one's racial background, most often to move toward social privilege. But one could also "pass" across the gender line, across lines of ethnic affiliation, across the ever-present bounds of social class. Like countless African Americans who risked exposure by passing as white in the workplace while returning home every night to their black families, King and Lind passed part-time, reluctant to give up all the pleasures and benefits of the world to which they had been born.[35]

Like King, Lind found in New York's poorest neighborhoods an unfamiliar and vibrant life that contrasted sharply with his middle-class upbringing. He moved to the city in the early 1890s to attend college but soon found his missionary work in the slums of New York more instructive than any lecture. The city itself became his stage. Using the phrase favored by contemporary guidebook writers, he notes that he set off on his first "nocturnal ramble" in search of sexual partners by donning an old suit and stuffing money in his shoe. Then, after carefully going through his clothes to be certain he carried no clue to his identity, he stealthily crept out of his "high-class boarding house," pulled a hat down over his eyes, and carefully hid a key across the street so "that it could not be stolen and I thereby rendered unable to let myself in on my return." At last, he writes, he was "transformed into a sort of secondary personality inhabiting the same corpus as my proper self."[36]

Lind pursued his double life for many years, never losing his sense of fear. If he glimpsed a familiar figure as he left his home he would "cross to the other side of the street and make a feint of ringing a doorbell."[37] But invariably, his anxiety about discovery would be alleviated by "blissful intoxication," as a train whisked him away to a distant neighborhood where he could feel more secure in his alternative identity. Only a few times did someone who knew him as one persona encounter him as the other. Counting on his clothes to serve as a reliable and definitive marker of his class identity, Lind simply denied that he was the person they imagined.[38]

Dress provided a powerful clue to one's tastes and values, class and educational background; it could reveal (or disguise) one's very identity. A rash of poseurs in late-nineteenth-century New York suggested how gullible Manhattanites could be, how apt to infer a person's character from his clothes. A con man "dressed in the height of fashion" successfully passed himself off for a year as the son of the Chicago meatpacker Philip Armour. For three years, another con man represented himself as the New York socialite Walter B. Lawrence, cadging money on the pretense of having lost his wallet. When the real Walter B. Lawrence complained to the Charities Aid Society about this disturbing situation, he learned "it was a frequent occurrence, and that my case was similar to hundreds of others they knew about."[39] Even a policeman, the detective James K. Price, found himself victimized by a young man who assumed his identity with the help of a borrowed sheriff's badge.[40] Dress could make, or unmake, the man. Clarence King, perhaps possessed of an old Pullman porter's coat, understood that.

KING'S FRIENDS RESIGNED THEMSELVES to his mysterious comings and goings, to the difficulties of tracking down a man who lived between hotels and club rooms. In May 1888 John Hay went off to King's office in search of his friend only to be told he was off in California and would return "in a week or a month." But then he went to the Brunswick and "there, in the middle of the shrimps, sat King." He had his usual assortment of maladies, Hay wrote to Henry Adams, "but he looks well and fit."[41] Even his closest friends had no idea how or where King passed his time, or precisely how he earned his living. They accepted his mystery as a part of his charm.

King's distracted inattentiveness seemed a consequence of caring for his mother, now living on her own in New York in a rented home at 12 East Eleventh Street, as fragile and high-strung as ever with "shattered nerves and broken spirits" as well as a "morbidly anxious mind."[42] "Poor Mother," King wrote to Hay in August 1888. "Would that her electricly [sic] charged mind and consuming spirit might find some pacific quenching medicine that should lessen the fire which is burning her frail nerves to ashes." King and his half sister, Marian, shouldered the burden of her care. "If you knew the difficulties of my situation in all its respects and phases," he told Hay, "you would not blame me for consenting to seek a quiet drudgery from which I frankly see that I may never emerge."[43] Hay undoubtedly understood this as a reference to King's ever-present need to earn a living in order to support his mother and his half siblings. King gave no hint that summer of 1888 that his life contained anything other than crushing work and family obligations.

His silence was, at the very least, dissembling. Even as he pursued his secret meetings with Ada in the summer of 1888 and they began, however tentatively, to consider marriage, King complained to Hay about women. No one could compare with Mrs. Hay, he wrote to his friend. "Women there are who have the best of the nineteenth century in their hearts and hands, but if there are any besides Mrs. Hay who have all that and the doric strength of nature too, I don't know where they live...and have their being."44 When a friend asked, over breakfast at the Brunswick, why King had never married, King replied, "Woman is too one-sided—like a tossed-up penny—and I want both sides or none."45 His public dissatisfaction gave no hint of his private affairs.

Nor did his writing. In October 1888, a month after his marriage to Copeland, King published an essay in the *North American Review*. His critical examination of the recent literary characterizations of women seemed to betray his sentiments about the real thing. Nothing about the women featured in contemporary realistic fiction—with their "incredible meanness" and the "primeval monkey-scale of their average intelligence"—appealed to him. The English created only "distorted and diseased creatures," while the French realists "flung woman naked in the ditch and left her there scorned of men, and grinning in cynical and shameless levity over her own dishonor." The women in American literature illustrated the "sawdust stuffing of their middle-class democratic society." So King posed a rhetorical question. "Out of it all, is there one figure for weary eyes to linger upon: one type of large and satisfying womanhood, natural in the rare and ravishing charm of a perfect body; sweet with the endowment of a warm, quick, sympathetic temperament; sound and bright in intellect; pure and spiritual with a soul...[undimmed by] the jar of modern conflict?" King found his ideal in the "Greek Venus in the Louvre, who is only perfect goddess because she is perfect woman"; a woman with a "rich femininity" and a "Doric strength," a "calm warmth" and an "irradiating aura of love."46 By professing his undying adoration for the unattainable perfection of a marble statue, King threw his friends off his scent. Who would suspect he had found real love with an African American nursemaid?

In September 1888 James Todd and Ada Copeland exchanged marriage vows in a small ceremony at the home of Ada's aunt, Annie Purnell. Ada's pastor, the Reverend James H. Cook of the Union American Methodist

Episcopal Church on East Eighty-fifth Street, conducted the wedding service before a handful of witnesses. One, then a young girl, later recalled the organ in the apartment that day, as well as "a big wedding cake, all kinds of candy, chocolates, bon bons, nuts and different kinds of food." If the event offered evidence of King's financial resources, it also testified to Copeland's social ambitions. The groom—possibly wearing a suit once seen in the Century Association dining room, or perhaps an old Pullman porter's coat—placed a ring on the bride's finger. The gold and silver overlay on the ornately patterned gold band symbolically intertwined as one and reaffirmed that the groom was a man of means. But no identifying names or dates personalized the wedding ring. King took care not to mark it as a personal memento of a particular day.[47]

Perhaps Clarence King noted to himself how modest the ceremony seemed, how different from the large church services and elaborate receptions he had attended in Newport and New York. But Ada likely viewed the festivities differently, less a diminished version of something more grand than a joyful embrace of all that her own parents and grandparents had been denied. Slave wedding rituals came in all forms, from the traditional "broomstick wedding," in which couples jumped over a broom handle, to informal religious services involving clergymen and elaborate ceremonies in the "big house" arranged by the planter. But few weddings took place without an owner's approval. And for all their importance within the slave community as rare celebrations of individual desire and will, they almost always reinforced the slaveholders' power and control. Slaves noted that the white preachers who presided over their weddings never said "till death do you part." One white minister expressed the reality: "Until death or distance do you part." Slave masters retained the ultimate threat: anyone who misbehaved could be separated from his or her spouse. And in truth, not even good behavior necessarily assured the stability of a marital relationship. The mere desire for financial gain might compel a slaveholder to separate a married couple.[48]

For the Copeland-Todd wedding ceremony to take place in a home instead of a church was not unusual. But the guests might have wondered why the groom—without family or friends—should be so alone.

. . .

KING GREW UP WITHIN his mother's United Congregationalist faith. His religion, he once quipped, was like his teeth: both were inherited and both were sound. But the intense piety of his youth, so evident in the long, searching letters about faith he exchanged with his friend Jim Gardiner, waned as he grew older.[49] He invoked a more pantheistic notion of a deity—of a "God, who is also Nature"—at the conclusion of *Mountaineering in the Sierra Nevada*, and as an adult turned toward a faith less stern than that of his boyhood, even flirting with the more emotional spiritualism of African American Christianity.[50] James Hague recalled that while investigating a north Georgia gold mine, King once "attended a religious meeting of a colored congregation, assembled in a large barn-like and frigid meeting-house, without any heating facilities whatever, except the large hot stones and bowlders which many of the old women brought with them." King addressed the meeting and, notwithstanding the bitter cold, "much enjoyed the fervent spirit of the prayers and the hymns and soul-saving exhortations." He promised to buy the congregants a large stove, and so he did. Returning to the area a few years later, he asked a white driver whether the church was still doing well. "I should say so!" the driver replied. "There ain't a fence-rail left in this neighborhood within two mile of that meetin'-house." Hague dismissed King's generosity as an amusing gesture.[51] But the anecdote hints at King's fascination with the African American church and suggests how he could use stories to deflect his friends from any probing queries about his innermost feelings or beliefs.

When Ada Copeland proposed that her pastor perform their marriage ceremony, King might thus have agreed not just to please her but because he himself felt drawn to the practices of African American worship. Perhaps James even presented himself to Cook, and to Ada, as a fellow member of the Union American Methodist Episcopal Church. Not a member of the New York congregation—Cook surely knew all his own parishioners—but a member somewhere else, maybe in Baltimore, the place Todd claimed as his hometown. Membership in the Union American Methodist Episcopal Church, an African American sect, would reaffirm what Todd had already implied by identifying himself as a Pullman porter: he was black. Certainly, everyone else in the church was.

Cook likely accepted the groom's story, whatever doubts he might have had about his appearance or the story of his past. What would Todd's background matter in light of the prospective bride's evident happiness? It would be a blessing to help launch his parishioner into a better life.

IF ADA AND HER AUNT lived largely within the social confines of Manhattan's black working-class community, the Reverend James H. Cook had a higher public profile. In the mid-1860s he helped found the Coachmen's Union League Society in New York to provide "good-fellowship" and insurance benefits to "negro coachmen employed in public stables or by private families," the very men who drove the fashionable carriages that King watched from the Brunswick Hotel. He donated his time to black fraternal organizations, raised funds for black refugees from the South, and anointed himself a champion of the downtrodden. In 1880 he went to the Tombs prison to pray with a soon-to-be-executed murderer named Chastain Cox. When Cook's congregants threatened to disrupt any funeral service for the convicted criminal at their church, Cook improvised a hasty service at the undertaker's and bought the burial plot himself.[52] He was a familiar figure at political gatherings and civil rights events, and in 1890, a year after being appointed a bishop of his church with responsibility for some twenty-two congregations in the Northeast, he joined an interracial group of New York clergymen to fight corruption in Tammany Hall.[53]

For much of his life as a black man, James Todd lived beyond the notice of those who shaped African American community life in New York; he could not afford much social scrutiny. But at the moment of his wedding, when he brushed up against the Reverend James H. Cook, he crossed paths with someone who might have heard of Clarence King and his well-connected friends. It would prove King's most public moment in black city life.

. . .

JAMES AND ADA TODD sealed their marriage with a religious ceremony but never obtained a civil marriage license. They thus had a common-law marriage, a partnership acknowledged by New York since 1809 and recognized as legally valid in most states by the late nineteenth century.[54] In having a family celebration but eschewing a legal record, they made what at first seems an odd choice for a couple concerned about privacy. Those who wish to keep their partnerships secret often turn to civil licenses, which can be obtained from the municipal authorities without involving family, religious authorities, or—aside from the obligatory legal witnesses—any friends or acquaintances at all. But in this case, civil documents likely seemed more threatening to the charade than any more public religious service. James Todd likely felt uneasy about appearing in a municipal office to identify himself and wary of leaving behind a paper trail of his deceptions. In 1888 Manhattan's official "certificate of marriage" required both bride and groom to report their names, ages, and parents' names, and asked the groom to record his occupation. The form also requested the applicants to designate their "color." The directions were simple: "If of other races, specify what." No one needed to clarify the official meaning of the phrase. In the nation's largest city, "white" remained the norm; everything else was a racial deviation from the standard. To obtain a civil marriage license, James Todd and his bride would have to not only fill out the form but find two witnesses to swear to the truth of everything—including their names and racial identities.[55]

No laws prohibited King and Copeland from taking out a marriage license as a white man and a black woman. Interracial marriage was not illegal in New York in 1888, as it was throughout the South. Nonetheless, it remained uncommon. Scant data exist for 1888, but even as late as from 1908 to 1912, a mere 10.4 interracial marriages per year appear in the New York City records.[56] Even accounting for common-law marriages and unofficial partnerships, the number is strikingly low. And the practice thus remained a topic of curiosity, particularly among King's social set, with alliances between white men and black women the most curious and titillating of all. "It is almost invariably the black man and the white woman," the *Boston Herald* reported in 1888, noting a supposed one hundred to two hundred interracial marriages in Boston that year. "It is very rarely that a white man marries a black woman."[57] The *New York Times* fed its readers' fascination with interracial marriage with a steady diet of stories about the criminal fate of the "white groom and colored bride" in such places as Vicksburg and Galveston, Shreveport and Memphis, Baltimore and Kansas City, all aimed at emphasizing the seeming strangeness of the practice.[58] Even if such marriages were legal in New York, they remained unnerving and destabilizing to the status quo.

When the activist Frederick Douglass wed his white secretary Helen Pitts in 1884, in the most prominent interracial marriage of the day, blacks protested along with whites, demonstrating that not even political prominence could shield one from the broad cultural antipathy toward interracial unions. Douglass showed "contempt for the women of his own race," some African Americans charged. But Douglass, whose African American wife had died a year and a half earlier, never shied from the publicity or notoriety engendered by his act. Alluding to his own suspected heritage as the son of a slave woman and her white owner, Douglass remarked that his first wife "was the color of my mother, and the second, the color of my father."[59]

King sometimes made light of race. He once joked, for example, that the skin on one side of his body temporarily turned "a coffee color" after lightning struck him on a Nevada peak in the summer of 1867.[60] The very ease with which he could jest about becoming black—whether on a mountain peak or in the African American neighborhoods of Manhattan—suggests his fundamental racial self-assurance as a white man. Unlike the dark-hued Ada Copeland, unlike Frederick Douglass whose mother was incontrovertibly black, Clarence King could choose how people perceived his racial identity. He could play at race and return to the white world whenever he chose. He could live as a black man within the embrace of Ada's family and church, and move out into the world to earn his living as a white scientist. It would be hard to embrace blackness as a playful masquerade if you had been born into slavery or had grown up in a world where dark skin circumscribed every aspect of your life. If race might sometimes seem to King a superficial marker shed as easily as a mask, Ada likely knew it to be something with deep, abiding repercussions.

And yet King's ability to see race as a mutable biological or social fact, less fixed than fluid, allowed him to envision a world in which race did not matter. "Miscegenation," King once told a friend, is "the hope of the white race." The friend dismissed the remark as one of King's "whimsical ideas."[61] But King meant it. He truly imagined an America without race.

King laid out his startling racial theories three years before his marriage, in an 1885 review of the designs submitted for a new monument to the late president and Civil War general Ulysses S. Grant. Some called for a structure in a distinctively "American" style, he wrote in the *North American Review*, but how could there be a true national style when the American people remained so fragmented and diverse? Americans of European, African, and Asian descent, bound together by a single government, might compose a *nation*, but they did not constitute a truly American *race*. King envisioned a future "when the composite elements of American populations are melted down into one race alloy, when there are no more Irish or Germans, Negroes and English, but only Americans, belonging to one defined American race." Only then would Americans become conscious of their own "ideals and aspiration" and find a true and distinctive form of cultural expression.[62]

In resorting to the metallurgical metaphor of "amalgamation" and employing the idea in such utopian terms, King echoed an older radical strain of thinking about racial and ethnic mixing in the United States that had all but disappeared in the wake of Reconstruction. The word first emerged in late-eighteenth-century England to denote the mixing of diverse peoples through intermarriage or cultural exchange, as with the blending of the Saxons and Normans. Similarly, in early-nineteenth-century America, the word usually referred to the admixture of immigrants of diverse ethnic origins. But by the early 1830s, it applied mainly to relationships between

African Americans and Americans of European origin. Even in the North, the term provoked spirited debates among the radical abolitionists, more conservative racial thinkers, and the working-class whites who saw black laborers as a threat to their own economic interests. In May 1834 concerns over amalgamation triggered a three-day race riot in New York City, with white mobs attacking black residences and singling out for special attention the homes of radical white abolitionists and the churches of ministers rumored to have performed interracial marriages. In the aftermath of the violence, the American Anti-Slavery Society in New York publicly disavowed all support for racial intermarriage, and most white abolitionists in the city retreated from their defense of interracial social relations.[63]

Over the coming decades, as the nation slipped ever closer to civil war over the issue of slavery, only a few intellectual outliers continued to use the metaphor of amalgamation to characterize positively the future of the country. Wendell Phillips, Boston's fiery abolitionist, spoke approvingly of the "United States of the United Races" in 1853, and in an 1863 Fourth of July oration thundered that he was "an amalgamationist to the utmost extent." He proclaimed, "I have no hope for the future...but in that sublime mingling of races, which is God's own method of civilizing and elevating the world."[64]

Raised on abolitionist rhetoric by his mother and grandmother, King grew up admiring Phillips.[65] But Phillips died in 1884, and when King penned his essay about the amalgamation of the American race a year later, Phillips's particular way of thinking about racial equality had all but vanished from the intellectual landscape. Indeed, the very word "amalgamation" had been largely supplanted by "miscegenation," a new term made popular by a pseudoscientific pamphlet of 1864, *Miscegenation: The Theory of the Blending of the Races, Applied to the American White Man and Negro.* The pamphlet was an elaborate hoax, purportedly written by a radical abolitionist. It called upon all good Republicans to support interracial marriage as the logical extension of the war to free the Negro and the only way to assure the continued vitality of the white race. Its anonymous authors, David Croly and George Wakeman, were, in fact, Democratic newspapermen, who intended their extreme argument to inflict damage on the Republican Party. Since the term "amalgamation" originally referred to the union of metals, it was a "poor word" to use to describe the melding of races, they argued. They coined their own new word from the Latin *miscere*, to mix, and *genus*, race.[66] The term "amalgamation" once evoked neutral or positive meanings, but "miscegenation" would be, from the start, a judgmental and pejorative term meant to evoke the intrinsic horror of interracial mixing.

In invoking the metaphor of amalgamation and the vision of a raceless America in 1885, King harkened back to an all but vanished tradition of radical racial thought. Not even Frederick Douglass, who so admired King's grandmother as an "excellent woman and a true abolitionist," could imagine the racial future of the nation with King's determined optimism.[67] Writing in the *North American Review* in 1886, where King had published his own thoughts about racial mixing just six months before, Douglass argued that the Negro would not remain a separate and distinct race but "will be absorbed, assimilated, and will only appear finally, as the Phoenicians now appear on the shores of the Shannon, in the features of a blended race." He neither advocated nor deprecated such racial mixing. "I am not a propagandist," he explained, "but a prophet."[68] King, for all his reluctance to make his own mixed marriage a matter of public record as Douglass had done, voiced a more radical view. Racial mixing was not simply inevitable but desirable: it would improve the vitality of the human race and create a distinctively American people.

We live in "the age of energy," King wrote in 1892. Soon "we shall whisper around the globe" and "flight through the upper air will be a daily matter of course." Technology seemed destined to transform the world, but what about the "new table of biological commandments" emerging from Darwinism? "We have been quick to adopt railways, but we cannot realize heredity." He thought humans could banish incompetence, insanity, and disease through sound breeding, thus anticipating the language of eugenics, which would emerge in the early twentieth century as a science concerned with the biological improvement of humankind. But while eugenicists generally concerned themselves with the preservation of an imagined racial "purity,"

King sounded a different note. He saw racial amalgamation as the path to the improvement of the white race.[69]

He might sometimes have imagined his marriage to Ada Copeland as a subversive political act, one that became increasingly effective as she gave birth to each of their five children, and King—in his own secret way—helped father a new raceless nation. Yet imagining the marriage as a sly political gambit on King's part seems as wrong-minded as dismissing it as self-absorbed hedonism. King loved Ada, and she loved him back. Their relationship rested on devotion and passion, even if it was grounded in deceit.

King held sentimental ideas about marriage. "To religion and marriage we may ever turn as to final expressions of the inner nature of man," he wrote in 1875. "His attitude toward the God whose unseen presence he can but feel, and his treatment of the mother of his children, at once fix his place in the scale of manhood and nobility."[70] For thirteen years he would remain devoted to Ada and their children, at no small cost to his own financial and emotional well-being. By virtue of his class and his race, his wealth and his social connections, King held all the cards of social privilege, and like others of his station he might simply have asked Copeland to become his mistress. But one imagines Ada resisting that idea; she sought a respectable life. And for all he did to keep his marriage a secret, King likewise seemed to value the stability of a real home. So James Todd consented to a religious wedding and he gave his wife his family name. If it was not quite his true, legal name, it was nonetheless a name that, at least in her world, would link them together as family.

WHEN JAMES TODD MARRIED, he crossed the color line. From now on, his private assurances to Ada served as his warrant that he belonged in her world. If she believed him to be a person of African descent, it would be as a black man that he moved through her world of churchgoing friends, curious urban neighbors, and Georgia relations. And as that identity became fixed, it would become increasingly difficult for him ever to confess or untangle the deceptions he spun out for her when he first encountered her on the streets of Manhattan. From now on, Clarence King would be a part-time black man.

King's journey as a black man would take him away from his familiar haunts and diminish his ability to move freely and openly in the world. At the same time, however, it would allow him to have an intimate connection to the woman he loved and to create for himself a real home. Clarence King could travel anywhere in New York. The black railroad porter James Todd could not: even as he built a rich emotional life, he would have to live within the more restrictive confines of a black working-class and middle-class world. And yet, if for James Todd New York seemed a newly diminished place, for his new bride it likely seemed magnificently enlarged and full of possibilities. By marrying James Todd, Ada grasped a kind of security her own slave parents never had. Her marriage asserted her place in the world, her independence, her ability to make her own choices. It marked her passage out of a life of domestic service and into a world where she could be a wife, a mother, and the mistress of her own home, and for a while even have servants of her own. In the world that Clarence King and Ada Copeland created as Mr. and Mrs. James Todd, he moved away from social privilege, she moved toward it, and together they created a family.

Family Lives

ADA TODD'S NEW LIFE CENTERED ON HER HOME. SOON AFTER her marriage, she settled into an apartment on Hudson Avenue in Brooklyn, a cobblestoned road lined with two- and three-story buildings that stretched from the East River down along the edge of the Brooklyn Navy Yards toward the busy intersection of Fulton and Flatbush avenues.[1] It was an old street, its Belgian-block paving rutted by the grooves of long-abandoned stage car tracks and "full of pitfalls for the truckman as well as the family carriage."[2] As one inspector of Brooklyn's streets complained, "A ride over the cobblestones is equal to a month in the penitentiary and a walk on the sidewalk on a windy day to a term in purgatory."[3] Ada's two-story building, at number 291, stood catty-corner from a blacksmith's shop.[4] Just a few blocks away, almost equidistant, lay Washington Park (later Fort Greene Park), with winding footpaths laid out by King's old friend Frederick Law Olmsted and Calvert Vaux, and the more forbidding grounds of the Navy Yards. The shipbuilding facility stood hidden away behind a high brick wall that concealed the huge storehouses, covered sheds, dry docks, and ironworks sprawled out along the East River's Wallabout Bay. Ada's immediate neighborhood, then as now known as Vinegar Hill, contained a mix of residential buildings and small businesses, chiefly bars and stores, as well as factories and slaughterhouses. In 1890 Brooklyn's population was just 1.3 percent black. This particular neighborhood, however, had been largely African American ever since the Civil War.[5]

In 1885 a municipal health survey pronounced the condition of Hudson Avenue "bad." "Garbage and refuse choke the gutters and decaying animal and vegetable matter lies till it rots to nothing."[6] On some days the smoke from the iron foundry down the block hung thick in the air. And the stench of the nearby stock pen, the slaughterhouse, the tallow-rendering facility, and the skin-salting plant could become almost unbearable. "At certain periods of each week," the *Brooklyn Daily Eagle* reported, "when the proprietors are boiling offal or rendering fat the odor that fills the air is so bad that it prevents those working in neighboring factories from continuing their labor, and a good deal of the unusually large amount of sickness in the neighboring tenements can be traced...to conditions produced by the slaughter houses." The people in the neighborhood "say that they cannot eat their meals with any relish and cannot sleep at night because of the odor."[7] But a woman like Ada Todd, newly freed from the necessity of work and living in her own home for the very first time, might find that the space and privacy outweighed the stench of the street.

Ada now had an independence and privacy she could only have dreamed of as a boarder in her aunt's tenement apartment or as a live-in domestic. On this dusty, smelly, sometimes rowdy street, she could eat whenever she wanted to, invite friends into her home, step out to walk any time of day. She might not live in the heart of Brooklyn's black society, among the older families with fortunes derived from successful careers as caterers or dressmakers whom James Weldon Johnson described as "positively rich." But down the street there lived a few African American families whose birthday parties drew attention from the society pages of New York's black newspapers.[8] From her own apartment on Hudson Avenue, Ada might glimpse the possibilities of such a life. She, too, might become a person of note in her community, the sort of woman others might read about in the society pages or acknowledge on the streets.

She lived surrounded by an urban landscape of sounds as well as smells: the clip-clop of horses on the cobblestones, the more distant sounds of steam-powered trains, the cries of street vendors hawking food or selling old clothes. Brooklyn began electrifying its trains in 1890, even as

Manhattanites continued to travel in horse-drawn cars and steam-powered trains. Ada's neighborhood soon rattled with the noise of an elevated train that rumbled by less than two blocks away. The new electric trains could hurtle through the streets at thirty miles an hour, roughly six times faster than the horse-drawn trolleys. But with their speed came danger. Though they had "the weight and power of locomotives," write two New York historians, "their brakes were still those of a horsecar."[9]

Near the elevated tracks of Ada's neighborhood stood the bars and poolrooms where African American residents sometimes gathered in the evenings. A group of neighbors petitioned the mayor in the summer of 1891 to complain about the late-night singing, dancing, and conversation "of a very vile character" by "a lot of lazy disreputable, blasphemous negroes of the male and female sex" that disrupted the local peace. But the police found the small restaurant at the center of the complaints to be quiet and orderly. "Hudson avenue stands vindicated," reported the *Brooklyn Daily Eagle*. The police "do not pretend that Hudson avenue is a second garden of Eden, a perpetual paradise, a community of celestial virtue. They do not assert that its inhabitants are eminently fitted, without preliminary preparation to join the angelic choir. What they contend is that the picture of drunkenness and disorder...is overcolored." The complainants lived in the "improved tenement flats" recently built in the middle of the block, "right in the midst of a dense colored population, mostly of the lowest order, who occupy buildings which are old and dilapidated." The police dismissed their complaints and defended the rights of the residents of the old tenements to sit out on their stoops on hot summer nights.[10]

The block that lay at the very center of Ada Todd's world lay at the periphery of her husband's. To reach Hudson Avenue, in downtown Brooklyn, King would slip out of his midtown clubs and head down to the ferry docks at the southern tip of Manhattan to board a boat across the East River, immersing himself in what one traveler called "the rushing crowds, the stamping teams and yelling teamsters, the tooting whistles, the rattling windlasses and clanging chains."[11] Or he might catch a crowded train to make the six-minute trip across the Brooklyn Bridge, that engineering marvel that spanned the East River, arching high over the ferries and freighters, schooners and steamboats that crowded New York's great harbor. Finally, said one of the speakers at the dedication of the bridge in 1883, the " 'silver streak' which has so long divided this city [Brooklyn] from the continent is now conquered, henceforth, by the silver band stretching above it, careless of wind and tide, of ice and fog, of current and calm."[12] By the spring of 1888, 487 cable railway trains a day made the crossing from Manhattan to Brooklyn, leaving as often as every minute and a half and depositing riders at a train terminal at Fulton and Sand streets, just eleven blocks from Ada's apartment.[13] King would walk from there to the apartment, transforming himself, somewhere along the familiar route, into James Todd, the black Pullman porter.

The Brooklyn Bridge knit together Manhattan and the independent city of Brooklyn, making it possible to imagine a truly unified metropolis, which was made real on January 1, 1898, when Manhattan, Queens, Staten Island, Brooklyn, and the Bronx joined together to form Greater New York, a single city of some three million souls. Railroads and bridges, telegraphs and telephones: such marvels annihilated space and distance, bringing the distant near. But a man like Clarence King, who sought to keep his two lives at a safe divide, might view these technological innovations with mixed feelings. He probably settled his wife in Brooklyn for a reason. With each subsequent move, he relocated her farther from his own midtown Manhattan haunts.

One imagines that as King traveled from Manhattan to Brooklyn, then walked to Hudson Avenue, he would prepare mentally, calculating how to drop the burdens and pleasures of one life to assume the guise of another. He might subtly alter his appearance or modify his behavior. Maybe he changed his clothes, stuffing his jacket into his bag and pulling out a Pullman porter's coat. Perhaps he adopted more colloquial speech to conceal his Newport and Ivy League antecedents, or took care to leave his business papers behind at his club or in his residential hotel rooms. By 1891, more than a million people commuted into and out of Manhattan every day.[14] In the anonymity of that crowd King could slip into character, perhaps talking to strangers on the train or the boat, spinning stories about his life as a porter, or just chatting about his neighborhood in Brooklyn. Perhaps, though, he just became silent, steeling himself to walk through the busy streets of Brooklyn as James Todd, bracing himself to leap into the newness of an invented life.

ABOUT THE TIME HE set up the new household with Ada in Brooklyn, King secured a new place to live in Manhattan. He could not wholly abandon his other, more public life; nor did he wish to. He valued his friends and family too much to risk their disapproval, and he relied for his livelihood on his reputation as an eminent geologist. To be James Todd, he needed to earn his living as Clarence King. So even if he continued to use his midtown clubs as a place to receive his mail, entertain his friends, and conduct informal business, he still needed a residential foothold in the city in order to maintain his public and professional life. Soon after his wedding, he moved from the Brunswick Hotel to the Hotel Albert, farther downtown at the corner of University Place and East Eleventh Street.[15] Its location reflected the complicated calculus of his new life. It stood just a few doors away from his mother's temporary residence on East Eleventh Street, and at the same time put him closer to Brooklyn. He could probably expect more privacy here. The residents and employees of the Brunswick, who had known him for years, would be more likely to note his comings and goings.

The Albert advertised itself as an "ideal fire-proof building" with "suites of two to six rooms; elegantly furnished; cuisine and service unsurpassed," and it attracted a literary and artistic clientele. Among his new neighbors, King could count two art dealers, a college treasurer, a journalist for the *New York Tribune*, and the enterprising "Miss Minnie Swayze, teacher, reader and lecturer," who offered elocution lessons in her rooms. His neighbors included a few more-troubled souls as well, like forty-seven-year-old Miss Frances Rhind, who leapt to her death from her parents' fourth-floor window, and George North Dalrymple, the flamboyant Englishman and would-be writer who drank his way through his family funds and went to jail for dodging his hotel bills. King's new residence lacked the social cachet of his last one, attracting midwestern retail merchants rather than the fashionable members of the "coaching set."[16] It had the advantage, however, of cheaper rents.[17]

Even so, to maintain two households took more than King had. In October 1888, a month after he married, King turned to John Hay for a $6,000 loan (more than $135,000 in 2007 dollars). It would prove the first of at least six loans King requested from Hay over the next three years. From the start, he sustained his secret life with crushing debt.[18]

Ada later claimed that she accompanied her husband to Washington, Newport, and Boston.[19] But it seems improbable that King could protect his secret if James and Ada Todd traveled together on the trains or ships that Clarence normally used for his trips along the Northeast coast. The potential social awkwardness of running into an old acquaintance would be too great, threatening to unravel his deceptions on both ends. Perhaps his friends would believe that Ada was a family servant or a relative of King's black valet, Alexander Lancaster, who began working for him at about this time. But lying to them in Ada's presence or even responding to the name they called him would expose his deceptions to his wife. A casual greeting from a passerby—"Clare!" or "King!"—could call everything into question.

King kept his friends uncertain about his whereabouts in the fall of 1888, during the first month or two of his marriage. He turned down a chance to travel to Fiji then with Henry Adams, though Adams jokingly promised that they could drink blood from empty skulls. "He does not seem to know," King wrote to Hay, "that enemies are impossible to me among archaic peoples, and that if a sudden mad thirst for blood drinking should ever overtake me I should as a matter of choice begin with the Americans."[20] He breathed not a word of his marriage, even to his closest friends, and remained maddeningly elusive. Finally, in November, he made his whereabouts known to John Hay. From Altoona, Pennsylvania, King wrote that he was on his way to the therapeutic spas at Hot Springs, Arkansas, and had "told no one except Mother" about his travels.[21] His back pain—variously described as "gouty rheumatism" or "deep muscular rheumatism"—seemed unbearable.[22]

King's friends knew of his back troubles, even if they never quite understood their source, and they tended to view the pain as a stimulant to King's astonishing physical vigor. King "has been very ill this winter," Hay wrote to a friend in the spring of 1887, "but there seems to be great recuperative forces somewhere about him always, and he gets out of bed for a ramble of five thousand miles and thinks nothing of it."[23] In the summer of 1887, however, King underwent some sort of operation. Henry Adams knew of it, though he remained vague on the details. "The ruffian seems well and bright," he reported to Hay that August. "[King] says that his operation worked like a charm, and that he has been very well since, but it will have to be repeated."[24] By the end of the year, though, King was confined to bed with an illness he deemed "the most serious of my life." He contemplated "the giving up of everything for a struggle to get well."[25] Whether King's trouble stemmed from an old injury, the painful inflammations of gout, or arthritis, he usually just called it rheumatism, a nonspecific term for a variety of medical disorders involving chronic, often intermittent pain.[26] The combination of hot bath treatments and repeated minor surgeries also suggests the possibility of a pilonidal cyst, a painful abscess at the base of the tailbone.[27] While he courted Ada Copeland, the pain had seemed tolerable. But now it was not.

Ada likely stayed behind when King left her, just two months after their marriage, to travel south—part of the way on segregated railway cars—in search of relief for his back pain. Presumably, she had quit her job when she married the railroad porter. With her newfound time, independence, and money, she could settle into her new house and begin to find her way around Brooklyn. In Hot Springs, meanwhile, King registered at the fashionable Arlington Hotel and protected his privacy in the rambling three-story frame hotel by securing a special room with a private entrance to the baths and arranging for his meals to be brought to his room. He might have an endless curiosity about the exotic peoples he met in his travels, but he had scant patience with the social set, whether in Manhattan or at a hot springs resort. King grumbled to Hay that the doctors' prescription for his pain involved an unbearably long sixty-day regimen of thirty baths on alternate days. He wrote nothing of Ada, but she seemed to preoccupy him. As never before, his letters focus on race. Arkansas seemed "the most barbarous and terrible place" he had ever been in. He told Hay that he was "interviewing a lot of Negroes about the recent notices to leave in various parts of Arkansas" and expressed shocked indignation at the governor's refusal to protect them. The entire South seemed a mockery of American civilization, led by "lying Jesuitical Brigadiers" and great bodies of ignorant people. Thankfully, the blacks were "rising as fast as the laws of Evolution will permit." King cut short his visit to return to New York, ostensibly to tend to business, perhaps to be with Ada. It was "lonesome" in Arkansas, he told Hay. He returned feeling better, but in a peculiar reference to his complexion, remarked that he was "nigger gray."[28]

King's surviving correspondence with his friends catalogs his continuing spinal pain, his struggles with depression, his worries about his mother, and the vicissitudes of his work life. But still not a word about his married life. By asking his friends' indulgence for his various health and financial worries, he suggested a source for his distracted inattentiveness and frequent absences and deflected probing questions about his personal affairs. His friends knew that he moved his mother back to Newport so that he could go down to Mexico during the summer of 1889 to tend to a mine, but then he disappeared from their lives for a while. He resurfaced in New York in the fall, elusive as ever, canceling dates at the last moment, pleading the necessity to be elsewhere, compelling his friends to write to business managers to figure out where he was. "I have drudged away here, sometimes worn down to the quick of my nerves," he wrote to Hay from New York in October 1889, "and then coming up again all right." He felt "low" in spirit, he explained, and missed Hay's companionship. He again dreamed of moving to Washington with his mother and half sister, Marian, because, he wrote to Hay, "I would rather have you than all New York." King did seem in the "depths of low spirits," Henry Adams reported to a friend, and very "low in mind." Adams surmised the problem must be money.[29]

It was, in part. But it was also more complicated than that. King threw out hidden clues to his friends. In October 1889, after Adams completed the first volume of his massive *History of the United States of America during the Administrations of Thomas Jefferson and James Madison*, King made

light of his own inability to sit down and write any of the "vast historical works" he always had in mind.[30] Writing to Hay about the depression
that descended upon Adams when he finished his book, King said, "It's
evidently a horrible thing to finish one's magnum opus. I who will never
begin mine may always have the gentle tonic of perpetual gestation, the soft
genial pride of an important bellyful, with none of the throes of printing
and none of the ghastly hollowness of collapsing sides. Can a man have a
second magnum opus? Is the intellectual womb capable of a second fecun-
dation?"[31] The teasing metaphor of the pregnant man hinted at King's powerful secret: James Todd had become a father.

Ada Todd gave birth to a son sometime in 1889; no surviving documents
record the precise date.[32] Clarence named him Leroy, a variation of *le roi*,
French for "the king," an inside joke that only King could appreciate. Just as
the pseudonymous James Todd honored his true father by becoming a "James,"
his son honored them both by becoming a "King." The echo of names proved
prescient: Clarence King disappeared from young Leroy's life just as his own
China-trader father had disappeared from his: in a dutiful search for money.

"Now in middle age, I am poor," the forty-seven-year-old King complained to Adams in September 1889, "and what is worse, so absorbed in the
hand to mouth struggle for income that I see the effective literary and scientific years drifting by empty and blank, when I am painfully conscious of
the power to do something had I the chance."[33] In November he borrowed
another $11,000 from Hay (nearly $255,000 in 2007 dollars).[34] Later that
year, he went west to check out a mining project in Colorado. He returned
to New York early in the new year, expecting to set off for Florida and Cuba,
but turned west again to investigate some mining prospects in California,
where the memories of his earlier ventures left him feeling "rheumatic and
gray and dull." From California during the bleak winter of 1890, King came
close to unburdening himself of his secrets, half-begging Hay to press him
to reveal what weighed so heavily on his spirit. "When can I be with you
long enough to open up my soul to you," he wrote, "for there grows over me

a dread but you should forget what sort of fellow there still is under all the load of hard things which cover me up and hide me....I wish I could write as I feel but that no longer seems possible."[35]

In March 1890 King turned to Hay for another loan, explaining that he had left some money behind to see his mother and half brother, George, through the winter, but needed an additional $450 by April to help George continue his painting studies in Paris.[36] Alluding to the collateral he put up for previous loans, King reminded Hay that all his "bric a brac" was "yours long ago as everything else I have belongs to you."[37] Hay, ever generous, sent the money to George Howland in Paris. In May King signed a promissory note to Hay for a stunning $26,000 (nearly $611,000 in 2007 dollars), backing it up with two chattel mortgages. The debt incurred since his wedding, only one and a half years before, now totaled more than $43,000 (over $1 million now).[38] "He handles vast interests," Hay wrote of King to William Dean Howells, "but cares so little for money that he gains very little. A touch of Avarice would have made him a Vanderbilt—a touch of plodding industry would have made him anything he chose." Hay puzzled over his talented friend: why did his brilliance and charm not bring him economic rewards? "I fear he will die without doing anything," Hay wrote, "except to be a great scientist, a delightful writer, and the sweetest natured creature the Lord ever made."[39]

As a man of liberal racial thought (and a generous one at that), Hay might have understood King's true dilemma. Though never a radical abolitionist, Hay grew up with strong sentiments against the "defiant and ungrateful villainy" of slavery and, as Lincoln's private secretary, watched the president struggle over the issue of freeing the slaves. Lincoln's Emancipation Proclamation, which took effect on January 1, 1863, struck Hay as "lightning from a clear sky" that "[melted] with a flash four million shackles."[40] Later, as an essayist and a historian—penning among other works a ten-volume history of Lincoln with coauthor John Nicolay—he continued to focus on the vexing American dilemma of race. In 1879 he helped lead a relief effort in Cleveland to support the black Exodusters fleeing the Deep South for Oklahoma and Kansas. Later, he contributed generously to a Washington, D.C., group that established a model tenement program for the urban black poor. Though his racial views hardened in the 1890s, he remained in the public eye a powerful friend of blacks. Twice, Tuskegee Institute honored his service by inviting him to speak, and in Alexandria, Virginia, in 1894, a group of citizens established in his honor the John Hay Normal and Industrial School.[41]

Given Hay's deep personal friendship and his civic interest in the affairs of black Americans, why did King not share his secret? One imagines he feared disappointing the admiring friend who was bankrolling his life. But it likewise seems possible that Hay himself steered away from intimate talk, for he, too, had a secret. His wife, Clara, was the model of domestic respectability, and her family money allowed him to pursue the life of the gentleman scholar and diplomat. But since 1887 Hay had been in love with Nannie Lodge, the witty and charming wife of Massachusetts congressman Henry Cabot Lodge, a woman different in every regard from the pious Mrs. Hay. Hay's secret affair did not cross the bounds of race or class as King's marriage did, but it likewise threatened the stability of public reputations and professional lives. Henry Adams knew about Mrs. Lodge, and so did his own close companion, Elizabeth Cameron. But Hay confided in no one else.[42] For all their camaraderie and the seeming closeness of their long relationship, Hay and King shared a friendship defined and circumscribed by secrets.

In New York, King shuddered at his "real apathy of soul, and indifference of heart to the world," confiding to Hay that he went about his work "mechanically" and beset by loneliness.[43] If his depression was real, his seeming openness was not. As always, King's words led his friends to imagine that his life held few pleasures, that his problems were largely financial. Hay perceived that every financial struggle of King's "gets him deeper in the mire, costs him something of life as well as money."[44] By late spring 1890, however, Ada Todd was pregnant with her second child. Of that world of physical intimacy, that part of his life where he found a comforting and affirming joy, King continued to tell his friends nothing. Hay thought it would benefit King's "immortal soul" to just "drop everything" and sail away to the South Pacific with Henry Adams.[45] But King could not go.

He sailed, instead, to England in June with his valet, Alexander Lancaster. Like James Marryatt, who played a similar role during the survey years, Lancaster was black. A light-skinned man of mixed racial ancestry, Lancaster was born in April 1863 in Petersburg, Virginia, a year before the town came under siege by Union troops.[46] His mother, like Ada's, was most likely a slave. The details of his early life and the circumstances of his initial meeting with King remain unclear, but he remained in King's employ until at least 1900.[47] Lancaster's life, King told a friend, "was in his work."[48] It was either Lancaster or Marryatt, that friend later recalled, who "came to be an invaluable assistant in geological underground work, observing with great acuteness, although without scientific knowledge, indications which more learned men might have overlooked."[49]

King traveled to England to testify in a trial involving ongoing troubles with the Anglo-Mexican Mining Company and to scout around for investors for another mining project in Idaho (the trip caused him to miss the ceremony at which Brown University awarded him an honorary LL.D.). He then moved on to talk to financiers in Paris, accompanied by his old New York friend Abram Hewitt, who was now retired from his public career as a congressman and short tenure as mayor of New York (1887–88).[50] When Hewitt became ill, King insisted he return to England with Lancaster as his personal attendant. In the Paris train station, solicitous officials grabbed their luggage and escorted them to a special railway car, insisting that Lancaster lead the way. Only later did Hewitt and Lancaster learn that the officials had mistaken the servant for "a certain Oriental Prince, who, attended by an English companion, was expected to leave Paris for London by the same train... with the result that Alexander was mistaken for the expected Prince and Mr. Hewitt for his gentleman-in-waiting." One of King's friends later reported that "Alexander bore with becoming dignity the honors thus unwittingly thrust upon him, while, at the same time, he failed in no respect in his duties to Mr. Hewitt."[51] To King's associates, the mix-up became an amusing story about how clueless the French could be. But Lancaster likely took it as something else. If he did not already know from close observation of King's life how easily one could assume an alternative identity, he surely did now.

King treated Lancaster as both a companion and an employee, someone who might occasionally be taken into his confidence but who would never cross the bounds of overfamiliarity. Surely Lancaster knew more about his employer's whereabouts at any given moment than King's close friends did, or than Ada Todd herself could have known. If he knew his employer's secret, however, he did not broadcast it.

IN EARLY JANUARY 1891, with Ada set to deliver her second child in just a few weeks, King traveled to Newport, with "the rather heavy heart I carry about," for the wedding of his half sister, Marian, and Lieutenant Clarence P. Townsley, an army man.[52] Like King, Townsley knew the West. But as a veteran of the Fourth Artillery's Apache campaigns of 1881, he knew it better through the sight of a rifle than the eyepiece of a surveyor's tool. Now, after a tour as a drawing instructor at the U.S. Military Academy at West Point, he served at Fort Adams, the massive masonry fort that guarded the entrance to Newport Harbor.[53] Marian's formal gown, Townsley's military dress, the fashionable crowd, all marked this as a social event vastly different from King's own wedding in a midtown Manhattan tenement some two years before. The Congregationalist wedding took place at Mrs. Howland's house, "in the English style, only members of the household being present." But the *New York Times* pronounced the large reception that followed "quite brilliant," as Townsley's military associates mingled with the bride's Newport friends and family, including her grandmother Sophia Little, now ninety-two and "widely known for her philanthropic work."[54] King might have recalled that no mother or grandmother had witnessed his wedding; no cousins, no neighbors, no old school friends shared his celebratory cake. He returned to New York shortly after the ceremony but fretted about returning to Newport to care for his mother, who worried that Marian's marriage to a military man promised nothing but "poverty and homelessness." "The grim realities of arithmetic," Mrs. Howland wrote, "are veiled by the rosy mists of joyful hope."[55] The marriage triggered another bout of fragile health. "My mother suffers from insomnia," King told Hay, "all of which is due to Marian's horrible mismarriage. It really is too heartbreaking to see a girl fling herself into the dust."[56] He clung to the high ground and consoled Mrs. Howland over Marian's seemingly ill-chosen spouse.

IN THE VERY EARLY morning of January 24, 1891, Ada gave birth to a baby girl at her Hudson Avenue home. Hours later, a tremendous blizzard hit New York, snapping virtually all of the city's electrical poles, plunging the metropolis into "impenetrable darkness" and leaving the streets an impassable mess of broken wood and tangled wires.[57] Manhattan had begun to bury the forest of poles that had sprung up along its streets over the past decade, hiding in underground conduits the thicket of wires put up by competing electrical firms, the nascent telephone and telegraph companies, and the city's police, fire, and burglar alarm services. But in Brooklyn, the process moved more slowly.[58] Toppled electrical wires made Ada's street perilous and left her apartment cold and dark. Inside, with Leroy and her newborn daughter, she would have only a gas lamp and candles for heat and light. When the white Canadian-born physician P. E. Kidd filed the formal birth certificate two days later, he left blank the space recording the child's first name. Her father, perhaps delayed by the winter storm, had not yet been to see her or helped to pick her name.[59] Like other fathers, he might even have chosen to stay away during the birth, leaving Ada's care to kindly neighbors, female relatives, a midwife, or a Brooklyn physician like Kidd who could be paid in advance to attend the delivery.

That a white physician should care for Ada was not unusual. So many of the city's African American residents preferred white doctors that in 1889 a black physician complained in New York's African American newspaper, the *New York Age,* that the black community's faith "in their own medical men is much like that of doubting Thomas...we are just as capable in diagnosing and just as skillful in treating the various diseases to which flesh is heir as our white historical brothers."[60]

In the chaotic aftermath of the storm, it would be difficult to get word to her husband, even if Ada knew how to find him. She would not know to look for him at the Hotel Albert or think, once the wires were repaired, to send a telegram to Newport, where Clarence King had told friends he would be for a few weeks.[61] She probably imagined him off on a train somewhere and had no recourse but to wait for him to reappear.

So Ada herself gave Dr. Kidd the information he needed to fill in the formal Brooklyn Certificate of Birth: mother's full name, Ada Todd; age, thirty; maiden name, Ada Copeland; birthplace, West Point, Georgia. She instructed Kidd to identify the father as James Todd, a forty-nine-year-old porter, born in Baltimore. And she told him what he could probably see for himself: this was her second child. With these spare words, Ada Todd entered the first account of her life into the historical record.[62]

The birth certificate form provided no space to designate the parents' race. But Dr. Kidd had to indicate the race of the baby. He looked at the mother and struck out the word "white." This was a "colored" child.[63]

When James Todd reappeared at the snowbound family apartment, he named the baby Grace Margaret, in honor of the infant sister Clarence King had lost in childhood. As with the names James and Leroy, he slyly honored his birth family, a gesture meaningful to no one but him.

DURING THE MONTHS FOLLOWING Grace's birth, King frustrated even his most devoted friends. He wrote to Hay that he could not come to Washington because he had to visit his mother in Newport and could not join him in Europe because he was too worn out. He complained about his health, worried about his finances, seemed to struggle to get nowhere, all the while sinking deeper into debt. "If he would stop struggling, he would get on well enough," Hay wrote to Adams. "He owes nobody but those who will never bother him." Hay lectured King like a "Dutch uncle." Still, he found him "just as good company as ever if he were not so infernally busy that you can never get him to stay more than a half a day anywhere."[64] Indeed. Along with the dinners at the Century Association, the trips to Newport, and the struggles to earn a living, there was, unbeknownst to his friends, that family in Brooklyn.[65]

King kept up his bluff joking about women. While traveling in Tahiti and Samoa in 1890–91, Henry Adams wrote long letters about the "old gold" girls he found there. But King took ironic comfort in knowing that neither Adams nor his traveling companion, the painter John La Farge, could appreciate them as much as he did. Indeed, Adams's indifference to women seemed exasperating. "It is too late for him to get a rise from his solar plexus," King joked to Hay; "the girls stir only his gray matter."[66] Just as well, King decided. "I love primal women so madly that I should have acted with jealousy had they discerned her." He let himself imagine Adams's new Kodak camera, which contained "somewhere in the sacred coil of its umbilical center...the faint potentiality of a face waiting to be developed by reagents more sensitive than the vision of either of our friends. A face which will touch and enchant me."[67] And so he danced and feinted around his friends, hinting at his feelings but hiding the ways in which he had acted on them. His pronouncements seemed safely abstract. "People are looked at in only two ways," King wrote to Hay, "with the brain and with the heart. If you take the former method you initially classify and judge people by their *differences* with other people usually yourself. If you see them with the heart you have your conceptions on the *similarities* between them and some other people usually yourself."[68]

ADA TODD'S WORLD MUST have felt more cramped than her husband's, with two small children keeping her all but housebound. Leroy, newly weaned, would be learning to walk during the winter and early spring of 1891, and baby Grace would demand her mother's constant attention. By late spring, Ada was pregnant again, for the third time in as many years. One imagines her exhausted and grateful for her husband's visits, however short or infrequent they might be. He might bring groceries or money and provide her with some fleeting moments of respite from the unending care for the children. Sometime during 1891, James Todd helped Ada and the children move to a quieter, more residential neighborhood farther east in the northwestern part of Bedford-Stuyvesant, the area then home to the large majority of Brooklyn's black residents.[69] During the 1890s, housing conditions for Brooklyn's black residents, previously regarded as more "healthful" than those in Manhattan, began to deteriorate.[70] But for Ada, this move represented another step up in the world. For her husband, it meant more strain.

In the spring of 1891, King borrowed another $1,800 from the ever-generous John Hay.[71] King seemed "far from well," Hay remarked.[72] "Here *all* is shadows," King confessed that summer to Mrs. Hay. Looking in on his family in Newport he found his grandmother infirm and irritable, his mother full of worrisome symptoms, and his half brother, George, on the verge of consumption. It all pointed to "a dreary present and sad enough outlook."[73]

The Todd family's new apartment at 72 Skillman Street was in a narrow, attached three-story building a block from the brewery and the gutta-percha factory that stood down the street near the intersection with Flushing Avenue.[74] The air hung heavy with smells on hot summer days, but the malt and burning-rubber-like odors likely seemed an improvement over the stench of the Hudson Avenue slaughterhouses. Moreover, this block had a more residential feel. The neighbors in the Todds' building included workingmen—a trimmer, a ship joiner, a porter—and several widows.[75] St. Mary's Episcopal Chapel stood catty-corner across the street. Some southern blacks found New York a cold place that lacked the neighborly conviviality of small-town southern life. James Weldon Johnson, a native Floridian, counted himself fortunate to feel an instant connection to the city from the moment of his first visit to his Brooklyn relatives in 1884. But, he wrote, "if among other requirements for happiness, one needs neighbors; that is, feels that he must be on friendly terms with the people who live next door, and in addition know all about them; if one must be able to talk across from front porches and chat over back fences; if one is possessed by a zeal to regulate the conduct of people who are neither neighbors nor friends—he is not born for a New Yorker."[76] Though occupied by her children, Ada had always been a resourceful and generous woman. One imagines her in that new apartment on Skillman Street, reaching out to the neighbors who could provide help and companionship as she made a home for her family, despite her husband's frequent absences. A Pullman porter might make a good living, but she had known from the start that he would never provide a conventional domestic life.

DURING THE LAST WEEK of August 1891, perhaps about the time that Ada was settling into the new apartment, King traveled to the nation's capital to attend the Fifth International Congress of Geologists. Some 250 scientists from around the globe convened in the halls of Columbian University (later George Washington University) to listen to formal papers about how to establish a uniform international system of geological nomenclature, classification, and cartography. One can imagine the gatherings: the reunions of old friends and colleagues, the sighting of old classmates, the excited introductions to scientists one knew only through publications. In the evenings, the talk would spill over into receptions and the restaurants and hotels of downtown Washington. Through the cacophony of English, French, and German, one might catch snatches of familiar gossip about the United States Geological Survey or arguments about the newest theories emerging from Europe, the latest buzz about new mineral deposits in the West, or complaints about government support for science. A kind of éminence grise of the gathering, King would feel at home here, surrounded by old and new colleagues and much sought after by the younger participants who knew of his writings and his central role in establishing the western American surveys. As the founding spirit and first director of the USGS, he had established the agency for which so many of them worked.

One of the younger geologists in the crowd might have caught King's attention. The "real" James Todd was there, fresh from a summer of fieldwork for the USGS near Vermillion, South Dakota. One can only wonder whether he walked over to introduce himself to King, the man who had preceded him at Yale and the USGS and left behind such legions of admirers.[77]

Such an imagined meeting would surely unnerve King. If he had known of Todd before, by name and reputation, he could now meet him in the flesh: his ghostly doppelgänger come to life.

THE SITUATION IN NEWPORT worsened in late summer, and from Washington King raced to his mother's home. Mrs. Howland was ill, his grandmother was failing, and an invalid cousin helped round out a household that, as he wrote to Hay, seemed conceived in the "pigments of sorrow and trials." The three servants had just left, and it fell to King to care for the ailing women until he could "break in" new domestic help. But temporary help arrived in the guise of a "grandly barbaric Congo woman" named Augusta—"seventy years old, black as ink, erect as a palm"—who brought in her "tribe" of female relations to run the household until King could hire a permanent staff. "Accordingly," he wrote, "wherever one goes a dark figure of the tribe flits past one. They are all very black and very silent, all have teeth like glistening ivory, all pass on in a broad smile." To the "grim calvinistic scotch propriety" of his mother's house, they brought a world of mysterious spices, "songs of the Guinea Coast," a "soft native Congo slur," and an open gaiety of expression. King's spirits improved and even his mother felt amused. "Civilization so narrows the gamut!" King wrote to Hay. "Respectability lets the human pendulum swing over such a pitiful little arc. That it's worth it now and again to see human beings when feelings have no inflexible bar of metal restraining their swing to the limits set by civilized experience and moral law."[78]

Even in his mother's house (or perhaps *especially* there), King pushed back against propriety and convention, and longed for other worlds.

THERE IS NO KNOWING precisely where King was when his son Leroy became ill sometime in 1891. Recently weaned so that his mother could nurse the new baby, Leroy would be especially vulnerable to food- and milk-borne bacteria, a particular concern in an era without a safe supply of unadulterated milk. He would also be subject to diseases transmitted by insects and to the so-called "weanling diarrhea," a leading cause of death for the young of all racial and ethnic backgrounds. In 1890 New York, more than 40 percent of all deaths occurred among children under five, a disproportionate number of them black.[79] A decade later, despite improved street sanitation and a safer food supply, black babies in the city still died at more than twice the rate of white infants, with two out of every seven black children dying before the age of one.[80]

Whatever the source of his illness, Leroy died around his second birthday. No death certificate survives to record the details. No letters document his parents' grief. For Ada, that grief would be made more intense by her isolation. She probably did not know how to find her husband or get word to him to rush home to see their sick toddler. For James Todd, grief might be compounded by guilt. In all likelihood, he was gone during Leroy's illness, and without old friends who knew of his loss, he could share his despondency with no one but his wife and whomever she had summoned for support. To the growing list of things about which he could not speak to his mother or his closest friends, he now added the death of his son, whose name slyly carried on the King family name. Knowing nothing of his friend's tragedy, Hay attributed King's despondency to his ongoing financial troubles and confided in Adams that King "*patauges* in the mire as if his life depended on his getting out—and gets deeper in all the time." Hay felt "despair about him. I cannot make him do what he ought, even though I offer to stand the racket."[81]

Ada delivered a baby girl at home on January 31, 1892. Dr. Kidd again attended her and noted on the birth certificate that this was Ada Copeland Todd's second child, not her third. In this age of high infant mortality, the number of live births mattered less than the number of living children. With a stroke of the doctor's pen, Leroy disappeared from the historical record. Kidd recorded the facts as Ada related them, much as she had just fifty-three weeks earlier, when Grace was born. She was Ada Todd, born Ada Copeland in Georgia thirty-one years ago. The baby's father was James Todd, a "Porter on Pulman Car," born in Maryland fifty years earlier.

No evidence documents his presence at this birth. Ada seemingly took it upon herself to name her daughter, invoking an old southern tradition of naming girls. The baby would be called Ada, after her.[82]

Where was King? He spent the months of January and February offering a constant stream of apologies to friends, excusing himself from engagements, demurring from prospective trips, perhaps creating a kind of cloak of invisibility around himself so he could slip away to spend time with Ada and their children. From the Century Association, he apologized to Hay for not repaying his debts. He had to keep his financial "wreck" from his mother, he explained, because she was "incapable of standing another great shock in life. She has suspected that I have been in trouble but I have been forced to keep up appearances with her and time has made her apprehension fade away." He had spent his whole life "trying to envelope some members of my family with a neighborhood of sustaining sympathy to create a change of the moral climate which should give them cheer." It was very hard to describe "the power of suffering" his family seemed to have, and even he was not free from the "soul-ache" which afflicted them. He was so hard up, he said, he might have to sell his geology books. But that "open advertisement of my ruin" would make it even harder to find work.[83]

If not complaining about his finances or his mother, King often griped about his health. Six days before his daughter Ada was born, he told Hay, with a peculiarly apt turn of phrase, that he had been in bed for two weeks with a weak heart: "A baby would whip me with one hand." He had to stay close to home and regretted he could not come to Washington to visit. Later, he sent word that dinners at the Century were out because his doctor had forbidden him to go out in the evenings. Next he wrote that a relapse would keep him in bed for ten days.[84] If nothing else, he had learned from his hypochondriacal mother that ill health could excuse almost anything. Having shaken his friends off his trail, King could disappear into the city, cross the Brooklyn Bridge, and ride the elevated train down Myrtle Street, reemerging on Skillman Street as a peripatetic railway porter named James Todd.

No evidence survives to describe life inside the Todds' Skillman Street

apartment or to suggest how Ada and her little girls fit into their new community. But a letter from King to his old California survey colleague William Brewer (now a professor at Yale) suggests that Ada might have extended
to her southern relations the sort of assistance in New York that her aunt
Annie Purnell once provided for her. In May 1892 King wrote to Brewer
in New Haven to ask a favor. Would Brewer help him "carry out a piece of
charity" for a "poor Alabama black boy"? Since Ada herself was born within
a few miles of the Alabama border, the boy might have been her relative,
perhaps a younger brother or nephew come north to New York. Mourning
her son and struggling to take care of her two baby girls, Ada might find a
teenage boarder difficult. For all he could help by running errands, picking up food, or tending to small details around the apartment, he would
be expensive to clothe and feed. Hard to supervise, he could already have
fallen into bad company on the streets. In 1886 a local African American
newspaper had observed that only three hundred black children attended
school while five thousand were "playing and loafing" in the street.[85]

"New York is a bad distracting town" for such a boy, King told Brewer.
He explained that the boy was illiterate, having "worked from the cradle up."
So he asked Brewer to inquire what it would cost for a local African American family in New Haven to care for the boy "and give him a good room
where he can study and where he can have a stove in winter and include his
washing, also what it would cost to get someone to give him instruction in
reading and writing." King hoped the lady of the house could teach the boy
enough that he could then go on to night school. He felt reluctant to give a
lump sum of money to the boy, and like a benevolent uncle (which perhaps
he was) King asked whether he might give Brewer a sum of money to dole
out monthly for expenses. "I would not ask so much of you," he concluded,
"did I not know that you share my pity for these poor blacks."[86]

King's peculiar situation blinded him to the true racial views of his
friends and made it hard for him to see what he did not wish to know.
Brewer might have some empathy for "poor blacks," but he considered the
"mongrel crowd" that resulted from mixed-race marriages to be as "repul-
sive as the mongrel dogs which are apt to be their companions." Quoting

the African explorer David Livingstone, Brewer told an academic gathering that "God made the white man and God made the Black man, but the Devil made the half caste."[87] To such a colleague, King seemed willing to entrust the fate of the young black boy he hoped to rescue from the streets of New York. No record survives of Brewer's response.[88] But, as ever, King's beneficent impulses had painful consequences. Before leaving a few weeks later for Florida to investigate a phosphate mine, King wrote to John Hay to ask for another $2,000 in loans.[89]

Everyone seemed to need King's help that summer of 1892. Early in the summer he rushed to Atlanta to help his half sister, Marian, and her own newborn child while her husband, Lieutenant Townsley, hovered near death with typhoid fever.[90] He had to go, he explained to Hay. The consequences of staying away might prove "very grave and lasting." Should Townsley die, King wrote, Marian's life "from a mere economic point of view would have been a life long burden to me." King could imagine his friend chastising him for turning his attention from business to family. "You sometimes blame [me] for over anxiety and over devotion to my family," he wrote, "but it has been a peculiar and very unfortunate family with abundant sorrows and reverses that I had no hand in, beside which my mother is of exaggerated [*sic*] nervous organization with the keenest power of suffering and I am the only one on earth who have [*sic*] never hurt her (I mean within the family) and the only one who has the power of softening the pain of wounds that never heal." The burden of it all had "taken the charm I once had away from me," King acknowledged, and his life might seem "fruitless." But he really had no choice.[91] In October he asked Hay for yet another $2,000 loan.[92]

In the autumn of 1892 Ada Todd became pregnant again, for the fourth time in as many years. Beyond such physical evidence of her intimacy with her husband, virtually nothing survives to chart her feelings toward him. But the surviving fragments of King's letters reveal him to be a man deeply in love.[93] When he was apart from Ada, he dreamed of her. "My darling, tell me all about yourself," James Todd begged from one of his many trips. "I can see your dear face every night when I lay my head on the pillow and my prayers go up to Heaven for you and the little ones. I feel most lonely and miss you most when I put out the light at night and turn away from the work of the day. Then I sit by my window in the starlight and look up at the dark night sky and think of you. Lonely seems my bed! Lonely is my pillow! I think of you and dream of you and my first waking thought is of your dear face and your loving heart."[94]

He waited anxiously for the letters Ada wrote in return. "My dearest," her husband wrote from the road, "I cannot tell you how delighted I was to see your handwriting again. To see something you had touched was almost like feeling the warmth of your hand."[95] Ada addressed her mail to "James Todd," presumably in care of an intermediary or to the general delivery post offices or hotels where her railroading husband said he would stop.[96] Since she had not traveled west herself, she would not know which hotels were frequented by black Pullman porters and which by prominent white scientists. And surely, the charming and beguiling Clarence King could persuade a hotel clerk to let him have the mail addressed to James Todd, no matter how he had registered. The trains whisked King across the country to pursue his business ventures far from Ada's knowing eyes. But they also carried the correspondence that kept them close. For all he waxed rhapsodic about "primitive" women, King had reason to be grateful that Ada could read and write.

Early in their marriage, Ada and James Todd took on the domestic roles that would govern their family life. To Ada fell the care of the children, the management of the household, the day-to-day details of life in Brooklyn. Often alone during her husband's frequent business trips, she might turn for support to the small network of relations and Manhattan church friends that she had developed before her marriage or to her new neighbors. But her husband brought no new friends or relatives or even work colleagues into her world. When he returned home, he almost surely came alone, falling back into Ada's world, never asking her out to join his.

James, by contrast, assumed the responsibilities for the financial support of his family. Traveling across the nation as Clarence King, the geologist and mining consultant, he had a network of colleagues and friends, old connections and new associates that to Ada would have seemed inconceivably broad. And yet, he kept coming home to her. She and the children provided the still point in his increasingly unsettled world.

IN LATE 1892 KING spent some time with Ada and the children in Brooklyn, then traveled to Chicago to talk to investors about his phosphate interests in Florida.[97] "Everywhere was slack-water," Henry Adams wrote of that dull fall. Even the presidential contest between Grover Cleveland and Benjamin Harrison stirred little interest. King, predictably, favored Harrison, the Republican candidate, out of a steadfast loyalty to the party of Lincoln. "With King," explained Adams, "the feeling was chiefly love of archaic races; sympathy with the negro and Indian and corresponding dislike of their enemies."[98]

America seemed tired that fall, Adams wrote, wearied not just by the lackluster election but by the stirrings of a global economic crisis that "helped to dull the vibration of society." The nation seemed caught up in the reckless pursuit of money, bereft of values, dangerously ignorant of its own past. "Thus, in 1892," he wrote, "neither Hay, King, nor Adams knew whether they had attained success, or how to estimate it, or what to call it; and the American people seemed to have no clearer idea than they." Clarence King's case seemed particularly puzzling. "King had played the ambitious course. He had played for many millions. He had more than once come close to a great success, but the result was still in doubt, and meanwhile he was passing the best years of his life underground." Adams's characterization of King's life was more apt than he could have known. "For companionship," Adams wrote of King, "he was mostly lost."[99]

That dispiriting fall was the prelude to an economic collapse and a financial depression that, as Adams wrote, caused a "massacre of my friends who are being cleaned out and broken down by dozens."[100] Banks collapsed, speculative investments disappeared, the stability of family fortunes teetered. Following months of economic uncertainty and anxiety over the nation's diminishing reserves of gold, the stock market fell sharply in May 1893. Mines, smelters, and factories began to close, and the railroads that carried the raw and finished products also began to fail. By August, one million people were out of work. At year's end the unemployment figures stood at three million. All told, during that dark year, some fifteen thousand businesses and more than six hundred banks failed.[101] "We live uncontestably above our means," Junius Henri Browne wrote in *Harper's Monthly* in December 1893, "because our means seem insufficient, and we cannot adjust them to our ever-growing wants."[102]

The year 1893 began for King with a familiar sort of juggling: the society parties, an essay on the age of the earth published in the *American Journal of Science*, trips back to Newport to visit his mother.[103] But over the summer, while suffering from a recurrence of his excruciating spinal pain, he learned of the failure of the National Bank of El Paso, which he had organized in 1886. As the principal stockholder, he was brought close to ruin by the friend he had installed as president of the bank. "I have lost everything," King confessed.[104]

In the midst of all this, on July 19, Ada delivered a son in the Skillman Street apartment. Dr. Samuel E. Stiles, a white physician with a private practice in Brooklyn, attended the birth, and Ada told him what she had told her previous doctor. The baby's father was a Pullman car porter named James Todd, who had been born in Maryland. He was now fifty-one, and she was thirty-two. Her maiden name was Ada Copeland (or "Copleyen" as the physician misspelled it), and she was from Georgia.[105] Although she later claimed to be a year or two younger, the information she provided on her children's birth certificates consistently established her own birth date as late in 1860. Dr. Stiles noted for the record that her infant son, later to be named Sidney C. (for Clarence or, perhaps, Copeland), was "colored." A glimpse of the mother sufficed to make a determination of the baby's race.[106]

Within a month of Sidney's birth, Clarence King was off visiting his mother during the height of the Newport social season. Before leaving New York, he had gone to see his physician. He felt anxious. Due to his worries over the El Paso bank failure, he said, he had scarcely been able to sleep for weeks.[107] But in the early fall of 1893 he headed west to investigate a mine in British Columbia.[108] King wrote to Ada, "My first duty in these hard times is to make enough for your expenses and on that I will use all my strength."[109] Back home in late October, after a month in Canada, King caught word of the engagement of Arnold Hague, his old Yale classmate and a member of the Fortieth Parallel survey. Remarking on the surprising news to Frank Emmons, King mused that he would soon "be left alone on the chill ocean of bachelorhood."[110] And to Hay he let slip an inadvertent double negative that hinted at the truth: "It always takes years for me to realize that I have not yet to marry a woman."[111]

Breakdowns

NEWSPAPERS ACROSS THE COUNTRY CARRIED THE STARTLING words: "Clarence King in an Asylum."[1]

On October 29, 1893, an unusually cool Sunday afternoon, a large group of visitors crowded into the lion house in Manhattan's Central Park to watch the big cats and an "interesting pair of hippopotami." The Menagerie provided one of the city's few free public attractions for working-class families, and as one official recalled, on Sunday afternoons, "no greater crowds gathered anywhere in New York than in this part of Central Park." Just recently, the park commissioners had acknowledged the crowd's ethnic diversity by ending the practice of giving the animals Irish names.[2]

On this particular autumn Sunday, the visitors in the animal house noticed a short bearded man in the crowd acting peculiar and agitated. Two police detectives observed him fly into a rage, then followed him outdoors to the ball field and arrested him for disorderly conduct. The distraught man identified himself as Clarence King, a resident of the Union League Club.

King insisted that the police send for Samuel Parsons, his former Yale classmate and rowing companion, now the park's superintendent of planting. While Parsons searched for someone to post bond, an officer booked King at the East Sixty-seventh Street station. King claimed Newport as his home, and mining as his occupation. By late that evening, when Parsons returned with the bail money, King had so annoyed the police court judge with his efforts to make him dismiss the case, the judge imposed a $10 fine. King protested that the judge was persecuting him for "refusing to vote for Isaac H. Maynard," a local Democratic Party politician, and he denied any responsibility for the altercation in the lion house. The crowd jostled him against an African American butler, he said, and the ensuing commotion was not his fault.[3]

Two physicians examined King and pronounced him "suffering from mental disturbance with occasional acute symptoms." On Halloween night, they and three of King's close friends sought legal help, and a judge committed King to the Bloomingdale Asylum for the Insane.[4] Two friends agreed to cover the costs of his hospitalization. Charles W. Gould, the lawyer friend with whom King had been staying in recent days, put up part of the money. Lloyd McKim Garrison, the attorney, poet, and grandson of the abolitionist leader William Lloyd Garrison, put up the rest.[5] At some $40 per week, King's care cost more than that of all but a handful of the other 313 patients. Apparently, he got a comfortable room.[6]

King's friends told reporters that the normally neat and dapper King had recently become "very slovenly and careless about his appearance and his dress. His beard and his hair grew unkempt, he wore soiled linen, and his clothes looked worn and old." He seemed to avoid his old friends, to respond "strangely" whenever anyone spoke to him.[7] Just recently he had set out on an errand, pronounced it done, but actually forgotten what he was to do. John La Farge told Adams that King had found himself "walking in certain streets without any notion of how he came to be there." King's agitated state makes it hard to know precisely what happened in the lion house, but Central Park was the sort of place where his separate worlds might collide. One wonders whether the black butler might have greeted him as "Jim" or "Todd," perhaps even reminding King that he had seen him on those very streets he walked "without any notion of how he came to be there." In his anxious state, King might imagine an altercation easier to account for than a double life.[8]

Only in hindsight did King's closest friends perceive his erratic behavior as part of a disturbing and ongoing pattern. "King was a man of remarkably robust physique," Frank Emmons wrote shortly after King's death, "and showed throughout his physically arduous life powers of endurance that are rarely equaled; yet it was one of the penalties of the highly sensitive and nervous organization, which rendered possible his marvelously acute and delicate perception, that he was subject to sudden and almost unaccountable break-downs in which he suffered intensely."[9]

King's physician, Dr. Rufus P. Lincoln, told the press that an old bout of catarrh and asthma had left King weakened, and the recent strains of his professional life had worn "severely on his nerves as well as physical vitality." The failure of the National Bank of El Paso and King's deep sense of obligation to his professional responsibilities "brought about the condition of his present nervous depression, which, at times, assimilates melancholia." King's friends reported that the patient had some awareness of his own condition. Indeed, King accounted for his behavior with carefully chosen words that seemed to forestall investigation of whatever stories might emerge. He explained that "nine-tenths" of the time he felt all right, but could sometimes lose himself and later have no recollection of what he had done. Loath to believe anything serious could befall King, his friends considered his condition nothing more than what might come to anyone "who brooded too much over himself."[10] It was just "partial lunacy," reported the *Washington Post*.[11]

But whatever King's affliction, the strain of his double life surely compounded it. Even now, under tremendous stress, he could not and would not speak openly of his wife and his children. If, as one psychologist suggests, deep secrets are "the currency of close relationships," King's closest relationships were bankrupt.[12]

Charles Gould, the friend with whom he resided at the time of his breakdown, would later write a nativist diatribe on the supremacy of the white race.[13] King likely knew Gould's views; how could he share his family situation with a man like that? Even ill, he remained under tremendous stress to be watchful and alert. An accidental slip of the tongue could jeopardize all.

Racial passing—like the assumption of a false name, the construction of a fictive job, or the invention of an alternative class identity—requires a careful attentiveness, what one scholar calls a kind of "voluntary amnesia" that involves erasing family ties and letting go of the acquired habits of a lifetime. A "hazardous" business, Nella Larsen called it in her 1929 novel *Passing*, "this breaking away from all that was familiar and friendly to take one's chances in another environment, not entirely strange, perhaps, but certainly not entirely friendly."[14] For five years, King had lived under the threat of discovery in his white world as well as his black one. And now, at Bloomingdale, he would need to remain on constant alert, erasing from his conversations all mention of Ada, his children, that home he and his wife had created together in Brooklyn. Even in the confines of a mental hospital, he could find no relief from the fraught doubleness that ruled his world.

Dr. Lincoln did not consider King's hospitalization to be absolutely essential, but he thought it best "in view of the fact that he had no family that he should go to some place where he could have good nursing and absolute freedom from care."[15]

Even if Ada saw the newspapers, none of which illustrated their stories about King's hospitalization, she would have no reason to suspect that the man caught ranting and raving in the lion house was her husband, the responsible railroad porter. King was "a bachelor," reported one of the New York papers, who called Newport home but "spent much of his time in this city, staying either at the houses of his friends or at clubs of which he was a member."[16]

HENRY ADAMS SENT WORD of King's breakdown to John Hay in Europe. It "does not make me gay," he wrote. Adams blamed King's troubles on the financial panic sweeping through the nation, as if that might lessen the seriousness of his friend's problem. All his acquaintances, he said, "have been, are, or ought to be in asylums; but those who are not, are getting wives, which proves their superior fitness for the other alternative."[17] In that "disastrous year" of 1893, an escape into an asylum often seemed "the only way to escape hopeless ruin and collapse."[18] Adams himself lost money in the collapse of the banks. "Men died like flies under the strain," he recalled, "and Boston grew suddenly old, haggard and thin."[19] Adams thought King's madness made him the archetypal man of his age.

At Bloomingdale, King joined the last group of patients to be treated on the hospital's old grounds in Harlem Heights, set high on a rise at 117th Street, where the hospital's brick and stone buildings lay scattered across grassy lawns. Most of the patients could wander at will, "harsh measures and all unnecessary confinement being strictly prohibited." When it opened in 1821, the hospital boasted peaceful views of the Hudson River and surrounding countryside. But as the city encroached on the solitude of the place, hospital officials made plans to relocate to White Plains in the summer of 1894, making the old Morningside Heights property available for an expansion of Columbia College. What King called his "house of madness" would soon be overrun by professors. He joked with Adams, "I shan't like it so well a few weeks hence when Columbia College moves in here and displaces these open, frank lunatics with Seth Low [the university president] and his faculty of incurables so I better move out now."[20]

James Hague visited King frequently at Bloomingdale. James Gardiner came nearly every day. "If anything can drive him to sanity," Adams quipped to Hay, "I think Gardiner can do it; he would drive me to a much further region."[21] After several years with Ferdinand V. Hayden's survey, Gardiner had served for a decade as director of the New York State Survey (1876–86) and as a consulting engineer for and member of the state board of health (1880–86). Now he worked in private industry as an officer and a mining adviser for several American and Mexican coal and railroad companies. He had remarried in 1881, and King so disliked his wife—the straitlaced daughter of an Episcopal bishop—that he delighted in provoking her with off-color stories. The dinner invitations stopped. But the old friendship forged in boyhood endured. After King's death, it would be Gardiner—not Hay or Adams—who stepped in to deal with all the messy details.[22]

The "merciless agony" of King's spinal trouble "crazed and nearly killed me," he wrote of his time in Bloomingdale. "It seems as if the human organism could not survive such suffering."[23] In late November, James Hague reported to Hay that King still felt "weak and restive," but his spinal inflammation was improving, and there had been no sign of "mental disturbance" since his first week of hospitalization. His mental derangement seemed "a disease of the body rather than of the mind."[24]

Gardiner went to Philadelphia to seek out S. Weir Mitchell, a leading expert on nervous disorders, who echoed King's own thoughts about the debilitating effects of modern life. "Civilization!" King once joked to a friend. "Why, it is a nervous disease!"[25] Mitchell agreed, and he argued in his book *Camp Cure* (1877) that "the surest remedy for the ills of civilized life is to be found in some form of return to barbarism." In 1869 the American physician George Miller Beard coined the term "neurasthenia" to describe the effect of modern industrialized society upon the nervous energy system, particularly of the elite and well-to-do. Chronic fatigue and weakness, worry, and neuralgia all made up what Beard later called the "American nervousness."[26] Mitchell found urban life similarly "perplexing and trying by its intricacy: so many wheels must be kept moving in order to the fulfillment of social, domestic, civil and professional duties that in the hurry of well-filled lives we are rarely kept at rest."[27] While Beard treated his patients with electrical therapies designed to stimulate their nerves, Mitchell advised a different therapeutic approach to the ills of modern life. He confined his female patients to bed and packed his male patients off west, to find the "peace of soul" required to restore their virile manliness.[28]

Mitchell's writing sent a generation of eastern men west to toughen up. Teddy Roosevelt, so sickly as a child, returned from his South Dakota adventures of 1884–86 a healthy poster boy for the ranching life. Mitchell's cousin Owen Wister, who first went west in 1885, eventually dropped his halfhearted legal career to become a writer. His book *The Virginian* (1902) became the archetypal western, a tribute to manly western ways as an antidote to the complexities of eastern urban life.[29]

Mitchell advised a contemplative engagement with the out-of-doors, recommending that his male readers take with them into the wilderness a camera, a sketchbook, "a book or two of geology," and some sample scientific instruments. He urged them to be open to the particular manly enjoyments of camp life and to take pleasure in "the contact with the guides, woodmen and trappers, and the simple-minded manly folk who live on the outposts of civilization."[30] His newest patient, Clarence King, the celebrated author of *Mountaineering in the Sierra Nevada*, a man who first headed out west with "a Bible, a Table of Logarithms, and a volume of Robertson's sermons," might under other circumstances seem Mitchell's ideal.[31] "Nature is the greatest medicine for my soul," King wrote to Hay the very year of his breakdown.[32]

As a novelist himself, Mitchell drew upon his clinical experience to inform the psychological portraits of his literary characters. And just recently he had written about a man with a fractured, double life. His novel *Characteristics* (1892) considered the problem of "double consciousness," describing the sudden disappearance of a married man "of refined and scholarly tastes, a student of Oriental languages," who reappears as a rough and unkempt store clerk married to an older, uneducated woman. The man retains no memory of his previous life. But through literary sleight of hand, he returns to his original young, wealthy wife at the end of the novel, wholly recovered from his plight. Mitchell proposed that his subject's second, aberrational personality stemmed directly from the first: the man sought the affections of an untutored woman as temporary respite from the stress of civilized life.[33]

Mitchell examined King and detected an "anaemia [*sic*] of the left lobe of the brain and equally of the whole left optical system" but declared the patient's troubles "wholly functional and not organic." Seemingly unaware of King's uncanny resemblance to his troubled fictional character, he recommended that his patient remain at Bloomingdale to rest. A western camp cure seemed ill advised. Mitchell told King that once recovered, his health should be as good as ever. "This I cannot believe," King quipped to Hay, "but who am I that I should doubt Weir Mitchell?"[34]

THE WEST LOOMED LARGE in the national imagination in that depression-riven year of King's breakdown. On July 12, 1893, a young historian from the University of Wisconsin named Frederick Jackson Turner delivered an after-dinner talk on "The Significance of the Frontier in American History" to the scholars gathered in Chicago for the annual meeting of the American Historical Association. Across town at the great Columbian Exposition, Buffalo Bill Cody staged his own version of American frontier history to considerably larger crowds. Turner's story lacked the galloping horses, Indian battles, and burning houses of Cody's extravaganza, but it made the same imaginative point: America's frontier past was over.

The 1890 census report that triggered Turner's remarks declared the nation's "frontier of settlement" gone: "At present the unsettled area has been so broken into by isolated bodies of settlement that there can hardly be said to be a frontier line." For Turner, this mattered, because the nation's westward expansion—more than the Revolution, more than the Civil War—seemed the defining fact of American life, the source of American political democracy and the distinctive national character. On the frontier, settlers left behind the influence of Europe, reverted to primitive conditions, and in the struggle to adapt emerged newly and distinctively American, with "that coarseness and strength combined with acuteness and inquisitiveness; that practical, inventive turn of mind, quick to find expedients; that masterful grasp of material things, lacking in the artistic but powerful to effect great ends; that restless, nervous energy; that dominant individualism...and withal that buoyancy and exuberance which comes with freedom."[35]

Turner ended his speech on an elegiac note. If the frontier had disappeared, how could America renew its national spirit or maintain all that was good and fresh and distinctive about American life? Obliquely, he raised a question about the future of those men—like Clarence King—so well suited to the earlier age of westward expansion. How would they find their way in the newly industrializing, urban world of late-nineteenth-century America? Four hundred years after Columbus sailed to America, the frontier was at last gone. "And with its going," Turner wrote, "has closed the first period of American history."[36]

Turner's frontier thesis echoed an enduring strain of American popular thought about the physical landscape as a source of the nation's distinctive culture.[37] King himself had written a few decades before that "the conquering and peopling of a broad continent within the short span of a single century remains the most extraordinary feat in the annals of the peaceful deeds of mankind." The heroes of this epic tale were men not unlike himself. "The sons of the pioneers are the true Americans; in the century's struggle with nature they have gathered an Antaean strength, and, flushed with their victory over a savage continent, believe themselves the coming leaders of the world." King thought the Civil War only "a furious, dreadful interruption" in this larger story of the nation's westward march.[38] But in the 1890s surely he, too, looked backward with a wistful air. He and his colleagues had mapped the West. But the future of the region no longer hinged on the work of a few free-spirited and government-supported scientist-explorers. It depended instead on the well-capitalized corporations that could wrest more of its natural resources from the earth. When King went west now, it was never as a pathfinder, but as a hired gun.

Turner synthesized popular thinking about westward expansion with powerful metaphors and persuasive historical examples, capturing brilliantly a broader cultural anxiety about industrialization, the integration of immigrants into American life, and the shifting role of masculinity in Victorian America. S. Weir Mitchell's neurasthenic man was a creature of the post-frontier West. In an earlier age, when muscular masculinity played an important role in the settling of the West, such a man might have found his natural calling on the frontier—fighting Indians, clearing a new settlement, even surveying the land for the federal government. But the proving ground for young men was shifting from the open plains to the boardrooms and factories of the East's great cities, with debilitating consequences for America's men. The economic depression of 1893 catalyzed American unease about the future and played off these deeper anxieties about the direction of American life.

WHILE THEY CONSULTED WITH his physicians, King's friends also ran interference with his mother. Mrs. Howland wanted to visit her son, but King had no desire to see her at Bloomingdale. He had always protected her from his financial problems, his medical worries, the daily uncertainties of his life. And just now he had little spirit for soothing her perpetual anxieties. But a few days before Christmas, Mrs. Howland closed her house in Newport and told friends she was off to New York to collect her son, "quite himself again mentally," in order to travel south with him for the winter.[39]

King, however, had other plans. Come with me, he begged Adams in a New Year's Eve note written from his hospital room. He envisioned a sailing trip to the Windward Islands in the southern Caribbean, with a few months on the British island of Dominica, and he promised "a light opera bouffe effect" to be given "by the extremely characteristic darkeys with their chatter and bandannas, with something serious and orchestral in the way of gumbo and pepperpot." His release from Bloomingdale seemed imminent, and they could then sail as soon as his servant, Alexander Lancaster, returned from South Dakota, where he had gone to secure a divorce. Even in Sioux Falls, the nation's divorce mill, the procedure required a temporary residency of three to six months. But, as one observer noted, "if the defendant puts in an appearance the Dakota decree is legal even in New York State."[40] King explained to Adams that since Alexander was a trained nurse, "You need have no fear of my suffering a recurrence of disability, and even if I do you could cut my acquaintance and leave me to Alexander." Somehow King ditched his mother.[41]

King had never been to Dominica, but the very idea of the island fired his imagination. He used his connections to secure introductions to the island's elite and contemplated "doing" the island, once he felt well enough to practice geology. But first, he wrote to a friend, he would "lie in the shade of some palms and continue the practice of patience and rest till the fire goes out in my poor nerves."[42]

To a friend, King sent the information necessary to secure passports for Alexander Lancaster and himself. He described himself as fifty-two, with a "florid" complexion, hazel eyes, and hair "gray and scant." He was five feet six inches tall, 166 pounds, and by profession a geologist. His "man" was precisely the same height, a thirty-one-year-old mulatto from Petersburg, Virginia, with black hair and eyes, by profession "valet of professor."[43]

King's desire to bring Lancaster suggests an unusual closeness and hints at the possibility that King might have confided in his servant. Although Lancaster was smart, dutiful, and ambitious, his later career within the New York municipal government bears all the hallmarks of a quid pro quo, a possible reward from King for his discretion and loyalty. In the mid-1890s, while still working for King, Lancaster began his ascent through the ranks of the city patronage system, moving from a position as messenger for the all-powerful commissioner of street cleaning, Colonel George E. Waring, to a job as "Inspector of Scows and Tug Boats" and doorkeeper for Waring's office, controlling access to the commissioner and his largesse.[44] King had known Waring, a fellow Newporter, for decades; well enough, it seems, to ask a favor.[45]

KING LEFT BLOOMINGDALE ON January 5, 1894, after a stay of just over two months. The discharge notice stated simply: "Form of Insanity: Acute Melancholia." From this particular form of depression it pronounced him "recovered."[46]

Ada and Clarence probably did not communicate during his hospitalization. Ada could not visit. And until the tail end of his stay, King could not write. Letter writing "has been next to impossible to me during all my illness," he told Hay a few weeks after leaving the hospital, "and strange to say next [to] impossible to those for whom I have the most feeling—my Mother and you."[47]

But James Todd likely reappeared in Brooklyn in January 1894 after a not-uncharacteristic two-month absence to tell his wife about an imagined train trip, leaving an envelope of money on the kitchen table when he left again within two weeks. This time he would be gone for three months. His three children, the eldest scarcely three years old and the youngest not yet able to crawl, would hardly recognize him when he returned. He would be in their memory little more than a smell, a tone of voice, a man who carried treats in his pockets. And Ada would welcome him back.

. . .

AT THE BEGINNING OF February 1894, King and his "man" Alexander joined Adams in Tampa to sail for Havana. King had been "fiercely curious" to see Cuba ever since reading "Mrs. Horace Mann's poor but instructive 'Juanita,'" a novel that explored the island's vexing problems of race and slavery through the eyes of a naive New England visitor.[48] And he fantasized about what the tropics might do for all those cold New England women for whom he felt such scorn. He dashed off a short story, never published, about the emotional and erotic awakening of a New England spinster as she sailed on a small boat through the "languorous golden air," ever closer to Cuba: "Oh that some strong Christian man would call me his own and I could lay my head on his breast and cry for joy."[49] As always, the warm humid air of the tropics (and the darker-skinned women who lived there) seemed intertwined for King with dreams of romance and fantasies of escape.

To Adams, Havana seemed as "noisy and fascinating" as ever, but King sought a more erotic sort of entertainment and protested that "the ideal Negro-woman is más allá, lejos [farther away], not at Havana...but at Santiago de Cuba, where the charming little plaza is the evening resort of five hundred exquisite females, lovely as mulatto lilies and graceful as the palm tree." He did not find his ideal there either. Adams reported that King "had lived only on this dream of unfair women, and he could not believe that it was thin air." His unrealized ideal now seemed "geographically vague." We will seek her out on some other islands, Adams wrote to Hay, and then return through Mexico, "certain to find her there anyhow, because King knows her well in Central America and Mexico." Even as they searched, King had begun to seem quite well.[50]

Adams felt colorless by King's side, "a drag—perhaps even a drug" acting upon the frenetic energy of his friend. And yet he enjoyed observing King, "whose restless energy will last till ninety, [fret] himself because the women have no charm."[51]

Hard-pressed to keep up with his friend, Adams struggled to amuse him. "Had I been a Cuban negro, it would have been easy, or a Carib or a brigand," he later recalled, "but unless I could find some way of reverting, step by step, through all the stages of human change, back to a pithecanthropos, or much better, a pithecgunai, I could not keep King occupied for twenty-four hours."[52] The British consul in Santiago, F. William Ramsden, arranged for a colleague to lend them his country house for a month. This "loan of...Paradise," high up in a narrow mountain valley, became their base. While Adams sketched and read, King tramped about "geologizing."[53]

At first all went well. But "within very few days," Adams reported, "King showed signs of coming to the end of his interest in science and landscape. Even paradox failed to stimulate him." Adams feigned an interest in geology to buoy King's flagging spirits. But he finally realized that his friend's "real interest was not in science, but in man, as he often said, meaning chiefly woman." King regarded the male "as a sort of defence thrown off by the female, much like the shell of a crab, endowed with no original energy of his own; but it was not the modern woman that interested him; it was the archaic female, with instincts and without intellect." Intellect seemed a defective instrument, but it was all the male had to rely on. The female, however, "was rich in the inheritance of every animated energy back to the polyps and the crystals."[54]

King often left Adams at home and disappeared into the streets and back roads of Santiago. "Within ten days he knew all the old negroes in the district," Adams recalled, "and began to go off at night to their dances." He gathered tales of political unrest, glowed with stories of "brigandage," thrived on stories of the coming revolution. Later, he published several essays calling for the United States to support Cuba's overthrow of Spanish rule. "Why not fling overboard Spain and give Cuba the aid which she needs...?" King asked. "Which cause is morally right?—which is manly?—which is American?"[55] But Adams quickly observed that Cuba held for King attractions greater than coffee or cigars or talk of politics. As he had observed of his friend so many times before, "if he had a choice among women, it was in favor of Indians and negroes."[56]

In mid-March, after a month in Cuba, Adams and King sailed on: to

Puerto Rico, to St. Thomas, where they were stuck for two weeks in a small-pox quarantine, to Martinique, and on through the British West Indies. Finally they landed in the Bahamas. Adams found it dreary, but reported that "King manages to amuse himself with the habits and manners of the Bahama niggers, who are a peculiar type." After a fortnight around Nassau, they returned to Florida, King's initial dream of Dominica foiled by inconvenient sailing schedules.[57]

By late April, Adams had King with him back in Washington, "well and gay," but worried that his friend might find New York depressing when he finally returned. King ought to leave New York at once, Adams told a friend, "and stay out of it."[58] King seemed "more steady, quiet and sane than I ever knew him," Adams wrote, "but he has still to face the intense depression which New York never fails to excite in every sane mind.... He had better geologize the negro with me in eastern Cuba."[59]

SOMETIME AROUND MAY DAY, King took the train from Washington back to New York, caught a local train to cross the Brooklyn Bridge, and transferred to the elevated line that would carry him out to the Bedford-Stuyvesant neighborhood of Brooklyn. King's "Cuban dream" was over.[60] After more than three months, James Todd was home. The children must have looked at him with shy curiosity, Ada with relief. She would not have heard from her husband. No matter how anxious he felt about her welfare, James Todd the Pullman porter could not send his wife a letter postmarked on a distant island. Not even Mr. Pullman's vast empire extended that far.

"How hard and cold and hateful the whole face of New York is with its veneered parvenues, and its ebb and flow of vulgar, clumsy, jostling peasantry," Clarence King wrote to Adams from the Century Association after being back in the city for less than two weeks. He would rather be a stow-away in the hold of a southbound steamer "than dwell in the tents of the Metropolitan Club." He tried his best, he told Adams. "I drivel away like all the rut and the optimistic lie rolls from my sinful tongue in oily stream." Next week, he would even go to the country home of his old friend, the journalist Whitelaw Reid, "to pass some days amidst marble, truffles, tapestry and nasal commonplace and I am going to be breezy and effective and talk like a genuine 'American' and be truly popular." It would make you sick, he told Adams.[61]

Every midtown dinner party seemed to demand of King a kind of painful charade. "I shall go to the Metropolitan Club," he wrote Hay, "and make myself beloved of all the stable boys whom fate has raised to the nth power and chum with all the huxsters manquée and carry off the role of a good sensible American bourgeois cad, to the Queen's taste." His intense dislike for "things New Yorkan" had driven him into isolation, and to make a living he would have to crawl out. He "would go back into this hated thing called society and make myself as popular and commonplace and like the average as I can (and I know I can do it) till I get some of the dollars them fellers are in and then!!! Then my beloved tropical islands!!!"[62]

King despised the infernal struggle for money. Like his friends, he wondered how someone with his talents could be so bad at making it. To Hay, whose financial generosity kept him afloat, he vowed to try harder, by suppressing his natural inclinations and adopting the cutthroat tactics of the self-made millionaires he viewed with such scorn. "No matter how much I hate the people and the life no one shall see it or know it. I am going in not as a skirmishing amateur in the part but as a man who means blood and loves the road that leads to it," King wrote. "I have sinned I owe in allowing my nature to influence my life. I shall do it no more till I am able to say to my nature 'at last it is your turn, be free!'...I have been a practical duffer and have not had the real life which my secret soul longs for. Now I am going to be practical all the time with all the energy and the brains I have got left and silence the cries of the soul till I can break the chains."[63]

If King had found in Brooklyn the "real life" for which his soul longed, he did not tell Hay.

In mid-June, within six weeks of arriving home from Cuba, King was off again, to check out some mines in the upper Columbia River region of the Pacific Northwest for prospective investors in Chicago. James Todd presumably told his family he would be off on a long train trip west.[64] Ada might have felt apprehensive, her customary worry over her husband's frequent absences now compounded by worry over her family's safety. A fatal shooting down the street in late May—the consequence of a landlord-tenant dispute among Italian immigrants in a boardinghouse—ended in a violent scuffle with the police in broad daylight, right on Ada's corner.[65]

But her husband left. By mid-July King was in Colville, Washington, investigating a mine. He had hoped to break away for a bit to join John Hay and Henry Adams, who were vacationing in Yellowstone National Park. But a Pullman strike derailed his plans. Angered by layoffs and wage cuts precipitated by the company's response to the financial crisis of 1893, the Pullman workers had gone on strike in May 1894, and by late June sympathetic railroad workers across the country were boycotting trains carrying Pullman cars. For once, Clarence King and James Todd could share the same excuse for not showing up on time.[66] In this "glorious sea of mountains I am pacified and the tranquility of my soul comes back," King wrote to Adams. But he dreamed at night of the sailing ship that would carry him back to the tropics.[67]

King seemed distant to his friends that summer of 1894 he spent away from New York. "You have often complained that I told too little of my life in my letters," King wrote to Hay from Spokane. "That old habit of silence about myself (on paper) has come in well these days when there is only a dull and sad story to tell."[68] Adams hung about the Knickerbocker Club for three days in late September waiting for King to reappear so that they could plan a fall trip to Trinidad and Martinique. Alexander Lancaster assured him his employer would show up any moment. But King never appeared; a large stack of mail sat waiting for him, unopened, at the Century.[69]

And then he returned "in fine form," John Hay thought, and too busy "trying to make a living or swindle some foreigner" to accompany Adams to the Caribbean.[70] King felt tortured by "neuralgia"—presumably a recurrence of the nerve pain in his back—as he engaged in the "more or less fruitless struggle for mere board money." He dreamed of going to Santo Domingo or Venezuela, but for now would settle for South Carolina, simply to be warm. But even there he could not travel until he had made enough money to pay for his trip and to cover the living expenses for his mother and stepbrother while he was away. He was detained, he told Adams, "by the vulgar problem of the daily loaf."[71] He headed back west to investigate some mining ventures in the fall of 1894, but returned to New York as depressed as ever, just after Christmas and a holiday spent with his mother in Newport. "This place will not do for me!" he wrote to Adams. "I must avoid it in the future! Really I am more at home with populists than these hard mechanical victims of respectability."[72]

King faced more than the usual family dramas that Christmas with his mother. Mrs. Howland had just testified for a friend in a peculiar legal case revolving around a secret identity, a mental breakdown, and an illicit family that might have made King wince at its uncanny similarity to the hidden drama of his own double life. One imagines Mrs. Howland eager to talk about her minor role in the unfolding scandal and her son loath to hear a word about it.

Mrs. Howland had traveled to Boston in early December to testify in the sensational case of William H. King, who was not a close relative but a member of another Newport family involved in the China trade whose "family connections were such as to afford him access to the highest social circles of that period." William King had alarmed his family with the "eccentric" ways he spent his China-trade money on the Continent. In 1866, as he was about to wed, his brothers dramatically appeared to whisk him off to an insane asylum. For twenty-seven years he lived at the McLean Asylum near Boston, and then in August 1893—just a few months before Clarence King's breakdown at the lion house—a mysterious Mrs. E. Webster Ross of Boston filed legal papers to secure William King's release. She refused to disclose her connection to the man but maintained he was illegally detained. The courts rebuffed her, and William's family moved him to an asylum in Newport. Mrs. Ross persisted in her claims, but the courts refused to admit her as a party to the case unless she disclosed her connection to King. Finally, she presented herself as his niece, and thus his would-be heir. And then she made an even more startling claim: she was his daughter. The *New York Times* reported in early December 1894 that Mrs. Ross "avers that King and her mother signed in Boston a marriage agreement which they regarded as a common-law marriage and that she is the offspring of the union."[73] To support her claim, she summoned witnesses. As the *Times* reported, "Mrs. Ross names as a witness Mrs. F. K. Howland of [Newport], a highly-respected lady, mother of Clarence King, the scientist of New-York."[74]

The odd parallels must have stunned Clarence King: a Newport King committed to an asylum, a common-law marriage, an unacknowledged child, a man imagined as a bachelor revealed as a family man, the idea of a secret life unfolding unbeknownst to one's family. It is difficult to imagine how Clarence and his mother talked about the case that Christmas in Newport. Or, indeed, how they talked about it later. When William King died in 1897, his estate was worth some $30 million. Mrs. Ross came forward with a new story. The deceased was not actually "William H. King," member of the Newport family. That King had disappeared in China in the 1840s (just as Clarence's father had), and Ross's uncle took his name when he fled the United States to avoid prosecution for a crime. She now said the man incarcerated all those years was Pelatian Webster Gordon, and she was his only living heir.[75] King likely felt discomfited by the stories of madness and illicit children. His mother, though, had to come to terms with being deceived by someone she trusted.

KING COULD SCARCELY KEEP afloat. Hay saw him in the spring of 1895 and told Adams their mutual friend "was too busy to talk to me much, being engaged in the same futile pursuit of elusive wealth which has been for years so distressing a sight for his friends."[76] By September, Hay reported, he had no idea where King could be: "He has vanished into space."[77] And then he reappeared, "deader broke than ever," claimed King.[78] Adams offered to give him money either for some stories or for the Turner painting *Whaler*, one of the gems of King's art collection, which was already serving as collateral for a loan King had accepted from Hay. "This is pure friendship on my part," Adams confessed to Hay. "I want neither the one nor the other."[79] But he forked over $2,200 for the painting (more than $56,000 in 2007 dollars), which King gratefully accepted to "clean up the mosquito swarm of unpaid bills."[80] To Hay, King wrote, "Oh! When shall I be free once again and stand as I once did!"[81]

New York "provokes me almost to homicide," King wrote to Adams in late November 1895. A recent visit with John Hay had made him forget his misery, he said. And he added a cryptic note: "To love someone is the single medicine, and God knows I have reason to love Hay as he will one day see." King said he was holed up reading Cervantes.[82] And then, in December's dark cold, he headed west to Cripple Creek, Colorado, to render an expert opinion on a mine for a group of London investors.[83]

Ada provided comfort, as always. "I thank God that even if I am forced to travel and labor far away from you," her husband wrote to her, "[I] have the daily comfort of remembering that far away in the east there is a dear brown woman who loves me and whom I love beyond the power of words to describe. If it were not for the vision of your dear self, and my absolute confidence in your love and your being true to me in act and thought at all times I fear I should not have the faith and courage to struggle on away from you."[84]

KING'S TRAVELS BECOME A continuing catalog of frustrations and disappointments, of complaints and cryptic allusions to his friends. The year 1896 found him back in California and the Pacific Northwest. He was in Brooklyn that summer. Ada's new pregnancy offered proof of that. But King remained elusive to his closest friends. An exasperated Henry Adams could only hope he would "some day give sign of life."[85] By late 1896, he had heard King was "far away in the west or in Mexico, and stays there to escape New York."[86]

When King wrote to Adams in the spring of 1897, asking his old friend to accompany him to Mexico, he promised to "execute in advance an assignment of half the brown girls we meet." To Adams the note seemed plaintive and sad, a desperate effort to stave off middle age with a kind of playful gesture toward the past. "[I]t was instinctive with him to call for companionship on his own youth, and he was really thinking not of me, but of the pine woods of 1870; the Sierras; the Rockies; and the brown girls. We both knew that it was all over; that thenceforward his energies were to be thrown away; that the particular stake in life for which he had played was lost, by no fault of his, but by those strokes of financial bad luck which brought down fully half of the strongest men of our time."[87] King revealed nothing, of course, of his pregnant wife.

When he traveled, King often felt vital and necessary; his expertise had real value in the business world. But the long hours on trains, the nights alone, could also make him feel worn out and lonely, driven to despair by his unending need for money. "My darling, I knew all your feelings," King wrote to Ada from one of his fruitless business trips. "I knew just how you love me and how you miss me and how you long for the days and nights to come again when we can lie together and let our love flow out to each other and full hearts have their way. Your letter gave me true joy. I read it over and over and felt like a new man."[88]

IN LATE 1896 OR early 1897, despite the tightening vise of his financial woes, King helped Ada and the children move to a quiet residential district of large single-family homes on the Long Island Rail Road line a good distance from the rough chaos of Hudson Avenue or the more tempered atmosphere of Skillman Street, farther still from his midtown Manhattan clubs. That distance might help King relax a bit about the possibility that his two worlds might collide. Certainly, the new house would make Ada the instant envy of the neighbors she left behind. The two-and-a-half-story unattached brick and frame house stood on a spacious lot (75 by 138 feet) at 48 North Prince Street in Flushing, set high on a gentle rise of land among the trees of the old Prince family nursery. Next door, at number 42, stood a veritable three-story mansion, with a circular drive, a carriage house out in back, and an impressive four-story tower that faced the street. The two yards ran back to the railroad tracks, where the children could see and hear the commuter trains bound for Manhattan pulling in and out of the nearby station. In their spacious new eleven-room house on a block of tree-filled yards, the Todd children tasted an unfamiliar sort of freedom. They might not be old enough to explore the neighborhood on their own, but they could race out the back door to run in the grass, make noise without disturbing the neighbors downstairs, and find places to hide and play in their own big house. Flushing took pride in itself as "one of the garden spots of Queens"—counting its trees among "its greatest attractions"—and retained the feel of a village. A contemporary guidebook pronounced the community's population, "if the term may be used in this country, somewhat aristocratic."[89]

With their move to Flushing, the Todds acquired more than a nicer house. They obtained new social identities. For Ada, it was largely a matter of social class. Here, in this freestanding house, she quickly established herself as a middle-class matron, well supported by her husband, who devoted her days to her three children and to preparations for the fourth, already on the way. For her husband, though, the move affected not just his economic identity but his alleged profession and, eventually, the very story of who he was.

When an agent stopped by the Todds' new home to gather information for an 1898 business and residential directory of Queens, someone—most likely Ada—reported that James Todd was a "clerk."[90] Either James or Ada could be the original source of the story. If James had told his wife about a new job, we might imagine that the would-be railroad worker realized the implausibility of a porter footing the bill for such a large rented home, wanted to assure his wife he would stop all his traveling, or perhaps just sought to stay home more himself. Maybe he worried that his more worldly neighbors in Flushing would doubt that such a light-skinned man could really be a Pullman porter. Or perhaps he felt tired of inventing exotic travel stories for his children. In any case, his new neighbors knew James Todd as a "clerk," a job title that could describe a wide range of work, but seemed to support a stable and respectable middle-class life.

Down the block, on South Prince Street, lived another clerk named James Todd, a coincidence that likely bemused the neighbors even if it confused the local postal carrier. And on North Prince Street lived immigrants from Germany, England, Ireland, and Poland, families supported by men who had found work as policemen, machinists, and clerks. Just to the south of the Todd house, in the large mansion on the corner, lived an extended family of German immigrants, some seventeen people in all, including three servants and three boarders. Frederick Kirpae, the self-styled professor of music who headed the household, might have been the music teacher Ada hired for her children. His seven- and eight-year-old daughters—almost the same age as Grace and young Ada—likely became their playmates. Just north of the Todds', at number 50, lived Mary Chase, a widow from Rhode Island who ran a small boardinghouse and employed a live-in black house-keeper, the widowed Deborah Peterson. Peterson was the only other black resident of the street. Queens was 98 percent white, North Prince Street not much different.[91]

On April 26, 1897, a lovely spring day, Ada gave birth to her fifth child, a boy named Wallace Archer Todd.[92] Perhaps her husband was with her, perhaps not. It was the sort of day that presented Clarence King with stark options.

The celebratory events of the day might have drawn him to Manhattan. Tens of thousands of Civil War veterans and curious residents, lured by cut-rate train fares, had gathered to celebrate the dedication of the new River-side Drive memorial to President Grant. The *New York Times* reported that American flags flew "from one end of the Greater New York to the other with a profusion that causes every patriot's heart to fill with pride." Aging soldiers, recalling the defining moment of their youth, donned old uniforms to walk the streets. The temporary tomb that had marked Grant's grave since his death in 1885 came down on April 26, the day of Wallace's birth. The next day, some one million onlookers lined the streets as fifty-five thousand men paraded to the presidential reviewing stand in Riverside Park where William McKinley, the last Civil War soldier to serve as president, watched the unveiling of the new tomb.[93] In the celebratory spirit of the day, few paid attention to the social and political failure of emancipation or the dismal state of race relations in an increasingly segregated nation.

. . .

ON THE DAY THE old tomb came down, some of the dignitaries in town for the Grant event gathered farther downtown at Madison Square Garden to attend a performance of Colonel Buffalo Bill Cody's Wild West show. King enjoyed Cody's show, and James Hague's children long recalled their delight in attending a performance with him. King secured seats so close to the arena that one of the Indian performers, who recognized him, pulled his horse up in front of the children to greet them with a memorable "How."[94] On this particular afternoon, the audience included two Union soldiers, General Nelson A. Miles and General Oliver Otis Howard, who had gone on to high-ranking commands in the Indian Wars. Their onetime nemesis Chief Joseph also sat in the stands. Joseph was one of the genuine heroes of the Indian Wars, his epic 1877 flight from General Howard and two thousand American troops already the stuff of legend. He had led between six hundred and seven hundred Nez Percé men, women, and children nearly 1,200 miles across the Northwest before surrendering to General Miles just thirty miles short of the Canadian border he had hoped to cross to safety. And now he was here, with the generals, at the matinee. Joseph shook the generals' hands. Buffalo Bill rode up to the chief and pronounced him "the Napoleon of them all." But Joseph declined General Howard's invitation to ride with him in the grand parade the next day, joking that he was too heavy to ride. He said he had to get out of New York because he could not breathe. His memory seemed more acute than the generals'; there would be no lighthearted rewriting of the past for him.[95]

King might have spent those nostalgia-washed days of late April in the reviewing stands of Riverside Park, in the crowds at Madison Square Garden, or at one of the festive receptions at the Union League Club, where he could relive his own memories of the 1860s and '70s, when he had been such a commanding presence in the public eye. Alternatively, he could have stayed in Flushing, close to Ada and their newborn son. But if he was in New York at all, he was soon gone, returning to the West, the one place where his own particular talents should have equipped him to succeed. What the "clerk" James Todd told his wife he would be doing on an extended trip away from home cannot be known. But by the ninth of May he was in Arizona, en route to California and the Pacific Northwest.[96]

In midsummer, King collapsed with mild heart failure in Telluride, Colorado, where he went for the North American Exploration Company.[97] By August he was in Seattle, outfitting an expedition for the Klondike and expressing cautious optimism about the prospects for the Alaskan goldfields. "The rush in many respects is most illogical," he said, correctly predicting that many of the would-be argonauts would never get to the goldfields before the winter snows. "Yet it is readily to be accounted for if the accounts of the new district are true, as I have no reason to doubt they are." He allowed himself an uncharacteristic moment of ebullience about the American future: "I believe we are about to enter a century which will open up vast resources and will be the grandest the earth has ever known. Before the end of the twentieth century the traveler will enter a sleeping car at Chicago, bound via Bering Straits for St. Petersburg, and the dream of Governor Gilpin [the first territorial governor of Colorado] will be realized." America would at last have her passage to India.[98]

But not in King's lifetime. He gained nothing from his investigation of the Klondike, from the ensuing trips to Mexico, to California, to the copper fields of Arizona. Over the last few years, he confessed to Hay, he had been as "lonely and isolated as an anchorite" and in his own odd way had come to love the "uncomplicatedness" of it all. "You have always thought my alleged savagery of soul a mere attitudinizing but you were wrong."[99]

His friends sensed a mounting despair. "What an abject idiot he is not to chuck it all and come to us, as I am eternally begging him," John Hay, who had recently been appointed ambassador to the Court of St. James's, wrote to Henry Adams in 1897.[100] King could collect fees as an expert witness: he testified before the Supreme Court of British Columbia in April 1899 and in a fight between two of the copper titans of Butte, Montana, in February 1900. He could sustain his occasional enthusiasms: he ventured to the Klondike himself in the summer of 1900 and returned, said a friend, "simply bubbling over with pleasure." And he could keep up outward appearances. In January 1900 he dined with President and Mrs. McKinley at a supper hosted by John Hay, who was now secretary of state and the man who presided over the cabinet. From the nation's capital, King headed west to Butte with his valet, Alexander Lancaster, who saw to it that he went into the mines each day in clean and neatly pressed clothes.[101]

All the while, though, he dreamed of Ada. From Butte, King wrote to her, explaining that he had been ill from a dog bite. He promised to write more regularly now and to telegraph soon to let her know what to do about renting the house for another year. Then he put aside business. "Ah, my darling, I lie in the lonely hours of night and long to feel your warm and loving arms about me and your breath on my face and the dear pressure of your lips against mine." Tired, weary, ground down from his unending search for money, King looked homeward for comfort. "My dearest, I love you with all the depth and warmth of my whole heart and will till I die. I pray for you all. God bless you."[102]

A few months later, on his way to Alaska that summer of 1900, King passed ten days in Seattle, dining each night with an old friend at the Rainier Club, a West Coast version of his New York haunts. King's dinner companion, Alexander Becker, recalled that when a mutual friend from the East joined them for several days, King delighted in teasing the easterner, "especially on his pretended preference for colored women—a bait to which our friend would rise every time; and I am not sure which he enjoyed the more keenly—our friend's indignant wrath and protestations, or my appreciation of his delicious humbuggery."[103] Far from home, King flirted with disclosure, testing how his friends might react if he revealed the truth about his own "preference for colored women." As always, though, he stopped short.

Becker later recalled with pleasure the week he spent with King in Seattle following the geologist's trip to the goldfields, never suspecting his friend had withheld from him any confidences. "We were almost inseparable," he wrote, "...and there were few matters of interest in any line in the past, present, or future, that we did not discuss more or less fully but always with a rare unity and sympathy of feeling that was simply delightful." As a physician,

Becker marveled at King's robust health. He "thumped and pounded and listened" to his chest and pronounced that he'd never found "more perfect thoracic contents." King seemed "really pleased" at the verdict.[104]

In Flushing, Ada Todd, the "clerk's" wife, had settled into the big house on North Prince Street with two black live-in servants, Phoebe Martin and Clarine Eldridge, to help with the daily chores. Born in 1867 and already widowed, Martin was a New Yorker, perhaps the same "Phebe Martin" who lived previously in the tenement at 149 West Twenty-fourth Street, where Ada and James had married in Annie Purnell's apartment in 1888. Eldridge, born in New York in 1886, was just a girl.[105] To watch her four children, Ada hired a young woman named Henrietta (later Henrietta Williams), an old acquaintance who, as a child, had attended the Todd wedding. All told, Ada Todd later recalled, she had five servants, "including a nurse and music teacher for her...children, and a cook, a maid, and a laundress."[106] She had known Henrietta, and in all likelihood Phoebe, for a long time, since before her fortunes changed. And in hiring them, as well as a young adolescent who probably had few options in life, she created an extended-family household in her big North Prince Street house that blurred the sharp lines between employer and employee. Many among New York's African American elite preferred English servants to African American domestics, on the grounds that black employees did not always show proper deference to black employers.[107] But Ada Todd chose a different path, perhaps recalling herself what it felt like to be a young black woman alone in the city, to work for someone else, to have little space or privacy of her own.

"It was always pleasant there," Henrietta Williams testified later about her time in the North Prince Street house.[108] A reporter would later characterize family life in the big house as "one of well-adjusted domesticity."[109]

As Ada thrived, her husband struggled. "Ever since I put that ring on your finger I have worked and prayed for you," he wrote to Ada, "and will do so till God parts us by death."[110] But money remained a source of tension. He had to work too hard, be on the road too much. From afar, he apologized for pushing Ada to exercise greater economy. "I think you are a good housekeeper and manager," he wrote, "and know that you don't waste money. Our family has grown expensive and I will struggle to keep you and them up well. God bless you my own—my only one."[111]

ON JANUARY 2, 1900, in the very month that Clarence King dined with the president, Ada Todd hosted a party to ring in the new century and celebrate her own increasingly secure status in a world of striving, middle-class black women. She must have beamed with pleasure and accomplishment to see mention of the event "hosted at the residence of Mrs. Ada Todd" in the Flushing society section of the *New York Age*, the weekly chronicle of the city's African American political and social life.[112] The paper's society pages focused on the activities of the city's black elite, members of such groups as the exclusive Society of the Sons of New York, a social group limited to native-born black New Yorkers of proven wealth.[113] Perhaps it was her big house, maybe just the splendor of the party. But somehow the former nursemaid who was born a slave had arrived. The paper had not taken note of either her wedding or the births of her children. Back then, she might not have cared or even suspected that her own family activities could be worthy of note. But now she felt confident enough to step into black society and knew how to bring her party to the attention of the *Age*'s local reporter. That she read the *New York Age* and felt she should appear in its gossip columns suggests a confidence about her own racial identity, perhaps even a sense of the advantages conferred upon her in a color-conscious world by having such a fair-skinned black man as her husband.

She would not then have noted the irony of the social notice that linked her to the larger community of black New York: "On Tuesday evening a masquerade party was given at the residence of Mrs. Ada Todd on Prince street. A goodly number gathered and many varieties of costumes were represented."[114] Her guests all arrived in disguise. Her husband might have been there. But if so he, too, wore a mask.

8

Endings

WHEN HE KNOCKED ON THE DOOR OF 48 NORTH PRINCE STREET in Flushing, Edward V. Brown, the census man, had already had a long day. It was June 5, 1900, his second day of work, and since morning he had counted 159 people, for some recording more than twenty items of data. Brown normally worked as a clerk at a guarantee company. But he had taken a leave these first two weeks of June to become an enumerator for the twelfth United States census. Like most of the other fifty thousand foot soldiers in this "white tape army," named for the binding of their official portfolios, he was working in his own neighborhood to help ensure that he would know his way around and have the confidence of the local residents. Nonetheless, Brown could not know everyone he interviewed, and he wore a badge to identify himself as a census official. Beyond being urged to be "friendly and polite," he had not received much training, and it would take him eleven long days to complete his census of district 665 in the third ward of Queens. For each name on his list he would earn 2½ cents. It was not much money, but he could take pride in performing a civic duty. As a local paper noted, "A stream cannot rise above its source and the census cannot rise in accuracy above the standard established by the enumerators."[1]

When Brown called on the Todds' residence, someone—most likely a servant or perhaps a child—invited him in to ask his questions. There remained a few weeks in the school year, but the school day had ended before he called, and Grace, age nine; Ada, age eight; and Sidney, age six, were home with their three-year-old brother Wallace.[2] Despite their spacious home on this nearly all-white street, the children probably attended a segregated school, perhaps the recently built Washington School on Union Street, a few long blocks away. "Flushing, Jamaica and Hempstead each have large and flourishing separate schools for negro children," the *Brooklyn Daily Eagle* reported earlier that spring, all permitted under an 1894 state law that allowed communities to establish "separate schools for children of African descent." That would change in the fall with a new law prohibiting mandated racial segregation in the state's public schools. According to the Brooklyn paper, the end of segregation "caused more dissatisfaction in Flushing than in any other borough."[3]

Brown entered the home to speak to Ada Todd, the lady of the house. Her husband, James, was away. So Brown marked his census form to indicate he had seen seven of the home's eight residents: Mrs. Todd, her four children, and the two servants. Phoebe Martin and Clarine Eldridge likely answered questions about their own backgrounds. Mrs. Todd, though, could have been the only source for the information about herself and her family.[4]

Brown would not have asked anyone here about race. He could glance around the room and make that determination by sight. The Todd children had light complexions, and an observer encountering them with their father might perceive them as "white." But Brown met them by their mother's side. He looked at Ada Todd, the four children, the two live-in servants, and carefully recorded their race: "black." With the same word he described the absent James Todd.

Beginning in 1850, census agents had the option of designating mixed-race persons as "mulatto." And in 1890, an era of increasing anxiety over racial purity, they had been directed to indicate just how *much* "black" blood people had. Were they "black," "mulatto," "quadroon," "octoroon"? Brown, however, had few choices when it came to describing the Todd household. The new census regulations for 1900 specified that if his subjects were not "white," "Chinese," "Japanese," or "Indian," they could only be "black," meaning they were either "negro or of negro descent."[5]

It thus became impossible to claim a mixed racial or ethnic heritage. Any trace of African heritage trumped all trace of European ancestry. Nevertheless, the aggregate census data of 1900 made it impossible to ignore the increasing diversity of the nation itself. As Henry Gannett, official geographer of the twelfth census, said, "The average adult American is a statistical octoroon."[6]

ADA TODD SPUN OUT the facts of her life for Edward Brown. She deftly subtracted two years from the age she had provided on her children's birth certificates and said that she had been born in Georgia in December 1862. "The reluctance of the woman to tell her age is, of course, proverbial," noted a Brooklyn reporter covering the census takers' work, "and it is probable that the enumerators will use up more time in getting an answer to this question than any other." Some women also hesitated to answer questions about their marital status, which, as the reporter delicately put it, "may involve the uncovering of family secrets."[7] In that regard, Ada had nothing to hide. Yet she told the census agent that she married her husband, James Todd, in 1882, some six years earlier than her actual wedding date—an odd lie (if not a slip of the recorder's pen).

Finally, Ada answered Brown's queries about her husband. She said he was a traveling steelworker, a black man born in the West Indies in January 1842 to two West Indian parents. She explained that he emigrated to the United States in 1870 and later became a naturalized citizen. With that, James Todd, the erstwhile Pullman porter and clerk from Baltimore, had a new identity.[8]

And our understanding of Ada's involvement in the family charade gets a bit more complicated.

James Todd's new profession seems plausible enough. A Pullman porter might retire from traveling to become a clerk and later a steelworker. But the shifting story about James's birthplace was something else: the Baltimore story and the West Indian tale could not both be true. Ada consistently spoke of Baltimore to the doctors who filled out the children's birth certificates, and now she told the census taker her husband was foreign born. Perhaps she had learned something new about her husband. In that case, she must realize he had misled her before. Or was she somehow complicit in a false story about his birthplace?

Public documents record the story that James and Ada Todd told the world, but they do not reveal what they said to each other. More than any other bit of evidence, the story Ada told the census taker in 1900 raises the fundamental question: what did Ada know about James's true identity, and when did she know it?

Ada's life centered on her home and her children and her effort to construct for herself a solid and respectable life. She valued the approbation of the friends who had gathered at her home only a few months earlier to celebrate the beginning of the new century. And she was not a fool. She had made the rare leap from rural Georgia to New York, found a job, married, run a household full of children with scant help from her husband, and worked her way up from penniless servant to middle-class matron. Nonetheless, it seems possible she believed her husband's stories. James Todd might travel a lot, but he provided for the family. She had every reason to trust him and not ask too many questions about his work. Even if she harbored some doubts, she would want to believe. And so when her husband revised his story to clarify that although he had once lived in Baltimore he was actually born in the West Indies, she might just take it on faith.

Nonetheless, Ada's report to the census taker compels one to wonder whether she might have been a partner of sorts in the family charade, at least in this piece of it. If her husband explained that it would be easier for them to rent the North Prince Street house and fit into this white neighborhood if he pretended to be West Indian, then she would tell that story to the world.

Later events would prove that Ada did not know her husband's real name or professional identity. But by changing her story about his birthplace, she suggested that she had some sense that all might not be as it seemed.

. . .

KING COULD HAVE HAD several reasons for inventing the West Indian story, some romantic, others practical.

He had entertained licentious fantasies about the tropics ever since his trip to the Hawaiian Islands in 1872, where he danced in that "merry Kala-kauan fête" and "came perilously near falling in love with the Princess."[9] His Cuban sojourn of 1894 rekindled his imagination, and to traveling companion Henry Adams, King confided in 1895 that he dreamed of spending his declining years—"if I have any left over from my ridiculous trials and absurd tribulations"—in Dominica.[10] It was now a British island where the descendants of African slaves, whose French patois reflected a complicated colonial past, lived alongside descendants of the indigenous Caribs, who had spotted Columbus's ships some four hundred years before. King knew little about the place. Its tropical warmth and racially mixed population offered lure enough. Like the idealized Mexico of novelist Helen Hunt Jackson's *Ramona*, the West Indies promised a place free of the racial rules and assumptions that circumscribed life in the United States. On an island like Dominica, one could freely love across the color line. King's increasingly complicated life made a *future* in the West Indies highly improbable. But with an invented story, he could grab a Caribbean *past.*

James Todd—who once told stories about his railroading adventures—probably knew enough to pass as an island man, as long as no one asked too many questions about his life there thirty years before. A gifted linguist, talented mimic, and captivating storyteller, King could no doubt talk about the Caribbean if he needed to, perhaps in a Caribbean-inflected lilt. A handful of "black" West Indians lived in the Newport of King's youth, working as servants, painters, or barbers, and among Newport's seafaring community there no doubt circulated more stories of island adventures.[11] One of King's own grandfathers, many generations back, had even been a resident merchant in the West Indies.[12] As an adult, King picked up stories about the islands from Jim Marryatt, his Jamaican-born valet of the survey years, and gathered experiences of his own on his extended trip with Henry Adams.

But if the fiction of a West Indian birth fed into King's tropical fantasies, it also lent greater plausibility to his efforts to pass as a black man. In the Caribbean the determination of racial identity focused less on ancestry—as in the United States—than on complexion and class. Appearance and behavior mattered more than heritage.

As the directions to the census takers of 1900 suggest, the hardening edge of American racial thought at the end of the century had effectively erased the possibility of a category of mixed-race "mulattoes" with an intermediate status between black and white. If such people had once held a special status that set them apart from "blacks," new state laws obliterated the distinction between peoples with different degrees of African heritage.[13] Some states designated as legally "black" all people with one-eighth Negro blood; other states set the hurdle at one-sixteenth. A person with a single great-grandparent or great-great-grandparent of African stock—no matter what his own appearance or experience—could be "black" in the eyes of the law. The Supreme Court affirmed this in 1896 in the infamous case of *Plessy v. Ferguson,* ruling that Homer Plessy, a man with only one African American great-grandparent, could be compelled to ride in a segregated railcar set aside for blacks. In a decision that held sway for more than half a century, the Court thus declared that "separate but equal" accommodations did not violate the equal protection clause of the Fourteenth Amendment.[14]

But if mixed-race people in the United States in the late nineteenth century found themselves legally classed as "black," mixed-race people in the West Indies more often found themselves classed with "whites." In the 1855 census of Grand Cayman Island, for example, "blacks" constituted one category; "white and coloured" another. "It was found impracticable to distinguish between the white and coloured population," explained the missionary census takers. "The greater proportion of these...are persons of colour, but, of course, of various shades of complexion."[15] One's class or job or behavior could all shade a colored person toward whiteness in the eyes of his neighbors. Racial heritage—the so-called one drop of blood—did not dictate one's social status or legal privilege or serve, as in the United States, as the sole determinant of race.[16] "A mulatto is not a negro, he is as much a white man as a black," a correspondent wrote to the *Brooklyn Daily Eagle* in 1902, complaining about its characterization of the people in the Danish West Indies. "In the West Indian Islands one would be laughed at for calling a mulatto a negro."[17]

In claiming a West Indian birth, James Todd thus created a plausible explanation for his light skin and racial identity. In the West Indies, there would be no stigma attached to being a "coloured" man who looked like he did, and no reason to deny an African heritage.

THE WEST INDIAN STORY also worked to King's advantage in other ways. In 1870, the year of Todd's alleged emigration to the United States, just 100 "colored" and 389 "white" West Indians lived in New York City.[18] Thirty years later, no one would be likely to inquire about his connections to anyone among this small cohort of early island immigrants. Indeed, a West Indian birthplace would deflect the sorts of questions Ada's friends and neighbors might ask about James Todd's putative Maryland relations and save him from queries that might expose the fraud of his story.

A West Indian identity would also enhance Todd's status as a black man. The island emigrants of color were, as a group, wealthier, better educated, more skilled, and lighter complected than the southern blacks who settled in New York in the late nineteenth century. And they created an elite subgroup within the city's larger black community, with their own churches and social organizations. To even enter the United States each Caribbean immigrant had to post a $30 bond to demonstrate his financial means and have a relative or guardian guarantee financial responsibility for his care.[19] The poorest islanders could not come north.

By 1900, the West Indian community in New York included about 3,800 immigrants, both white and black. Many of the "coloured" West Indians there, as elsewhere, hung on to their foreign citizenship to assert their social superiority over American-born blacks and shield themselves from some of the most virulent forms of racial discrimination.[20] The writer James Weldon Johnson recalled that while traveling by train through Florida in 1903 he was asked to move to a segregated car. But when the conductor heard him speaking Spanish to his black Cuban companion, the two men received permission to remain where they were.[21] The same system extended to other foreign-born blacks. A black New Yorker told the sociologist Mary White Ovington that he might not be admitted to a fashionable restaurant as a "southern darkey" but could enter as the "Prince of Abyssinia."[22] The West Indian James Todd could present himself to strangers as a man of somewhat higher social standing than the James Todd from Baltimore. And yet, by claiming to be a naturalized American citizen, he could set himself apart from most West Indian New Yorkers in 1900 and avoid a too-close association with a tight-knit community where people might pose uncomfortable questions.

In every way, then, the fiction of a West Indian birth upped the social status of a black man who had heretofore claimed to be from Maryland. And it resolved once and for all the question that might have lingered in the minds of Todd's new acquaintances. Since an act of Parliament abolished slavery throughout the British Empire in 1833, a British West Indian of Todd's age would have been born into freedom. By contrast, an African American born in Baltimore in 1842 might once have been a slave.

Although the earliest written record of the West Indian story appears on the census forms of 1900, James Todd might first have floated the story of a Caribbean birth when he moved his family to Flushing in 1896 or 1897. A West Indian identity would give him greater social cachet and access to a housing market that discriminated more openly against American-born blacks. Moreover, by claiming to be a colored West Indian, he could present what *looked* like an interracial family as one in which husband and wife were simply different shades of darkness, a more acceptable option in a community that still harbored segregated schools. That a white landlord should believe his story—as Ada and her friends did—suggests how readily Americans of both races embraced the idea that "one drop of blood" trumped all other markers of identity, including complexion.

For all its usefulness, however, the fiction of a West Indian birth complicated Todd's would-be life as a Pullman porter. Simply put, West Indian men would not likely hold such a job. The Pullman Company discouraged the employment of West Indians because they seemed less willing than native-born blacks to adopt a subservient role with white passengers.[23] A "clerk," Ada called her husband when they first settled in Flushing. "Steel wks—traveler," Edward Brown, the census taker, wrote later in the summer of 1900. That particular designation clarified little, possibly because Ada herself found it hard to explain how her husband spent his time. "Traveling steel worker" could describe an unskilled worker searching for work or an itinerant strike-breaker as easily as a highly skilled laborer selling his expertise to the highest bidder. The size of the Todds' rented home, like the size of their household staff, suggested Todd was a man of means. But more than 60 percent of work-ers in the American steel industry in 1900 made less than 16 cents an hour, and just over 5 percent made as much as $25 per week.[24] Even at the upper end of the pay scale, a skilled worker lucky enough to find steady employ-ment of sixty hours or more per week would be hard-pressed to support that large household on North Prince Street. The job title better explained James Todd's long absences from home than the spacious yard or the servants who helped Ada run the house. As a geologist and mining expert, though, King knew something about metals and he had spent time around heavy equip-ment and the men who fixed and maintained machines. In a casual backyard conversation about the steel industry, he could probably pass muster.

A HANDFUL OF UNDATED letters from James to Ada Todd clarify noth-ing about the deception that lay at the heart of their relationship. But they suggest that as Ada came to feel more and more secure in her world of black mothers and children, house servants and party guests, James Todd felt increasingly anxious. His wife's increased social visibility and confidence threatened his own precariously built life. Ada sought to move out before the public eye, but James needed to remain invisible.

"The reason I did not come to the house," James wrote to Ada, "was because I thought there were more boarders there and it will not do to have too many people seeing us."[25] His cryptic words, presumably alluding to the boardinghouse next door at 50 North Prince Street, suggested that something might be threatened by the very *sight* of James and Ada, the very light-skinned man and the dark-complected woman with the four young children. It seems easy to understand why Clarence King remained fearful of being recognized in Ada's company. Her dark complexion as well as her class background threatened Clarence King's social and professional identity; his desire to keep their relationship secret had led to his deceptions in the first place. Yet, since Ada did not know that her husband *was* Clarence King, she would not understand the need for discretion on that score.

She might, though, understand that James Todd's light skin could threaten her own social standing; not so much if people understood him to be a very light-skinned "black" man, but if they surmised he was white. To *look* white was good; it was more problematic to *be* white. The white boarders next door might harbor the common social prejudices against interracial marriage, and blacks might respond with equal discomfort. As W. E. B. DuBois observed in 1899, "For, while a Negro expects to be ostracized by the whites, and his white wife agrees to it by her marriage vow, neither of them are quite prepared for the cold reception they invariably meet with among the Negroes."[26]

Ada herself seemed to accept her husband as a very light-skinned person of African descent. The confidence with which she staged that costume party and allowed herself to be written up in the black society pages suggests a comfort with her racial identity and social station. One imagines that in the color-conscious world of black society, where light skin tone conferred social privilege, she thought she had married "up." Ada Todd would thus accept her husband's peculiar appeal to secrecy as a project of mutual self-interest. "The more important thing to us of all others," he wrote to her, "is that the property which will one day come to me shall not be torn away from us by some foolish, idle person talking about us and some word getting to my old aunt."[27] Those words, as much as anything, prove that James continued to deceive his wife. The perpetually broke Clarence King might entertain fantasies of a fabulous inheritance. But instead of a wealthy aunt, he had only a difficult and financially dependent mother.

The false words nonetheless contain a simple truth: James Todd desperately hoped to keep his marriage to Ada a secret from his family and friends.

Ada played by James's rules, at times even leaving letters for him at a local mail drop. "Yesterday I went over to Brooklyn to give the rent money to Mr. Thomas to pay next Monday," James wrote to Ada in an undated note, "and there I got your love letter. Here is a $100 order. Write me if you receive this and the $50 in bills I sent yesterday."[28] Her family's financial security seemed to hinge on her discretion. "For the sake of our darling babies we must keep the secret of our love and our lips from the world," James explained. "God sees and knows our love and I believe He blesses us. But this cold and prejudicial world would prevent the little ones from getting the property I want them to have." He told Ada he loved her "all the time." And he concluded, "P. S. Carefully burn my letters!!"[29]

James's furtive behavior might not necessarily signal to Ada any deep or abiding deception. She might believe him to be "James Todd," a man of African heritage, whether from Baltimore or the West Indies, who did indeed earn his living on Pullman cars or in the steel industry. Such a man might still have an elderly aunt of means. And that aunt might have any number of reasons for disapproving of her nephew's marriage to a much darker woman from the South who had been born into slavery. At the very least, however, Ada had to understand that James had secrets, and that he came from a family she would never be permitted to meet. She might suspect or even believe that having left his job as a Pullman porter, her light-skinned husband was now passing for white in the workplace. In that case, she would understand his appeal to her discretion. Their family life depended on his earnings.

And so she acceded to his wishes. "My darling," he wrote on one of his long business trips. "It will be only four weeks before I can see your dearest face again." He professed his love and then continued. "Write me a nice letter and have it ready by Friday, for by that time I hope the gentleman will be ready to take you some money. I don't care for him to see the children. Always have the parlor looking nice, and when he comes put on a nice dress or a nice wrapper."[30] An intermediary might be the simplest means of delivering money to Ada in his absence. But one wonders at the instructions to hide the children. Maybe King worried that the "gentleman," a white friend, perhaps, might understand the idea of a consort but feel repelled by the mixed-race children (perhaps resembling their father) who offered such tangible proof of an interracial affair. Or perhaps he worried about the stories his children could tell about their father's mysterious rich friend. Conversely, the "gentleman" might be a black acquaintance of King's—someone like his valet, Alexander Lancaster—whom he could trust to keep his secret. A black visitor at Ada's home might excite less curiosity from the neighbors than a white one. But why hide the children?

Whatever Ada imagined, though, whatever doubts she harbored, she felt loved. "Ah dearest," James wrote to her, "I have lain in my bed and thought of you and felt my whole heart full of love for you. It seems to me often that no one ever loved a woman as I do you. In my heart there is no place for any other woman and never will be. My whole heart is yours forever."[31]

King's words conveyed his deep and passionate devotion to his wife. But they also hinted at the man he somehow *wanted* to be. Whatever he wrote, he could not give himself wholly to Ada. There was too much he had to hold back to keep his secret safe.

IN AUGUST OF 1900, while King was wrapping up his investigation of the Alaskan goldfields and Ada was home with the children, readying them for their transfer to an integrated school, the West Side of Manhattan erupted in racial violence. In his book *Black Manhattan,* James Weldon Johnson depicted that riot as the culmination of the "dark and discouraging days" African Americans had experienced in the late 1890s. With the promise of Reconstruction gone, lynchings rampant in the South, and Jim Crow laws everywhere denying people equal protection under the law, the Negro had lost heart, he said. And "nowhere in the country was this decline in the spirit of self-assertion of rights more marked than in New York....But the riot of 1900 woke Negro New York and stirred the old fighting spirit." It was a "brutish orgy," he wrote, "which, if not incited by the police, was, to say the least, abetted by them." The recent decision to integrate the public schools notwithstanding, race relations in New York had reached their nadir.[32]

The trouble began on the evening of August 12, 1900, when an African American man named Arthur Harris left his sweltering tenement room on Manhattan's West Forty-first Street to buy a cigar and grab a drink at a nearby saloon at the corner of Eighth Avenue. His wife followed later to bring him home. While she waited outside the saloon for her husband, a white plainclothes policeman named Robert Thorpe approached her and accused her of soliciting. When Harris came out to the street, he saw the white officer grabbing his wife. "I didn't know who he was and thought he was a citizen like myself," he later testified. Thorpe pummeled Harris and called him names. Harris took out a pocketknife, stabbed Thorpe in the stomach, and fled. The policeman died in Roosevelt Hospital the following day.[33]

On August 15 the neighborhood erupted with what the *New York Times* called "the wildest disorder that this city has witnessed in years." A scuffle between a white man and a black man outside the house where Thorpe's body lay exploded into a full-blown race riot. More than one hundred policemen swinging nightsticks tried to clear the streets. Scores of wounded blacks flooded Roosevelt Hospital; many more stayed home, afraid to move through the streets in search of medical help. The "police were not too active in stopping the attacks on the negroes," the *Times* reported, "and even went so far as to use their clubs on colored men who had been arrested." The police, "according to their own statements, are feeling vindictive against the colored people generally."[34]

By late August, the street rioting abated. Two people were dead, countless numbers were wounded, and hundreds of black people had been arrested. As various black and white political groups convened to assess the future of local race relations, and a police board began to investigate allegations of police brutality, a group of black West Indians living in New York sought diplomatic protection. Some two hundred city residents prepared a petition to the British consul, alleging that they had been brutally attacked "by the mob in the recent riots, and that the police, instead of giving them protection, actually urged and incited the mob to greater fury."

Their foreign citizenship could not protect them from the racial animus of the crowd.[35]

Ada and James might both have read of the riots with some anxiety: Ada from her home in the largely white neighborhood of Flushing; her husband from far across the continent as he prepared to return home from the Alaska gold country. Ada undoubtedly understood racial violence in a personal, visceral way that her husband could scarcely comprehend. She might rarely talk about it, but no fond memories of her family or her childhood friends in Reconstruction Georgia could ever obliterate what she had likely heard about or seen for herself: the random beatings and attacks, the burned homes and schoolhouses, the Ku Klux Klan attacks on her black neighbors and the white people who associated with them. She would know from family stories that before the war slaves could not walk the rural roads of Troup or Harris County without passes from their owners or overseers. An ex-slave from Harris County named Rias Body recalled that "patarolers" would ride all night: "If the 'patarolers' caught a 'Nigger' without a pass, they whipped him and sent him home."[36]

Ada Todd might worry that not even her nice house in Flushing could necessarily protect her and her children from the angry violence of racial hatred, its unpredictability and intensity, its deep psychological roots and harsh physical brutality. Though turn-of-the-century New York scarcely harbored the same all-pervasive racial tensions as the Deep South, the violence unfolding on the streets of Manhattan might yet stir in Ada a deep sense of unease and make her pause to question the safety she thought she had grasped in fleeing Georgia and building her new middle-class life. Clarence King might understand mob violence in an abstract way and feel grateful his children were too young to go off on their own through the streets. But he could scarcely grasp the power of the dark memories that likely haunted Ada as she waited alone, at home, for her husband to return. He knew London and San Francisco, Shakespeare and James. But there were some things that Ada knew better than he did.

King liked to imagine his light-complected, mixed-race children as the harbinger of a new, distinctively American people. But Ada knew differently. In the eyes of their neighbors, their teachers, their friends, and the law, their children were unalterably and irrevocably black.

KING RETURNED EAST IN August 1900 while racial tensions still gripped New York. He stopped to visit Hay at his summerhouse in New Hampshire around Labor Day; then, presumably, James Todd came home to Flushing.[37] One imagines the tempo of the household picking up with his arrival: the children clamoring for the gifts he always had in his pockets, the servants eager to please, Ada basking in his presence and in the satisfaction of having kept the family on such an even keel during his long absence. But one also imagines the summer's violence casting a shadow over the household—the parents talking in hushed tones late into the night about the tense racial situation in Manhattan, the children's prospects in their new racially integrated school, how their "West Indian" family could navigate the tricky shoals of racial politics. The children may have begged their father for stories of his summer adventures. The eldest were old enough to talk to neighbors and share family stories with friends. So James could tell only those stories that might safely get around the neighborhood. Perhaps even Ada did not know he had been in Alaska. A traveling "steelworker" would have spent his summer indoors, in the fierce heat and noise of a factory.

By late in the fall, though, James Todd was gone again, and the household resumed its usual rhythms. King traveled to Arizona to investigate some copper mines near Prescott. He fell ill there with whooping cough. Around Christmastime, he saw a doctor in Chicago, who discovered a "thumbnail"-sized spot of tuberculosis on King's lung. But pressed for funds and with a grim sense of duty, King continued on to Missouri, stopping in St. Louis before heading on to a mine in Flat River. "I have been desperately ill for ten days trying not to have pneumonia," he wrote a friend just before the new year, "and am generally used up and worn out." He fantasized about giving up the job and heading "to the South, which is always home to me, and try to heal up." But he went to the mine instead. Ten days of work stretched into thirty, and by the time the job was done, King's tubercular infection was the size of a hand. That robust good health he had had in Alaska just a few months before was gone.[38]

Back east in February 1901, King probably stopped briefly in Flushing before heading south, pausing in Washington to see Henry Adams, then continuing on to Florida and the Bahamas. On his way back north in late April, he again called on Adams, who pronounced him "fairly gay even in paroxysms of coughing." King tried "to bid good-bye, cheerily and simply telling how his doctors had condemned him to Arizona for his lungs." But Adams sensed the seriousness of the illness. King's tuberculosis seemed "pronounced" and no longer confined to his lungs. "He must go to Arizona at once, and ought to have gone there three months ago." Adams wrote that he, Hay, and King all knew "that they were nearing the end, and that if it were not the one it would be the other." From Washington, King headed north to see his mother and to visit with Ada and the children. By early May, he was back in the West. John Hay was there, too, making an official trip as secretary of state through the territories of New Mexico and Arizona, where at every stop crowds called for statehood.[39]

Many years later, Henrietta Williams, the Todd family nursemaid, recalled that Mr. Todd was home in Flushing the night before he left for Arizona and assured Ada he had given money to "Mr. Gardiner," who would take care of her and the children.[40] Thirty years after the fact, subsequent events had burnished her memory. Perhaps King had taken Gardiner into his confidence by now. But it is not clear.

King went west "to die," as Ada later recalled.[41] The eldest children likely sensed something different about this leave-taking, no matter how much their parents tried to shield them. James and Ada both knew it might be the last.

By letter, written before or after he left for Arizona, King instructed Ada to leave New York.[42] He wanted her to move the children to Toronto, using the money he had received from two friends to buy a house, taking care to find something desirable and reasonable. And on May 9, 1901, Ada took her children north. It would have been no small undertaking to close up the big house, discharge the servants, pack up the children's belongings, and get all four of them ready to leave behind a familiar world. Grace, her oldest child, was ten; Wallace, the youngest, not quite four. Ada might know more about the world than she did as a young woman leaving rural Georgia to move to New York and have more money in her purse. She might let herself imagine that Canada would be a kind of racial Eden, unmarked by the stark fault lines that defined racial life in the United States. But it would feel daunting to be responsible for the children in a new place where she probably knew not a soul. King had a vague knowledge of Toronto from his involvement with a local mining company, and he directed Ada to enroll the children in the Logan School, which he understood to be the best school in the city. It proved useless advice. Sir William Logan had founded the Geological Survey of Canada in 1842, but no Toronto schools bore his name, and it remains unclear just what Ada arranged for the children's education.[43]

Ada crossed into Canada at a moment when race relations had dipped to a new nadir. Canadians took pride in providing a legal refuge for runaway slaves, particularly in the years following the Fugitive Slave Act of 1850, as the United States lurched toward civil war. But legal safety had never been equivalent to social equality. Canada, too, had established segregated schools, seen cities erupt in racial violence, and tolerated the rise of a scientific racism that deemed people of African descent particularly ill suited to the cold Canadian climate. In the years following the Civil War, many of the American blacks who had fled to Canada returned south across the border, and in the final decades of the century, the population of African Canadians actually declined as a more virulent form of cultural racism took hold in Canadian culture. In the entire Dominion of Canada in 1901 there lived only 17,437 reported "Negroes," just over half in the combined regions of Upper Canada, Canada West, and Ontario, the province that included Toronto. Some citizens, both within and outside the government, began to articulate the idea of closing the borders to those who could not "assimilate." Toronto town councilman William P. Hubbard, the light-skinned son of freeborn parents, thought his city was the least racially prejudiced one in Canada. But Ada's new neighbors would not necessarily be any more welcoming than those among whom she had lived in Flushing.[44] Perhaps she imagined this sojourn as a brief respite from the ugliness in New York. Perhaps, though, she sometimes wondered if her husband had sent her off into exile, compelling her to leave the neighbors, the mothers, the gay masked partygoers who had become her friends.

KING TRAVELED WEST. HE failed to improve in Prescott. He nearly died of heart failure there, he wrote to Hay. He moved on to Pasadena, where he hoped another doctor might help. But by August, he had lost about forty pounds and suffered days on end from fevers that kept his head "swimming and throbbing." Still, he could muster the old spirit to write to Hay with heartbreaking "grace and tenderness" about the tragic death of Hay's son, Del, a rising young light in the McKinley administration who fell to his death from a window while attending his third class reunion at Yale. "What would I give to be well and with you," wrote King, "to take my share of the passing shadow and the coming light. But I am a poor, sick, old fellow, uncertain yet of life or of death, suffering more than my lot, and simply waiting till nature and the foe have done their struggle."[45]

Half lost in his own sorrow and "savage, unreasoning grief," Hay still saw the tragedy of King's situation. "There you have it in the face!" he wrote to Adams. "The best and brightest man of his generation, who with talents immeasurably beyond any of his contemporaries, with industry that has often sickened me to witness it, with everything in his favor but blind luck, hounded by disaster from his cradle, with none of the joy of life to which he was entitled, dying at last, with nameless suffering, alone and uncared for in a California tavern."[46]

King had a bushel of mail but no strength to open the letters. For seven weeks he did not write even to his mother. By late August he still felt weak, but could drop her a line now and then and get off some notes of sympathy to Hay and his wife.[47] Still, he said nothing about Ada and the children to either Adams or Hay.

In other matters, though, Hay became King's confidant, drawn newly close through the shared bonds of suffering and intimations of human mortality.

Now they could forgo all talk of politics, all bluff talk about their travels, all sharp jokes about their mutual friends. They were just two aging men, each face-to-face with a future utterly beyond his powers to control. Forgive "my sad ramble of dull talk," King wrote to his old friend in late August, "but I have no one else to say it to."[48]

Thanking Hay for his "superhuman" kindness and generosity over the years, King acknowledged receipt of yet another check, just arrived at his Pasadena sickroom. Then he took up the question that Hay and Adams had discussed between themselves. How could it be that such a prodigiously talented man, "the best and brightest" as Hay put it, should be dying alone and broke? "I have been trying to understand," King wrote, "why a man as well endowed with intelligence as I, should have made such a failure of many matters as I have."[49]

Adams had pondered the same question since King's breakdown in 1893, an event that seemed to him "singularly full of moral." Years later, in his memoir, he tried again to understand King's particular tragedy. "In 1871 he had thought King's education ideal, and his personal fitness unrivaled. No other young American could approach him for the combination of chances—physical energy, social standing, mental scope and training, wit, geniality, and science, that seemed superlatively American and irresistibly strong. . . . The result of twenty years effort proved that the theory of scientific education failed where most theory fails—for want of money." Money alone could make permanent and valuable what one achieved through sheer brainpower or hard work. "Education without capital," Adams wrote, "could always be taken by the throat and forced to disgorge its gains."[50]

King had been as well equipped as any man to seize the opportunities afforded by American expansion into the West in the decade after the Civil War. He helped engineer that expansion, harnessing federal resources to map the region's contours, catalog its natural wealth, and imagine how it could fuel the growth of American enterprise. But with the West mapped, its vast stretches of sparse settlement crisscrossed by railroads, its natural resources increasingly in the hand of large corporations, imagination and bravery were no longer enough. Nor was intellect. Scientific knowledge and personal bravado now mattered less than capital and corporate know-how.

LIKE ADAMS, KING FOUND it hard to understand the tragic lessons of his life without talking about money, that incessant undertow of the Gilded Age. Money in the bank—more than one's family, more than one's books— seemed the hallmark of success in life, however fleeting its rewards. "During the last six or seven years," he wrote to Hay from his sickroom, "I have constantly lifted my technical work and had at least a practice that yielded enough to cover my ten or twelve thousand of expenses of my dependents and myself." Here, for all the frankness of his tone, King knew Hay would imagine the family to which he referred: his mother, his grandmother (who died in 1893), his artist half brother George; Marian, at least, had been taken care of since her marriage to Captain Townsley. To Hay, now gripped by the grief of his own son's death, King could say nothing of Ada and their four surviving children—Grace and Ada, Sidney and Wallace. Nor could he reveal what he knew himself about the ways in which the loss of a child could sear a father's heart. Leroy's death, a decade before, remained his own intensely private grief. To Hay, though, he could speak of money, the lingua franca of their late-nineteenth-century world.[51]

"Two thousand has covered my own cost of life and you know that it is not much to keep a decent position with," King wrote to Hay. "I have check stubs for $275,000 spent on my family in the last 35 years but besides that I ought to have made abundant money. But I feared that I stayed too long in pure science and got a bent for the philosophical and ideal side of life too strong for any adaptation to commercial affairs.

"I might have taken a college position and abandoned the family to sink. But really, whenever the moment came, I could not do it and struggled on my wavering way.

"I believe I could have done better in pure literature, but the door seemed always shut in my face." Now, he told Hay, he could do nothing. "Till this fever or I die out, I can only hope and wait."[52]

King deluded himself in imagining that "pure literature" might have proved a path to riches. But his failure to pursue a literary career had always puzzled his friends, who thought *Mountaineering in the Sierra Nevada* and the short story "The Helmet of Mambrino" such evidence of his talent. "If he had given himself to literature, he would have been a great writer," Hay thought. "The range of his knowledge, both of man and nature, was enormous; his sympathy was universal; his mastery of the word, his power of phrase, was almost unlimited."[53] And there had been so much *talk* of writing.

Since adolescence, King had imagined himself a literary man. In the spring of 1876, with the survey fieldwork behind him, he told his mother, "I *must* write a novel." Mrs. Howland replied that fifteen years of solitude and geological fieldwork seemed "a poor sort of preparation for the successful writing of fiction." Not at all, retorted King. "Geology itself is chiefly a matter of the imagination—one man can actually *see* into the ground as far as another; best training conceivable in constructive imagination."[54]

King's friends never knew precisely what he had in mind, but they had every reason to believe he was at work on something. King wrote to Hay in the fall of 1885 to explain that a careless chambermaid had straightened up his room at the Brunswick Hotel and tossed all his papers into the trash. It was a "horrid loss." "All my mss.—including what little I had done on the English novel, all the London notes. My unfinished Hadrian & the odds & ends—are gone."[55] Two years later, he was at work on a novel tentatively called "Santa Rita," gathering local color among the "dear old ranches" of California.[56] Research into the saint's biography gave him pause.[57] It did seem odd to name his romance after a fifteenth-century woman with a weeping head wound who endured an abusive marriage and ended up in a convent. But King's California trip put him in high spirits. He sent long letters to Hay about the different women he had observed, delightful sketches Hay found "full of comparative gynaecology." King "is in delicious vein," Hay told Adams in the summer of 1887, just a few months before King met Ada Copeland; "he ought to write his novel now."[58]

King hinted to friends that he was hard at work but rebuffed their inquiries with vague excuses. "I have a sort of grim, muttering sound in my ear that seems as if you were taking me to task for not writing literature," King wrote to Hay in the summer of 1888, "but if you saw my life you would not. If you knew the difficulties of my situation in all its respects and phases, you would not blame me for consenting to seek out a quiet drudgery from which I frankly see that I may never emerge."[59] In the late 1890s, he told a friend that he was working on a collection of studies "of the American woman, young woman or girl," a kind of domestic version of the book he had planned about the barmaids of London, and he later suggested it was nearly done. It consisted of three stories about women: "One of the Rocky Mountain one of the California and one of the semitropical type." There should be a manuscript somewhere, King's friend mused after King's demise. "I can not remember that he ever said in so many words that he had committed his results to paper. But I had not doubt upon that point in my own mind. And the stories were charming."[60]

But there was no novel, no collection of amusing or charming stories to be unearthed among King's papers. He squandered his literary treasures in conversation, Hay concluded. "There were scores of short stories full of color and life, sketches of thrilling adventure, not less than half a dozen complete novels, boldly planned and brilliantly wrought out,—all ready for the type or the pen."[61] But they never came to fruition. "The greater part of what he did was never published," conceded Frank Emmons, "and very likely never even written."[62] King liked to work things out in his head before putting pen to paper. With the creative work done, writing seemed tedious. "His brilliant talk exercised and fatigued the same faculties as if it had been pen-work," King's engineer friend Rossiter Raymond wrote. "If he felt the impulse of utterance he wore it out in talking, and often threw away upon the transitory entertainment of a few what might have been the enduring delight of a multitude."[63] Perhaps, Emmons speculated, King had such a refined literary taste he avoided writing for fear nothing could meet his own expectations.[64] Perhaps, as Raymond supposed, he was just stretched too thin. A man might be a "darling of society" and still write in his spare time, or combine a literary career with an active business life. But to do all three, Raymond thought, would be impossible.[65]

From his sickroom, King complained to Hay that he failed in the field of literature because the door seemed always shut in his face. But that door did not slam before him. As King walked into his secret life, he slowly pulled it shut behind him. For many years, the imagination and curiosity, the energy and spirit that might have sustained his literary fiction instead sustained his life. He acted out on the streets of New York and in the drawing rooms of Flushing what he could not let himself explore on paper or expose to the scrutiny of his colleagues. His most dazzling words were spun not for his Century Association friends, who so admired his verbal play, but for his wife and his children, their neighbors and friends, all people oblivious to the studied artfulness of his tales. As Hay and others noted, King's talk sparkled more brightly than his written words. "James Todd" was his greatest fictional work of all.

As King lay on his deathbed and pondered his failed literary career, Owen Wister was finishing *The Virginian*, the western novel that established the very conventions of the genre—the strong silent hero, the admiring woman, the shoot-out between good and evil on the deserted street of the frontier town. A Harvard-educated Philadelphian, sent west by S. Weir Mitchell in 1885 to recover from a mental breakdown, Wister created in his literary alter ego a hero with the self-confidence he could never quite muster himself, a model for the modern western man King had never been able to be.

The Virginian, Wister's fictional hero, was a natural aristocrat of modest birth and common sense endowed with a strong moral code and a deep masculine bravery. In the fluid world of the ranching West, he rose to the very top of the social order. But he could foresee the imminent demise of the open-range cattle industry and knew he would need more than his gun and innate sense of frontier justice to become "well fixed for the new conditions." So he bought land with coal that he knew would serve the needs of the expanding rail lines.[66] Wister's cowboy-turned-entrepreneur thus moved effortlessly from Frederick Jackson Turner's frontier into the more industrialized West of a twentieth-century nation. In his own life, however, Clarence King could not pull it off. He might have the Virginian's natural talents, and they had served him well in his years as an explorer. But he lacked the Virginian's economic foresight and business skill. He was a man with a middle-class income running with a more moneyed crowd. He never figured out how to parlay an old set of skills into the tools that would help him triumph in the new corporate economy of the Gilded Age.

FROM HIS SICKROOM, KING likely followed news of the attack on President McKinley by a self-proclaimed anarchist at the Pan-American Exposition in Buffalo, the stories of his uncertain recovery, and the reports of the president's eventual death on September 14, 1901. Theodore Roosevelt, the youngest president ever inaugurated, was sworn in as his replacement. King must have thought of Hay: in a few short months he had lost to unexpected and violent death both his son and the man he served as secretary of state. He likely thought of Roosevelt, to whom Wister would soon dedicate *The Virginian*, a fellow western spirit King had known for years.[67] The rough-and-tumble world of Washington politics had once been King's world. Now, even with an old friend in the White House, it likely felt unimaginably far away. King was dying alone and broke.

By October, King had moved from Pasadena to Phoenix in a last-ditch effort to salvage his health. The very day he left California, he called on the writer George Wharton James. "It is one of my constant regrets that I was not at home to greet him," James later wrote. "To my wife he was the same courteous, happy, debonair gentleman in spite of the fact that he must have known...he had no expectation of living much longer."[68] Frank Emmons called on King in Phoenix in mid-October. He found his friend feverish, suffering from hip pain, sometimes able to walk into town but often dependent on a horse-drawn carriage to carry him home.[69]

King wanted mail from Ada; he needed to know how she and the children were faring in Canada. But he feared letters addressed to "James Todd" would not be delivered. His caretakers thought the man coughing away in the sickbed was Clarence King. So "James Todd" wrote to his wife the letter clarifying once and for all that she had not been party to the deception all these years: he said his name was really "Clarence King."

As if his stunning words could ever slip her memory, he directed her to write his name in her Bible, so "you can refer to it if you forget it."[70]

After more than thirteen years, King had finally told his wife who he was. At least in part. Although he disclosed his name, nothing survives to tell whether he also disclosed his race or his birthplace, his family background or his profession. One imagines he felt a sense of incredible relief, and perhaps a sense of freedom that was the odd inverse of the one that had filled him with anticipatory joy when he first crossed the Brooklyn Bridge to become "James Todd." With his newfound freedom and lightness of being probably came newfound fears: about his mother's feelings should she learn the truth, about how his colleagues would respond and whether his scientific reputation would be subjected to critical revision.

But he needed Ada to know his name. And he wanted to protect his mixed-race children. There was no wealthy aunt, no inheritance windfall. But he could at least acknowledge his role as a father and give his family a heritage that included his old Newport world of senators and abolitionists, China traders and merchants. And maybe, at least in the utopian world of the raceless America that he had once imagined, those children might even be proud to be Kings and would reap the social benefits due the man who had helped to map the West.

Ada opened her husband's letter in Toronto. Perhaps James's disclosure confirmed what she had imagined all along: her husband had a deep secret. But she might have just stared at the letter in disbelief before carefully folding it away among the treasured items to which she would hold tight over the coming years.[71] For thirteen years she had been "Ada Todd," and with that name as the tangible marker of her shifting fortunes, she had left behind the world of domestic servitude, claimed an identity as a mother, established herself as an employer, and found her own place in New York's African American social world. The family's name provided the most fundamental, seemingly solid, part of their identity as they moved across Brooklyn, to Queens, and then across the border to Toronto. If they were not "Todds," who were they? And if Ada's husband had lied about his name, how else had he deceived her? She might sometimes harbor doubts about his birthplace or the nature of his work. But to learn now that even his name was a fiction must have shaken her to the core, made her pause to wonder not only who he was but who she was herself.

The distance that now lay between her and her old New York friends perhaps made the situation easier. She would not have to stumble in confusion over what to say to the neighbors, to her friends at church, to the other mothers at school. But she would not have the deep comforts of old friendship either. She had just introduced herself to her new Toronto neighbors as "Ada Todd." To whom would she turn now, as she pondered what to tell the children?

King wrote to Ada again in late October, trying to help her negotiate the family's new life in Toronto, giving her hope even as he felt so despairing himself. "I cannot express to you what a relief it is to me to have you get away from that place where you have lived so long and comfortably but where so many people felt curiosity about you and me," he wrote. Ada's successful party and James's claims to be a black West Indian notwithstanding, perhaps the neighbors gossiped. The well-dressed children, the dutiful servants—not even these markers of middle-class life could erase the neighbors' curiosity about this family in which the ever-present wife and the often-absent husband looked and seemed so utterly different.[72]

Or perhaps it was only King who was nervous. As Ada found her own, more solid niche in the public world, he may have felt his secret threatened, worried about the possibility of being recognized with Ada on the street. In Flushing she was likely out and about more than she had been when the children were small, when she seemed to be pregnant all the time, when she had to do more of the domestic work herself. As she stepped out into the world and claimed for herself a broader public sphere, King may have felt that his would have to shrink. The world they could occupy together safely, comfortably, and without the scrutiny of family, friends, or neighbors was little bigger than the house they shared with their children.

Ada would have a fresh start in Toronto, far from the prying eyes of neighbors and the smoldering memories of the racial tensions that had racked New York the year before. But King's own secret would also be safer there, far from accidental discovery by an acquaintance on the street, or the idle gossip of knowing servants. King coached Ada on how to explain her family situation. "Whenever anyone asks about your husband tell them that you and your husband have agreed to separate and that you do not like to discuss your family matters." For years, King had kept his own secrets; now he asked Ada to keep secrets as well, to be wary of the easy banter with which she might spark new friendships with her Toronto neighbors or with the parents of her children's classmates.[73] Perhaps she felt more free in Toronto, far from those nosy neighbors. But not likely. As long as she was ignorant of King's identity, or at least uncertain about who he was, she could move through the world with a certain self-confidence, slowly building up a new world of social relations in Brooklyn and then Queens. Any social uneasiness was King's problem, not hers. But now she would have to erect a social wall between herself and her new acquaintances and hide behind the lies her husband asked her to tell.

Her husband's newly disclosed name might reveal little to Ada about his past or his public life, his family or even his race. It would be possible to know his name but remain unaware of his government service, his heroic exploits in the field, his books, his many scientific articles and political essays. The very name "Clarence King" would not necessarily trigger any bells of recognition for her.

KING SUGGESTED TO ADA that he had been dissembling about his name in order to preserve the family inheritance he had mentioned before. "You know it is my strongest desire and intention in life that we should be legally united just as soon as we can do so without risking the loss of the little property which will come to me, and it would be very awkward for you to keep talking to people of me and my coming."[74] The allusion to a "legal" union suggests that James and Ada had discussed their common-law marriage before, perhaps in a conversation over whether secrecy would be the only way to preserve his inheritance. Ada might sense that James had hurt his family by marrying across class lines or by wedding a woman so much darker than he. She might suspect he had some reason for avoiding the formalities of a civil marriage license. Keeping up his brave front, King laid out for Ada a scenario of what could happen after he received the inheritance and they legalized their marriage. "You might want to take my name at that time and have the children's name changed in the New York State Court at Albany so as all to have my name. I have studied it all out and consulted a good lawyer about it and my only wish before God and for you is to do the very best thing for us all and I am perfectly sure that what I have advised you is the best."[75] He likely imagined, but could not write, that this was what she should do after his death. What would his reputation matter then? Perhaps his name could help Ada or shield his mixed-race children from the worst impulses of a Jim Crow America. And even if she assumed his name, perhaps word would never get back to his mother in Newport or even his friends in New York.

From Washington, Secretary of State John Hay kept in touch with King's doctors. The move from Pasadena to Phoenix seemed to help a bit. Even in his illness, King remained a charmer. His California doctor pronounced him a "rare, sweet soul"; his Phoenix physician thought him the "most delightful creature" he had ever met.[76] Adams wrote from Paris to assure Hay that he would help rescue King from his ongoing financial nightmare. Frank Emmons, who had heard that King was "destitute," tried to raise a "thousand or two" from King's closest friends. From such a distance, what else could one do?[77] Other friends worked to have Yale present King with an honorary degree. The answer from New Haven came back a polite "no."[78]

As when King recuperated at the Bloomingdale Asylum, it was James Gardiner, his old boyhood friend, who stayed in closest touch, keeping King's other friends informed. At some point King asked Gardiner to bring to him "a package of papers" stashed in a black trunk that James Hague had been storing for him.[79] It was time, perhaps, to make final arrangements for his mother and for Ada and the children, to settle his debts to Hay, to make plans for the disposition of his worldly goods. When King died, however, his only will was the one he drew up in 1886, two years before his marriage to Ada. It left everything to his mother.[80]

By mid-December, King's death seemed only a matter of time. "The doctors say he cannot live," Gardiner wired to Hay; "may live for a few months."[81] King had written hopefully to his mother, telling her he would be home in April. Later she would call her failure to be with him those last months her "one bitter and inconsolable regret."[82] He discouraged visitors. "It was part of his characteristic unselfishness that he effectually discouraged all offers on the part of friends and relations to visit him," recalled Emmons, "visits which might have cheered his last lonely days in that far distant region."[83] But one imagines it was not so much "unselfishness" as an anxiety about all the arrangements for Ada and the children that remained undone, and worry about what his friends and relations might learn if they engaged in a long talk with his doctor. Evidently, King had confided in his physician and told him about his secret family in Toronto. When the TB took its inevitable course, he wanted someone to convey the news to Ada.

King's acquaintances knew nothing of his correspondence with Ada. King's only concern was "his poor, old mother," recalled one Phoenix friend, G. W. Middleton. But when death seemed imminent he did everything he could to keep her from coming west herself. He "had me to go and wire to Gardiner that he did not want any of his relatives to come," Middleton recalled. "His love for his mother was the most beautiful thing that I ever saw."[84]

Nonetheless, King's brother-in-law, Clarence P. Townsley, rushed west by train.[85] He likely felt compelled to represent the family, remembering that King had raced to his side as he hovered near death some years before. Perhaps Townsley learned of King's secret family as he maintained his death watch. But if he did, he kept his counsel. No evidence suggests he ever contacted Ada. And no whiff of family scandal tainted his subsequent rise through the military ranks.

On December 23, 1901, Ada celebrated her forty-first birthday and helped the children get ready for a Christmas far from the family and friends with whom they had marked the holiday in the past. The weather in

Toronto was gray and damp; the rain would soon turn to sleet and snow.[86] Far off, under Phoenix's winter sun, Clarence King clung to his wit, even as his strength failed. When his doctor remarked that the heroin seemed to have gone to his head, King whispered his last recorded words: "Very likely, many a heroine has gone to a better head than mine is now."[87]

At 2:00 a.m. on Christmas Eve day, King died in his sleep. He was not quite sixty years old.[88]

Edmund Clarence Stedman, a longtime friend, provided a tribute to the *New York Tribune* a few days later. After lauding King's humor and wit, his loyalty and charm, Stedman remarked, "In some ways Clarence King's life seemed pathetic to those who really knew him. His devotion to his nearest kindred was beautiful, but there should have been even dearer ones to bear his name and mourn his loss."[89]

King's physician, Dr. R. W. Craig, a recent arrival from Illinois who was just setting up his medical practice in Phoenix, indicated on the death certificate that King was a married man. He sent a telegram to Ada in Toronto with news of her husband's death. And on the death certificate, where the form asked for a description of the deceased, Craig struck out the word "color," and typed "American."[90]

Craig intended nothing ironic. He simply meant to record King as a citizen whose color seemed normal and therefore beyond notice. He was "American," not "Indian" or "Mexican" or "Black," the categories of "color" in Arizona Territory that confused ethnicity and heritage, citizenship and appearance. Once, King had imagined an America in which the "composite elements of American populations are melted down into one race alloy, when there are no more Irish or Germans, Negroes and English, but only Americans."[91] To the end, he must have clung to the hope that somehow his own children might live as "Americans," unmarked by difference in the great national melting pot.

IT WAS SURELY A grim Christmas around the Todd household in Toronto. The following day, the local papers carried news of yet another race riot in

New York. Two white boys stoned two black girls, and within hours armed battle had erupted on a Harlem street, with more than one hundred men fighting on each side with guns, stones, and razors.[92] Ada Todd must have felt utterly alone, unsure where to go, uncertain where the money to support her family would come from now. She must also have inferred that the funeral of the man she now knew to be "Clarence King" would be planned by those family members and friends she had never been permitted to meet, and that neither she nor the children would be invited to attend.

King's friends placed death notices in the New York papers, and Townsley accompanied his brother-in-law's body back east.[93] If he had heard about King's secret life, he would have much to ponder, including how to protect his own reputation. Now a captain in the Artillery Corps and stationed at Fort Monroe, Virginia, he had a promising army career ahead of him.[94] If he learned anything in Phoenix, he seems to have kept it to himself.

An obituary ran in the *New York Times* on Christmas Day, focusing on King's western survey work, saying little about the last twenty years of his life. King was "an alert and fascinating thinker," noted the reporter, "with a charm wholly his own in personal intercourse, and a heart, the kindness of which seemed to grow with each of the countless manifestations of it. He will be deeply and tenderly mourned by numerous friends, and by none more than by the humble ones whose needs he constantly sought out in modest and unfailing ministration."[95] In Washington the staff of the United States Geological Survey gathered for a memorial service and listened to King's successor, John Wesley Powell, eulogize his old colleague.[96]

To JAMES HAGUE, KING once joked, "If there were any graceful and inoffensive way of doing it, I wish it could be intimated in my life and engraved on my tombstone that I am to the last fibre aristocratic in belief, that I think the only fine thing to do with the masses, is to govern and educate them into some semblance of their social superiors."[97]

And so King wished to appear to his friends: a man of inbred grace and intelligence, unquestioned social superiority, and physical skill; a gentleman who believed in the proper order of things. Yet, for some thirteen years with Ada, he was someone else, and as James Todd he found the physical intimacy and rich emotional life that had eluded the celebrated Clarence King. The great tragedy of his life had nothing to do with his financial insolvency or his unrealized literary promise. It lay, rather, in his inability to breach his divided worlds and do the right thing by the people he loved. And if that inability stemmed in part from personal choice or economic need, it also reflected the constraints of a world that offered few choices to a man like Clarence King who loved a woman like Ada Copeland.

King gave to his family and his closest friends an illusion of openness; his endless willingness to talk and write conveyed a sense of frank emotional intimacy. "I have never known a more perfect human tie than that which bound my son and myself. We were one in heart and mind and soul," said King's mother after his death.[98] But no one truly knew King, and he could not admit, even to himself, all the seeming paradoxes of his life. The man who had once gained fame by exposing the great diamond hoax of 1872 had for thirteen years mounted a tremendous deception of his own.

His friends, though unaware of his double life, thought "paradox"— that state of "exhibiting inexplicable or contradictory aspects"—lay at the very heart of King's character. King relied upon paradox, wrote his friend William Cary Brownell. "I fancy he thought that things capable of settlement had been settled long since." The art of discussion, Brownell added, engaged King more than any resolution or conclusion ever could.[99] Henry Adams characterized his old friend in much the same way: "Above all he loved a paradox—a thing, he said, that alone excused thought. No one, in our time, ever talked paradox so brilliant."[100] Or lived it so vividly.

AT TEN IN THE morning on New Year's Day 1902, King's funeral service took place at the Brick Presbyterian Church in Manhattan. The skies were fair, but the temperature hovered in the low teens as King's friends roused themselves from sleep after a subdued and somber New Year's Eve.[101] William Dean Howells recalled it as a day of "intense cold" with a "piercing bleakness of the sunshine."[102] The pallbearers included Arnold and James Hague, Gardiner, Emmons, and George Becker, all friends from the western survey years; Edward Cary, a friend from the Century Association; the eminent painter Albert Bierstadt, just weeks away from death himself; and Henry Adams, who had received news of King's death while returning home from a trip abroad.[103] William Dean Howells sat in the pews along with the painter R. Swain Gifford and a delegation of fifty from the Century. John Hay, for whatever reason, remained in Washington, perhaps tending to urgent matters of state. The mourners took note of what a distinguished gathering it seemed to be. "King had the gift of friendship," one observed.[104] But the assembled crowd remembered the man who had lived by his words with silence. No one delivered a eulogy. Two hymns, a Bible reading, and a brief prayer made up the service, and by 11:00 a.m. it was done. The pallbearers carried the coffin out of the church at Thirty-seventh Street and Fifth Avenue, and by 1:00 it was on a train to Newport. Emmons and Gardiner, along with the Townsleys, accompanied the body to Mrs. Howland's house. A dozen people gathered the following morning for a simple service in her parlor. Then King was laid to rest in Newport's Island Cemetery beside the graves of his two infant sisters and next to the plot reserved for his grieving mother.[105]

PART THREE

Ada King

On Her Own

ON A SPRINGLIKE DAY IN MID-MARCH 1902, NOT QUITE THREE months after her husband's death, Ada walked into the *New York Herald* office at Fifth Avenue and Twenty-third Street to hand the clerk a brief paid advertisement. A day or two later, on March 19, it appeared among the personal announcements on the paper's front page: "Will C. King's friend who saw A. Todd and children off on train please call on same? 942 3d Ave."[1] Ada had inserted a similar ad in the paper once before, from Toronto, shortly after learning of her husband's death.[2] When no one replied, she packed up her house and her children to return to New York. With few resources, four small children, and no independent income of her own, she needed help to get to the trust fund her husband had promised her. She had to hope this second ad would work.

While she sorted things out, Ada took temporary lodgings on Third Avenue near Fifty-seventh Street. On a largely white block, crowded with immigrants from Ireland and Germany, her apartment building at number 942 stood out because its residents were nearly all African Americans, mostly small families and the boarders they took in to help ends meet. Whether she and the children occupied their own apartment in the eight-unit building or shared a crowded suite of rooms with others, they likely felt worlds away from their old eleven-room home set among the orchard trees in Flushing. Their rooms perched above a paint store and a commercial space that housed everything from political gatherings to coin-operated peep shows.

Instead of keeping an eye on her children as they played in a yard out back, Ada had to mind them out front, as they played alongside the electric street-cars that hurtled up and down the street, beneath the deafening rattle of the Third Avenue elevated train.[3]

Ada left behind no trace of how she found an apartment here on Manhattan's East Side. The spare listing of names in the 1900 census, however, hints at a possible family connection. A black Virginia-born waiter named Emanuel Copeland lived in the building. He had moved to New York as a young man, sometime before 1880, and found work as a domestic servant. Perhaps coincidence brought Ada to the same building as this man who shared her maiden name. But when the white Copelands of Troup and Harris counties emigrated from Virginia to Georgia with their slaves in the decades before the Civil War, they left behind broken black families as well as white ones. At least eight Virginia-born black Copelands lived in Harris County during Ada's childhood there. Scant evidence survives to document whether the former Copeland slaves in Virginia and Georgia maintained their ties across the miles and years. But in New York City, the mere existence of a shared name might compel one southern-born black Copeland to reach out to another.[4]

ADA'S AD WAS EXPLICIT but discreet. Anyone who knew about her relationship to Clarence King would recognize her at once. But neither the cryptic names—"C. King," "A. Todd"—nor the reference to an earlier encounter would mean much to anyone not already in the know. Clarence's letters to Ada always counseled discretion and now, even after her husband's death, she continued to play along, disclosing nothing that might expose her peculiar family situation to public light. Indeed, she likely resorted to a public ad only because she had no other way to contact her husband's business associates. Many years later, she maintained that in 1901, just before he left for the Southwest in his futile effort to regain his health, King told her she could turn for help to his friend James Gardiner: "I have left $80,000 with Mr. Gardiner. You need never worry."[5] Such money—the equivalent of more than $2 million in 2007—would certainly erase her financial worries.[6] But if she actually knew Gardiner's full name, she seemed not to know a more private way to find him.

Ada's ad found its intended target. Gardiner sent his secretary Howard Dutcher to Ada's Third Avenue apartment.[7] Dutcher called on Ada as Gardiner's agent. Nonetheless, he might have known King himself, since he moved in similar circles as a member of the Union League Club and secretary of the Mexican Coal and Coke Company.[8] Dutcher would seem an improbable figure to comfort the grieving Ada Todd. Several years later, in divorce proceedings, his wife would accuse him of conducting a not-very-secret affair with their maid and characterize him as an abusive drunk who once beat her so badly she "was unable to appear in public for some time."[9]

Nonetheless, Dutcher did as he was told. He asked Ada for evidence that she was "Mrs. Todd" and took the letters from Clarence that she offered as proof.[10] Then, on Gardiner's behalf, he struck up a financial agreement with the new widow and began delivering to her monthly checks of $65 (about $1,600 in 2007 dollars). He also set about finding her a better place to live.[11] By the summer of 1902, Ada and the children were back in Flushing, in a single-family house at 42 Kalmia Street for which someone else paid the rent. In July 1903, acting on Gardiner's orders but without Ada's knowledge, Dutcher purchased the home for approximately $2,200, and two months later he transferred the deed to Gardiner.[12] Ada's monthly stipend dropped to $50. She knew nothing about the ownership of the house or the precise source of her monthly check. She understood only that her husband's friend Mr. Gardiner looked after her and took care of the house payments and taxes. With good reason, she imagined that the money for the house, as well as her monthly stipends, came directly from her husband's estate.[13]

Kalmia Street was an unpaved dirt road, a block long, extending between Golden Avenue and Jamaica Avenue, just east of the marshland along Flushing's Mill Creek. It lay a mile and a half south of the Todds' North Prince Street residence, in a newer, less-settled part of town. Indeed, when she moved in, Ada had only one other neighbor on the north side of the street. Her frame house, two stories high in the front and one story high in the back, had a stable in the backyard, an accommodation to a soon-to-fade mode of transportation on the streets of New York. It sat on a lot twenty-five feet wide, but with the adjacent lots still undeveloped, the yard had a spacious feel.[14]

The Kalmia Street house did not measure up to the large house on North Prince Street, but it offered more space and privacy than Ada's cramped apartment on Third Avenue. Fireplaces graced the downstairs living spaces, a bay window brought morning light into the dining room, and the kitchen opened onto an enclosed sunporch at the back of the house. Little touches—like the stained glass in the vestibule door and the handsome carved wooden banister that led upstairs to the three bedrooms—gave the modest house an air of elegance.[15] Moreover, the house boasted a convenient location, close enough to a world of shops and schools that Ada knew and relatively far from the handful of Gardiner intimates who now knew of Ada's existence.

At some point King must have confided in his old boyhood friend—in a quiet conversation, one imagines, rather than through a written disclosure, and with strict admonishments to keep secret the stunning news. Gardiner himself might have been the man who carried letters and money to Ada during King's prolonged absences, or saw her and the children off on the train to Toronto, and if not him, a trusted associate working on his behalf. When King died, he stepped in to help Mrs. Howland with her duties as executrix of her son's estate. But he kept the news of King's secret family close to the vest. Half a century later, Gardiner's daughter claimed that her father's black servants knew about King and his secret life. But they, too, kept silent.[16]

Gardiner was discreet. He intended to preserve King's reputation and to spare Mrs. Howland from scandal. But King's messy financial affairs made it essential that Gardiner speak to Hay, to whom King was so hopelessly in debt. Whether Hay told Adams remains unknown; a government official would know better than to commit the revealing words to paper. But King's startling private life seemed to remain more or less a secret, never getting into the papers or becoming a topic of public speculation. Whatever Hay, and possibly Adams, knew about King they kept to themselves. In a memorial address prepared for the Century Association, Adams remarked, "We were his slaves, and he was good to us. He was the ideal companion of our lives."[17] If he felt stunned or disappointed by his friend's behavior, he gave no hint.

Almost immediately, King's friends set out to memorialize him. Frank Emmons sat down to write a memoir of King for the *Engineering and Mining Journal* within forty-eight hours of his friend's death and sent it off in the mail even before the funeral.[18] Three weeks later, Rossiter Raymond proposed to James Hague that they collaborate with Gardiner and Emmons to create a biographical volume on King's life.[19] The Century Association assumed sponsorship of the project, and Hague agreed to head the special memorial committee that would compile a book of "personal memoirs" solicited from King's intimates.[20] Henry Adams took his time, laboriously writing out his recollections in longhand. "Of course I cannot, or perhaps I ought to say brutally—will not—write anything about King that shall not be carefully prepared and compared," he wrote to Hague. "One must do one's utmost for such an object."[21] John Hay carefully typed his memories on little six-by-four-inch pieces of paper.[22] Raymond submitted an essay he had prepared for the American Institute of Mining Engineers, and Emmons adapted his memorial tribute for the *American Journal of Science*. Daniel Gilman, the founding president of Johns Hopkins University, submitted a brief contribution. Longer tributes came from Hague, William Dean Howells, John La Farge, and a handful of old Century Association friends. Gardiner, for whatever reason, contributed nothing.

Hague opened the book with King's own short story "The Helmet of Mambrino," the tale of the author's search for Don Quixote's helmet that originally appeared in *Century Illustrated Magazine* in 1886. King's friends had always hailed it as sparkling proof of his literary genius. The poet Edmund Clarence Stedman argued that King captured "the very soul of Spain in the flask of his translucent English."[23] John Hay ventured that the "exquisite idyll of *The Helmet of Mambrino*" proved that no one felt more keenly than King "the melancholy charm of Castile."[24] One friend went so far as to say that the story "disclosed the exquisite delicacy of [King's] literary touch, which rivaled that of Howells or James, and an even rarer quality of wit than Bret Harte's."[25] But the overly effusive praise failed to mask a widespread disappointment that King left behind so little writing. "It makes me wonder at geology," Henry Adams wrote, "when I think that this is all that remains of the most remarkable man of our time."[26]

His friends illustrated the story with a photograph of the author dressed for his quixotic search in the tight-fitting green velvet suit he had worn on his romp through Spain. Arms akimbo, hands tucked awkwardly into the small, waist-high pockets, King gazes at the camera with an amused grin, his dark hat set rakishly off center on his head.[27] In both words and image, he projected his puckish charm from beyond the grave.

As Hague gathered material for the book and marketed it through direct solicitations to libraries and associates of King's, Mrs. Howland watched anxiously over the editors' shoulders.[28] "I have been very careful with my papers," she told one of Clarence's friends, "and had a special Yale locked cupboard built in my chamber closet to hold them—all on the subject of Clarence's life and death. I wanted them at hand and yet secure." The self-appointed keeper of her son's flame, she begged to read the essays submitted for the book in order to assure their accuracy and apologized that she did not feel quite up to writing herself "as my grief sweeps me away when I attempt it."[29] When the book appeared in March 1904, she thanked the editors: the volume "brought solace to a heart much saddened by the untimely breaking of a tie that was almost ideally perfect in its strength and tenderness."[30]

Clarence King Memoirs: The Helmet of Mambrino remains a key source of anecdotal information about its subject's life. The contributors preserve the flavor of King's talk, the quality of his presence, the sheer energy and vivacity that characterized his public life. More than anything, they convey their extraordinary and admiring devotion to a man who seemed so much more capable than they. Even those who did not know King, noted a critic in the *New York Tribune*, "will feel, when they put down this memorial, that they have made a valuable friend."[31] King, said a reviewer for the *New York Times*, had a "genius for friendship."[32]

Unable to contribute a personal reminiscence herself, Mrs. Howland channeled her grief into an effort to reissue *Mountaineering in the Sierra Nevada*, which had gone out of print. Within weeks of her son's death, she had Hague rummaging through King's storage lockers with King's servant, Alexander Lancaster, in search of the original printing plates. The plates never turned up, but she and Hague nonetheless prevailed upon Scribner's to republish the book. The publishers released it in November 1902, less than a year after King's death, touting it as a "classic of humor, of romantic adventure and of nature description rivalling Ruskin in vividness and power."[33] A "genuine classic of American literature," proclaimed the *Brooklyn Daily Eagle*. "Its style of description and narrative combines a virility and picturesqueness with a flueness [*sic*] of language rare in the chronicles of explorers; its adventures are thrilling, yet told with singular modesty and respect."[34]

King's friends gave some thought to publishing a book of his letters. Gardiner told Hay that "in earlier years [King] wrote many interesting letters to his mother." But in the spring of 1904, Mrs. Howland was "run over" in the street in Newport, by a horse-drawn carriage one presumes, and became too frail to go through the old papers she had so carefully preserved in her bedroom safe. Around the same time, Hay lost many of his letters from King to a leaky roof. The project went nowhere.[35]

KING LEFT HIS FINANCIAL affairs in a mess. The outdated will written before his marriage left everything to his mother, but it seemed uncertain that he had any assets at all. Two mortgages executed in 1890 and secured with personal property gave John Hay an interest in King's extensive art collection and about $76,000 in National Bank of El Paso stock (presumably worthless since the bank collapse in 1893) as security for three loans that totaled $43,000. No records of security for Hay's subsequent loans survive; without any real estate to his name, King would have secured those with personal property, too, if they were backed up at all. Fortunately for Mrs. Howland, King's creditor could afford to be magnanimous: he had no compelling need to call in his old loans. Two months after King's death,

Hay entered into a trust agreement with Gardiner, transferring to him whatever interest he might have in the King estate, the funds to be used for the benefit of King's mother. In March 1902 Mrs. Howland submitted her son's will for probate. In its final accounting of the estate, the Surrogate's Court of New York County declared in June 1903 that the estate had no assets at all.[36] Mrs. Howland's eventual stipend came from Hay, not her son. She had known nothing of her son's indebtedness, she wrote to Hay. "It was from mistaken kindness and the ever watchful tenderness with which he sought to guard my declining years."[37]

Ada knew nothing of her husband's debts or the disposition of his estate, nothing of the agreement between Hay and Gardiner. And no one informed her when Gardiner put King's art collection up for auction in March 1903 through the American Art Association. For two nights, crowds of art patrons and King associates filled Mendelssohn Hall on Fortieth Street, near Broadway, to bid on King's pictures. Some came to ogle the eleven Claude Monets up for sale from another collector. Others showed up to obtain a memento of King or get a glimpse of what he had kept in storage for so many years. His sixty-nine watercolors included a small Turner of an English seaside scene, a picture of a water lily by his friend John La Farge, some landscapes by Gustave Doré, and dozens more works by minor nineteenth-century European painters that he had purchased in the early 1880s. King's twenty-six oil paintings included landscapes by his friends— Albert Bierstadt, Gilbert Munger, and R. Swain Gifford—and a collection of sixteenth- and seventeenth-century Dutch and Flemish religious paintings that he had purchased abroad. King never lived with the things he amassed. He had no gentleman's house to house his gentleman's collection.[38] In the home he shared with Ada Todd there hung only a picture of little value, a large reproduction print of a floral still life by the nineteenth-century French artist François Rivoire, housed in a heavy period frame. Ada held on to it for the rest of her life.[39]

The sale of the paintings realized nearly $35,000; the books, textiles, and Asian art auctioned off to "large and fashionable" afternoon crowds brought in still more.[40] Many years later, the auction would prove a point of contention in Ada's claims to her husband's estate. To whom did the art truly belong? Had it been left in trust for Ada? Or did it belong to King's benefactor, John Hay?[41]

Unaware of the various legal and financial proceedings involving her husband's estate, Ada pressed her own claims. In May 1902, just a few weeks after locating Gardiner through her newspaper ad, she visited him at his office at 14 Church Street in Manhattan. According to her, he confirmed that he held a fund in trust for her and the children.[42] When Gardiner again sent Dutcher to her home to interview her in 1903, she turned over several letters from King reiterating the existence of the trust. She never saw those letters again.[43]

Despite her monthly stipends and Gardiner's assurances, Dutcher's threatening behavior made Ada suspect something was amiss. "Mr. Dutcher said that if I made any outcry or tried to bring this before the court that they would stop giving me anything," she later said.[44] She went repeatedly to Gardiner's office to press her claim. William Winne, who became Gardiner's secretary in 1904, assumed the role of Gardiner's "go-between" with Ada Todd. He recalled "these people coming in the office from time to time making complaints that were unjustified." Ada would "come in the office and make a rather loud complaint," he said, "and it was rather objectionable." To avoid any face-to-face confrontations, he changed the way Ada received her stipends around 1908: he stopped giving checks directly to Todd and arranged for her monthly remittance to be channeled through the Legal Aid Society.[45]

Between 1902 and 1906, as Gardiner and his associates continued to stonewall her, Ada Todd contacted at least two attorneys. She needed professional counsel to get control of her trust fund or to renegotiate a stipend that would better reflect the income generated by such a sizable estate.[46] When her first two lawyers dropped her case, Ada persisted with a determined self-confidence. By June 1906, she had enlisted the help of Philadelphia attorney Everett J. Waring, one of the most eminent African American attorneys in the country.[47]

To find a black attorney at all took some doing. Only about ten African

American lawyers worked in New York City in 1901, W. E. B. DuBois noted in his study of the "Black North," and the 1910 federal census recorded just thirty-two black male attorneys in the entire state.[48] To find a black attorney in Philadelphia would require even more resourcefulness, and in a period during which residential telephones were a luxury, communication across such a distance would be difficult and expensive. But Ada might imagine that a well-known civil rights lawyer like Waring would be particularly sympathetic to her claims. Not every attorney would take on a case that pitted the word of a penniless and anonymous black woman against a prominent white man and his well-to-do friends. After years of struggle with Gardiner, Todd had to understand that her late husband was white, whatever he had once led her to believe, and had powerful friends who would fight to protect his name. Her very existence threatened not just King's public reputation but the more private memories of his friends. To acknowledge her prominent role in his life meant facing up to the fact that they had not known their friend Clarence nearly so well as they thought.

Born in Springfield, Ohio, in 1859, Waring grew up in relative privilege as the light-skinned son of a mulatto school principal and his white wife. He did not like being called a "colored" man, and in 1878 (or so he claimed) he coined the term "Afro-American." "Strictly speaking," he said, "people not white are colored, and 'colored' applies to Indians, Chinese, Japanese, Italians, and Spaniards, but these people are known by their ethnic names." Americans of African descent, he argued, deserved their own ethnic designation as well.[49]

By the time Ada Todd found him, Waring had become a high-profile advocate for African American clients. He earned his law degree from Howard University in 1885, won admittance to the District of Columbia bar, then joined a test case that successfully challenged a Maryland law restricting blacks from practicing law within the state. On October 10, 1885, he became the first African American admitted to the Maryland bar. Soon afterward, he challenged the legality of the Bastardy Act, a state law that permitted white women—but not black women—to seek financial support from the father of an illegitimate child. Although he lost the case, the experience launched his career in civil rights law.[50]

Waring's most celebrated case took him all the way to the nation's highest court. The case of *Jones v. United States* involved Waring's client Henry Jones, one of eighteen black employees of the Navassa Phosphate Company accused of murder in the Navassa Island riot of 1889. The island was a tiny speck of Caribbean land, of value only for its rich guano deposits. When a group of black American workers rioted against their white American supervisors in September 1889, the legal issues involved not just their guilt but the jurisdictional question of who owned the island: Haiti or the United States. The case eventually reached the Supreme Court, and in 1890 Waring and his associate, Joseph S. Davis, became the first black attorneys to present an oral argument there. Waring lost the case. And his law career in Maryland ended in 1897, with the collapse of an African American–managed bank that he had helped to charter. He retreated briefly to the Midwest, where he became "the only colored man who ever sat on the Bench in the State of Ohio," then moved back east to Philadelphia to reestablish his law practice. And there, Ada Todd found him.[51]

Waring's association with Todd did not last long, however. Perhaps he doubted the legitimacy of her claim or concurred with the probate court that King's estate had no assets. He represented her during the summer of 1906, but Ada had a new attorney by March 1907, a white Legal Aid Society lawyer named Albert Bridgham.[52]

Ada's switch from Waring to a Legal Aid attorney suggests her practical perseverance. If she could not find a lawyer to take her case on a contingency basis, she would find one to work for free, even if it meant giving up a more high-stakes trial. New York's Legal Aid Society, an outgrowth of the older German Legal Aid Society, had been incorporated in 1890 to "render legal aid, gratuitously if necessary, to all who may appear worthy thereof and who, from poverty, are unable to procure it." By 1911, the agency handled some thirty-four thousand cases a year.[53] With Waring, Ada might have mounted a high-profile case involving issues of race and judicial fairness.

With a Legal Aid lawyer, she would appear in court as just one more poor woman pressing for rent money.

But Ada Todd's association with Bridgham lasted less than a year, scarcely longer than her relationship with Waring. Perhaps Bridgham, too, came to doubt the legitimacy of her case, or maybe Ada began to doubt his commitment to it. But she persisted with her claims. By February 1909, she was working with J. Douglas Wetmore, perhaps the most prominent black attorney in all of New York.[54] At only a few moments in her life had Ada brushed up against prominent social and political leaders of black society— when she married with the blessing of the Reverend James H. Cook, when she worked briefly with Waring. But this would prove a more long-lasting connection. She and Wetmore worked together for the next five years.

BORN IN FLORIDA IN 1870, "Doug" Wetmore grew up in Jacksonville, a close friend—later a college roommate and a law partner—of the writer James Weldon Johnson.[55] In Johnson's memoir *Along This Way*, he appears as "D.," a suave and self-assured young man of striking physical beauty. In contrast to himself, Johnson wrote, D. seemed "more mature and far more sophisticated" with a "racy style of speech." Moreover, Johnson explained, "he was extremely good looking, having, in fact, a sort of Byronic beauty.... But speaking of his face as pale does not convey the full truth; for neither in color, features, nor hair could one detect that he had a single drop of Negro blood."[56]

Wetmore played his racially ambiguous appearance to his advantage. In Jacksonville, where the community knew his family, he lived as a light-skinned black, and when he roomed with Johnson at Atlanta University, a historically black institution, no one doubted his identity as African American. But when Wetmore attended the University of Michigan Law School in 1896–97, his fellow students and teachers assumed him to be white, and Wetmore did not correct them. Several months went by before he realized that no one in Ann Arbor knew of his African American descent, and he let his inadvertent passing continue uncorrected.[57] Returning to Jacksonville,

Wetmore resumed his black identity and joined his old friend James Weldon Johnson in a law practice. In 1905 Wetmore won election to the Jacksonville city council and that same year became the lead attorney for *Florida v. Patterson*, a test case challenging streetcar segregation in Jacksonville.[58]

Wetmore won a stunning victory in June 1905. The Florida Supreme Court ruled in his favor, with a direct challenge to the "separate but equal" public accommodations sanctioned by the United States Supreme Court in *Plessy v. Ferguson* (1896). But the victory proved short-lived. Within the year, the state supreme court ruled differently in two similar cases—both unsuccessfully argued by Wetmore—and upheld the Jim Crow segregation laws on Florida's streetcars.[59] Nonetheless, the black papers proclaimed Wetmore a hero for "his fearless championing of the cause of his people where gross injustice and mean unfairness ran high."[60]

In the spring of 1906 Wetmore moved to New York City. He purchased a half interest in the Brooklyn practice of African American attorney Rufus L. Perry, and opened a Manhattan office for the Legal Bureau of the Afro-American Council, which he served as chief counsel.[61] Founded in 1898, the black civil rights organization headed by *New York Age* publisher T. Thomas Fortune was shaped largely by the conservative racial policies of his friend Booker T. Washington. The group was in its waning days by 1906, riven with dissent over the proper way to press for black rights and fading in importance beside the newly organized Niagara Movement. It survived, in name only, until 1908, and in 1909 the new National Association for the Advancement of Colored People succeeded the Niagara Movement as the nation's preeminent black civil rights organization.[62] Nonetheless, Wetmore used the Afro-American Council as a bully pulpit. In the fall of 1906 he pressed President Theodore Roosevelt to appoint a federal commission to investigate the conditions of black life in the South, now veering perilously toward "anarchy."[63] And several weeks later, he protested Roosevelt's dishonorable discharge of the African American soldiers of the Twenty-fifth Infantry implicated in a notorious riot in Brownsville, Texas.[64] "Beyond the shadow of a doubt," Wetmore wrote to the *Evening Post*, "[Roosevelt] has deserted the colored man completely."[65]

In the spring of 1907, as the Afro-American Council struggled to remain afloat, Wetmore solicited private clients by placing ads in Fortune's paper, the *New York Age*.[66] His legal partner, Rufus Perry, the son of a prominent minister, already had a high public profile, and Wetmore soon brought in his own share of work.[67] In 1908 he defended a black fraternal group, the Improved Benevolent and Protective Order of Elks, against a charge they had usurped the corporate identity of the older and similarly named white association.[68] And in 1909 he took up the cause of Ada Todd, the widow wronged by her husband's powerful friends.

Ada might have found Wetmore through church connections or a newspaper ad, through mutual friends within Brooklyn's black community or through her own involvement in political causes. Her association with him provides the briefest of glimpses into her life outside the confines of her home. Her name is absent during these years from the Flushing social notes published at regular intervals in the *New York Age*. No surviving records document her church membership or her political beliefs, her participation in social clubs or her other leisure activities. Her connection to Wetmore, though, hints at her sophistication about working the legal system, her familiarity with Wetmore's political activities, and her continuing sense that the larger, more principled issues at stake in her case merited the attentions of a high-profile attorney.

Wetmore represented Ada Todd from 1909 to at least 1914, but she never abandoned her own extralegal efforts to press her case. In 1910, for example, she again called on Gardiner, who showed her the deed to her house and said he would record it in her name and turn it over to her.[69] When Gardiner died in 1912, though, the deed to the house remained in his possession. Wetmore pursued other targets. He corresponded with the firm representing the King estate and visited with the head of the Legal Aid Society on Ada's behalf.[70] Something about the case of the prominent white man who passed himself off as black might have intrigued him. He knew from firsthand experience how porous the color line could be.

About the time he took on Ada Todd's case, Wetmore began experimenting again with his own racial identity. He dissolved his partnership with Rufus Perry and set up a downtown Manhattan practice where, according to James Weldon Johnson, "his clientele was almost entirely white." In Manhattan social circles, Wetmore began to pass as white with his new white girlfriend. "She knew that he was colored," Johnson wrote, "but her family did not."[71] And increasingly, as he let people make their own assumptions about his racial heritage, Wetmore augmented his practice of civil rights law—a profession in which his race might be known or assumed by his clients—with a career in real estate.[72] He floated between New York's racial communities, much as Clarence King had done, suggesting his racial affiliation by his actions, letting people assume whatever they wished. He married his white girlfriend, divorced her, and around 1920 married another white woman from the Deep South. Johnson observed that southern white women possessed a "strange and strong attraction" for Wetmore. "A situation which combines the forbidden and the unknown close at hand could not do less than create a magnified lure.... Dame Nature never kicks up her heels in such ecstatic abandon as when she has succeeded in bringing a fair woman and a dark man together; and vice versa."[73]

Even as he moved in white circles, however, Wetmore kept up his connections in the black community. Johnson proclaimed him "the only man I have known to 'pass'—and I have known numbers of them—without feeling it was necessary to 'pass up' his colored friends."[74] After Wetmore's suicide in the summer of 1930, the *New York Age* likewise commented on his ability to move seamlessly across the city's racial landscape: "Native of Florida, He Came to New York and Built Up Large Law Practice, Mostly with White Clientele, but Kept Race Contacts." The paper also noted that both of his wives were Jewish, as if Jews constituted a separate racial category within a binary world of black and white.[75] It did not note that when the census taker had knocked on his door a few months earlier, Wetmore reported his race as white. According to official records, the only "Negro" person at his residence was the family maid.[76]

From Wetmore's perspective, Ada Todd might seem an interesting client, a woman precluded by her race from getting fair treatment from her husband's powerful friends, and a client who could understand how racial perceptions shaped social realities. But eventually, just as his predecessors had, he dropped the case.

While Wetmore served as attorney to Ada Todd, he served as muse to James Weldon Johnson, becoming the model for the protagonist in *The Autobiography of an Ex-Colored Man* (1912), Johnson's great novel about racial passing in American life. Written in the first person and published anonymously, the book purports to be the confessional memoir of a man who repudiated his mother's race to pass as a white man, like his father. But the book was not a true autobiography. It was a work of social fiction deeply informed by personal experience and Johnson's own familiarity with Wetmore, his light-skinned friend who journeyed across the color line. Unwittingly, Ada stood between two of the most compelling racial passing stories of the day: that of her husband, the privileged white scientist who passed as a part-time black man, and that of her lawyer, the prototype for Johnson's "ex-colored man" who hid his black heritage to pass as white.

When the fair-skinned protagonist of Johnson's book moves to New York to begin a new chapter of his life, he lets others determine his race, just as Wetmore had done. "I finally made up my mind that I would neither disclaim the black race nor claim the white race," he explains, "but that I would change my name, raise a mustache, and let the world take me for what it would; that it was not necessary for me to go about with a label of inferiority pasted across my forehead."[77] He lets others perceive him as white, marries a white woman, expresses relief that neither of their two children betrays his racial heritage. "There is nothing I would not suffer to keep the 'brand' from being placed upon them," the "ex-colored man" remarks as he resigns himself to his future in the white world. And yet he remains a man haunted, left to feel "small and selfish" beside the "gallant band of colored men who are publicly fighting the cause of their race." Tortured by his deceptions, beset by feelings of racial betrayal and moral cowardice, Johnson's "ex-colored man" confides his secret in a private manuscript that never discloses his name. Ruefully he muses, "I have sold my birthright for a mess of pottage."[78] Like Clarence King, he feels trapped. The public disclosure of his deceptions would hurt the people he loves the most; the cost of psychological freedom from his lies feels almost too high to bear.

AS HER LEGAL EFFORTS to claim King's estate foundered, Ada Todd quietly asserted her connection to Clarence King in another, more personal way. Without staging a public announcement, filing legal papers, or making any scandal-provoking claims, she simply claimed his name. She needed no legal help. All her life, her name had changed without benefit of official sanctions. In this age before driver's licenses and Social Security cards, few native-born Americans had official identity papers. Foreign-born residents might have immigration records or naturalization papers, veterans might have military records, and Americans seeking to travel abroad might possess a passport. But as Clarence King understood, most of the nation's citizens asserted their identity by simply speaking their name. No piece of legal paper had recorded the moment an enslaved child called Ada became a free person called Ada Copeland; no legal document marked the moment Ada Copeland became Ada Todd. Now, no official record would mark her transformation into Ada King. She would do that herself, slowly, and in fits and starts.[79]

For some years after she moved to the Kalmia Street house, Ada listed herself in the Queens residential directory as "Todd, Ada, wid. James."[80] But in 1908, after years of trying to prove her married identity through legal channels, she gave a different name to the man gathering information for the directory: Ada King, widow of Clarence.[81] Clarence King's old Manhattan world remained so far from Ada's life in Flushing that this public use of his name stirred no interest at all.

Ada's new identity seemed tentative, easier to test out in a street directory than in an official federal record. In the federal census of 1910 she reverted to her old name, again calling herself Ada Todd. The census taker described her as a widowed woman living in a household with her four children and a black boarder named Henrietta Evens, who worked as a "notions peddler." Neither of Ada's daughters, nineteen-year-old Grace or eighteen-year-old Ada, had a job. Sixteen-year-old Sidney peddled vegetables. Wallace, almost thirteen, still attended school. But even as she clung to the family name "Todd," Ada subtly altered the children's identities. She told the census taker her children's father was born in Rhode Island—not Baltimore, as she reported on their birth certificates, or the West Indies, as she told Edward Brown in 1900. Bit by bit, she claimed for her children a new heritage. She might not be ready to give them a new surname (or to change the name by which she had been known for twenty-two years), but she could share with them what she now knew of their father's history.[82]

Frederick Bachner, the census agent who called on the Todds at their Kalmia Street house on April 25, 1910, recorded Ada as a "black" woman and designated her children "mulatto." The rules for racial categorization had shifted again. Although the 1900 census did not allow for the designation of mixed-race persons, the government now directed census enumerators to designate as "black" all persons "who are evidently fullblooded negroes" and to categorize as "mulatto" those "having some proportion or perceptible trace of negro blood."[83] Since the census form included no questions about the race of the children's deceased father, Bachner would have made his racial categorizations on the basis of visual examination or, perhaps, what he learned from Ada. For the first time, the children appeared in an official record as people of mixed racial ancestry.[84]

OVER THE NEXT FEW years, the Todds gradually became Kings in the official records that marked their public lives. But the racial identities of the children remained fluid. With their light-colored skin, they had a kind of social flexibility that Ada did not. They could sometimes let others *imagine* their racial identity and—like their father—sometimes assert what they wished it to be.

On March 17, 1913, Clarence and Ada's youngest daughter, Ada, age twenty-one, wed Virgil H. Hite in a municipal ceremony at City Hall in Manhattan. Their official wedding certificate is a skein of untruths.

Hite described himself as a twenty-two-year-old white man, born in Hot Springs, Arkansas, now living at 42 Eighth Avenue, Whitestone, Queens, and working as a clerk. The age was a lie; Hite was only nineteen. The twenty-one-year-old bride gave her name as Ada N. King, the first time she used that surname for a public record, and the only place her middle initial ever appears. She gave her address as 942 Third Avenue in Manhattan, the place where her family had found temporary shelter over a decade earlier when they returned to New York from Toronto after Clarence King's death. But nothing suggests Ada actually lived there. In 1910 she lived with her mother and siblings in Flushing, and in later life she always stuck close to home. Moreover, between 1900 and 1910 the apartment building on Third Avenue had lost its black residents and become entirely white. A clerk recorded her father's name as "Clarence Archie" King. That untruth possibly has a longer backstory. King might not have revealed his true middle name, Rivers, to his wife. "Archie" evokes Wallace's middle name, Archer (and perhaps even reflects the recording clerk's error). Perhaps James Todd told his wife that Archer was his own middle name, and that he wanted to pass it along to his son. But even if young Ada made an honest mistake in relating her father's name, she deliberately lied about her address. Perhaps Ada did not wish to be tied to her mother's address, or even to her mother, in such an official document. For with this marriage certificate, she staked out a new identity of her own, and not simply that of Virgil Hite's new spouse. Young Ada swore to the alderman who performed her civil ceremony that she was white. Her sister, Grace, and Grace's fiancé, James A. Burns, witnessed the ceremony and testified that the information on the marriage certificate was "correct, to the best of [their] knowledge and belief."[85]

In a formal studio portrait made sometime after her marriage, Ada indeed looks like someone viewers might assume to be white. Seated on an ornate bench, turning slightly to face the photographer, she has her mother's round face, full cheeks, and slightly bemused expression. But the hair pulled back in a bun looks fine and wavy, and her light skin, set off by a dark flower-print dress with a wide lace collar, gives no hint of her mother's racial classification.

A few months after Ada's wedding, on September 3, 1913, Grace King and James Burns returned to City Hall in Manhattan for their own civil marriage ceremony. Burns, a twenty-two-year-old soldier from Coldwater, Michigan, gave his address as Fort Totten, the old Civil War–era military base in Whitestone, Queens, near the juncture of the East River and Long Island Sound. Grace provided dissembling information, much as her sister had done. She identified her father as "Clarence King" and her mother (as the clerk recorded it) as "Ada Coapun." She, too, said she lived at 942 Third Avenue, in the building she had occupied briefly as a child. And she claimed to be white, just like the groom. Her sister, Ada Hite, witnessed the wedding and testified to the truth of the racial claim.[86]

Clarence King and Ada Todd had never obtained a civil marriage license, probably because King felt reluctant to commit his lie to paper. But if a civil license seemed potentially threatening to King's secret, his daughters found it the easiest way to preserve their own. Each swore to the whiteness of the other.

No photographs of Grace survive.[87] Apparently, neither her appearance nor that of her sister raised any serious concerns on the part of the city officials who certified their marriage licenses. But their ploy had a cost. Neither could marry with her mother by her side. To pass as white in City Hall, they would have to leave their dark-complected mother at home. Her physical appearance would threaten their claims to a new racial identity.

If the King girls' new husbands knew about their family background, each might go along in order to conceal his wife's racial heritage from his own family or to live with greater ease in a white community. James Burns, who served in a segregated all-white military unit, might have found it particularly difficult to introduce a black wife to his friends.[88] A state senator from Brooklyn, William Carswell, had recently introduced a bill in the legislature to forbid interracial marriage in New York, making it a misdemeanor punishable by a $500 fine with a possible one-year prison term.[89] The bill went nowhere, but it sparked a renewed public debate about race. And so the burdens of a family secret continued into a new generation. One thing is certain: if either Burns or Hite ever met his mother-in-law, Ada Copeland

Todd King, he would know that his wife possessed a mixed racial heritage. In any case, neither man remained part of the King family for long.

Burns swore on his marriage certificate that he had never been married before, but he had a three-year-old son named Clarence. The name likely provoked ironic smiles around Ada King's household when Grace brought the boy home to live at her mother's house while her new husband returned to his military quarters. Clarence King now had a namesake, a small white child, no blood relation to him or his wife, who would be raised within the embrace of his family.[90] Ada King now had two white sons-in-law, a white grandchild, and two daughters who sometimes, if not always, passed as white. If she had denied the racial complexity of her family before, as she embraced the myth of her husband's African American heritage, there was no denying it now.

Despite her marriage, Grace continued to live in the family home. In April 1914, seven months after her wedding, she gave birth to her daughter Thelma in Ada's Kalmia Street house. Fifteen months later, on July 16, 1915, she delivered there her second daughter, Grace Margaret. The attending physician identified the baby as her mother's third child, apparently imagining young Clarence to be her natural child as well. He noted that the father was "white," the mother "colored." He did not designate the "color" of the baby. But there could be no doubt. The child of a "colored" woman would share her mother's racial classification.[91]

Just after Christmas that year, both the elder Grace and her infant daughter contracted pneumonia. On January 5, 1916, baby Grace died, and her mother, Grace King Burns, died less than forty-eight hours later, a few weeks shy of her twenty-fifth birthday. On their death certificates, their Flushing physician—the same man who had attended Grace in child-birth—again had to describe their race. This time, he pronounced them both "black" rather than "colored," an expression of just how fluid and arbitrary the racial categories could be.[92]

Grace had asked her mother and siblings to watch over her children, and the elder Ada now found herself the guardian of Clarence and Thelma Burns, her two small grandchildren—one by marriage, one by blood. Their father, James Burns, effectively disappeared. After leaving the military, he became a policeman for the Long Island Rail Road. He soon drifted back to the Midwest, where he picked up work as an itinerant carny in small two-bit sideshows.[93] Ada provided the family stability and her home became the focal point of family life. After her divorce in 1916, Ada Hite moved back to her mother's house and resumed using the name "Ada King."[94] "Marry in haste, repent in leisure," the elder Ada told her children.[95] Her daughter's ex-husband, Virgil Hite, headed back to Arkansas to look for work and eventually joined the military.[96]

WHILE THE KING GIRLS claimed white identities to pass, however briefly, across the color line, the federal government categorized their brothers as "colored." The Brooklyn clerks who registered Sidney King (now using his father's true surname) for the World War I draft in June 1917 described him in words as a stout man of medium height. But they indicated his race without resorting to language. Military rules directed the officials to prepare draft registration cards in a particular way: "If person is of African descent, cut off this corner." The military clerks looked at Sidney and quietly snipped off the lower left corner of the form. No photographs of him survive; if he resembled his sisters he might have passed as white. But King told the officials that since March he had served in the Fifteenth Regiment of the National Guard, New York's celebrated segregated unit, later renamed the 369th Infantry and popularly known as the Harlem Hell-fighters. Sidney presented himself to the military as a man some two years younger than he really was, born in 1895 rather than 1893. It made little difference. The military accepted Sidney as a private and assigned him to the Fifteenth Regiment's Company H, an all-black unit.

The New York troops faced their first battles in their own country. "I am sorry to learn that the Fifteenth Regiment has been ordered here," commented Spartanburg, South Carolina, mayor J. F. Floyd upon learning that the troops would train nearby, "for with their northern ideas about race equality, they will probably expect to be treated like white men. I can say right here they will not be treated as anything but negroes."[97] But the troops ultimately distinguished themselves overseas, earning honors for their heroic service in France, where they served alongside French soldiers and withstood shell fire for 191 days. Denied a place in the farewell parade when they left for Europe, the soldiers of the 369th demanded a victory parade upon their return. And in February 1919, New Yorkers crowded the sidewalks of Fifth Avenue to watch the veterans march by. Those hoping to hear the regiment's celebrated band play jazz were sorely disappointed; this was the solemn march of proud men who had withstood the horrors of war.

Sidney King, however, did not march with them. When the Fifteenth shipped out for France on November 12, 1917, King stayed behind in New York. Five days later, he received an honorable discharge from the military. A hearing board of officers found him unfit for duty under the terms of U.S. Army Regulation 148½, which provided for discharge "when an enlisted man is inapt, or does not possess the required degree of adaptability for the military service, or gives evidence of habits or traits of character which serve to render his retention in the service undesirable, or is disqualified for service, physically or in character, through his own misconduct." King family lore explained Sidney's disability as shell shock. It was not; he never saw combat. Sidney seemed to have inherited the King family disposition toward melancholy and emotional instability.[98]

Sidney's younger brother, Wallace, registered for the draft on June 5, 1918, having turned twenty-one since the previous year's sign-up. The local draft board officer described him as a builder's clerk of medium build, with dark brown eyes and black hair. And then, taking note of his complexion, he clipped off the lower left corner of Wallace's registration card.[99] The King sisters had entered briefly into a white social world by virtue of their marriage certificates, but their brothers' military registration records consigned them to a black world circumscribed by the rules of a Jim Crow military. In late August 1918 Wallace joined Company A of the Sixty-third Pioneer Infantry; relegated, like most African American soldiers during World War I, to a supporting role in construction. Due to lingering fears about the capabilities of black troops, only about 11 percent of the 404,308 African

Americans in the army received assignments to combat positions.[100] Wallace earned a promotion to corporal in November and left the military with an honorable discharge in December 1918, a few weeks after the armistice that marked the war's end.[101]

Some African Americans criticized the Jim Crow military, but most concurred with W. E. B. DuBois, who in 1918 argued, "*first* your Country, *then* your Rights." Writing in *The Crisis*, the official organ of the National Association for the Advancement of Colored People, DuBois contended that a look back at Negro military service throughout the nation's history proved "we have gained [our rights] rapidly and effectively by our loyalty in time of trial."[102] Whether Wallace and Sidney King registered for the military draft out of a sense of patriotism, obligation, or political expediency, it was certainly not from any sense of family tradition. Their father had done all he could to avoid military duty.

Their extended family, though, boasted a proud military tradition. While King's two nephews, of whom he may or may not have been aware, served their country as second-class soldiers, King's brother-in-law, Clarence Townsley, the husband of his half sister, Marian, continued his rise through the military ranks. In August 1912 President Taft appointed Colonel Townsley superintendent of the United States Military Academy at West Point. In 1916, now a brigadier general, Townsley left West Point to serve overseas; in late 1917 he returned to North America to assume command of American interests in the Canal Zone.[103] While the men in Sidney's and Wallace's segregated units fought literally and figuratively to assert their full citizenship, Marian Townsley—the King boys' aunt—fulfilled her own supporting role by sewing and knitting for her country under the auspices of the Hudson River War Relief Committee, alongside women named Roosevelt, Vanderbilt, and Astor.[104]

IN THE DECADES FOLLOWING World War I, official records and the rare newspaper story provide the only glimpse of life inside the King household, offering little more than a brief glance at family life. The federal census agent who called on Ada's Kalmia Street house in January 1920 recorded the family in the census as "Kings" for the very first time. The elder Ada reported that she owned her house, that she had no job, that she was a fifty-seven-year-old widow. The census agent recorded her as "mulatto," the first and only time her race would be noted this way, whether by her own prompting, the agent's own visual determination, or a decision based upon the examination of her fair-skinned children. All three of Ada's surviving children lived with her; whatever had impelled her to stray so far from home had not been passed down to the next generation. The younger Ada worked as a "forelady" in a nut factory. Sidney did manual labor for a building contractor. Wallace, a pianist, picked up jobs from time to time by playing in a band. Grace's children, Clarence and Thelma Burns, now nine and five, lived there as well. One black family lived down the street, but most of the residents of this solidly working-class block were native-born whites.[105]

The only evidence of difficulties within the Kalmia Street household comes from later court documents. On September 22, 1921, Ada King appeared before the supreme court of Kings County, New York, to ask that her eldest son, Sidney, age twenty-eight, be declared incompetent. The emotional instability that surfaced during his brief military career now manifested itself as schizophrenia. Ada could no longer care for him, particularly with small grandchildren around the house. The court ordered Sidney institutionalized at Kings Park State Hospital and appointed his mother as his legal guardian. She deposited a small sum of money for Sidney's benefit and use, and every year for the next twenty-one years, the hospital accounted for the funds. Sidney would never leave the hospital. He remained there, an "inmate" as the census records called him, until his death in 1942.[106]

With Grace dead and Sidney institutionalized, Ada's remaining children, Ada and Wallace, remained close to home. Indeed, they would never leave. Their own modest incomes supplemented the monthly checks that Ada continued to receive through the Legal Aid Society. Her efforts to learn the true source of that money went nowhere. After Gardiner's death in 1912, the money came as regularly as before, and some unknown source continued to pay the taxes for her house. With this outside help, Ada King raised her grandchildren, giving them the accoutrements of a middle-class life that she could never have imagined for herself as a young girl in Reconstruction Georgia.

There are few traces of the King family in the historical records until November 13, 1929, when the younger Ada King found herself swept up in a murder dubbed a "petter's shooting" by the local tabloid. She was in a parked sedan in a deserted section of Bayside, Queens, with a married used-car dealer named John Ancona, when several men drove by and "without warning fired a fusillade of shots." Seriously wounded in the abdomen, Ancona kept his nerve and told Ada to "beat it and keep out of trouble." For a day, he lingered, insisting to authorities that he had been alone in his car. But after the police found Ada and took her to the dying man's bedside, Ancona confessed that they had been together. The police questioned their families, and while they detained Ada as a material witness to the shooting on $10,000 bail, they sought her former husband, Virgil Hite, for questioning. She had not seen him in four years, Ada insisted. In a photograph that appeared in the *New York Daily News*, Ada looked more like a proper middle-class matron than a woman caught up in a sordid nighttime shooting. Stylishly dressed in a knee-length dress, dark pumps, and a fur-trimmed coat, she sits erect in a chair, legs together, hands folded neatly on her lap. She appears to have a fair complexion, and her wavy shoulder-length hair lends her a youthful look. Through dark round-rimmed glasses she looks calmly at her unseen interlocutor. The police released Ada; the murder remained unsolved.[107]

Several years later, when news of the elder Ada's marriage to Clarence King became public, the black press in New York resurrected the story of the Ancona murder. A reporter for the *Amsterdam News* suggested that the younger Ada "inherited her mother's fateful lure for white men—a lure which was even intensified, some admirers believe, by the lighter complexion for which she thanked her white father." He fashioned Ada—and by association her mother—as a temptress. The "same fascination" that drew Clarence King "to the arms of a chocolate-hued servant girl in the '80s of the last century," the reporter declared, "was transmitted to a daughter of the mixed marriage and lured a white father of five children, forty years later, to his death."[108]

A few months after the Ancona incident, in April 1930, a federal census agent again captured a spare portrait of the King family: Clarence King's widow, Ada, lived in the house on Kalmia Avenue (Kalmia Street had been renamed a year or two before) with her daughter, Ada, her son Wallace, and her grandchildren, Clarence and Thelma Burns. The older Ada did not work. The younger Ada worked as a saleslady in what the census agent called an "apartment store." Wallace played jazz piano in a band, picking up gigs in restaurants. Clarence, now nineteen, worked as a showroom clerk. Thelma, about to turn sixteen, attended school. In response to the census agent's question, the family replied, yes, they owned a radio. But when asked whether she owned or rented the house, the elder Ada said she lived there in "trust," implying that someone owned the house *for* her. In 1910 and again in 1920, she had told census agents she owned the house herself. The change seems to signal her growing awareness that something remained irregular about the title to her home. She had not, after all, ever received the deed that Gardiner had promised.[109]

But the most peculiar part of the 1930 census records concerns the family's racial designations: every member of Ada's immediate family was classified "Negro." The rules had changed again. In 1910 and 1920, when the official racial categories for the federal census distinguished between "Black" and "Mulatto," the King children had been recorded as persons of mixed race. But the option to claim a mixed racial heritage disappeared in 1930, not to be regained until 2000. In 1930 any visible trace of African blood made one "Negro" or "Black." And so, the younger Ada, who was once characterized as a mulatto and considered fair enough to marry as a white woman, became a "Negro" again in the eyes of the federal government, as did Thelma, who had three white grandparents, and Clarence, who likely had four.[110] More than forty years earlier, Clarence King had exploited this particular system of racial categorization to declare himself a black man, despite his very light complexion. And now his children and grandchildren became "Negroes" in the eyes of the census taker, not necessarily because of their own appearance but because of their evident familial connection to the dark-complected Ada King.

Only Sidney—an "inmate" in a state mental institution—acquired the racial designation his sisters had once claimed for themselves and the unmarked status his father had wished for all his children. When the census takers at the state hospital recorded the name of Sidney King, a veteran of a segregated military regiment, they carefully noted his race: "white." Whether they actually observed him or interviewed him remains unknown. But certainly they did not see him by his mother's side when they assigned him a race.[111]

EVEN IN HER HOUSE of adult children, the elder Ada called the shots. Thelma later recalled her as a regal and demanding woman, a stickler for propriety and formal good manners. Wallace wore a hat and a tie whenever he left the house; the younger Ada never went out without a hat, a purse, and gloves. Wallace, in particular, demanded the same of his niece, insisting that Thelma, too, never leave the house without a pair of ladylike gloves and neatly done-up hair. One summer, when she was around sixteen, Thelma went to Missouri to visit her father. For several weeks she appeared as an extra in his carnival sideshow, obligingly permitting herself to be "sawed in half" day after day, as James Burns tried to lure paying customers with a glimpse of a mysterious animal that had "killed a flock of chicken and 2 of his dogs." But back at the Kalmia Avenue house, a stricter decorum prevailed. Thelma took ballet and tap-dancing lessons and, to improve her posture, walked around the house with a book balanced on her head.[112]

At some point, Ada left the Union American Methodist Episcopal Church in which she had been married, perhaps because the small denomination had no congregation in Flushing. But she had a deep and abiding familiarity with the Bible, and family members recalled how she often cited her favorite religious injunctions: "Do unto others..." and "The meek shall inherit the earth." In Flushing Ada joined a Catholic church, and she raised her grandchildren as Catholics, insisting that Thelma sing in the church choir and participate in various youth activities. Thelma's daughter would later recall that after church on Sundays the King family would sit down to a formal supper, with food that evoked Ada's southern girlhood: fried chicken and biscuits or baked chicken with dressing. Ada raised her own chickens in the backyard and she killed them herself. Raising and butchering poultry, a familiarity with the Bible, wine-making, and an insistence on a strict regimen of home remedies—all offer tantalizing glimpses of the hidden world of Ada's Georgia youth. In the house on Kalmia Avenue, vestiges of the rich and distinctive African American culture of southern cotton country mixed with the trappings of Ada's upwardly mobile social aspirations and, later, with the stirrings of the new black world emerging in Harlem in northern Manhattan. Wallace learned to play the piano, and jazz and honky-tonk often resounded from the neat two-story house. And as Thelma grew older, she sometimes slipped away from her grandmother's orderly home to ride the subways to Harlem to dance at the Cotton Club, finding in that racially mixed club and others the sort of allure that had once beckoned her grandfather Clarence King.[113]

While she raised her young grandchildren, Ada dropped her persistent efforts to press for money from her husband's estate. She had been threatened before and understood that the stakes were high. She could not afford to lose her monthly stipends from the Legal Aid Society. But during the mid-1920s, she again contacted an attorney to explore the possibility of mounting a case. She turned to a white man this time. Martin W. Littleton Jr. was the son of the famously conservative (and famously high-priced) attorney who had defended D. W. Griffith's *Birth of a Nation* to its New York critics and earned recognition from *Time* magazine as "one of the world's richest lawyers."[114] The elder Mr. Littleton had successfully defended Harry K. Thaw, the accused killer of architect Stanford White, and Harry F. Sinclair, who was charged with bribing Secretary of the Interior Albert Fall in the Teapot Dome scandal of the mid-1920s. The *New York Times* deemed him "an outspoken foe of socialism, communism and radicalism in general."[115] But his namesake was just starting his legal practice in 1924 and took on less high-profile cases. Sometime between 1924 and 1929, when he became assistant district attorney in Nassau County, Martin W. Littleton Jr. became another in Ada King's long string of attorneys. Like all the rest, he apparently counseled her to drop her case.[116]

In 1931, with her grandchildren poised to move out on their own, Ada, now close to seventy, finally found an attorney to press the claim to her husband's estate that she had first tried to initiate almost three decades before. Her lawyer later explained why it had taken her so long. "It must be remembered," Herman Schwartz wrote, "that the plaintiff, Ada King, was a negress and her children of half blood, and that the children were small and the needs for keeping them clothed and educated were great, and for that reason the enforcement of their claim was delayed.... After the children had reached maturity and it was possible to proceed without endangering their means of livelihood, this action was begun, especially as Ada King is getting on in years, and may not have much longer to struggle with the ingratitude that the white persons on earth show."[117]

10

The Trial

ON A COOL, CLEAR AFTERNOON IN LATE FALL 1933, ADA KING finally got her day in court.[1] On Monday, November 20, she sat before Justice Bernard Shientag of the New York Supreme Court and, in a quavering voice "filled with emotion," told her story.[2] She appeared nervous, a reporter noted, and the court "had to urge her to speak more slowly and distinctly."[3] But she began at the beginning: her meeting with Clarence King, their marriage in 1888, the birth of their five children (she gave a self-deprecating chuckle as she confused their birth dates). She described their happy family life in the big home on North Prince Street, where servants helped her run the household. And she related in some detail what her husband told her as he prepared to leave for Arizona in a futile attempt to recover his health. King explained that he had left $80,000 for her and the children with his close friend Mr. Gardiner. "He hoped he wouldn't die," Ada recalled, "because he had a great interest in his children and had an education planned for them."[4]

Ada King carefully examined the letters from her husband that had been introduced as evidence. She verified King's handwriting in a handful of original manuscripts and scrutinized the content of the typed transcripts also submitted by the defense. And then, as one reporter put it, "a score of torrid love letters, allegedly from King to his dusky wife were read into the records."[5] The case really hinged on financial issues—King's debts, the disposition of his estate, his verbal promises of a trust fund. But Ada had to prove that she was married to Clarence King, and she wanted to show the world that he loved her.

The press hung on every word of King's letters, breathlessly quoting excerpts for their readers. And the very private life of Clarence King and Ada Copeland, otherwise known as James and Ada Todd, became the stuff of public speculation. It was "a two day sensation," wrote a reporter for the black press, a tale of sex, race, and false identity made all the more salacious for its evocation of famous names and a hint of social scandal.[6]

The mainstream press focused on Ada King's race: "Colored Woman Sues as Widow of Society Man"; "Mammy Bares Life as Wife of Scientist"; "Old Negress Suing Estate, Reveals Love."[7] A New York tabloid described her as a "huge, kinky-haired, pleasant-faced colored woman of 70 years."[8] Her race seemed to render her both an improbable plaintiff and an improbable spouse for the distinguished Clarence King. The black press played the story differently, extending its empathy to Mrs. King and painting her husband as the one whose race merited notice. Even so, the *Amsterdam News* evoked the stereotype of a black "mammy," characterizing Ada as a "stoutish, grandmotherly type." The *Chicago Defender* remarked that she "still bears marks of a once beautiful woman."[9] The *New York Age* headlined its coverage, "Court Hears Suit for $80,000 against White Man's Estate."[10]

Clarence King's luster had faded in the decades since his death. In 1908 the sculptor Louis Amateis cast King's likeness in bronze for the elaborate new door at the west entrance of the U.S. Capitol that celebrated the role of the arts and sciences in the "apotheosis of America."[11] In 1921 Yale University carved King's name in stone over an entryway in Branford Court, its new neo-Gothic "memorial quadrangle." King was the only graduate of Sheffield to be honored in the new Yale College buildings. As an early chronicler of the project wrote, "There are few names carved upon these stones that represent so great a wealth of human genius."[12] But by 1933, when Ada finally appeared in court, the press could barely explain who he was. Reporters misidentified him as a "man who made his fortune in the Arkansas oil rush in the '90s"; "an oil millionaire"; "the scion of an old New York family."[13] His alleged marriage seemed an odd and distant story from the so-called mauve decade, a popular term for the 1890s. Ada King's presence in a Manhattan courtroom, however, brought his story back to light.

Even for a generation of Americans unfamiliar with Clarence King, the trial provided the prurient fascination of a social scandal made all the more engaging because it played out against a backdrop of intractable worries about money and race. The Depression left all Americans in 1933 uncertain about their economic fortunes, easy prey for stories of poor women being swept off their feet by wealthy men or penniless girls rising to middle-class comfort. And the news from abroad, as well as home, underscored the continuing social potency of race. In Hitler's Germany, the plan "to multiply and 'purify' " the German race seemed to be gaining steam, and the very week Ada appeared in court Nazi leaders expressed delight at the rising German marriage rate.[14] Closer to home, President Franklin Roosevelt entertained pleas to intervene in the case of the so-called Scottsboro Boys, a group of black teenagers falsely accused of raping two white women in the racially tense world of Jim Crow Alabama.[15] These more prominent unfolding stories served as background for the King trial, priming newspaper readers to see Ada's story in terms of the broader themes of class and race. But at its core, this remained a deeply human tale. As one reporter remarked, "Love knows no race, creed or color."[16]

THE FINAL CHAPTER OF Ada King's thirty-year effort to gain control of the money her husband left her opened on March 30, 1931—more than a year and a half before Ada finally appeared in court—when she and her children Wallace and Ada filed a formal complaint in the New York Supreme Court. Since Sidney's mental illness rendered him legally "incompetent," his mother represented him, too. The complaint targeted a large group of defendants associated with Clarence King's long-dead friend James Gardiner and focused on a straightforward question: where was the money Clarence King left for his family?[17]

The Kings' attorney, now a thirty-three-year-old Russian immigrant named Morris Bell, laid out Ada's case.[18] As the lawful wife of Clarence

King, she was entitled to the trust fund he had created for her. Bell contended that before King died in 1901 he transferred to Gardiner money and property totaling around $80,000. Gardiner accepted it with the "express agreement" that he would hold it in trust until King's death, use it for the benefit of Ada and her children, and eventually transfer the money to her.[19]

Gardiner had confirmed the trust's existence to Ada, Bell said, and provided her with monthly checks, "which monthly installments in lesser amounts, she still receives from a source unknown to plaintiffs."[20] Since Gardiner's death in 1912, Ada no longer had any idea who controlled her money or even where the stipends came from.

Her complaint targeted Gardiner's executors, heirs, and former secretaries—everyone who might know the details of his financial affairs or have a continuing interest in his estate. Ada long suspected that one of Gardiner's secretaries, either Howard Dutcher or William Winne, controlled her trust. But they would never tell her a thing. She could not even describe for the sake of her lawsuit the precise nature of the property held in trust.

The Kings' questions, if not their demands, seemed straightforward: where was the money, how much was there, how had it been disbursed, who controlled it? But the defendants maneuvered to delay the case, hoping that Ada and her attorneys would give up in frustration. They flat-out refused to say where the money came from. An "unnamed benefactor," they insisted.[21] For two and a half years, the case slowly wound its way through the discovery phase of the proceedings.

BOTH SIDES HAD MUCH they wanted to know. The seven Gardiner heirs named in Ada's complaint claimed absolute ignorance of the legal situation and urged the judge to dismiss the case.[22] The three trustees of Gardiner's estate likewise expressed legitimate bewilderment. Who was Ada King?

Attorney Henry W. Jessup, who represented the three trustees of Gardiner's estate and most of the family members named in the complaint, derided Ada's assertions as baseless and without legal merit, especially after so many years. Why had she made no claims before? Jessup's life mirrored those of his well-heeled clients. Born in Syria to American missionary parents, he was a Princeton graduate who now lived on Manhattan's Upper East Side with his wife, a grown son, and a black West Indian–born servant. Like Clarence King, he belonged to the Century Association. And he was something of a polymath: an authority on estate law, a novelist, a legal writer, and a frequent contributor to the letters column of the *New York Times*, sounding off on everything from college football to the "regretted paucity of white horses in the modern scene."[23] His clients likely viewed him as a man of discretion who could keep their names out of the paper. After all, they contended, they had no idea what this case was about.

The contrast between Jessup's life and that of the Kings' lawyer, Morris Bell, echoed the social divides that separated Ada from her husband's associates. Bell lived with his in-laws on a polyglot street in the Bronx. His father-in-law ran a grocery store; his wife worked as a secretary. He harbored doubts about Ada's case but took it on after "constant and determined pressure from the plaintiffs." Although the Kings could not afford his fees, they promised a percentage of the money they recovered.[24]

The case seemed a clash of David versus Goliath. It pitted Ada and her children against the sort of powerful men Clarence King knew well but from whom he hid his secret family. King had kept his worlds separate during his lifetime, but now, more than three decades after his death, they collided in a courtroom. Two of the trustees of Gardiner's long-settled estate were retired attorneys long active in New York civic affairs. John S. Melcher, who summered near the Gardiner family vacation home in Northeast Harbor, Maine, spent fifteen years on the Grievance Committee of the New York City Bar Association, and in retirement served as president of the New York Society for Relief of the Ruptured and Crippled.[25] Seth Sprague Terry, an active political reformer and a leader of the New York Society for the Suppression of Vice, served from 1895 to 1898 as New York City's commissioner of accounts. Like King, he was a clubman, and he took pride in his stamp collection and in an ancestry he traced back to the *Mayflower*.[26]

The third Gardiner trustee named in the suit, retired investment banker

George Foster Peabody, was an even more improbable defendant. He had just completed a remarkable forty-six-year stint as a trustee of Hampton Institute, the historically black school in Virginia, where he had created a special library collection devoted to African American history. A reporter covering the trial for the black press identified him as "a widely-known patron of Negro art and education" and "a backer of the Southern Commission on Interracial Co-operation."[27] Others knew him as a passionate advocate for women's suffrage and free trade, a champion of world peace, a proponent of government ownership of the railroads. To acknowledge his philanthropic largesse, the University of Georgia had named its distinguished journalism awards in his honor. Moreover, Peabody would have known something of Ada King's childhood world. Born in 1852 in Columbus, Georgia, about forty miles south of her home near West Point, he moved to Brooklyn in 1866, just after the Civil War. But he retained his Georgia ties and in 1923 acquired property in Warm Springs, not far from Ada's girlhood home. Peabody subsequently introduced Franklin D. Roosevelt to the therapeutic waters at Warm Springs, and there Roosevelt later established his "Little White House." Indeed, the president was in Warm Springs when Ada took the witness stand in New York.[28] Anyone searching for traces of Ada Copeland in the still-rural part of Georgia where she grew up will come upon the Little White House museum and FDR State Park, lasting legacies of the president's friendship with the man Ada now targeted in her complaint.

Not until Jessup found William Winne, the Gardiner secretary also named in the complaint, did he and his clients have a clue as to what this case was all about. Winne, at least, "was conversant with the occasional relations which [Gardiner] had to the plaintiffs," and he had met Ada King.[29]

THE PRETRIAL PHASE OF the lawsuit stretched out for more than two years. Time, money, and social power all lay with the defendants. They moved slowly, hoping the seventy-year-old plaintiff would simply give up. Ada King did not, but her lawyer did. When the defendants refused to give straight answers about the money, Morris Bell dropped the case. He said he had taken it against his better judgment, and in August 1931, with no quick solution in sight, he quit.[30] Ada promptly hired another attorney. Herman Schwartz, like Bell, was a Russian Jewish immigrant.[31] He became Ada's eighth legal adviser in a struggle that had gone on for nearly three decades, and he would be the one to finally take her case to trial.

Schwartz pressed Winne, who became Gardiner's stenographer and secretary in 1904, to be explicit about the source of Ada's monthly checks. But Winne evaded the question. "Not one cent I have transmitted to the Legal Aid Society since 1912, for the benefit of these plaintiffs, came from Mr. James T. Gardiner or anyone else interested in this Estate." He coyly explained where the money did *not* come from. But he refused to identify its source.[32]

Winne explained that shortly after King's death, "a non-resident friend" who wished to keep King's "financial and personal memory free of attack and criticism, provided moneys with which to pay his debts and to provide for the support and maintenance of the said King's aged mother." When this friend learned about Ada, he feared "the shock to King's aged mother, Mrs. Howland, of this scandalous claim." He then "voluntarily provided, from time to time, about $50 a month to be paid to [Ada] for her support and maintenance" and gave Gardiner $2,000 to buy her a home. Later, he supplied additional money for home repairs and property taxes. Winne said that he transmitted the monthly checks to Ada during the benefactor's lifetime. Following this unnamed donor's death, Winne said, he received money from an anonymous family member "interested because of the father's interest in the good name of his friend, Clarence King."[33]

In other words, Ada had no trust fund. Her monthly cash came from a secret benefactor. And it was hush money meant to keep her quiet and to protect Clarence King's good name from the taint of scandal.

Steadfastly refusing to identify Ada's mysterious benefactor, Winne—the figure on whom the defense rested its case—attacked Ada's character. "The self-styled Mrs. King," he called her. "From time to time," he claimed, "and especially since the children have grown up and proved more or less shiftless and unwilling to earn their self-support, they and their mother have made claims." He conflated character and race. He spoke of "these negro plaintiffs," as if their skin color denoted their moral probity, and contrasted "the negro claimants" to "Clarence King, a distinguished American," as if an American identity hinged on whiteness. He suggested that Ada's previous lawyers had dropped the case because it had no merit.[34]

In November 1931 both sides filed motions for bills of particular, requesting that they be supplied with more detailed answers to specific questions before going to trial.

For her part, Ada King had to account for her long delay in filing a legal complaint. She explained that she and her children had been threatened and told that their monthly allowance would end if they initiated legal action. She had long tried to learn more about the trust, but Gardiner and his associates had deliberately concealed "the true facts." Her family had waited a long time to file charges, but it was "no fault of their own."[35]

Ada's lawyer again pressed Winne to disclose the name of the Kings' secret benefactor. But Winne refused, replying that "he is long since deceased and his address is unknown to this defendant." As for the financial records charting thirty years of cash disbursements, he professed to have nothing.[36]

"Why all this mystery?" asked Ada's lawyer. Surely, this mysterious "friend" must be "a person who made monthly payments to the plaintiffs, not merely out of charity and from his own funds, but in fulfillment of an equitable and legal obligation" held by Gardiner. Why wouldn't Winne disclose his name?[37]

But Winne would not reveal what he so clearly knew. As his attorney explained, they didn't "intend to expose another set of people to a suit of this character. Their names have been preserved anonymous for nearly thirty years; the statute has run against your clients, so far as we are concerned doubly, and the question of who has been doling out charity to your clients for thirty years is wholly irrelevant to the issues in this action, so long as the money doesn't come from our decedent or any of his children or representatives."[38]

"It is difficult to understand why you are so determined to make a secret of the identity of the person," replied the Kings' attorney.[39] He could draw only one conclusion. There was no mysterious benefactor. And if there was no charitable benefactor, there must be a trust fund. From evidence submitted by the defense, Schwartz now knew about the sale of King's art collection in 1903. And that, he thought, must be the source of the original trust.

THE JUDGE OVERSEEING THIS pretrial discovery phase of the case sided with the Kings and ordered Winne to reveal the source of Ada's monthly stipend. But Jessup continued to disparage "this negro-plaintiff, calling herself Ada King." The attorney counseled Winne not to disclose any names in order "not to unleash these plaintiffs on the trail of another set of defendants."[40] And he again asked the judge to dismiss the case. His clients would give Ada clear title to the Kalmia Avenue house; they had no stake in that. But her claims about a trust fund were preposterous. The plaintiff, "calling herself Ada King, claims to be the widow of one of the most distinguished and brilliant and nationally known geologists and men of letters of the nineteenth century. The executors of Mr. Gardiner are three well-known, honorable and highly reputable members of the New York community. It is inconceivable that they could have converted a trust fund of Eighty Thousand Dollars; or of any amount."[41]

Jessup then posed a rhetorical question: why would these "negro plaintiffs" continue to accept $600 a year for thirty years, if they knew they were entitled to a fund of $80,000, or the yearly interest of $4,000? "Making all allowance for the fact that they are poor and ignorant people," he said, "they are certainly chargeable with the knowledge and skill of seven successive legal advisors." Ada's race made her prone to dissembling and foolish behavior; his clients' whiteness and elite social status, on the other hand, seemed proof of their moral probity. Jessup suggested that the Kings ought not be allowed to make charges "of such a character against people of repute and integrity."[42]

The Kings' attorney thought claims about the credulity of human behavior worked both ways. In fact, a benevolent donor seemed less likely than a misappropriated trust fund. Why should his clients believe that their money came from someone "out of the rare goodness of his or their generous hearts?" *That* seemed "incredible." The defendants continued to "submit to the court the fantastic and mysterious explanation involving a non-resident, unknown benefactor, whose identity, they insist, must be kept a secret. Surely, the court will not permit this veil of mystery to remain drawn so that the plaintiffs' just demands will be forever obscured." The Kings could draw only one conclusion from the defendants' case: "A substantial trust fund rightfully belonging to these plaintiffs, is being concealed."[43]

Schwartz felt frustrated, and he complained to the judge about the defense's prejudicial language. They "repeatedly referred to the plaintiffs as 'negroes,' in a manner contemplated to prejudice these plaintiffs," Schwartz contended. "It is true that the plaintiff Ada King, widow of Clarence King, deceased, is a negress and that Clarence King was white. But when the proper time comes, it will be made apparent that the relationship which existed between the plaintiff Ada King and her deceased husband was one of deep love and devotion, notwithstanding that they were persons of different race."[44]

The *Chicago Defender* picked up news of the lawsuit. "Millionaire's 'Love Wife' Sues for Share in Huge Fortune: New York Aristocrats Shocked by Suit of Oil King's 'Maid.' " The paper set the tone for the coverage by the black press. This was the story of a secret alliance between "the scion of a wealthy white family and a Race woman."[45]

In early 1932 a judge denied yet another defense motion to dismiss the case and charged the defendants $10 in court costs.[46] He ruled that no statute of limitations applied to Ada's claims to the house she had occupied for thirty years, nor to her efforts to obtain the trust. "Since the payments are alleged to have been made with trust moneys...and in recognition, in part at least, of a trust obligation, the defense of a statute of limitations cannot be sustained."[47] The *Defender* reported that Mrs. Ada King, "the inamorata of the now dead scion of an old New York family," had at last achieved "a measure of legal recognition" in her long legal struggle.[48]

But the press had little grasp of the true facts of the case, and Wallace King refused to clarify anything for the reporters who knocked on the family's Kalmia Avenue door. Even the local black papers spun out a tale of untruths about the African American woman who allegedly met her white husband while he was prospecting for oil in Arkansas. When his search "became successful," reported the *Amsterdam News,* "he made a fortune and returned to New York with her and established her in the Flushing home which he purchased for that purpose."[49] No matter that the Arkansas oil boom occurred in the early 1920s, two decades after King's death, or that Ada moved into her Flushing home only after her husband died.[50] Accurate reporting took a backseat here to more sensational stories about interracial sex and the rags-to-riches tale of a poor black woman. Both the *Amsterdam News* and the *New York Age* mistakenly reported that Mrs. King still lived in the very house her husband had bought her at the start and that there she raised their two children (not their four or five).[51] An *Amsterdam News* reporter dredged up the old story about the younger Ada's involvement in the 1929 John Ancona murder case, implying that the current financial dispute might somehow trigger a new investigation of that unsolved crime. And he underscored the "startling similarity" between this case and the 1927 case of Letitia Brown, a black "former maid," and Carleton Curtis, "the millionaire scion of a socially prominent white family," which had provided such salacious gossip for the press a few years before.[52] The King trial promised a comparable story.

THE DEFENSE DEFIANTLY PREPARED for trial. They would not disclose the name of the benefactor who provided "for these negroes after Mr. King's death—the reason being to spare his aged mother the shock of learning of this liaison." They accused the plaintiffs of mounting little more than "a fishing expedition to discover another group of people" remarkable only for their kindness and generosity.[53] And they argued that the plaintiffs had waited too long to press their claims: "Assuming that these negro plaintiffs are ignorant and misguided, it is obvious that the Statute of Limitations has run against the assertion of a claim—thirty years after the death of a distinguished man whom, it is now claimed, had married, or agreed to marry, the negro plaintiff, Ada Todd, claiming to be Ada King."[54] They would not only raise doubts about Ada's matrimonial claims but in effect put her race on trial, questioning the integrity of any "negro" plaintiff.

When Ada arrived in Justice Bernard Shientag's Manhattan courtroom on Monday, November 20, 1933, she and her son Wallace braved the *Daily News* photographer who stood in wait for the "colored mammy."[55] The old phrase evoked a buffoonish image that belied the seriousness of the moment and predisposed readers to doubt Ada's credibility. In a picture taken as they exited the courtroom, Wallace looks anxious as he escorts his mother past the press. Formally dressed in his coat and tie and ever-present hat, he protectively steers his mother through the crowd. Ada, by contrast, appears bemused, with the slight hint of a smile on her face. She wears a long fur-trimmed coat and a dark, close-fitting hat; a "smart outfit," thought one reporter for the black press.[56] She looks younger than her seventy-some years.

The press outnumbered the principals in the courtroom of Justice Shientag, a former labor lawyer and state industrial commissioner, who had been elected to the New York Supreme Court in 1930.[57] The Kings' attorney, Herman Schwartz, now had help from Harris J. Griston, an Austrian-born lawyer and Shakespeare scholar.[58] And the defendants had new counsel altogether. The elderly Henry Jessup had handed the case over to George W. Martin of Emmett, Marvin & Martin, a law firm founded in 1805 that once counted Franklin Delano Roosevelt among its partners.[59]

The trial took an unexpected turn at the very start. In their opening statement, the defense again denied the existence of any trust fund. But finally, they revealed the source of Ada King's money.

Her secret benefactor was Clarence King's old friend John Hay.

WILLIAM WINNE, GARDINER'S ONETIME secretary, at last related what he knew. He testified that the nation's secretary of state had provided the money for Ada King's house. And the checks she subsequently received every month for more than thirty years all came from the extended Hay clan: first from Hay, then from his widow, then from their son-in-law Payne

Whitney ("one of the richest of Americans"), and finally, after his sudden death in 1927, from his widow, John Hay's daughter Helen Hay Whitney. Mrs. Whitney had suspended the monthly stipends when the Kings commenced their legal action, but she had secretly paid the taxes on the Kalmia Avenue house right up to the present day.[60]

The defense described James Gardiner as the link between the Kings and the Hay family. "Mr. Gardiner was a prominent and respected citizen of New York," they explained, "and undoubtedly regarded the situation that he discovered about a year after King's death as a terrible nightmare which he was obliged to see through to the finish because he was King's oldest friend." Since Gardiner himself was not wealthy, "he reported the matter to Mr. Hay."[61]

Winne explained—with a sometimes confused chronology—how the payments worked. After King's death, Hay transferred to Gardiner all of King's art collection and whatever else he held as collateral for unpaid loans, instructing Gardiner to sell it and establish a trust fund for the maintenance of King's mother, Mrs. Howland. Hay made additional payments into the fund so that Gardiner could also write Ada King monthly checks, and he provided Gardiner with $2,000 to purchase a home for Mrs. King. After John Hay's death in 1905, Gardiner stepped out of the arrangement and Clara Hay provided money for Ada's family directly to Winne. In the beginning, Winne himself gave Ada the money. Later, after various altercations, he funneled her monthly stipends through the Legal Aid Society. After Mrs. Howland died in 1911, John Hay's executors, his sons-in-law Payne Whitney and James Wadsworth, met with Gardiner to do an accounting of the trust fund, and Gardiner turned over to them the remaining assets. The two men agreed to continue on their own their family support of Ada King and her children. Wadsworth—later a U.S. senator and then a congressman from New York—knew about the arrangement. But Whitney, and then his widow, handled the payments.

It was stunning news. But as Winne admitted, neither he nor the other defendants had any receipts, account books, or bank records to back their claims.[62]

. . .

ADA'S ATTORNEYS—WHO HAD no paper trail either—seized the moment to offer an alternative version of events. They contended that because Clarence King sought "to placate his family and friends, and yet to protect his wife and children," he could not put in writing the covert agreement he made with James Gardiner. "His family and friends were Newport society people. His wife was a negress. The children were of half blood. If the miscegenation, or the intermarriage of black and white were disclosed to the public, particularly as matter of record, it would obviously prove embarrassing to his family and friends, who did not view the colored race and miscegenation in the same favorable light as Clarence King. Under these circumstances, it is, of course, obvious why it was impossible to have the trust appear in writing, without defeating the end which was sought."[63]

Ada's attorney explained that shortly before his death King asked Gardiner to accept his art collection in trust for Ada and the children. The existence of this art collection had been known to Ada's legal team for only a short while, but it seemed to account for the funds she had received all these years.

King and Gardiner "shared each other's confidence," argued Ada's attorney, Harris Griston. "They were like Damon and Pythias. He knew Clarence King's love for the colored people, and particularly of his marriage with Ada King and of their offspring. To what person other than this intimate friend, who was fully familiar with all of these circumstances, should Clarence King have turned, in order to make arrangements for his loved ones, and save his family and friends from embarrassment?" King's relatives would have been "aghast" at his secret marriage, and he could not afford to bring more people into his confidence while protecting Ada's privacy. "It is obvious, that the only person he could have turned to logically, to execute this trust, and the person who should have been willing to accept that trust, was his intimate and life long friend, Gardiner."[64]

King had a love for his wife and children "so sublime and so beautiful" it would be unthinkable for him not to provide for them after his death.[65] But to prove King's good intentions, the plaintiffs had no legal documents. And to prove his affection for his family, they had only a handful of old love letters, along with the recollections of Ada King and a single one of her friends.

The twenty or so Clarence King letters, "yellowed and crumbling with age," introduced into the trial came from two sources.[66] Ada brought some herself, including the one written toward the end of his life in which her husband told her to enroll the children at the Logan School in Toronto. The defense team introduced four letters into the trial. Ada King said that she had long ago provided six letters to Gardiner to prove her relationship to Clarence King and to document his statements about the trust. But instead of bringing these original letters into the courtroom, the defense brought carbon copies of typed transcripts. And instead of bringing six letters, they brought just four. These included the key letter in which Clarence King revealed to his wife his true name, and another in which he directed her to move to Toronto. Ada identified these as truncated copies of longer communications. She accused the defense of deleting the passages that referred to the trust.[67]

ASIDE FROM ADA HERSELF, the plaintiffs' attorneys called just one witness, Henrietta Williams, of Brooklyn; she was a "negro," the papers clarified.[68] Mrs. Williams testified that as a six-year-old she had attended the Todd wedding. "It was the first wedding I ever saw," she said, "and I guess I remembered it. They had a cake with white icing and candies—chocolates and all kind." Later, as a teenager, she moved into the Todd family house on North Prince Street to help Ada care for her children. "Mr. King was always at home when he wasn't traveling," she testified, "and when he was away, he always brought presents to all of us." Mrs. Williams recalled for the court one of the last conversations Clarence King had with his wife. "The very night he left for Arizona, we were all in the living room sitting around after dinner when he told her she mustn't worry because he had given Mr. Gardiner money to take care of her and the children all their lives."[69] After Mr. King's death, Mrs. Williams sometimes accompanied Ada on her visits to Gardiner's office.[70]

Clearly, Henrietta Williams was Ada King's confidante. The judge questioned her closely on her recollections of the wedding, dubious that she could retain such vivid childhood memories.[71] Ada's lawyer could account for this. "How many weddings does the court believe, Henrietta Williams attended, in which a socially prominent white man and a negress were married?"[72] The defense, too, tried to trip her up. They got her to identify a photograph of President Garfield as a portrait of Clarence King, a disingenuous ploy, since their bearded faces and receding hairlines gave the two men a passing resemblance.[73] Moreover, as Williams explained when asked to read something in court, she had broken her glasses a year ago and could not see well. The defense attorneys even insinuated that she had been paid to appear in court. They asked about her finances. She replied that she and her husband were out of work, but that she earned some money singing in choirs. Asked how she could afford to wear pearls and a fur coat, she responded that they came from friends who "know I have nothing and they have things, so they give to me. We get some money that way, too, and food."[74] Mrs. Williams understood that a poor black woman had to prove her respectability in court through her outward appearance. She thus took care to dress well. But her well-born interrogators turned that against her, implying that she was dissembling in every regard.

When Ada King took the stand and spoke in her quavering voice she gave her first and only public accounting of her life with Clarence King. Despite the many complexities of their relationship, her account was spare, focused on details that would prove their common-law marriage and establish the existence of the trust fund her husband created for her. She said that she met King while she worked as a nursemaid for a family in downtown Manhattan, explained that a Dr. Cook married them in 1888 at the home of a friend on West Twenty-fourth Street, and laughed as she tried to recall the birth dates of the five children born between 1889 and 1897. She claimed that she traveled with her husband to Washington, Boston, and

Newport, though that claim seems hard to square with any other surviving evidence. She recalled the address of her old house on Skillman Street in Brooklyn and described the large home in Flushing where she once lived with five servants, including a cook, a maid, and a laundress. She explained that before he left for Arizona "to die" her husband reassured her that he had left $80,000 for her with Mr. Gardiner. She kissed him good-bye, for the very last time, as he boarded the train west.

Ada King said she was in Toronto when her husband's physician in Phoenix contacted her to inform her of King's death. She returned to New York and placed her ad in the paper, trying to find Gardiner. "I wanted to find out how I was going to live," she testified. Gardiner's secretary, Howard Dutcher, responded to the ad. He brought her money, gave her advice, and took "half a dozen letters from Mr. King in which he mentioned the trust fund." She never saw them again. "They were all my evidence, all my principal letters." She had not gone to court before, she said, because "they threatened me."[75]

For all that Ada King related in her testimony, however, she left much unsaid. No one asked her (nor did she reveal) anything about her maiden name or place of birth, the details of her first meeting with Clarence King, or what she really knew or believed about her husband's identity. Nothing came out in the trial about Clarence King's false identity other than the fact that he used the name "James Todd." No one commented on his alleged career as a Pullman porter, a clerk, or a steelworker. No one speculated about how he deceived his friends and led a double life. No one alluded to his shifting racial identities. And nobody ever raised the possibility that Ada herself had been deceived. As she tried to establish herself as the common-law wife of a loving husband, it was scarcely in Ada King's best interests to confess that she, too, had been deluded by James Todd, the mysterious man from Baltimore (or was it the West Indies?). The defense wanted to portray her as a fool, and she would not play into their hands.

At the conclusion of the trial, Justice Shientag expressed his skepticism about the plaintiffs' case. "The most that plaintiff has shown is that she lived with Clarence King and either was married or was his mistress; that for a short time before Clarence King went West for his health he wrote her letters which indicated that he was pressed financially, but he always indicated he would take care of her." Such letters, in conjunction with the chattel mortgage due John Hay, seemed to explain the situation. "Those people interested in Clarence King, in keeping his memory from their point of view unsullied, made these payments voluntarily to this woman; that is all I can see in this case."[76] But the judge agreed to delay his final decision until a review of the trial memoranda submitted by the two sides.

Ada King's lawyers mounted one last argument. Ada King knew the trust existed and the defense had not proved otherwise. The defense had failed to provide "one word of proof that Gardiner ever denied the trust" and had concealed the people—Gardiner's executors and Mrs. Payne Whitney—who would know about it. As a mere secretary, Winne could not be expected to know of Gardiner's secret arrangements with King. "What more do the plaintiffs have to prove to establish a case, and entitle them to judgment?"[77]

But the defense saw it differently, arguing that the trial established only three things: an affectionate relationship between Clarence and Ada King; the 1903 auction of King's art collection; and the fact that from shortly after King's death until the commencement of this legal action, Gardiner and then Winne made periodic payments to Mrs. King, who lived in a house in Flushing still held in Gardiner's name. But that was all. They insisted the plaintiffs had not proved the existence of a trust.[78]

Justice Shientag issued his final ruling in January 1934. He conceded that Clarence King had "great affection and love" for Ada King and that they lived together as Mr. and Mrs. James Todd, though "Clarence King was white and Ada King was a negress." But he ruled in favor of the defendants. The burden of proof lay with Ada King, and she had never established the existence of a trust. Nonetheless, since the defendants had indicated their willingness to let her gain legal possession of her Kalmia Avenue house, he directed that the title be signed over to her.[79]

The *New York Times* simply noted that "Mrs. Ida King, elderly Negro," lost her case.[80] The *Herald Tribune* likewise identified her as a "Negro" in its account of the ruling, but at least it got her name straight.[81]

The legal endgame played out in a matter months. One of Ada's previous attorneys, Morris Bell, went to court to get the money he thought due him. Since Ada had recovered no cash, he could only ask for a lien on her newly acquired house. The court rejected his claim.[82] In the meantime, her current attorney (also unlikely to get any money) filed an appeal of Shientag's ruling. An appellate court denied the appeal in September 1934.[83] Ada King had lost, and the monthly stipends she had relied on for over thirty years were gone for good. As the *Amsterdam News* put it, "she fought the group of wealthy white society folk to regain the trust fund" and she lost.[84]

Ada King and her family dropped from the public eye, their high-stakes gamble lost, and settled back into life in the Kalmia Avenue house. For whatever it was worth, they had established their familial links to Clarence King. And they had won the title to their home. But without their monthly stipends, without an unknown benefactor to pay their property taxes, without any hope of gaining the money they had always believed to be theirs, life became more difficult. Wallace picked up occasional gigs as a musician, and the younger Ada worked as a store clerk. Despite their newly straitened circumstances, however, the Kings retained their middle-class aspirations. Family stories would recall as a point of pride that the younger Ada continued to wear matching shoes and hats, and that neither she nor her niece, Thelma, would leave the house without nylon stockings, the seams arranged just so.[85]

CLARENCE KING REENTERED THE public consciousness, not so much because of the trial as in spite of it. The revelations about his secret family made it difficult to speak of King with the undying adoration that had characterized talk of him during his lifetime. Francis P. Farquhar, the director of the Sierra Club from 1924 to 1951 and an ardent student of California mountaineering, issued a new edition of *Mountaineering in the Sierra Nevada* in 1935 with a preface in which he described King as bold and impetuous, charming and vigorous. In passing, he noted that King's last ten years "were not happy ones," dogged as he was by "financial troubles and disappointments."[86] Neither here, nor in the introduction to a new edition of "The Helmet of Mambrino" published in 1938, did Farquhar allude to King's marital life. But in his "Mambrino" essay, Farquhar tried to second-guess the tone of disappointment he sensed in the memorial essays that King's friends had published after his death. The decline of King's final years seemed attributable to something other than "mere financial catastrophe." He seemed, indeed, a tragic hero, "in the sense of Aristotle—'One highly renowned and prosperous, whose misfortune is brought upon him by some error of judgment or frailty.' "[87]

Other writers felt compelled to pay lip service to the story about King's family, even if they scarcely knew what to do with something that seemed vaguely scandalous and undeserving of explanation. John Hay's biographer Tyler Dennett, writing in 1933, asserted without documentation that once Hay learned of King's marriage, King's "name was never again mentioned over the 'Five of Hearts' teacups."[88] Bernard DeVoto's stirring 1943 book on westward expansion, *The Year of Decision: 1846*, sought to resurrect King as one of the unsung scientist-heroes of American expansionism, but the taint of the trial colored his characterization. "Clarence King survives as a man to be mentioned in appraisals of our civilization through his friendship with a literary person of considerably inferior intelligence, Henry Adams, and through a rumor of scandal that has been attached to him."[89] Likewise writing in the wake of the trial, the great western novelist and historian Wallace Stegner remarked in 1954 that King ended up "defeated and damned," with "a clandestine Negro wife and five unacknowledged children."[90]

In the early 1950s, two scholars turned their hands to full-length biographies of King. Harry Herbert Crosby, writing a dissertation on King at Stanford under Stegner's supervision, pulled together a vast amount of published information and gathered personal memories from the daughters of King's old friends James Hague and James Gardiner. Nearly everyone who knew King admired him without reservation, Crosby noted, largely because he embodied the ideals of the age. But ultimately, he judged King "the most lavishly overpraised man of his time." Crosby had access to the court documents but gave only passing attention to the "colored woman who took King's assumed name and became known as Ada Todd," misconstrued where the family lived, and never speculated about the nature of King's double life. He hypothesized that in Ada, King had finally found a woman as devoted to him as the black nurse of his childhood had been. Ada, he said, "lived for him alone."[91] Concerned mainly with King as a writer and a representative man of his age, however, Crosby paid scant attention to King's secret marriage.

Working at the same time as Crosby, Thurman Wilkins, a lecturer in English at Columbia, was turning his own dissertation into the masterful biography that remains indispensable to anyone interested in King. Wilkins proved an indefatigable researcher. He tracked down a miner who had once worked with King; interviewed the Hague daughters; gathered manuscripts, government documents, and newspaper accounts; pulled together King's school records, the correspondence of his friends, the family genealogical material. "King ought to have written his own life," Henry Adams told a friend shortly after King's death, "and the world has lost a book of capital interest in losing it; but the world may go hang, for all it can get now."[92] Adams's regret became Wilkins's challenge.

First published in 1958, Wilkins's book tracks King's early education, his career as an explorer, the development of his scientific theories, and the politics of the surveys. It untangles King's complicated financial affairs, explores his many friendships, and lays out a detailed chronology of King's sometimes frenetic comings and goings. But in a biography of more than four hundred pages, Wilkins devotes only about five pages to Ada and the life King shared with her over a period of thirteen years. He did not uncover King's racial masquerade.

He describes King's meeting "Ada Todd"—imagining that to be her maiden name—and says, "She had a pleasant face, a warm dark, brown complexion, with splendid white teeth and the black kinked hair of the Negro race." He speculates that "she was no better educated perhaps than a primitive Greek Venus" and notes that before the law her relationship with King had "no status beyond that of libertine and kept mistress."[93] He draws evidence from newspaper accounts of the trial and even quotes from the court documents, but he never mentions the trial itself. Instead, he leaves his readers to imagine that King provided for his family by leaving with Gardiner an art collection (worth more than his debts) that would help with their support. Wholly invested in his subject, like so many biographers, Wilkins found it difficult to explore those aspects of King's life that seemed to him less than admirable.

Wilkins's discretion struck reviewers as just about right. The biographer Louise Hall Tharp, praising Wilkins's "absorbing" book in the *New York Times*, remarked that the author handled the "difficult matter of King's marriage...with compassion and taste."[94]

But despite his skill as a researcher, Wilkins missed one critical source of information: Ada King. During all the years he traveled around the country, digging records out of archives and tracking King's every move, he lived and worked just a subway ride away from her. And in 1958, the year his book came out, Wilkins took a new job at Queens College, barely a mile from the Kalmia Avenue home where Ada had resided for more than half a century.[95] He never met her. Thirty years later, when he revised his King biography and added a brief epilogue about the court case of 1933, Wilkins could only speculate about Ada's last years. He explained that the King children grew to "undistinguished maturity," that Ada King "grew enormously fat," that the court case came about because of her "greedy" attack upon the "quiet well-wishers" who sought to protect her family. He described the outcome of the trial, noted that Ada received title to the Kalmia Avenue house, and concluded his 413-page book: "...and presumably she continued to live there until her death over four decades after that of Clarence King."[96] Indeed, she had.

Had he sought her out in the 1950s as he first prepared his manuscript for publication, Wilkins would have found Ada King still living in the home bought for her through the largesse of John Hay, both she and the house links to a long-ago world of nineteenth-century America. Her son Wallace lived there, too. Like Wilkins, he was a veteran of World War II (one of a select group of Americans to serve in both world wars), and as he had for a very long time, he worked as a jazz musician, picking up jobs where he could.[97] Increasingly, he looked like his father: short, a bit stout, with a receding hairline. Like that father he barely knew, he remained devoted to his mother. He spoke the "King's English" and wrote in a neat, flowing script, his niece recalled, though he had finished just three years of high school.[98] And he was a stickler for proper manners. At home, he enjoyed a good game of poker or casino, liked to do crossword puzzles, and entertained friends by reading tea leaves. Wallace's sister Ada still lived at home, too, with her second husband, a white war veteran named William "Bill" McDonald.[99] While Wallace helped with the grocery shopping and cooking, the younger Ada kept up with the housecleaning and sewing. Since Sidney King's death at Kings Park State Hospital in 1942, Ada Copeland Todd King had kept her remaining two children very close.[100]

Over the years, the house had begun to show its age. The front porch sagged; patches dotted the plaster walls; the kitchen and bathroom fixtures seemed "old fashioned."[101] But the family still got out and about: to movies and shows in Manhattan, to the local parks, occasionally on out-of-town trips to Toronto or Vermont. The Rockettes at Radio City Music Hall remained a favorite, and for a meal on the town they might head to Chinatown or to Schrafft's. The house itself remained a gathering place for friends and neighbors. Ada liked to keep a record of it all by asking visitors to sign a lamp shade in the front room.[102]

Thelma Burns, the elder Ada's granddaughter, visited frequently, but her half brother, Clarence, an employee of the *Daily News* who lived more fully in an all-white world, had grown estranged from the family who had taken him in so long ago. After a brief first marriage, Thelma married John Leroy Thomas, a white air force veteran, in 1952. The snapshots of their wedding reception at Ada King's house show a racially mixed gathering. The Kings' friends had always included blacks and whites, and after the war Ada had taken in a German Holocaust refugee who lived with the family for a time. John Thomas understood what sort of family he had married into, but he took Thelma to live with him in an all-white world. She returned often to Kalmia Avenue to visit her grandmother and the aunt and uncle who had helped to raise her. But Ada King never visited Thelma at her suburban Long Island house; Wallace, who could pass on the street as white, came occasionally. Thelma's husband hinted that her mixed racial heritage should remain a secret, and many of her closest friends and neighbors never learned of her dark-complected grandmother. Like her aunt and uncle, Thelma had been raised to believe that family matters were private. Anxious about what her own children might look like, Thelma adopted two white infants in the 1950s. Those two girls became Clarence King's only great-grandchildren. A mixed marriage, Thelma told her daughter Patricia, is hard on children and not fair to them. It was part cautionary message, part reflection on what she had seen and learned growing up in her grandmother's house.[103]

On Friday afternoons Thelma would often take her girls on the long bus ride from their home in Uniondale to Flushing to spend the weekend with her grandmother Ada. They would make the trip again on Mother's Day, on Easter, and during the Christmas holidays. Even as Ada King approached one hundred, and her daughter Ada and son Wallace neared seventy, family dinners remained formal affairs, with everyone gathering around a nicely set table. Wallace no longer had the piano he once kept in the house, but the family still had a large record collection, and they played classical music at dinnertime.

Ada King remained active until close to her hundredth birthday, taking special pride in her home-baked pies. As she grew older, she spent more time upstairs in her bedroom, settled into a big burgundy leather chair near the window, where she could keep an eye on neighborhood comings and goings. Her great-granddaughter recalls her uncanny knack for hearing visitors approach up the front walk; Ada would shout downstairs for them to come up and visit. In a home filled with newspapers and magazines, she followed the news in the *New York Times* and *Daily News*, and kept on top of current events with *Time, Life,* and *National Geographic.* Ada also watched the television news and listened to the radio. Conversation around the dinner table sometimes focused on the latest films but often turned to politics and the nascent civil rights movement: this family could recall Reconstruction, the emergence of Jim Crow laws, the dismantling of the segregated military, and the end of "separate but equal" schools. And now, on television, they could watch the beginnings of a mass movement for equal rights in the Deep South, where Ada had been born so long ago.

By 1963, Ada rarely left her home. And so perhaps she sat in her chair—it was like a throne, her great-granddaughter recalls—watching television on August 28, as nearly a quarter of a million Americans gathered on the Mall in Washington, D.C. "I have a dream," thundered the Reverend Martin Luther King Jr. From the steps of the Lincoln Memorial, he harkened back one hundred years to the signing of the Emancipation Proclamation: "This momentous decree came as a great beacon light of hope to millions of Negro slaves who had been seared in the flames of withering injustice."[104] Ada Copeland Todd King, not quite 103, lived in a house bought for her by a man who had watched Lincoln draft that declaration of freedom. And she was one of the very last ex-slaves still alive to hear King's stirring words.

We cannot know what she thought of that speech, what memories ran through her mind as she listened to King articulate his vision of a nation where race did not matter. "I have a dream that one day on the red hills of Georgia the sons of former slaves and the sons of former slaveowners will be able to sit down together at the table of brotherhood.... I have a dream that my four little children will one day live in a nation where they will not be judged by the color of their skin but by the content of their character."[105] In their own way, she and her husband, another King, had once dreamed of that future for their four children, too.

Ada King died on April 14, 1964, at the age of 103. She had outlived her husband by more than sixty-two years. Her grave lies near that of their daughter Grace in Flushing Cemetery, far from her husband's final resting place beside his mother in Newport.[106]

Ada's two surviving children, Ada and Wallace, lived together in the Kalmia Avenue house until their deaths, just months apart, in 1981.[107] Their niece, Thelma, now wore the wedding band that Clarence King had long ago given to his bride, Ada Copeland. And she inherited Wallace's scant collection of treasured papers: a copy of his military record, the deed to the house, and a handful of faded newspaper clippings from a trial a half century before, the yellowing evidence of his family's brief brush with notoriety, when his mother risked all to prove to the world that she was Mrs. Clarence King.

Secrets

Secrets and silences haunt this story: secrets crafted to protect and to hurt; silences created by neglect and with intent. And at the root of all these unspoken words lies the ever-potent mix in American life of race and love and sex and class.

Ada Copeland did not *choose* for her childhood to disappear into the dustbin of history. The institution of slavery itself rendered invisible her early years, assuring that she would have no legal records to establish her birth date or identify her parents, no surname as a young child, no old photographs with which to reconstruct the world of her youth. She likely took little with her when she moved to New York, and once there, she would have found it difficult to get news from the older, mostly illiterate, relatives she left behind. Unnourished and uncorroborated, Ada's own memories of girlhood might fade away.

Distance and time, coupled with the legacies of illiteracy and poverty, eventually snapped the family ties. Today, the extended clan of African American Copelands from the area around West Point, Georgia, gathers every summer for a "homecoming" in the Bethlehem Baptist Church in nearby Pine Mountain Valley. From across the state and from more distant parts of the country, Copelands return to worship and visit together in a church that sits on land deeded to two of their African American ancestors—Scott and Ishmael Copeland—by a local white family in 1883.[1] Despite their deep roots here, however, they know no stories about the young woman named

Ada who left home so long ago to move to New York. And in New York Ada kept alive no memory of this extended southern family for her own children and grandchildren.[2]

Clarence King, by contrast, deliberately crafted the silences that make it so hard to discern the story of his private life. From the moment he met Ada Copeland, he began weaving a skein of lies too intricate to untangle even decades after his death. Acting from a complicated mix of loyalty and self-interest, reckless desire and social conservatism, he deceived his mother, his closest friends, his colleagues, and all the people who knew him in his public role. He also deceived the woman he married. If he, too, lived a married life unimaginably far from the world of his childhood, it was because he chose to live that way. And if his children never met his mother, it was because King calculated how to keep them apart. Florence King Howland died never suspecting she had four mixed-race grandchildren.

King lied because he wanted to and he lied because he had to. He loved Ada Copeland, but to marry her in a public way—as the white man known as Clarence King—would have created a scandal, cost him his friends, devastated his mother, and destroyed his livelihood. It would also have created an aura of scandal around his wife and children. In some ways, his deceptions made their lives easier. James Todd could leave his wife and children at home and then, as Clarence King, find the work (or borrow the money) to give them a comfortable life. Unaware of the scope of his secrets, Ada could move confidently toward black middle-class respectability. King's secrets protected him, but they protected her as well. Nonetheless, those secrets proved hazardous. King's double life demanded an inventiveness, an attention to detail, and a watchfulness almost exhausting to contemplate: his breakdown in 1893 provides but a glimpse of the hidden costs.

King perhaps hoped that his deathbed confession would free him and his wife from the consequences of his deceit. But his secrets weighed heavily on his family long after his death. James Gardiner and John Hay conspired together to ensure that the world would never learn of Ada King and her children. For more than thirty years, Hay and his family paid hush money to prevent Ada from speaking about her relationship to their famous friend. And even the Hays' generosity became the stuff of secrets, as the attorneys who represented Gardiner's heirs and executors in the legal battles of the early 1930s fought to keep hidden the name of Ada's mysterious benefactors.

For the King children and grandchildren, however, Clarence King's true identity proved a less burdensome secret than Ada King's race. They always honored Ada as the family matriarch; until her death she remained the center of the extended family world. But outside the home, in a twentieth-century America still riven by racism, the King descendants struggled with the meanings of Ada's racial heritage. Her dark skin, more than her husband's duplicity, became their cross to bear. Ada might have been the parent who loved them and raised them and helped them grow up feeling safe and secure, but it was Clarence who bequeathed to them the light complexions that let them reach for the privileges of whiteness in a race-conscious nation. The two King daughters concealed Ada's race in order to marry as white women. And when Ada's granddaughter, Thelma, married a white man, she concealed her grandmother's race from her suburban neighbors. Fearful of the "human stain," worried that her own racial heritage might show itself in the face of her children, she adopted two white infants. Clarence and Ada King had five children, but Thelma was their only surviving grandchild by blood. When she adopted children rather than having her own, Clarence King's dream of creating his own mixed American race met its end.

AFTER KING'S CLANDESTINE MARRIAGE came to public light in 1933, his biographers steered away from it, and even his most recent ones have followed suit.[3] Concerned more with King as an exemplar of American science than with what his life might reveal about the nation's complicated politics of race and class, they have focused mainly on his professional career. They have asked questions about King's contributions to the history of science, his role in the westward expansion of the late nineteenth century, his place in an elite circle of American letters. Now, however, in a historical moment when Americans find it easier to talk about race, to query the ways in which it has shaped and defined so many American lives, King's private affairs—rather than his scientific accomplishments—seem the richer vein to mine. As we ask new questions of that private life, our research inevitably takes new turns. Only now, then, does King's own racial passing come to light. And only now can we begin to discern the ways in which King's extraordinary life might help us think about broader social issues in late-nineteenth-century America: the possibilities and limitations of self-fashioning, the simultaneous rigidity and porousness of racial definitions, the fluidity of urban life.

In the end, however, this is not just the story of a celebrated white explorer who passed across the color line but also a tale about his wife. Ada Copeland Todd King might seem the chief victim of King's deceptions and of all the secrets that ensued. But she refused to play the victim. With long and steady persistence, she brought her marriage to public attention and left behind the evidence that lets us now move beyond the old questions about King's professional life to pose a new set of queries about the larger meanings of his private actions. In that New York courtroom Ada King offered up her hints, giving brief accounts of her wedding, her children, her family homes, and her long search for legal justice. And there, she set before the world the fading love letters her husband had sent to her so many decades before. By the time Ada steps, however briefly, into the public eye, she has been widowed for more than three decades. We glimpse her as a woman in her seventies, a practical woman working through the legal system to assert her rightful name, give her children their true familial identity, and claim the trust fund she believed to be hers. She had scant time for sentiment. She expressed no bitterness toward the man who deceived her by presenting himself as a Pullman porter and who, even on his deathbed, took no legal steps to protect her and her children. She simply sought to dispel the tangle of secrets that had shaped and constricted her family life since the day she married the man called James Todd.

Ada King's life might have begun in obscurity, in the rural cotton country of west Georgia, but in the court records and newspaper accounts of her

1933 trial she lives more vividly than her once well-known husband. Here, the trajectories of their separate lives cross, and Ada King becomes a figure more easily understood than the husband glimpsed only through memories handed down from his devoted friends. Three decades of financial support had hinged on her silence, but she would be silent no more.

THE STORY OF CLARENCE AND ADA KING is about love and longing that transcend the historical bounds of time and place. It is a story about the struggle between desire and duty, about the ways in which two people can rise above social expectations, about the ways in which both love and friendship can compel one to suspend disbelief or take crazy risks. But it is also a peculiarly American story that could take root only in a society where one's racial identity determined one's legal rights and social opportunities. At every turn it exposes the deep fissures of race and class that cut through the landscape of American life, cracks as deep and enduring as the geological features that the explorer Clarence King once mapped on his treks across the continent—rifts that are, in the end, even harder to explain.

Acknowledgments

THE STORY OF CLARENCE KING AND ADA COPELAND PIQUED MY curiosity many years ago when I first stumbled upon the passing reference in Thurman Wilkins's biography of King. How could a prominent figure like King lead a double life for thirteen years without ever being detected? For years, I encouraged my students to investigate the story, but no one pursued it. It haunted me. In our own age, the fleeting indiscretions of public figures attract an almost microscopic scrutiny. What was there about the late-nineteenth-century world that allowed King to pull off his secret life? I logged on to the recently digitized census records to see whether I might be able to find any trace of King's secret family. Within moments, I found the 1900 census records that described King, living under his pseudonym of "James Todd," as a black man. The possibility that King might have engaged in racial passing had never occurred to me. Nor, I think, to anyone else. I decided to write this book.

I began this book during a sabbatical year in 2004–5 as the Frederick W. Beinecke Senior Fellow in Western Americana at Yale University's Beinecke Rare Book and Manuscript Library. There could be no better place to work, and I am particularly grateful to George Miles, the library's curator of Western Americana, for his longtime friendship and support. My gratitude extends to the entire Beinecke staff, especially Frank Turner and Una Belau. The Beinecke Fellowship also gave me a connection at Yale to the Howard R. Lamar Center for the Study of Frontiers and Borders, where

Johnny Faragher, Jay Gitlin, and Edith Rotkopf served as my hosts, and I engaged in many useful conversations about this work with Lamar Center fellow Barbara Berglund. At Yale I also benefited from conversations with Jean-Christophe Agnew, Glenda Gilmore, Howard Lamar, Joanne Meyerowitz, David Musto, and Laura Wexler.

A research grant from the Gilder Lehrman Institute of American History helped jump-start my research in New York City archives, and a visiting fellow's connection to the Gilder Lehrman Center for the Study of Slavery, Resistance, and Abolition at Yale helped facilitate my access to other resources. I thank the center's director, David Blight, for his helpful comments on several portions of this manuscript.

Everyone who teaches at Amherst College has reason to be grateful for the school's generous support of faculty scholarship, through the acquisition of library resources as well as through more direct financial support. I am deeply indebted to the wonderful staff of the Frost Library who patiently and generously responded to my many acquisition requests and research queries, and I extend particular thanks to Susan Edwards for her help with my many questions about the federal census. Amherst also offered me financial support in the form of a senior sabbatical fellowship and a grant from the Amherst College Faculty Research Award Program, as funded by the H. Axel Schupf '57 Fund for Intellectual Life.

A fellowship from the Rockefeller Foundation provided a glorious month at the foundation's Study and Conference Center in Bellagio, Italy, where I drafted the final portions of this manuscript. I am grateful to Pilar Palacia and Elena Ongania for facilitating my stay, and to all of my fellow residents—particularly Susan Crile, Mary Brown Bullock, Brad Leithauser, and Mary Jo Salter—for their stimulating thoughts about my project.

I have also benefited from the comments of colleagues who offered feedback on earlier presentations of this work at the Gilder Lehrman Center brown-bag lunch series and the Lamar Center lecture program at Yale, the American History Workshop at New York University, and the City Seminar program at Columbia University, where Ken Cobb offered particularly useful suggestions. Colleagues also offered helpful advice in an Amherst College faculty work-in-progress seminar, and there I thank Martha Umphrey, Marisa Parham, and Rhonda Cobham-Sander. To my fellow seminar participants Hilary Moss, Karen Sánchez-Eppler, and Martha Saxton, each of whom read and offered comments on additional parts of this manuscript, I extend particular thanks for their friendship and advice. Several others have read and commented on portions of this book, and for their generosity and thought-provoking questions I extend thanks to Carol Clark, Sage Sohier, Jim Grossman, and Karen Merrill. Along the way, I also benefited from exchanges with other colleagues at Amherst and elsewhere, including Marcy Sacks, Laura Lovett, Margaret Hunt, Bill Taubman, Kim Townsend, Rich Halgin, Nancy McWilliams, Clyde Milner, Carol O'Connor, Natalie Dykstra, James Gregory Moore, and Eric Paddock.

Ann Fabian, Maria Montoya, and Virginia Scharff—wonderful friends and smart colleagues all—more than once helped me think through many of the pieces of this story, and I am grateful for their generous readings. A few brave souls actually tackled this entire manuscript and provided extensive feedback that much improved the book. Clifford M. Nelson, of the United States Geological Survey, patiently read my entire draft, gently setting me straight on matters relating to King's professional career. Hugh Hawkins, Dan Koffsky, Daniel Giat, and Martha Hodes also read the entire manuscript, and each took time to give me a careful critique of the work. My readers have all served as reminders that writing is not really the solitary task it so often seems. I have felt buoyed by my team in countless ways.

Several students provided me with useful research assistance. Caitlin Crowell offered valuable help at Yale, and at Amherst I received assistance from Katie Hudson, Mirza Ali Khan, and especially Mahesha Subbaraman. For additional research help, I am grateful to Adam Sandweiss Horowitz, Isabelle Smeall, James L. Gehrlich, Shawn Alexander, Alan Swedlund, Lewis Baldwin, Ed Townsley, Rodger Andrew, Neilson Abeel, Judith Schiff, Peter Blodgett, Ken Thomas, and Randall Burkett. A special word of thanks goes to Kaye Lanning Minchew and Forrest Clark Johnson III of the Troup County Archives in La Grange, Georgia, for assisting me on a research trip and responding to many subsequent queries.

My Santa Fe friends have offered moral support, useful feedback, and occasional lodging as I've worked on this project, and I send my thanks to David Margolis, Jeannie Moss, Charlene Cerny, Joe Chipman, Carol Mothner, Daniel Morper, Joan Maynard, and Jerry Richardson. A special word of gratitude goes to David Anderson and Phoebe Girard, who provided me with a wonderful writing hideaway as I completed this book.

My literary agent, Wendy Strothman, has been a good friend and supportive reader since first we met, and I am grateful to her and her associate, Dan O'Connell, for their ongoing help. At The Penguin Press, I received valuable editorial advice from Emily Loose and Scott Moyers, and give special thanks to my editor, Vanessa Mobley, and her assistant, Nicole Hughes, who helped shape this manuscript for publication.

Fortunate, indeed, is the historian lucky enough to find anyone else equally excited about hunting down the elusive clue. Josh Garrett-Davis, my former student at Amherst College, caught the bug early on and quickly proved an invaluable partner in this project, helping me trace the King family's movements across the changing landscape of Brooklyn and Queens. While Josh helped me in New York, Lea Dowd and her granddaughter Sarah welcomed me into their Georgia home and became my guides to the landscape of Ada Copeland's childhood. I thank Lea, too, for taking me with her to a Copeland family homecoming in the summer of 2004; it was a memorable experience for me, and I am grateful to the assembled family members who so patiently indulged this interloper's requests for stories.

When I began this project, I never suspected I would meet someone who had known Ada Copeland Todd King; I had not yet discovered that she lived to be 103. But then I found her great-granddaughter, Patricia Chacon. Patty has a trove of valuable family memories, and a keen sense of which might prove most useful to a writer. She and her husband, Edgar, opened up their home to me, and Patty generously shared with me her stories and family snapshots. I am deeply grateful to her for her trust and support, and for her willingness to share her ancestors with a curious outsider like myself.

In the end, of course, this is a book about a family. So I offer thanks to my children, Adam and Sarah, constant reminders of why family matters. And I dedicate this book to my parents, Joy and Jerry Sandweiss, who first showed me the value and power of familial love.

Martha A. Sandweiss
Pelham, Massachusetts
May 2008

Notes

PROLOGUE: AN INVENTED LIFE

1. On the weather, see "The Weather," *New York Times*, June 5, 1900, 1, and June 6, 3. For Edward V. Brown and his work on North Prince Street, see the Twelfth Census of the United States, New York, Queens, SD 2, ED 665, sheet 4, http://content.ancestrylibrary .com/Browse/view.aspx?dbid=7602&path=New+York.Queens.Queens+Ward+3.665.8&fn=Ad a&ln=Todd&st=r&pid=56465284&rc=&zp=50 (accessed July 20, 2007). On the racial break-down of Queens and Brooklyn, see *Census Reports*, vol. 1, *Twelfth Census of the United States, Taken in the Year 1900: Population, Part 1* (Washington, DC: United States Census Office, 1901), 631; for the percentage of foreign-born residents, see p. 669.

2. John Hay, quoted in Henry Adams, *The Education of Henry Adams* (c. 1907; repr., Sentry edition, Boston: Houghton Mifflin, 1961), 416; all subsequent citations are to the Sentry edition.

3. Adams, *Education*, 313.

4. Defendant's Exhibit C, Plaintiff's Trial Memorandum, *Ada King et al. v. George Foster Peabody et al.* (file no. 26821-1931; Records of the Supreme Court of the State of New York, New York County Clerk's Office), 171 (hereafter *King v. Peabody et al.*). See also below, pages 235–37.

CHAPTER I: BECOMING CLARENCE KING

1. William Dean Howells, "Meetings with Clarence King," in *Clarence King Memoirs: The Helmet of Mambrino*, comp. James D. Hague (New York and London: Published for the King Memorial Committee of the Century Association by G. P. Putnam's Sons, 1904), 148.

2. Adams, *Education*, 313.

3. Ibid., 312.

4. William Crary Brownell, "King at the Century," in Hague, *Memoirs*, 215–16.

5. Clarence King (CK) to James T. Gardiner (JTG), 15 Feb. 1873, Gardiner Collection, New York State Library.

6. Brownell, "King at the Century," in Hague, *Memoirs*, 219.

7. Edgar Beecher Bronson, *Reminiscences of a Ranchman* (Chicago: A. C. McClurg, 1910), 327.

8. Edmund Clarence Stedman, "King—'The Frolic and the Gentle,'" in Hague, *Memoirs*, 201.

9. Howells, "Meetings with Clarence King," in Hague, *Memoirs*, 142.

10. Stedman, "Frolic," in Hague, *Memoirs*, 209.

11. Brownell, "King at the Century," in Hague, *Memoirs*, 218.

12. Edward Cary, "King's 'Mountaineering,'" in Hague, *Memoirs*, 235.

13. Brownell, "King at the Century," in Hague, *Memoirs*, 219.

14. John Hay, "Clarence King," in Hague, *Memoirs*, 125–26.

15. Brownell, "King at the Century," in Hague, *Memoirs*, 221.

16. Ibid., 223.

17. Edward Cary, "Century Necrological Note," in Hague, *Memoirs*, 236.

18. On King's paternal ancestors, see Samuel Franklin Emmons, "Clarence King—Geologist," in Hague, *Memoirs*, 255–58; Thurman Wilkins, *Clarence King: A Biography*, rev. and enlarged ed., with the help of Caroline Lawson Hinkley (Albuquerque: University of New Mexico Press, 1988), 6–14; Jacques M. Downs, *The Golden Ghetto: The American Commercial Community at Canton and the Shaping of American China Policy, 1784–1844* (Bethlehem, PA: Lehigh University Press, 1997), 198–209, 369. See also Samuel Franklin Emmons, "Clarence King—Memoranda," box 35, S. F. Emmons Papers, Manuscript Division (hereafter Ms. Div.), Library of Congress (hereafter LC); and Rufus King, "Pedigree of King, of Lynn, Essex County, Mass.: 1602–1891" [printed genealogical chart], King Papers, Henry E. Huntington Library, San Marino, CA (hereafter HEH). The Wilkins biography remains the best source for the details of King's youth and professional life, and I am indebted to it throughout.

19. On Samuel's breakdown, see Downs, *Golden Ghetto*, 199. See also Wilkins, *King*, 9.

20. In "Senate of the United States. February 19, 1839. Submitted by Mr. Robbins... Senate Committee of the Joint Committee on the Smithsonian Institution," 25th Cong., 3rd sess., S. Doc. 234, serial set 340, session 3; Marlana Portolano, "Increase and Diffusion of Knowledge: Ethos of Science and Education in the Smithsonian's Inception," *Rhetoric Review* 18, no. 1 (Autumn 1999): 65–81. Although the Smithsonian Institution ultimately emphasized museum exhibition over conventional instruction or pure research, Robbins helped shape its broader educational mission.

21. See Emmons, "Clarence King—Memoranda," S. F. Emmons Papers, LC; Wilkins, *King*, 8–13; Emmons, "Clarence King—Geologist," in Hague, *Memoirs*, 258–59. Sophia Little's abolitionist activities and involvement with the Rhode Island Anti-Slavery Society can be traced through accounts in the *North Star* and *Frederick Douglass' Paper* during the years 1848–52. Julie Roy Jeffrey makes passing mention of Little's views on the antislavery movement and religion in *The Great Silent Army of Abolitionism: Ordinary Women in the Antislavery Movement* (Chapel Hill: University of North Carolina Press, 1998), 145–54. Little's own books include *The Birth, Last Days, and Resurrection of Jesus. Three Poems* (1841), *Thrice through the Furnace: A Tale of the Times of the Iron Hoof* (1852), *The Reveille, or, Our Music at Dawn* (1854), and *Pentecost* (1869). Emmons alludes to King's "rapid diction" in "Clarence King—Memoranda," [51], S. F. Emmons Papers, LC.

22. Wilkins, *King*, 9; Florence King Howland (FKH) to S. F. Emmons, 24 Feb. 1902, box 13, S. F. Emmons Papers, Ms. Div., LC.

23. James D. Hague, "Memorabilia," in Hague, *Memoirs*, 406.

24. Bronson, *Reminiscences*, 333.

25. FKH to S. F. Emmons, 17 Jan. 1902, cited in Wilkins, *King*, 14. In later years, Florence King Howland recalled it as her twenty-second birthday.

26. Rossiter W. Raymond, "Biographical Notice," in Hague, *Memoirs*, 305.

27. Daniel C. Gilman, "Clarence King's School-days," in Hague, *Memoirs*, 297.

28. FKH to C. W. Howard, 17 Jan. 1902, cited in Wilkins, *King*, 18n.

29. Clarence King, "Camp Forester, West Brattleboro, VT. 1859," A2, "Notebooks, Private," King Papers, HEH.

30. A Chinese phrase book by George L. Shaw is in A2, King Papers, HEH; see also Bronson, *Reminiscences*, 332.

31. The Asian art was sold at auction with the books from King's estate. See the advertisement for the American Art Galleries, *New York Times*, Mar. 7, 1903, 5.

32. Bronson, *Reminiscences*, 333.

33. Ibid., 338.

34. [J. T. Gardiner], "Clarence King's Boyhood," 2, box 2, A3, King Papers, HEH. This typescript reminiscence appears to be a joint production of King's friends James T. Gardiner, R. W. Raymond, James D. Hague, and S. F. Emmons. Although the authorship of different sections is not

always clear, Gardiner's contributions are obvious, as he was the only one of the authors to have known King as a youth. See R. W. Raymond to James D. Hague, 17 Jan. 1902, 11 Feb. 1902, and 19 Feb. 1902; James D. Hague to R. W. Raymond, 19 Feb. 1902, box 2, A3, King Papers, HEH. Thanks to Peter Blodgett, H. Russell Smith Foundation Curator of Western Historical Manuscripts, Huntington Library, for his assistance in sorting out the attribution of the typescripts.

35. Emmons, "Clarence King—Geologist," in Hague, *Memoirs*, 258–59.

36. Wilkins, *King*, 15–17.

37. See the entry for Clarence and Florence King in 1850 U.S. Federal Census, Town of Pomfret, Windham County, CT, sheet 380, http://content.ancestrylibrary.com/Browse/view.aspx?dbid= 8054&path=Connecticut.Windham.Pomfret.9&fn=Wm%20Florence&ln=King&st=r&pid= 18384080&rc=&zp=50 (accessed Jan. 8, 2006).

38. FKH to S. F. Emmons, 24 Feb. 1902, box 13, S. F. Emmons Papers, LC.

39. Bronson, *Reminiscences*, 338.

40. Emmons, "Clarence King—Memoranda," [52], S. F. Emmons Papers, LC. The "climate" in Boston proved against them, Emmons wrote.

41. "Sophia Louisa Little," in *Appleton's Cyclopaedia of American Biography*, vol. 3 (New York: D. Appleton, 1887).

42. Wilkins, *King*, 17–19.

43. [JTG], "Clarence King's Boyhood," 1–2, King Papers, HEH.

44. Gilman, "Clarence King's School-days," in Hague, *Memoirs*, 297.

45. Wilkins, *King*, 20–23.

46. As a boy, Gardiner spelled his name without an *i*. He returned to the traditional family spelling of the name later, and for consistency's sake, I've used the later spelling throughout.

47. Letter reprinted in *A Memorial of Lt. Daniel Perkins Dewey, of the Twenty-Fifth Regiment Connecticut Volunteers* (Hartford: Press of Case, Lockwood, 1864), 25.

48. CK to JTG, Sat. eve., [n.d. 1860], HM 27814, HEH.

49. Wilkins, *King*, 25; "Message of the President of the United States, communicating, in compliance with a resolution of the Senate, the instructions to, and dispatches from, the late and present ministers in China," 36th Cong., 1st sess., S. Ex. Doc. 30 (vol. 1032), 114.

50. Wilkins, *King*, 26.

51. CK to JTG, 2 Oct. 1859, HM 27809, HEH.

52. CK to John Hay (JH) [n.d. 1893], John Hay Collection, Brown University Library.

53. Cited in Raymond, "Biographical Notice," in Hague, *Memoirs*, 307.

54. King, "Camp Forester, West Brattleboro, VT. 1859," King Papers, HEH.

55. [JTG], "Clarence King's Boyhood," 1, King Papers, HEH.

56. James Gregory Moore, *King of the 40th Parallel: Discovery in the American West* (Stanford, CA: Stanford University Press, 2006), 10–11.

57. John Leander Bishop et al., *A History of American Manufactures from 1608 to 1860* (Philadelphia: Edward Young, 1868), 3:190; Henry R. Stiles, *A History of the City of Brooklyn*, vol. 3, chap. 12 (Brooklyn, NY: published by subscription, 1867–70), http://search .ancestrylibrary.com/cgi-bin/sse.dll?db=HistBrooklyn123&so=2&rank=0&tips=0&gsfn =george&gsln=howland&sx=&gs1co=2%2cUSA&gs1pl=35%2cNew+York&year=1860& yearend=&sbo=0&sbor=&wp=4%3b_80000002%3b_80000003&prox=1&db=&ti=5542 &ti.si=0&gss=angs-b&o_iid=21416&o_lid=21416&o_it=21416&srchb=p (accessed Aug. 10, 2007).

58. Wilkins, *King*, 25–26; "The Arctic. Additional Particulars," *New York Times*, Oct. 13, 1854, 1.

59. FKH to JH, 11 June [1882], cited in Wilkins, *King*, 29.

60. Wilkins, *King*, 29. On John Snowden Howland's age, see his entry in the 1870 U.S. Federal Census, Third Ward, City of Newport, County of Newport, RI, p. 30, http://content.ancestry library.com/Browse/view.aspx?dbid=7163&path=Rhode+Island.Newport.Newport+Ward+3.30 &fn=Florence%20K&ln=Howland&st=r&pid=9785013&rc=&zp=50 (accessed Jan. 10, 2007).

61. Clarence King, "Miscellaneous Notes, 1860," box A2, King Papers, HEH; CK to JTG, 26 Apr. 1860, HM 27812, HEH; Nancy K. Anderson, Ross Merrill, and Michael Skalka, "Albert Bierstadt: A Letter from New York," *Archives of American Art Journal* 40, no. 3/4 (2000): 28–31.

62. CK to JTG, 4 Jan. 1860, HM 27810, HEH.

63. King documents his churchgoing activities in his small pocket notebook "Miscellaneous Notes, 1860," King Papers, HEH.

64. CK to JTG, 20 May 1860, HM 27813, HEH.

65. CK to JTG, Sat. eve., [n.d. 1860], HEH.

66. CK to JTG, 25 Mar. [1860], HM 27811, HEH.

67. [JTG], "Clarence King's Boyhood," 1, King Papers, HEH; Raymond, "Biographical Notice," in Hague, *Memoirs,* 308.

68. See the entries for Sophia Little, Florence King, and Clarence R. King in 1850 U.S. Federal Census, City of Newport, County of Newport, RI, sheet 355, http://content .ancestrylibrary.com/iexec/?htx=View&r=5542&dbid=8054&iid=RIM432_842-0128&fn= Sophia&ln=Little&st=r&ssrc=&pid=12395818 (accessed Nov. 18, 2006).

69. CK to JH, [Mar.?] 1888, Hay Collection, Brown.

70. Wilkins, *King,* 21.

71. "Thirteenth Annual Meeting of the Rhode Island Anti-Slavery Society," *North Star,* Dec. 8, 1848; Frederick Douglass, "Letter from the Editor," *North Star,* Nov. 23, 1849; "Fourteenth Annual Anniversary of the Rhode Island Anti-Slavery Society," *North Star,* Nov. 30, 1849; Frederick Douglass, "Letter from the Editor," *Frederick Douglass' Paper,* Nov. 20, 1851; "Proceedings of the Rhode Island Anti-Slavery Society," *Frederick Douglass' Paper,* Nov. 27, 1851; Jeffrey, *Great Silent Army,* 147.

72. Douglass, "Letter from the Editor," *Frederick Douglass' Paper,* Nov. 20, 1851.

73. Sophia L. Little, "Purify the Sanctuary," *The Liberator,* Oct. 6, 1837, 162; "Poetry…from 'The Birth, Last Days, and Resurrection of Jesus,' " *The Liberator,* Jan. 21, 1842, 12; "The Branded Hand," *The Liberator,* Oct. 17, 1845, 168.

74. Sophia L. Little, *Thrice through the Furnace: A Tale of the Times of the Iron Hoof* (Pawtucket, RI: A. W. Pearce, 1852), 3.

75. Ibid.; "Literary Notices. 'Thrice through the Furnace. A Tale of the Times of the Iron Hoof,'" *Frederick Douglass' Paper,* July 16, 1852.

76. Little, *Thrice through the Furnace,* 121–22.

77. Gilman, "Clarence King's School-days," in Hague, *Memoirs,* 299.

78. A Graduate of '69 [Lyman H. Bagg], *Four Years at Yale* (New Haven, CT: Charles C. Chatfield, 1871), 39.

79. Russell H. Chittendon, *History of the Sheffield Scientific School of Yale University, 1846–1922* (New Haven, CT: Yale University Press, 1928), 1:74.

80. Gilman, "Clarence King's School-days," in Hague, *Memoirs,* 298–99; Chittendon, *History of the Sheffield Scientific School,* 1:81–127.

81. Chittendon, *History of the Sheffield Scientific School,* 1:82.

82. King comments on Marsh's youthful fossil discoveries in CK to JTG, 18 Mar. 1862, HM 27824, HEH.

83. CK to JTG, 10 Oct. 1861, HM 27821, HEH.

84. Clarence King, "Scientific notes, private" [notebook, c. 1863], A2, King Papers, HEH.

85. Hague, "Memorabilia," in Hague, *Memoirs,* 377–78.

86. CK to George F. Becker, Sunday, [Jan. 1894], box 2, George Perkins Merrill Collection, Ms. Div., LC. Thanks to Clifford M. Nelson of the USGS, for bringing this to my attention.

87. Chittendon, *History of the Sheffield Scientific School,* 1:76.

88. CK to JTG, 10 Oct. 1861, HEH.

89. Ibid., 18 Mar. 1862.

90. Ellsworth Eliot Jr., *Yale in the Civil War* (New Haven, CT: Yale University Press, 1932), 8, 13, 20,

28; Aaron Sachs, *The Humboldt Current: Nineteenth-Century Exploration and the Roots of American Environmentalism* (New York: Viking, 2006), 180–86.

91. Rufus King, "Pedigree of King," King Papers, HEH.

92. *Memorial of Lt. Daniel Perkins Dewey*, 28.

93. Moore, *King of the 40th Parallel*, 12.

94. CK to JTG, 28 July 1861, Gardiner Collection, NYSL.

95. CK to JTG, 18 Mar. 1862, HEH.

96. Wilkins, *King*, 38.

97. Ibid.

98. Declaration of Benjamin Baldwin, 11 Aug. 1862, Gardiner Collection, NYSL.

99. *Memorial of Lt. Daniel Perkins Dewey*, 32–33.

100. Thurman Wilkins made a concerted and unsuccessful effort to find King's name on Civil War enrollment lists. See Wilkins, *King*, 39n.

101. Rufus King, "Pedigree of King," King Papers, HEH. Although Rufus King claimed that William served with the famous Fifty-fourth Massachusetts Regiment, other sources suggest he served with Company C, Fourth Infantry Regiment, United States Colored Infantry. See William V. King, military record, http://search.ancestrylibrary.com/cgi-bin/sse.dll?indiv=1& rank=0&gsfn=william+v.&gsln=king&sx=&f9=&f14=&f6=&f10Day=&f10Month=&f10 Year=&gskw=&prox=1&f10=++&db=hdssoldiers&ti=5542&ti.si=0&gss=angs-d&fh=0& recid=713305&recoff=1+2+3 (accessed Jan. 6, 2007), and http://search.ancestrylibrary.com/ cgi-bin/sse.dll?indiv=1&rank=0&tips=0&gsfn=&gsln=king&sx=&f22=U.S.+Colored+ Troops&f5=Union&f20=4th+infantry&gskw=&prox=1&db=nps_civilwarsoldiers&ti= 5542&ti.si=0&gss=angs-d&fh=1&recid=3080700&recoff=3+14+15+16+17+43+56+61 &hovR=1 (accessed Aug. 10, 2007). See also Edward G. Longacre, *A Regiment of Slaves: The 4th United States Colored Infantry* (Mechanicsburg, PA: Stackpole Books, 2003), 86–87. Rufus King, when publishing his family genealogy in 1891, may simply have conflated other black regiments with the better-known Fifty-fourth Massachusetts. On William Vernon King's mother, Charlotte King, see Henry James, *A Small Boy and Others* (New York: Charles Scribner's Sons, 1913), 274–76, 388–95.

102. James, *A Small Boy*, 392.

103. On the mechanics of the 1863 draft, see "Final Report Made to the Secretary of War, by the Provost Marshal General, March 17, 1863 to March 17, 1866," in *Executive Documents Printed by the House of Representatives, During the First Session of the Thirty-Ninth Congress, 1865–66* (Washington, DC: GPO, 1866), 19–20. Reference courtesy of Robert Bonner.

104. Francis P. Farquhar, ed., "The Whitney Survey on Mount Shasta, 1862: A Letter from William H. Brewer to Professor Brush," *California Historical Society Quarterly* 7 (1928): 121–31.

105. Raymond, "Biographical Notice," in Hague, *Memoirs*, 315.

106. "His decision is fully as hard to unravel as mine," Gardiner wrote to his mother, with regard to King's career choice, October 26, 1862, cited in Wilkins, *King*, 41.

107. CK to George J. Brush, 30 Jan. 1863, cited in ibid.

108. Ibid., 42–43.

109. David H. Dickason, *The Daring Young Men: The Story of the American Pre-Raphaelites* (Bloomington: Indiana University Press, 1953), 75.

110. Moore, *King of the 40th Parallel*, 26.

111. Cited in Wilkins, *King*, 43; [JTG], "Clarence King's Boyhood," 2, King Papers, HEH.

112. King evidently mentioned *John Brent* to his friend Frank Emmons. The novel appeared after its author's death in the Civil War. Emmons, "Clarence King—Memoranda," S. F. Emmons Papers, LC.

113. *Memorial of Lt. Daniel Perkins Dewey*, 86–109.

114. Lieutenant Leander Waterman to Mrs. Dewey, ibid., 88.

115. Ibid., 23.

116. Clarence King, entry for Oct. 18, [1863], "Journal of Trip in Northern Sierra, Grass Valley, Northern Survey," D23, King Papers, HEH.

117. Clarence King, "Catastrophism and Evolution," *American Naturalist* 11 (Aug. 1877): 450.

118. William H. Brewer, quoted in Raymond, "Biographical Notice," 316.

119. J. T. Redman, "Reminiscences and Experiences on My Trip Across the Plains to California Sixty-One Years Ago When I Drove Four Mules to a Covered Wagon," typescript, 2, HM 20426, HEH.

120. David Dary, *The Oregon Trail: An American Saga* (2004; repr., New York: Oxford University Press, 2005), 289.

121. Cited in Moore, *King of the 40th Parallel*, 31, 39.

122. [JTG], "Clarence King's Boyhood," 2, King Papers, HEH.

123. Hague, "Memorabilia," in Hague, *Memoirs*, 378–81 (quote is on 380); Redman, "Reminiscences," 5.

124. Theodore Roosevelt, "Big Game Disappearing in the West," *Forum* (Aug. 1893): 768–69.

125. Redman, "Reminiscences," 5.

126. Ibid.

127. Moore, *King of the 40th Parallel*, 38–43.

128. Wilkins, *King*, 50; Moore, *King of the 40th Parallel*, 42–43.

129. JTG to his mother, Anne Terry Gardner, quoted in William H. Brewer, *Up and Down California in 1860–1864*, ed. Francis P. Farquhar (New Haven, CT: Yale University Press, 1930), 469n; Moore, *King of the 40th Parallel*, 68–69.

130. Quoted in William H. Goetzmann, *Exploration and Empire: The Explorer and the Scientist in the Winning of the American West* (New York: Vintage Books, 1972), 360.

131. Wilkins, *King*, 53; Charles W. Eliot cited in Wilkins, *King*, 53n.

132. Farquhar, "Introduction," in Brewer, *Up and Down California*, xviii–ix.

133. Brewer letter quoted in Raymond, "Biographical Notice," in Hague, *Memoirs*, 316.

134. Ibid., 317.

135. John Ruskin, *Modern Painters I*, 2nd ed. (London: George Allen, 1892), 265, 267.

136. Brewer letter quoted in Raymond, "Biographical Notice," in Hague, *Memoirs*, 318.

137. Clarence King, *Mountaineering in the Sierra Nevada*, ed. and with a preface by Francis P. Farquhar (1872; repr., Lincoln: University of Nebraska Press, 1997), 142. Unless otherwise noted, all subsequent references are to this edition.

138. Ibid., 193.

139. Brewer, *Up and Down California*, 525.

140. Brewer letter quoted in Raymond, "Biographical Notice," in Hague, *Memoirs*, 319. For an excellent discussion of King's interest in Tyndall and Ruskin, see Michael L. Smith, *Pacific Visions: California Scientists and the Environment, 1850–1915* (New Haven, CT: Yale University Press, 1987), 71–103.

141. Brewer letter quoted in Raymond, "Biographical Notice," in Hague, *Memoirs*, 321.

142. Goetzmann, *Exploration and Empire*, 372.

143. Clarence King, entry for Sept. 20, "Journal of Trip in Northern Sierra, Grass Valley, Northern Survey," D23, King Papers, HEH.

144. Ibid., entry for Oct. 19.

145. JTG to mother, 6 Jan. 1864, quoted in Moore, *King of the 40th Parallel*, 72.

146. King, "Journal of Trip in Northern Sierra," entry for Oct. 18, King Papers, HEH.

147. Goetzmann, *Exploration and Empire*, 373–74; Raymond, "Biographical Notice," in Hague, *Memoirs*, 327–29.

148. Moore, *King of the 40th Parallel*, 72–73.

149. JTG to his mother, 7 Apr. 1864, cited ibid., 76.

150. King, *Mountaineering*, 48.

151. Ibid., 60.

152. Ibid., 99.

153. Ibid., 71.

154. Clarence King, "The Ascent of Mount Tyndall," *Atlantic Monthly* 28 (July 1871): 369–84. King later adapted the piece for inclusion in *Mountaineering.*

155. King, *Mountaineering,* 74–75.

156. Ibid., 69–94.

157. Wilkins, *King,* 73.

158. King, *Mountaineering,* 95–111.

159. Edwin Tenney Brewster, *Life and Letters of Josiah Dwight Whitney* (Boston: Houghton Mifflin, 1909), 237–38, cited in Goetzmann, *Exploration and Empire,* 374.

160. Goetzmann, *Exploration and Empire,* 377.

161. King, *Mountaineering,* 164.

162. Ibid., 191.

163. CK to S. F. Emmons, 26 Aug. 1877, Clarence King Papers, American Philosophical Society (hereafter APS).

164. "George S. Howland," *Quarter Centenary Record of the Class of 1888: Sheffield Scientific School, Yale University,* comp. Percey F. Smith (New Haven, CT: Printed for the class, 1915), 114. Citation courtesy of Neilson Abeel.

165. Wilkins, *King,* 80; CK to William Henry Brewer, 25 July 1865, group 100, series 1, box 4, folder 100, William Henry Brewer Papers, Manuscripts and Archives, Sterling Library, Yale University; "Maritime Intelligence," *New York Times,* Nov. 2, 1865, citation courtesy of Patricia Chacon.

166. Raymond, "Biographical Notice," in Hague, *Memoirs,* 332.

167. Quoted in Wilkins, *King,* 85.

168. Gardiner letter included in Raymond, "Biographical Notice," in Hague, *Memoirs,* 335.

169. Wilkins, *King,* 89; Bishop et al., *History of American Manufactures,* 3:190.

170. CK to S. F. Emmons, 1 Apr. 1873, Clarence King Papers, APS.

171. Hague, "Memorabilia," in Hague, *Memoirs,* 382.

172. *Van Cott v. Prentice and Others,* 59 Sickels 45, 104 N.Y. 45, 10 N.E. 257 (Jan. 18, 1887); [JTG], "Clarence King's Boyhood," King Papers, HEH.

173. CK to Henry Adams, 25 Sept. 1889, cited in Wilkins, *King,* 89.

174. "Clare has paid me all that he owed." JTG to mother, 3 Nov. 1867, Gardiner Collection, NYSL.

175. Clarence King, "Preface," in *Mountaineering in the Sierra Nevada,* 9th ed. (Boston: Ticknor, [1874]), iv.

CHAPTER 2: KING OF THE WEST

1. W. W. Bailey, "Clarence King," *Hartford Courant,* Jan. 3, 1902, 14.

2. King's orders reproduced in Goetzmann, *Exploration and Empire,* 437.

3. Quoted in R. W. Raymond, "Biographical Notice of Clarence King," *Transactions of the American Institute of Mining Engineers* 33 (1902) (New York: Published by the Institute, 1903): 631.

4. S. F. Emmons, "Clarence King," *American Journal of Science* (March 1920): 224.

5. Raymond, "Biographical Notice," in Hague, *Memoirs,* 335.

6. [JTG], "Clarence King's Boyhood," 2, King Papers, HEH. Humphreys had directed the Office of Pacific Railroad Surveys in the 1850s.

7. Wilkins, *King,* 101–2. "Provided, That the same can be done out of existing appropriations," *U.S. Statutes at Large* 14 (1867): 457. Renewed by *U.S. Statutes at Large* 15 (1869): 318, which authorized the secretary of war to have prepared and published reports on the results of the Fortieth Parallel survey. Citations courtesy of Clifford M. Nelson.

8. Hague, "Memorabilia," in Hague, *Memoirs,* 385.

9. Goetzmann, *Exploration and Empire,* 433–35. For more on O'Sullivan, see Joel Snyder, *American Frontiers: The Photographs of Timothy O'Sullivan, 1867–1874* (Millerton, NY: Aperture, 1981);

Robin Kelsey, *Archive Style: Photographs & Illustrations for U.S. Surveys, 1850–1890* (Berkeley: University of California Press, 2007); Rick Dingus, *The Photographic Artifacts of Timothy O'Sullivan* (Albuquerque: University of New Mexico Press, 1982).

10. Wilkins, *King,* 103.

11. On the stability of King's staff versus the staff of the competing federal surveys of the period, see Clifford M. Nelson and Mary C. Rabbitt, "The Role of Clarence King in the Advancement of Geology in the Public Service, 1867–1881," in *Frontiers of Geological Exploration of Western North America,* ed. Alan E. Leviton et al. (San Francisco: American Association for the Advancement of Science, 1982), 31–32.

12. General background information on the so-called Great Surveys can be found in Goetzmann, *Exploration and Empire,* and Richard A. Bartlett, *Great Surveys of the American West* (Norman: University of Oklahoma Press, 1962). Bartlett revisited the history of the surveys in his "Scientific Exploration of the American West, 1865–1900," in *North American Exploration,* vol. 3, *A Continent Comprehended,* ed. John Logan Allen (Lincoln and London: University of Nebraska Press, 1997), 461–520.

13. See Nelson and Rabbitt, "The Role of Clarence King," in Leviton, *Frontiers of Geological Exploration*; Clifford M. Nelson, "Toward a Reliable Geologic Map of the United States, 1803–1893," in *Surveying the Record: North American Scientific Exploration to 1930,* ed. Edward C. Carter II (Philadelphia: Memoirs of the American Philosophical Society, 1999, vol. 231), 51–74.

14. JTG to mother, 2 Mar. 1867, Gardiner Collection, NYSL.

15. Wilkins, *King,* 104–5.

16. William Whitman Bailey, "To California with Clarence King" [memoir recounting 1867 trip], 23, HM 39965, HEH.

17. Charles Loring Brace, *The New West, or California in 1867–1868* (New York: G. P. Putnam, 1869), 14–15.

18. Ibid., 15–16.

19. Wilkins, *King,* 106–9.

20. Hague, "Memorabilia," in Hague, *Memoirs,* 391.

21. Raymond, "Biographical Notice," in Hague, *Memoirs,* 345–46.

22. George C. Parke to CK, 31 Aug. 1868, reproduced in Moore, *King of the 40th Parallel,* 335.

23. Hague, "Memorabilia," in Hague, *Memoirs,* 392.

24. Raymond, "Biographical Notice," in Hague, *Memoirs,* 346.

25. Hague, "Memorabilia," in Hague, *Memoirs,* 392.

26. See the entries for James Marryatt, 1880 U.S. Federal Census, City of San Francisco, County of San Francisco, SD 1, ED 14, 54, http://content.ancestrylibrary.com/iexec/?htx=View&r=5542&dbid=6742&iid=CAT9_73-0098&fn=James&ln=Marryatt&st=r&ssrc=&pid=43567686, and James Marryatt, 1880 U.S. Federal Census, Town of Eureka, County of Eureka, Nevada, SD 81, ED 16, 66, http://content.ancestrylibrary.com/iexec/default.aspx?htx=View&r=5542&dbid=6742&iid=NVT9_758-0417&fn=Jas.&ln=Marryatt&st=r&ssrc=&pid=43459628 (accessed Jan. 10, 2007).

27. See the entry for Florence Marryatt, 1880 U.S. Federal Census, City of San Francisco, County of San Francisco, SD 1, ED 14, 54, http://content.ancestrylibrary.com/iexec/?htx=View&r=5542&dbid=6742&iid=CAT9_73-0098&fn=Florence&ln=Marryatt&st=r&ssrc=&pid=14356364 (accessed Jan. 10, 2007).

28. Clarence King, *First Annual Report of the United States Geological Survey* (Washington, DC, 1880), 4, cited in Wilkins, *King,* 117–18.

29. "Clarence King's Boyhood," 8–9, King Papers, HEH. This is Emmons's piece of the manuscript.

30. CK to James D. Hague in J. D. Hague, "Clarence King's Notes for My Biographical Sketch of Him…," box 1, A1, King Papers, HEH.

31. JTG to mother, 26 Dec. 1867, Gardiner Collection, NYSL.

32. On the intense male friendships so characteristic of mid-nineteenth-century American life, see E. Anthony Rotundo, *American Manhood: Transformation in Masculinity from the Revolution to the Modern Era* (New York: Basic Books, 1993), esp. chap. 4.

33. JTG to mother, 26 Dec. 1867, Gardiner Collection, NYSL.

34. Mark Twain, "Letters from Washington," no. 9, *Daily Territorial Enterprise*, Mar. 7, 1868. On Twain's time in Nevada, see Effie Mona Mack, *Mark Twain in Nevada* (New York: Charles Scribner's Sons, 1947).

35. "Lively," *Daily Territorial Enterprise*, May 7, 1868, 3.

36. The Virginia City *Daily Territorial Enterprise* documents the community's rich social life.

37. S. F. Emmons, Diary, 1 Jan. 1868, box 1, S. F. Emmons Papers, LC; William Whitman Bailey, "Diary of a Journey in California and Nevada (1867–68)," 2 Jan. 1868, New York Botanical Garden Library.

38. Bailey, "Diary of a Journey," 3 Dec. 1867, New York Botanical Garden Library.

39. JTG to mother, 26 Dec. 1867, Gardiner Collection, NYSL.

40. Wilkins, *King,* 120.

41. See the entries for January and February in Emmons, Diary 1868, box 1, S. F. Emmons Papers, LC.

42. Emmons, Diary, 13 Apr. 1868, box 1, S. F. Emmons Papers, LC.

43. CK to William Brewer, 10 June 1868, group 100, series 1, box 4, folder 100, Brewer Papers, Yale.

44. Ibid., 27 Aug. 1868.

45. "Married," Virginia City *Daily Territorial Enterprise,* Sept. 8, 1868, 2. J. W. Rogers, in whose home the wedding occurred, is identified as Josephine's father in 1860 U.S. Federal Census, Township of Downieville, Sierra County, CA, 94. The 1870 census identifies J. W. Rogers as a mining engineer in Grass Valley, CA.

46. Emmons, Diary, 7 Sept. 1868, box 1, S. F. Emmons Papers, LC.

47. Ibid., 4 Dec. 1868.

48. Clarence King, "Misc. Notes 1869" [leather-bound daily diary], D17, King Papers, HEH.

49. Ibid., entry for May 24.

50. JTG to mother, 16 July 1869, Gardiner Collection, NYSL, cited in Moore, *King of the 40th Parallel,* 192. Harry Herbert Crosby asserts without documentation in "So Deep a Trail: A Biography of Clarence King" (Ph.D. diss., Stanford University, 1953, 146) that King brought Dean back to Newport in the fall of 1869 to meet his mother. As Gardiner's letter suggests, however, any meeting happened well before that. No record of it survives.

51. Hague, "Memorabilia," in Hague, *Memoirs,* 413. I've been unable to find any trace of Ellen Dean in the census records or to trace her subsequent fate.

52. FKH to JTG, 2 Apr. 1869, Gardiner Collection, NYSL.

53. See the entry for Florence K. Howland, 1870 U.S. Federal Census, Third Ward, City of Newport, Newport County, RI, 30–31.

54. FKH to JTG, 2 Apr. 1869, Gardiner Collection, NYSL.

55. Ibid.

56. CK to George Jarvis Brush, 7 Apr. 1869, cited in Wilkins, *King,* 132.

57. King, "Misc. Notes 1869," entry for May 19, King Papers, HEH.

58. CK to Mr. Davis, 9 Apr. 1880, quoted in Patricia O'Toole, *The Five of Hearts: An Intimate Portrait of Henry Adams and His Friends* (New York: Clarkson N. Potter 1990; New York: Ballantine Books, 1991), 31. Citations are to the Ballantine edition.

59. J. D. Hague, with geological contributions by Clarence King, *Mining Industry,* vol. 3, *Report of the U.S. Geological Exploration of the Fortieth Parallel* (Washington, DC: GPO, 1870). The Fortieth Parallel survey's eight volumes and two atlases make up *Professional Papers of the Engineer Department, U.S. Army, No. 18.* They are cited in *USGS Bulletin* 222 (1904).

60. Wilkins, *King*, 139–40; Bartlett, *Great Surveys*, 179.

61. CK to Humphreys, 10 Oct. 1870, King Survey Letter Book (R.G. 57, National Archives), cited in Wilkins, *King*, 143.

62. Wilkins, *King*, 55–56, 143–47.

63. Ibid., 147–48.

64. CK to Whitelaw Reid, 29 Jan. [1879], reel 153, Whitelaw Reid Papers, Ms. Div., LC.

65. Wilkins, *King*, 148.

66. CK to James T. Fields, 24 Feb. 1871, tipped into CK, *Mountaineering in the Sierra Nevada* (Boston: James R. Osgood, 1872), copy held in Special Collections and Archives, Frost Library, Amherst College.

67. [Clarence King], *The Three Lakes: Marian, Lall, Jan, and How They Were Named* (n.p., Christmas 1870). Reproduced in Francis P. Farquhar, "An Introduction to Clarence King's 'The Three Lakes,'" *Sierra Club Bulletin* 24 (June 1939): 109–19.

68. Wilkins, *King*, 154–55. He triumphantly reached his goal, or so he thought. Back in San Francisco later he rechecked his barometric reading and to his embarrassment discovered that in the dark and swirling clouds he had surmounted a peak a few hundred feet lower than the true summit. Two years later he returned and rectified his mistake, but by then he could not claim to be the first white man to stand on the great mountain's peak.

69. Adams, *Education*, 311. David Dickason suggests that Adams and King actually met very briefly, a few weeks prior, in early July when they crossed paths in a Cheyenne dining room, as King headed back east. See David H. Dickason, "Henry Adams and Clarence King: The Record of a Friendship," *New England Quarterly* 17, no. 2 (June 1944): 231–32.

70. Adams, *Education*, 309.

71. Ibid., 311–12.

72. Ibid., 312.

73. Ibid., 311.

74. Ibid., 312, 313.

75. Ibid., 313.

76. *Cheyenne Sun*, Oct. 24, 1877, cited in Wilkins, *King*, 231. On King's involvement with the ranching industry, see ibid., 230–42, and Bronson, *Reminiscences*, 28–30 and passim. In Cheyenne, King put up some $8,380 of his own money to form a partnership with his former field assistant N. R. Davis. Davis would manage the ranching operations, while King would be a hands-off partner. Over the next decade, the industry thrived, and King not only set up his secretary, Edgar Beecher Bronson, with a ranch but drew in his friends as investors. Emmons and Gardiner put up money, as did King's New York associates Congressman Abram S. Hewitt and Edward Cooper, the mayor of New York City. Only an occasional visitor to Wyoming, King nonetheless took pleasure in the paid-up membership that Bronson and Davis maintained for him at the elite Cheyenne Club. In 1877 the editor of the *Cheyenne Sun* imagined that King might become a real rancher: "We could not see why he should not grow up with the country and become one of Wyoming's cattle kings." When King finally sold off his ranching shares in 1882, he reaped some $120,000 (the equivalent of more than $2 million today).

77. Moore, *King of the 40th Parallel*, 221.

78. Wilkins, *King*, 167–70; Bronson, *Reminiscences*, 326.

79. Henry Adams, "King," in Hague, *Memoirs*, 172.

80. "Mountaineering in the Sierra Nevada," *New York Times*, Mar. 14, 1872, 2.

81. [JTG], "Clarence King's Boyhood," 8, King Papers, HEH.

82. Ibid.

83. King, *Mountaineering*, 293.

84. Ibid., 293–94.

85. Ibid., 100.

86. Ibid., 165.

87. Clarence King, "The Biographers of Lincoln," *Century Illustrated Magazine* 32 (Oct. 1866): 861.
88. King, *Mountaineering,* 122–23.
89. Ibid., 122.
90. Ibid., 128.
91. Ibid., 315.
92. Ibid., 282.
93. Ibid., 283.
94. Ibid.
95. Ibid., 114.
96. Ibid.
97. Adams, *Education,* 313.
98. King, *Mountaineering,* 228–29.
99. Ibid., 281.
100. "Clarence King's 'Mountaineering,'" *Scribner's Monthly* 4, no. 5 (Sept. 1872): 643.
101. Review, *Appletons' Journal of Literature, Science and Art* 7, no. 158 (Apr. 6, 1872): 388.
102. Howells, "Meetings with Clarence King," in Hague, *Memoirs,* 153, 155.
103. Goetzmann, *Exploration and Empire,* 377; Wilkins, *King,* 161n; Wallace Stegner, *Beyond the Hundredth Meridian: John Wesley Powell and the Second Opening of the West* (Boston: Houghton Mifflin, 1954), 243.
104. Henry Adams, "Mountaineering in the Sierra Nevada," *North American Review* 114, no. 235 (Apr. 1872): 445.
105. King, *Mountaineering,* 296.
106. This account of the diamond hoax comes from Wilkins, *King,* 171–85, and Bartlett, *Great Surveys,* 187–205. See also Robert Wilson, *The Explorer King: Adventure, Science, and the Great Diamond Hoax—Clarence King in the Old West* (New York: Scribner, 2006).
107. *San Francisco Chronicle,* Nov. 28, 1872, cited in Bartlett, *Great Surveys,* 203.
108. *Nation* 15 (Dec. 12, 1872): 380, cited in Wilkins, *King,* 185.
109. CK to S. F. Emmons, 30 Jan. 1873, Clarence King Papers, APS.
110. Ibid., 1 Apr. 1873.
111. CK to JTG, 15 Feb. 1873, Gardiner Collection, NYSL.
112. CK to S. F. Emmons, 30 Jan. 1873, Clarence King Papers, APS.
113. On the details of this arrangement, see below (chapter 4) and "In Trust: The Fortune Which John H. Prentice Gave to His Dead Friend's Family," *Brooklyn Daily Eagle,* Jan. 10, 1882, 4; "Secret Trust," *Brooklyn Daily Eagle,* Feb. 22, 1884, 4; *Van Cott v. Prentice and others.*
114. CK to S. F. Emmons, 30 Jan. 1873, Clarence King Papers, APS. In 1873 King would have drawn a government salary of a minimum $3,850 per year. Clifford M. Nelson, e-mail communication to author, Sept. 12, 2007.
115. Bronson, *Reminiscences,* 3.

CHAPTER 3: BECOMING ADA COPELAND

1. The earliest record of Ada Copeland's own story of her origins can be found on the birth certificates of her children. See below, chapter 6.
2. In 1860 Georgia's Troup and Harris counties, which encompass the West Point metropolitan area, together produced some 32,884 bales of cotton, each bale weighing 400 pounds. Troup County ranked as the state's fourth wealthiest county and among the state's top five slaveholding counties. See David Williams, *Rich Man's War: Class, Caste, and Confederate Defeat in the Lower Chattahoochee Valley* (Athens: University of Georgia Press, 1998), 206; Julie Turner et al., *Travels through Troup County: A Guide to Its Architecture and History* (La Grange, GA: Troup County Historical Society, 1996), 10.
3. "Testimony of John M. Ward," *Testimony Taken by the Joint Select Committee Appointed to Inquire into the Condition of Affairs in the Late Insurrectionary States, Georgia,* vol. 2 (Washington, DC: GPO, 1872), 1085.

4. Department of Commerce, Bureau of the Census, *Negro Population, 1790–1915* (Washington, DC: GPO, 1918), 57.

5. See the analysis of the 1860 census data in Williams, *Rich Man's War,* 198–208.

6. See Clarence L. Mohr, *On the Threshold of Freedom: Masters and Slaves in Civil War Georgia* (Athens: University of Georgia Press, 1986), esp. 20–67.

7. Louise Calhoun Barfield, *History of Harris County, Georgia, 1827–1961* (Columbus, 1961), 292.

8. On the utility of the slave narratives as historical testimony, see Ira Berlin, "Slavery as Memory and History," in *Remembering Slavery: African Americans Talk about Their Personal Experiences of Slavery and Emancipation,* ed. Ira Berlin et al. (New York: New Press, 1998), xiii–xxii; C. Vann Woodward, review of *The American Slave: A Composite Biography,* by George P. Rawick, *American Historical Review* 79, no. 2 (Apr. 1974): 470–81; David Thomas Bailey, "A Divided Prism: Two Sources of Black Testimony on Slavery," *Journal of Southern History* 46, no. 3 (Aug. 1980): 381–404.

9. See "Dink Walton Young, interviewed August 1, 1936," "Life Story as Told by Aunt Easter Jackson, Ex-Slave," "Rias Body, Ex-Slave, interviewed July 24, 1936," all accessible on "Born in Slavery: Slave Narratives from the Federal Writers' Project, 1936–1938," a digitized resource available at the Library of Congress American Memory Web site, http://memory.loc.gov (accessed Aug. 10, 2005).

10. Ada King, Certificate of Death, 156-64-404943, City of New York, Department of Health and Mental Hygiene.

11. Kaye Minchew, director, Troup County Historical Society, e-mail communication to author, Sept. 22, 2004.

12. 1850 U.S. Federal Census, Slave Schedule, Harris County, GA, http://content.ancestry library.com/iexec/?htx=View&r=5542&dbid=8055&iid=GAM432_91-0170 and http://content.ancestrylibrary.com/Browse/view.aspx?dbid=8055&path=Georgia.Harris .Dowdells.3 (accessed Aug. 13, 2007). The slaves seem to be residing on two separate tracts of land. A photograph of Copeland's house is published in Barfield, *Harris County, Georgia,* 611.

13. "Will of William Copeland Sr.," Harris County, GA, WB 2:82, 17 July 1858/April Session 1859, Harris County Courthouse, Hamilton, GA. Citation courtesy of Lea Dowd, Cataula, GA.

14. 1860 U.S. Federal Census, Slave Schedule, Harris County, GA, http://content.ancestrylibrary .com/iexec/?htx=View&r=5542&dbid=7668&iid=GAM653_146-0456&fn=Wm&ln=Cope land&st=d&ssrc=&pid=1368167 (accessed Aug. 13, 2007).

15. See advertisement placed by William Copeland, Jun., in the *Harris County Enterprise,* Jan. 9, 1862, 2.

16. See the entry for William Copeland, 1880 U.S. Federal Census, District No. 786, Harris County, GA, SD 4, ED 57, p. 22, and the adjacent pages of census records that document the black Copeland families living in the immediate vicinity. See also the entry for William Copeland, 1870 U.S. Federal Census, Hamilton Post Office, Harris County, GA, p. 250 (accessed on Ancestry.com).

17. "Inventory and Appraisement of Estate of Wm. Copeland... Recorded Georgia Harris County," Harris County Courthouse, Hamilton, GA. Citation courtesy of Lea Dowd.

18. Brenda E. Stevenson, *Life in Black and White: Family and Community in the Slave South* (New York: Oxford University Press, 1996), 182.

19. For the correlation between monetary value and childbearing potential, see Robert William Fogel and Stanley L. Engerman, *Time on the Cross: The Economics of American Negro Slavery* (Boston: Little, Brown, 1974), 76.

20. See the entries for Adaline Copeland and her family in the 1870 U.S. Federal Census, Hamilton Post Office, Harris County, GA, pp. 252–53.

21. See the entries for Scott and Adeline Copeland in the 1880 U.S. Federal Census, Valley Plains, District No. 786, Harris County, GA, SD 4, ED 57, p. 14.

22. Lea Dowd, personal communication to author, Aug. 7, 2005. For a not always accurate introduction to the local genealogies, see also Barfield, *Harris County, Georgia,* 665–68.

23. Lea Dowd, "Descendants of Dock Copeland," genealogical research report prepared for author, August 2005.

24. The records from the 1890 federal census are largely lost, an enormous loss for scholars of the American past. On the destruction of the 1890 census records, see Kellee Blake, "'First in the Path of the Fireman': The Fate of the 1890 Population Census, Part I," *Prologue* 28, no. 1 (Spring 1996): 64–81. Although it is widely reported that the records were completely destroyed by fire in 1921, Blake explains that many of the records, though heavily damaged, survived until 1934 and 1935, when they were destroyed as being of little use. Scott Copeland does not appear in the 1900 census. But the 1910 census records him as living in Militia District 726 in the White Sulphur Springs area of Meriwether County, Georgia, just north of the Harris County line on the road to Hamilton, and notes that he has been married to his present wife, Emily, since 1887 (see the records for 1910 U.S. Federal Census, White Sulphur Springs, Meriwether County, GA, SD 4, ED 4, sheet 10). This would imply that his first wife, Adeline, disappeared from his life between the time of the summer 1880 census and the moment of his remarriage. Although she seems too old for the Ada Copeland of our story, these dates do correspond to the time at which Ada left Georgia and moved to Manhattan: http://content.gale.ancestry .com/Browse/view.aspx?dbid=7884&path=Georgia.Meriwether.White+Sulphur+Springs.84 .20&rc=&zp=50 (accessed Aug. 13, 2007).

25. "The Price of Negroes," *Harris County Enterprise,* Jan. 9, 1862, 1.

26. Mohr, *Threshold of Freedom,* 212.

27. Williams, *Rich Man's War,* 20, 151–67; Mohr, *Threshold of Freedom,* 210–32.

28. See, for example, the ads in the *La Grange Reporter,* Mar. 3, 1865.

29. See Eleanor Davis Scott and Carl Summers Jr., eds., *The Battle of West Point, April 16, 1865* (Chattahoochee Valley Historical Society, publication no. 20, 1997).

30. "Excitement in Harris County" [from the *Columbus Enquirer*], *La Grange Reporter,* Dec. 8, 1865, 2.

31. "Are the Freedmen Abused?" *La Grange Reporter,* Feb. 16, 1866, 2.

32. Whitelaw Reid, *After the War: A Tour of the Southern States, 1865–1866,* ed. with an introduction and notes by C. Vann Woodward (1866; repr., New York: Harper Torchbooks, 1965), 367–68.

33. Quondam ["our own correspondent from LaGrange," Troup County, GA, Tuesday, June 4, 1867], "Affairs in Georgia," *New York Times,* June 10, 1867, 8.

34. "Report of Freed-People murdered or assaulted with intent to kill, in the counties of Harris, Troup and Meriwether during the year 1867," in "Freedmen's Bureau Report of Outrages Committed against Freedmen in Georgia," http://freedmensbureau.com/ georgia/gaoutrages2.htm (accessed Aug. 13, 2007).

35. *The Condition of Affairs in Georgia: Statement of Honorable Nelson Tift to the Reconstruction Committee of the House of Representatives, Washington, February 18, 1869* (repr., Freeport, NY: Books for Libraries Press, 1971), 134.

36. *Report of the Joint Select Committee Appointed to Inquire into the Condition of Affairs in the Late Insurrectionary States* (Washington, DC: GPO, 1872), *Alabama,* vol. 1, 70–77; *Alabama,* vol. 2, 1043–48, 1114–25.

37. "Testimony of V. J. Jones (colored)," in *Report of the Committee of the Senate upon the Relations between Labor and Capital,* vol. 4, *Testimony* (Washington, DC: GPO, 1885), 626.

38. Jacqueline Jones, *Soldiers of Light and Love: Northern Teachers and Georgia Blacks, 1865–1873* (Chapel Hill: University of North Carolina Press, 1980), 59 and appendix 1, 229.

39. Richard R. Wright, *A Brief Historical Sketch of Negro Education in Georgia* (Savannah: Robinson Printing House, 1894), 21.

40. "Testimony of Rev. E. P. Holmes (colored)," in *Relations between Labor and Capital,* 4:609.

41. "Testimony of C. S. Giddens," ibid., 4:651–52.

42. Department of Commerce, *Negro Population,* 419, 426.

43. Jones, *Soldiers of Light,* 62; Paul A. Cimbala, *Under the Guardianship of the Nation: The Freedmen's*

Bureau and the Reconstruction of Georgia, 1865–1870 (Athens: University of Georgia Press, 1997), 220.

44. "Testimony of W. H. Spencer (colored)," *Relations between Labor and Capital,* 4:577.

45. Wright, *Brief Historical Sketch of Negro Education,* 24.

46. Unsigned report, dated Augusta, GA, Oct. 8, 1868, in "Miscellaneous Lists and Memoranda," in U.S. Bureau of Refugees, Freedmen, and Abandoned Land, "Record of the Superintendent of Education for the State of Georgia, 1865–1872," record group (hereafter RG) 105-M799, reel 28.

47. John D. Withum, "Teacher's Monthly School Report, March 1868," in U.S. Bureau of Refugees, "Record of the Superintendent of Education for Georgia, 1865–1872," RG 105-M799, reel 21.

48. Daniel McGee, "Teacher's Monthly School Report, Sept. 1868," ibid., reel 22.

49. Fannie Neal, "Teacher's Monthly School Report, Dec. 1869," ibid., reel 24.

50. Eliza Brown, "Teacher's Monthly School Report, Dec. 1869," ibid., reel 24.

51. Clifford L. Smith, *History of Troup County* (Atlanta: Foote and Davies, 1933), 136.

52. James Weldon Johnson, *Along This Way: The Autobiography of James Weldon Johnson* (1933; repr., New York: Penguin Books, 1990), 110–12.

53. Wright, *Brief Historical Sketch of Negro Education,* 26.

54. "Testimony of Robert W. Williams (colored)," *Relations between Labor and Capital,* 4:617.

55. "Testimony of John Hill," ibid., 4:588.

56. "Testimony of Preston Brooks Peters (colored)," ibid., 4:569.

57. Turner et al., *Travels through Troup County,* 12.

58. Ulrich B. Phillips, *Life and Labor in the Old South* (Boston: Little, Brown, 1929), 123.

59. Twice in the early 1880s, "vicious" and "frightening" cyclones or tornadoes swept across Harris County, causing considerable destruction and even death. See "Swept Over by Cyclones: Buildings Blown Down and Many Persons Killed and Injured," *New York Times,* Apr. 16, 1884, 5; "A Cyclone in South Georgia," *New York Times,* Feb. 27, 1887, 10. Smallpox swept through the county in 1884. See "Quarantined against Small-Pox," *New York Times,* June 30, 1884, 1.

60. Ada Copeland's great-granddaughter Patricia Chacon recalls hearing no stories about Copeland's Georgia girlhood either directly from Copeland herself or from Copeland's children and grandchildren. Personal communication to author, Wilmington, NC, June 20, 2006.

61. Marcy Sarah Sacks, " 'We Cry among the Skyscrapers': Black People in New York City, 1880–1915" (Ph.D. diss., University of California, Berkeley, 1999), 21.

62. "Testimony of Tony Jenkins (colored)," in *Relations between Labor and Capital,* 4:635.

63. Sacks, " 'We Cry,' " 29.

64. The digitization of census records makes such calculations about the origins of large numbers of people much simpler. Using the databases accessible at Ancestry.com, for example, one can describe the makeup of Manhattan's and Brooklyn's black and mulatto communities by conducting a search using both race and birthplace as variables.

65. "The Slaves of New York City," *La Grange Reporter,* Mar. 19, 1869, 2.

66. "An Exodus Movement," *La Grange Reporter,* Aug. 17, 1879; "The Exodus in Northeast Alabama," *La Grange Reporter,* Sept. 4, 1879. For a general overview of the Exoduster movement, see Nell Irvin Painter, *Exodusters: Black Migration to Kansas after Reconstruction* (New York: Knopf, 1977).

67. Ada's son Wallace King supplied this information on her death certificate.

68. J. Wesley Hoffman, "Facts from Georgia," *New York Age,* Jan. 5, 1889, 2.

69. "Testimony of Tony Jenkins (colored)," in *Relations between Labor and Capital,* 4:637.

70. See Charles S. Mangum Jr., *The Legal Status of the Negro* (Chapel Hill: University of North Carolina Press, 1940), 215–17. Although Mangum cites segregation laws stemming mainly from the 1920s, he suggests that practice likely followed the older established rules for segregation on railroad cars. He also cites (p. 204) the ruling of *Hall v. DeCuir,* 95 U.S. 485 (1877), which held in

a case involving a Louisiana steamboat that the state civil rights acts enacted during Reconstruction prohibiting discrimination on public carriers were invalid with regard to interstate travelers.

71. Alexander Walters, *My Life and Work* (New York: Fleming H. Revell, 1917), 53.

72. Henry Hugh Proctor, *Between Black and White*, 133–34. For an overview of black life in New York City during this relatively understudied time period, see Marcy S. Sacks, *Before Harlem: The Black Experience in New York City before World War I* (Philadelphia: University of Pennsylvania Press, 2006).

73. Paul Laurence Dunbar, *The Sport of the Gods* (New York: Dodd, Mead, 1902), 81–82.

74. Ada identified "Annie Purnell" as her aunt in court testimony given more than forty years later (see *King v. Peabody et al.*, file no. 26821-1931, Records of the New York County Clerk's Office, Supreme Court of the State of New York, and below, chap. 10) and stated that in 1888 her aunt lived at 149 West Twenty-fourth Street. *Trow's New York City Directory* for the years 1882–89 records Purnell's move from 26 Minetta Lane to the West Twenty-fourth Street address. The directory entries note that she is the widow of John, and the 1887 entry identifies her profession as "washing." Annie Purnell's precise relationship to Ada is unclear. The loss of the 1890 census records in a disastrous fire in 1921 makes it difficult to know, with any assurance, which of the other people of that name living in New York either earlier or later might have been Ada's relative.

75. For the tenants of Purnell's building in 1880, see 1880 U.S. Federal Census, City of New York, County of New York, State of New York, SD 1, ED 343, 23–24. On the use of racial terms in the census, see below, 213, 264.

76. See the entry in *Trow's New York City Directory for the Year Ending May 1, 1888* (New York: Trow City Directory Company, 1888), 1595.

77. "Situations Wanted," *New York Times*, Jan. 5, 1886, 6.

78. Again, the digitization of the census records on such sites as Ancestry.com makes it possible to quickly scan the 1880 records to search for the living situations of Georgia-born blacks in the greater New York area. The *New York Age*, the city's preeminent paper for the black community, lends a more qualitative note to a quantitative story. It published a brief article on Mar. 30, 1889 (p. 3), about Georgia-born Jane Mitchell, who was found dead in her bed in her Seventh Avenue apartment. She was buried by her "Georgia friends," and the public administrator took charge of her effects in the absence of any kin.

79. Sacks, " 'We Cry,' " 34–35.

80. "Situations Wanted: Female," *New York Times*, Mar. 1, 1886, 6.

81. "Widow Tells of Ceremony and Children," *Amsterdam News*, Nov. 22, 1933, 2.

82. Wilkins, *King*, 358.

83. Mary White Ovington, *Half a Man: The Status of the Negro in New York* (1911; repr., New York: Negro Universities Press, 1969), 149; Isabel Eaton, "Special Report on Domestic Service," in W. E. B. DuBois, *The Philadelphia Negro: A Social Study* (1899; repr., New York: Benjamin Blom, 1967), 427.

84. Jessie Redmon Fauset, *Plum Bun: A Novel without a Moral* (New York: Frederick A. Stokes, 1929), 27–28.

85. Eaton, "Special Report," 452–54.

86. Lucy Maynard Salmon, *Domestic Service* (New York: Macmillan, 1897), 96; Eaton, "Special Report," 452; "Facts from Georgia," *New York Age*, Jan. 5, 1889, 2. On field wages around Harris County in the 1880s, see "Testimony of W. H. Spencer (colored)," *Relations between Labor and Capital*, 4:5.

87. "Testimony of Mrs. M. W. Farrer," *Relations between Labor and Capital*, 2:643.

88. Eaton, "Special Report," 468.

89. Department of Commerce, *Negro Population*, 156.

90. Salmon, *Domestic Service*, 286, 144, 97.

91. Eaton, "Special Report," 467. See also Daniel E. Sutherland, *Americans and Their Servants: Domestic Service in the United States from 1800 to 1920* (Baton Rouge: Louisiana State University Press, 1981), 114–17.

92. Ovington, *Half a Man*, 151.

93. Eaton (p. 470) found that in her sample group of black women domestic workers in Philadelphia, 66 percent said they turned to their church for recreational activities. She estimated that many of those who reported that they spent most of their leisure time at home also relied on church programs, bringing the total number of women involved in church affairs during their leisure time to 93.2 percent.

94. DuBois, *Philadelphia Negro*, 201.

95. James Weldon Johnson, *Black Manhattan* (1930; repr., New York: Knopf, 1940), 165.

96. For a history of this strain of Methodism, see Lewis V. Baldwin, *"Invisible" Strands in African Methodism: A History of the African Union Methodist Protestant and Union American Methodist Episcopal Churches, 1805–1980* (Metuchen, NJ: American Theological Library Association and the Scarecrow Press, 1983), and U.S. Bureau of the Census, *Religious Bodies: 1906* (Washington, DC: GPO, 1910), 444–46.

97. Baldwin, *"Invisible" Strands*, 92–95, 111–19.

98. Department of the Interior, Census Office, *Report on Statistics of Churches in the United States at the Eleventh Census: 1890* (Washington, DC: GPO, 1894), 48, 542.

99. Knowledge of Ada's church membership comes from her reference to her minister in *King v. Peabody et al*. Records from the church itself do not seem to have survived. On the church activities, see, for example, the ads for "A Dramatic Cantata," *New York Age*, Mar. 10, 1888, 3; "Third Re-Union," *New York Age*, Feb. 16, 1889, 13; "The Union A.M.E. Church," *New York Age*, Aug. 4, 1888.

100. Easter Jackson, interview included in "Born in Slavery," LC.

101. On religion in Troup and Harris counties during Reconstruction, see Barfield, *History of Harris County*, and Forrest Clark Johnson III, *Histories of LaGrange and Troup County, GA: A History of LaGrange, Georgia, 1828–1900*, vol. 1 (LaGrange: Family Tree, 1987).

102. DuBois, *Philadelphia Negro*, 204.

103. "Bishop James H. Cook," *New York Times*, Aug. 12, 1899, 7. Ada King refers to Cook as her pastor in the later court testimony reported in "Sues Gardiner Estate," *New York Times*, Nov. 21, 1933.

104. On the doctrine of the Union American Methodist Episcopal Church, see Baldwin, *"Invisible" Strands*, passim.

105. [Ida B. Wells], "The Model Woman: A Pen Picture of the Typical Southern Girl," *New York Freeman*, Feb. 18, 1888, reprinted in Miriam Decosta-Willis, *The Memphis Diary of Ida B. Wells: An Intimate Portrait of the Activist as a Young Woman* (Boston: Beacon Press, 1995), 188–89.

106. Ada's great-granddaughter Patricia Chacon, personal communication to author, Wilmington, NC, June 20, 2006.

107. Little scholarly work has been done on the lives of African American women in late-nineteenth-century New York, and the field remains ripe for further research. Kathy Peiss's book *Cheap Amusements: Working Women and Leisure in Turn-of-the-Century New York* (Philadelphia: Temple University Press, 1986) offers an excellent model for investigating women's lives but largely ignores the experiences of African Americans. Tera W. Hunter's *To 'Joy My Freedom: Southern Black Women's Lives and Labors after the Civil War* (Cambridge, MA: Harvard University Press, 1997) focuses on Atlanta and suggests how rich a comparable study might be of black women's lives in a northern city. Marcy S. Sacks's *Before Harlem* concerns itself with a broad range of issues beyond gender but introduces the reader to the range of sources that might support a more focused investigation of this little-studied period.

CHAPTER 4: KING OF THE CITY

1. Bancroft letter quoted in George Wharton James, "Clarence King," *Overland Monthly and Out West Magazine* 81, no. 6 (Oct. 1923): 36.

2. Adams, *Education*, 313.

3. Wilkins, *King*, 215–16.

4. Ibid., 206–20.

5. Ibid., 209.

6. JH to CK, 18 June 1870, Hay Collection, Brown.

7. On Hay, see O'Toole, *Five of Hearts;* Tyler Dennett, *John Hay: From Poetry to Politics* (New York: Dodd, Mead, 1933); Kenton J. Clymer, *John Hay: The Gentleman as Diplomat* (Ann Arbor: University of Michigan Press, 1975). Hay's life merits a full new biographical study. Hay's book *Castilian Days* was published by James Osgood, the same publisher who issued King's *Mountaineering* the following year.

8. O'Toole, *Five of Hearts*, 38.

9. Hay, "Clarence King," in Hague, *Memoirs*, 131.

10. King, "Catastrophism and Evolution," 470.

11. The debate continues. Geologist James Gregory Moore argues in *King of the 40th Parallel* (2006) that recent thought has swung toward a general acceptance of some of King's catastrophist views. "For example, it is well accepted that major meteoritic impacts and episodes of massive volcanism have assaulted the Earth across the eons with catastrophic results, thus shaping and accelerating physical and biologic evolution. Many of these catastrophes have been shown to occur at the boundaries of the great geologic eras and periods, boundaries that were originally discovered and defined because they marked the time that major extinctions and changes occurred in plant and animal life" (p. 269).

12. Goetzmann, *Exploration and Empire*, 464. For a more recent evaluation of King's science, see Kenneth R. Aalto, "Clarence King's Geology," *Earth Sciences History* 23 (2004): 9–31.

13. CK to Marcus Benjamin, 21 Aug. 1887, record unit 7085, box 3, folder 14 "King, Clarence," Marcus Benjamin Papers, Smithsonian Institution Archives; letter quoted in Clifford M. Nelson, "King, Clarence (Rivers)," in *New Dictionary of Scientific Biography*, ed. Noretta Koertge (Detroit: Charles Scribner's Sons, 2008), 4:120.

14. On the history of the United States Geological Survey, see Mary C. Rabbitt, *The United States Geological Survey, 1879–1989* (U.S. Geological Survey Circular 1050, 1989); Nelson and Rabbitt, "The Role of Clarence King," in Leviton, *Frontiers of Geological Exploration;* Clifford M. Nelson, "Clarence Rivers King (1842–1901)," in *The History of Science in the United States: An Encyclopedia*, ed. Marc Rothenberg (New York and London: Garland Publishing, 2001), 300–301. The most comprehensive history of the agency remains Mary C. Rabbitt, *Mineral, Lands, and Geology for the Common Defence and General Welfare*, 3 vols. (Washington, DC: GPO, 1979–86).

15. *U.S. Statutes at Large* 20 (1879): 394, quoted in Nelson and Rabbitt, "The Role of Clarence King," in Leviton, *Frontiers of Geological Exploration*, 32.

16. "Confirming and Rejecting," *Washington Post*, Apr. 4, 1879, 1.

17. [James D. Hague], "Biographical Sketch of Clarence King," typescript, 8, A1, King Papers, HEH.

18. Bronson, *Reminiscences*, 356.

19. Johnson, *Along This Way*, 49.

20. *Compact Edition of the Oxford English Dictionary*, s.v. "slumming."

21. Bronson, *Reminiscences*, 326–27.

22. Ibid., 356.

23. On the electrification of New York, see Edwin G. Burrows and Mike Wallace, *Gotham: A History of New York City to 1898* (New York: Oxford University Press, 1998), 1059–68.

24. For an interesting exploration of the night as a space with parallels to the frontier, see Murray Melbin, *Night as Frontier: Colonizing the World after Dark* (New York: Free Press, 1987). Thanks to Jean-Christophe Agnew for suggesting this book.

25. Norman Mailer, *The White Negro: Superficial Reflections on the Hipster* (repr., San Francisco: City Light Books, n.d.), [3]. Originally published in *Dissent* (1957).

26. Wilkins, *King*, 269–92; Nelson and Rabbitt, "The Role of Clarence King," in Leviton, *Frontiers of Geological Exploration*, 32–33.

27. For an illuminating and lively account of King's Washington circle, see O'Toole, *Five of Hearts*. My account of the group is informed by O'Tooles' excellent research. Her reference to the James story is on p. 72.

28. For the source of the group's name, see ibid., xvi.

29. Ibid., 69, for a photograph of the tea service.

30. Henry Adams [Frances Snow Compton, pseud.], with an introduction by Robert E. Spiller, *Esther: A Novel* (1884; repr., New York: Scholars' Facsimiles & Reprints, 1938), 19.

31. JH to Clover Adams, 14 Nov. 1881, Ms. 1146, Autograph Collection, Letters to Henry Adams, box 10, Theodore F. Dwight Papers, 1668–1915, Massachusetts Historical Society (hereafter MHS). Citation courtesy of Natalie Dykstra.

32. The best account of King's complicated mining ventures is in Wilkins, *King*, esp. chap. 16.

33. "Clarence King's Resignation," *New York Times*, Mar. 16, 1881, 4; Rabbitt, *Minerals, Lands, and Geology*, 2:54.

34. Wilkins, *King*, 308.

35. Ibid., 308–11.

36. JH to Clover Adams, 14 Nov. 1881, Dwight Papers, MHS.

37. "In Trust," *Brooklyn Daily Eagle*, Jan. 10, 1882, 4; "Secret Trust," *Brooklyn Daily Eagle*, Feb. 22, 1884, 4; *Van Cott v. Prentice and others*. Monetary calculations made with the help of www.measuringworth.com.

38. *Van Cott v. Prentice and others*. In 1887 the New York State Court of Appeals made a final ruling in Mrs. Howland's favor, agreeing that Prentice clearly intended the interest to go to the Howland family until the youngest child, George, reached legal age, at which point Mrs. Howland and the children should receive the principal of the trust. But it had diminished over the years, and Mrs. Howland's efforts to hold Prentice's executors responsible for the management of the funds failed.

39. FKH to JH, 1882, quoted in O'Toole, *Five of Hearts*, 109.

40. FKH to JTG, 8 May 1881, Gardiner Collection, NYSL.

41. Stedman, "Frolic," in Hague, *Memoirs*, 203–5.

42. For an excellent overview of King's time in Europe, see Wilkins, *King*, 312–35.

43. Clarence King, "The Helmet of Mambrino," *Century Illustrated Magazine* 32 (May 1886): 154–59.

44. Royal Cortissoz, *The Life of Whitelaw Reid* (London: Thornton Butterworth, 1921), 2:86, cited in Wilkins, *King*, 327.

45. Hay, "Clarence King," in Hague, *Memoirs*, 129–30.

46. Ibid., 124–25.

47. Wilkins, *King*, 317–25.

48. Stedman, "Frolic," in Hague, *Memoirs*, 207.

49. Howells, "Meetings with Clarence King," in Hague, *Memoirs*, 143–44.

50. Ibid., 144.

51. "Sanctum Chat," *Saturday Evening Post*, May 31, 1884, 8.

52. See Seth Koven, *Slumming: Sexual and Social Politics in Victorian London* (Princeton, NJ: Princeton University Press, 2004), 14–15, 187–88.

53. John Baker Hopkins, "Lazarus to Dives," *Eclectic Magazine of Foreign Literature* (Feb. 1887): 263.

54. Quoted in Leon Edel, *Henry James: The Treacherous Years: 1895–1901* (Philadelphia: J. B. Lippincott, 1969), 237.

55. Ibid., 237–38; George Monteiro, *Henry James and John Hay: The Record of a Friendship* (Providence, RI: Brown University Press, 1965), 98.

56. Raymond, "Biographical Notice," in Hague, *Memoirs*, 369.

57. Hay, "Clarence King," in Hague, *Memoirs*, 123.

58. F. H. Mason to JH, 1 Sept. [1883], cited in Wilkins, *King*, 320.

59. Raymond, "Biographical Notice," in Hague, *Memoirs*, 369–70.

60. Hon. Maude Stanley, "Country Holidays for Working Girls," *Outlook* 63, no. 6 (Oct. 7, 1899): 346.

61. F. H. Mason to JH, 18 Jan. 1884, cited in Wilkins, *King*, 321n.

62. Bronson, *Reminiscences*, 354; Henry James to JH, 13 May [1885], cited in Phillip Horne, ed., *Henry James: A Life in Letters* (London: Penguin, 1999), 176.

63. F. H. Mason to JH, 18 Jan. 1884, cited in Wilkins, *King*, 321n.

64. Ibid.

65. Raymond, "Biographical Notice," in Hague, *Memoirs*, 370.

66. Wilkins, *King*, 325–26, 333–34.

67. CK to "Haig," 27 June 1884, A1, King Papers, HEH.

68. Henry James, *Daisy Miller* (1878; repr., New York: Penguin Classics, 1987); Koven, *Slumming*, 169–80.

69. Wilkins, *King*, 334.

70. CK to D. C. Gilman, 27 Feb. 1885, cited ibid., 338.

71. John La Farge, "Clarence King," in Hague, *Memoirs*, 192.

72. *Catalogue of Valuable Paintings and Water Colors to Be Sold at Unrestricted Public Sale by Order of the Executors and Trustee of the Estates of the Late Clarence King, William H. Fuller and Theodore G. Weil the trustees of H. Victor Newcomb* (New York: Press of J. J. Little, 1903). Auction catalog, American Art Association, New York, March 1903.

73. La Farge, "Clarence King," in Hague, *Memoirs*, 192–95.

74. Adams, "King," in Hague, *Memoirs*, 166.

75. CK to Henry Adams (HA), 6 Oct. 1884, cited in O'Toole, *Five of Hearts*, 129.

76. Clarence King, "Household Expenses 47 Lafayette Place, NY [fall 1873]," A2, King Papers, HEH. In this small ledger book, King kept note of his payments to his servants. "Mary" starts work on Sept. 9, 1873, for $3 to $4 a week and works for King until Oct. 30. "Sarah Johnson" begins at $4 a week on Oct. 31. "Edward Schoales" begins at $35 a month on Oct. 8, 1873. Because the notebook ends at the end of the year, it is difficult to tell how long the servants stayed.

77. *Miller's Strangers' Guide for the City of New York* (New York: James Miller, 1867), 70.

78. *Taintor's Route and City Guides: City of New York* (New York: Taintor Brothers, Merrill, 1876), 26.

79. Edna L. Farley, *The Underside of Reconstruction New York: The Struggle over the Issue of Black Equality* (New York and London: Garland Publishing, 1993), 157.

80. "Personal Intelligence," *New York Times*, Apr. 8, 1881, 5; Apr. 28, 1881, 8; Apr. 30, 1881, 5; "Duke of Sutherland," *New York Times*, Apr. 27, 1881, 8.

81. On American vs. European plan, see *Rand McNally & Co.'s Handy Guide to New York City* (Chicago: The Company, 1895), 15.

82. "The Arts: Our Domestic Architecture," *Appletons' Journal: A Magazine of General Literature* 13, no. 302 (Jan. 2, 1875): 22. An image of the hotel can be found in Henry Collins Brown, *Fifth Avenue Old and New, 1824–1924* [New York, c. 1924], 57.

83. *Appleton's Dictionary of Greater New York and Its Neighborhoods* (New York: D. Appleton, 1879), s.v. "Restaurants"; *Rand McNally Guide* (1895), 115.

84. *Rand McNally Guide* (1895), 19.

85. Ibid., 16–17.

86. "New York City Directory, 1890," on Ancestry.com (accessed Aug. 15, 2007); *Trow's New York, New York City Directory for 1890* (New York: Trow City Directory, 1891); "Another Big Office Building," *New York Times*, Oct. 29, 1893, 21; "Punished for Contempt," *New York Times*, Apr. 2, 1880, 8; "Theatrical Gossip," *New York Times*, Mar. 9, 1887, 3.

87. "Eclipsed by Four Mules: The Tantivy's First Trip to Pelham and Gilmore's Practical Joke," *New York Times*, Apr. 27, 1886, 8.

88. Fifth Avenue Bank of New York, *Fifth Avenue Events: A Brief Account of Some of the Most Interesting Events Which Have Occurred on the Avenue* ([New York]: Printed for the Fifth Avenue Bank of New York, 1916), 49–51.

89. "City and Suburban News," *New York Times*, Jan. 14, 1887, 3; "Discussing Future Hunt," *New York Times*, Mar. 15, 1888, 3; "An Electric Convention: A Big Meeting at the Brunswick Hotel," *New York Times*, Aug. 30, 1888, 8; "City and Suburban News," *New York Times*, Jan. 14, 1887, 3; "Lee Talks for the South: Frank Words for the Southern Society Dinner," *New York Times*, Feb. 23, 1889, 5; "Soured by a Single Bad Egg," *New York Times*, Jan. 29, 1889, 5.

90. "The Professional Clubs: Influence of Outsiders on Their Management," *New York Times*, Jan. 10, 1887, 2.

91. For King's memberships and thumbnail descriptions of the clubs, see *Club Men of New York* (New York: Republic Press, 1893) and *Rand McNally Guide* (1895), 183–86.

92. On the mail drop-offs, see "Professional Clubs."

93. King named different clubs as mailing addresses in the 1893 and 1896 editions of *Club Men of New York*. He made frequent use of stationery from both the Century Association and the Union League Club during the 1880s and '90s, suggesting he was using both clubs as office spaces.

94. Edith Wharton, *The Age of Innocence* (1920; repr., New York: Charles Scribner's Sons, 1968), 126.

95. Wilkins, *King*, 345, 352–53.

96. Hague, "Memorabilia," in Hague, *Memoirs*, 411–12.

97. Walt Whitman, "Crossing Brooklyn Ferry," stanza 11, lines 121–22.

98. Earl Lind [pseud.], *Autobiography of an Androgyne* (1918; repr., New York: Arno Press, 1975), 47.

99. Ralph Werther [Jennie June, Earl Lind, pseuds.], *The Female-Impersonators* (New York: Medico-Legal Journal, 1922), 82.

100. *Rand McNally Guide* (1895), 140.

101. JH to Clara Stone Hay, 6 Dec. 1879, quoted in O'Toole, *Five of Hearts*, 66.

102. CK to JH, 30 May 1885, Hay Collection, Brown.

103. Ibid.

104. Ibid., June 1886.

105. Bronson, *Reminiscences*, 329.

106. CK to JH, 4 July 1886, Hay Collection, Brown.

107. Ibid., 30 May 1885.

108. Ibid., 28 July 1887.

109. Ibid.

110. Alfred Lord Tennyson, "Locksley Hall," lines 167–68.

111. CK to JH, 28 July 1887, Hay Collection, Brown.

112. Clarence King, "U.S. Geological Survey July 1867 Private" [small pocket notebook], D12, King Papers, HEH.

113. Clarence King, "Bancroft's Native Races of the Pacific States," *Atlantic Monthly* 35 (Feb. 1875): 172.

114. Helen Hunt Jackson, *Ramona* (1884; repr., New York: Penguin Books, 1988), 360, 362.

115. An odd short story informed by Helen Hunt Jackson's novel appeared in the African American newspaper the *New York Age* on June 2, 1888. A young black woman named "Ramona" is reunited with the love who she wrongly thought had rebuffed her through her kindly white patron "Helen Huntington."

116. CK to JH, 28 July 1887, Hay Collection, Brown.

117. CK to Samuel Barlow, BW box 184 (12), Barlow Collection, HEH.

118. CK to JH, 28 July 1887, Hay Collection, Brown.

119. O'Toole, *Five of Hearts*, 141–75.

120. CK to JH, 4 Aug. 1887, Hay Collection, Brown.

121. Clarence King, "Artium Magister," *North American Review* 147 (Oct. 1888): 382.

122. King, "Biographers of Lincoln," 868.

123. CK to JH, 18 July 1888, Hay Collection, Brown.

124. Wharton, *The Age of Innocence*, 335.

125. The earliest record of this name appears on the 1891 birth certificate for King and Copeland's second child, Grace Margaret Todd: Certificate of Birth, Brooklyn. 920, New York City Department of Records and Information Services, Municipal Archives.

CHAPTER 5: NEW BEGINNINGS

1. Burrows and Wallace, *Gotham*, 1148.

2. Johnson, *Black Manhattan*, 77; Sacks, "'We Cry,'" 140–43.

3. Hay, "Clarence King," in Hague, *Memoirs*, 130.

4. Sacks, "'We Cry,'" 140–46.

5. The earliest reference to Todd's false identity comes from Ada's statement to the physician who filled out her daughter Grace's birth certificate in Jan. 1891. See below, 171–72.

6. Robin Marantz Henig, "Looking for the Lie," *New York Times Magazine*, Feb. 5, 2006, 83.

7. Werther [pseud.], *Female-Impersonators*, 175.

8. The 1890 census identifies 23,601 persons of African descent living in New York County out of a total population of 1,515,301. See the Historical Census Browser, Geospatial and Statistical Data Center, University of Virginia, http://fisher.lib.virginia.edu/collections/stats/histcensus/php/county.php (accessed Aug. 2, 2007).

9. See, for example, Benedict Carey, "The Secret Lives of Just About Everybody," *New York Times*, Jan. 11, 2005, D1.

10. Carol Midgley, "Porn, an Affair, You're Gay: What's Your Secret?" *Sunday Times* (London), Apr. 29, 2005, http://www.timesonline.co.uk/article/0,,7-1589332_1,00.html (accessed May 1, 2005).

11. "1,000 Passing in Washington," *New York Age*, Sept. 16, 1909, 1. The article quotes the work of Ralph W. Tyler, whose own racial identity is documented in the 1910 U.S. Federal Census for the District of Columbia, SD 1, ED 155, sheet 4A.

12. On Florence King Howland's pseudonym, see CK to Whitelaw Reid, 29 Jan. [1879], reel 153, Whitelaw Reid Papers, LC. On Sophia Little's pseudonym, see Rufus Wilmot Griswold, *Female Poets of America*, 2nd ed. (Philadelphia: Purvey & McMillan, 1854), 107.

13. O'Toole, *Five of Hearts*, 168–69.

14. The 1880 U.S. Federal Census (accessed on Ancestry.com, Dec. 20, 2004) lists seven James Todds in New York City. Subsequent city directories list others.

15. "James Edward Todd," *History of Fremont County, Iowa* (Des Moines: Iowa Historical Company, 1881), http://www.rootsweb.com/~iabiog/fremont/fl1881/fl1881-ross.htm (accessed Oct. 21, 2004); "James E. Todd," Database: American Civil War Soldiers, Ancestry.com (accessed Oct. 21, 2004); "James E. Todd," Civil War Pension Index, Ancestry.com (accessed Oct. 21, 2004); *Biographical Record: Classes from 1868–1872 of the Yale Sheffield Scientific School* (New Haven, CT: Class Secretaries Bureau, Yale University, 1910). Todd is listed as a nongraduating student enrolled in 1870–71.

16. Charles Keyes, "Glacial Work of James Edward Todd," *Pan-American Geologist* 39, no. 1 (Feb. 1925): 1–14; "Todd," *History of Fremont County, Iowa;* "American Naturalist," *Forest and Stream; A Journal of Outdoor Life, Travel, Nature Study, Shooting, Fishing, Yachting* 11, no. 25 (Jan. 23, 1879): 514; James E. Todd, "The Missouri Couteau and Its Moraines," *Proceedings of the American Association for the Advancement of Science* 33 (1884), published independently (Salem, MA, 1885); *Washington, D.C., City Directory, 1890* (Washington, DC: R. L. Polk, 1890); J. E. Todd (state geologist), *Preliminary Report on the Geology of South Dakota* (Sioux Falls: Brown & Saenger, 1894); Frank Leverett, "Memorial of James Todd," *Bulletin of the Geological Society of America* 34 (1922): 44–51. With thanks for some of these references to Brenda L. Graff, reference librarian, USGS Library, and Clifford M. Nelson, geologist and historian, USGS.

17. Ironically, the name "James Edward Todd" again came to public attention in 1968, some eighty years after King and Copeland married, when a young white sailor by that name married a young black woman named Floria Marquite Mayhorn, in Memphis, Tennessee, in what the *Washington Post* called "this Old South city's first interracial marriage since Reconstruction" (Jan. 13, 1968, A5). Like King and Copeland, they were married by the woman's pastor, in a ceremony held outside the church.

18. Jack London's short story "South of the Slot" originally appeared in the *Saturday Evening Post* 181 (May 1909), 3–4, 36–38.

19. Nat Love, *The Life and Adventures of Nat Love* (1907; repr., Lincoln: University of Nebraska Press, 1995), 139.

20. From *Railroad Commission of Texas v. Pullman Co.*, 312 U.S. 496 (1941), cited in Judith Resnik, "Rereading 'The Federal Courts': Revising the Domain of Federal Courts Jurisprudence at the End of the Twentieth Century," 47 *Vanderbilt Law Review*, 1039.

21. "St. John and the Color Line—A Talk with a Pullman Palace Car Porter," *New York Freeman*, Mar. 7, 1885, 2.

22. Love, *Life and Adventures*, 131, 134, 135.

23. Resnik, "Rereading 'The Federal Courts,' " 1039.

24. Larry Tye, *Rising from the Rails: Pullman Porters and the Making of the Black Middle Class* (New York: Henry Holt, 2004), 33, 61.

25. Howells, "Meetings with King," in Hague, *Memoirs*, 136.

26. Study by Hornell Hart, cited in Louis Wirth and Herbert Goldhamer, "The Hybrid and the Problem of Miscegenation," *Characteristics of the American Negro*, ed. Otto Klineberg (New York: Harper & Brothers, 1944), 312–13.

27. "1,000 Passing in Washington," 1.

28. "Married a Negro Instead of a Cuban," *New York Times*, Sept. 28, 1888, 2.

29. Mark Twain, *Pudd'nhead Wilson* (1894; repr., New York: Bantam Books, 1981), 26, 142–43.

30. St. Clair Drake and Horace R. Cayton, *Black Metropolis: A Study of Negro Life in a Northern City* (1945; repr., New York: Harper & Row, 1962), 1:164–65. On the particular interest of early-twentieth-century social scientists in matters of racial mixing, see Joel Williamson, *New People: Miscegenation and Mulattoes in the United States* (1980; repr., Baton Rouge: Louisiana State University Press, 1995), 115–29.

31. R. Roberts, "Negro-White Intermarriage: A Study in Social Control" (master's thesis, University of Chicago, n.d.), cited in Wirth and Goldhamer, "The Hybrid," in Klineberg, *Characteristics of the American Negro*, 303.

32. Gunnar Myrdal, *An American Dilemma: The Negro Problem and American Democracy* (New York: Harper & Brothers [1944]), 164.

33. Walter White, *A Man Called White* (1948; repr., Athens: University of Georgia Press, 1995), 3.

34. David H. Fowler, *Northern Attitudes Towards Interracial Marriage: Legislative and Public Opinion in the Middle Atlantic and the States of the Old Northwest* (New York: Garland Publishing, 1987), 360.

35. Sociologists Louis Wirth and Herbert Goldhamer later called such people "segmental passers." Wirth and Goldhamer, "The Hybrid," in Klineberg, *Characteristics of the American Negro*, 302–3.

36. Lind [pseud.], *Autobiography of an Androgyne*, 47, 61.

37. Werther [pseud.], *Female-Impersonators*, 175.

38. Lind [pseud.], *Autobiography of an Androgyne*, 82, 161–65.

39. M. H. Dunlop, *Gilded City: Scandal and Sensation in Turn-of-the-Century New York* (New York: William Morrow, 2000), 126–28.

40. "Detective Price's Troubles: Life Made Miserable by a Man Who Assumed His Name," *New York Times*, Mar. 11, 1885, 8.

41. JH to HA, 19 May 1888, *Letters of John Hay and Extracts from Diary* (1908; repr., New York: Gordian Press, 1969), 2:146.

42. CK to Clara Hay, 7 Mar. 1888; CK to JH, 17 Apr. 1889, Hay Collection, Brown.

43. CK to JH, 12 Aug. [1888], Hay Collection, Brown.

44. Ibid.

45. Bronson, *Reminiscences*, 355.

46. King, "Artium Magister," 383.

47. Plaintiff's Trial Memorandum Relating to the Existence of the Trust [Mar. 1932], 2, *King v. Peabody et al.* (file no. 26821-1931; Records of the Supreme Court of the State of New York, New York County Clerk's Office); "Widow Tells of Ceremony and Children," *Amsterdam News*, Nov. 22, 1933, 2. On the convention of personalizing wedding rings in the late nineteenth century, see "Buying Wedding Rings," *Washington Post*, Nov. 25, 1883, 7. The wedding ring has descended through the King family and now belongs to the Kings' great-granddaughter, Patricia Chacon.

48. Eugene D. Genovese, *Roll, Jordan, Roll: The World the Slaves Made* (New York: Pantheon, 1974), 375–481; Herbert G. Gutman, *The Black Family in Slavery and Freedom, 1720–1925* (New York: Vintage, 1977), 273–77.

49. Wilkins, *King*, 26–27.

50. King, *Mountaineering*, 292.

51. Hague, "Memorabilia," in Hague, *Memoirs*, 408–9.

52. "Bishop James H. Cook," *New York Times*, Aug. 12, 1899, 7; "Ball of the Coachmen's Union League," *New York Times*, Jan. 11, 1895, 8; "Colored Odd Fellows' Jubilee," *New York Times*, Apr. 27, 1893, 10; "Aid for the Arkansas Refugees," *New York Times*, Mar. 30, 1880, 2; "His Last Day on Earth: Chastain Cox Ready to Meet His Fate," *New York Times*, July 16, 1880, 2; "Cox Expatiates His Crime," *New York Times*, July 17, 1880, 3; "The Burial of Chastain Cox," *New York Times*, July 18, 1880, 12.

53. "Fifteenth Amendment Celebrated," *New York Times*, Mar. 31, 1887, 5; "Clergymen in Politics," *New York Times*, Sept. 23, 1890, 1; "Bishop James H. Cook," 7.

54. See Ariela R. Dubler, "Note: Governing through Contract: Common Law Marriage in the Nineteenth Century," *Yale Law Journal* (April 1998): 1885–920.

55. Certificate of Marriage [1888], Health Department of the City of New York, Sanitary Bureau, Division of Vital Statistics. Thanks to Josh Garrett-Davis for retrieving this data from the forms on file in the New York City Municipal Archives.

56. Wirth and Goldhamer, "The Hybrid," in Klineberg, *Characteristics of the American Negro*, 277.

57. "Miscegenation in Boston," story from the *Boston Herald* reprinted in *New York Age*, Sept. 8, 1888, 2.

58. See "A White Groom and Colored Bride," *New York Times*, Apr. 6, 1885, 5; "Arrested for Miscegenation," *New York Times*, Oct. 4, 1885, 3; "Capt Lusk Assassinated: An Advocate of Miscegenation Riddled with Bullets," *New York Times*, Aug. 27, 1886, 5; "Held for Miscegenation," *New York Times*, Sept. 12, 1889, 3; "Charge of Miscegenation: Couple Arrested in Washington at Request of Maryland Authorities," *New York Times*, Aug. 6, 1900, 1.

59. Philip S. Foner, *Frederick Douglass* (1950; repr., New York: Citadel Press, 1964), 338.

60. Bailey, "Diary of a Journey," 99, New York Botanical Garden Library.

61. Robert Underwood Johnson, *Remembered Yesterdays* (Boston: Little, Brown, 1923), 26.

62. [Clarence King], "Style and the Monument," *North American Review* 141 (Nov. 1885): 443–44.

63. Leslie M. Harris, "From Abolitionist Amalgamators to 'Rulers of the Five Points,'" in *Sex, Love, Race: Crossing Boundaries in North American History*, ed. Martha Hodes (New York: NYU Press, 1999), 191–212; *Oxford English Dictionary*, s.v. "Amalgamation" and "Amalgamate."

64. "Testimony of Wendell Phillips from his speech at Framingham, Mass., July 4, 1863," reprinted in *Miscegenation: The Theory of the Blending of the Races, Applied to the American White Man and Negro*, [ed. David Croly and George Wakeman] (New York: H. Dexter, Hamilton, 1864), 66; Gary B. Nash, "The Hidden History of Mestizo America," in Hodes, *Sex, Love, Race*, 22.

65. CK to JTG, 25 Mar. [1860], King Papers, HEH.

66. [Croly and Wakeman], *Miscegenation*, ii.

67. Frederick Douglass, "Letter from the Editor," *Frederick Douglass' Paper*, Nov. 20, 1851.

68. Frederick Douglass, "The Future of the Colored Race," *North American Review* 196 (May 1886): 437.

69. Clarence King, "The Education of the Future," *Forum* 13 (Mar. 1892), 20–33; quote, 27.

70. King, "Bancroft's Native Races of the Pacific States," 165.

CHAPTER 6: FAMILY LIVES

1. The earliest recorded date of Ada's residence here is on the 1891 birth certificate for Ada's second child, Grace Margaret. On the geography of Brooklyn's black community, see Seth M. Scheiner, *Negro Mecca: A History of the Negro in New York City, 1865–1920* (New York: New York University Press, 1965), 22–25.

2. "Condition of Hudson Avenue," *Brooklyn Daily Eagle*, June 1, 1888, 1.

3. "A City Survey: The Condition of Brooklyn's Streets and Houses," *Brooklyn Daily Eagle*, May 9, 1885, 1.

4. [Sanborn Map Company Insurance Maps of New York], Atlas 66, New York (City), Brooklyn, vol. 2, 1887, sheet 42, Map Division, New York Public Library.

5. Craig Steven Wilder, *A Covenant with Color: Race and Social Power in Brooklyn* (New York: Columbia University Press, 2000), 118. On the Navy Yard, see *Rand McNally Guide* (1895), 195.

6. "A City Survey," 1.

7. See the Sanborn map and "A City Survey," 1.

8. See, for example, "A Birthday Social," *New York Age*, Jan. 28, 1888, 2; "Brooklyn Briefs," *New York Age*, May 19, 1888, 3; and Johnson, *Along This Way*, 202.

9. Burrows and Wallace, *Gotham*, 1068.

10. "Relief Asked from Alleged Nuisances in Hudson Avenue," *Brooklyn Daily Eagle*, Aug. 3, 1891, 4; "No Rioting: The Police Say That Hudson Avenue Is Peaceful," *Brooklyn Daily Eagle*, Aug. 7, 1891, 4; "Hudson Avenue at Peace," *Brooklyn Daily Eagle*, Aug. 8, 1891, 2.

11. Johnson, *Along This Way*, 47.

12. The Reverend Richard S. Storrs, as quoted in Alan Trachtenberg, *Brooklyn Bridge: Fact and Symbol*, 2nd ed. (1965; repr., University of Chicago Press, 1979), 124.

13. "The Traffic of the Cable Railway on the New York and Brooklyn Bridge," *Manufacturer and Builder* 21 (Feb. 1889): 32.

14. Burrows and Wallace, *Gotham*, 1058.

15. King is listed as a resident of the Hotel Albert in the "New York City Directory, 1890," http://search.ancestrylibrary.com/cgi-bin/sse.dll?rank=0&gsfn=&gsln=king&gskw=11th&prox=1&db=nyc1890&ti=5542&ti.si=0&gss=angs-d&ct=170103 (accessed Aug. 5, 2007).

16. "New York City Directory, 1890"; "Hotel Albert" (display ad), *New York Times*, Apr. 29, 1890, 7; "Death of Albert S. Rosenbaum," *New York Times*, Feb. 18, 1894, 7; "Obituary Notes: Arthur P. Yorston," *New York Times*, May 1, 1903, 9; "Business Troubles: New York City: Yorston Brothers," *New York Times*, Feb. 17, 1898, 5; "Death List of a Day: Gilbert K. Harroun," *New York Times*, Sept. 14, 1901, 7; "Western Merchants Organize," *New York Times*, Aug. 13, 1889, 2; "Educational Institutions: Miss Minnie Swayze," *New York Times*, Aug. 24, 1895, 9; "Is This Another Suicide?" *New York Times*, Dec. 15, 1890, 1; "Did Not Pay His Hotel Bill," *New York Times*, Oct. 19, 1890, 16.

17. For the relative cost of the Hotel Albert, see *Rand McNally Guide* (1895), 14–18.

18. JTG to S. F. Emmons, receipt dated 10 Feb. 1902, box 35, S. F. Emmons Papers, LC.

19. "Mammy Bares Life as Wife of Scientist," *New York Daily News*, Nov. 21, 1933, 3.

20. CK to JH, 12 Aug. [1888], Hay Collection, Brown.

21. Ibid., 5 Nov. 1888.

22. King complained about his "densely gouty state" to Hay, ibid., July 1888.

23. JH to Sir John Clark, 14 May 1887, *Letters of John Hay*, 2:112.

24. HA to JH, 4 Aug. 1887, in *The Letters of Henry Adams*, ed. J. C. Levenson et al. (Cambridge, MA: Belknap Press of Harvard, 1982–1988), 3:71.

25. CK to Clara Stone Hay, 30 Dec. 1887, Hay Collection, Brown.

26. The possibility of an undiagnosed tubercular infection is raised by King's later death from pulmonary tuberculosis. On spinal TB, see Robert F. McLain, M.D., and Carlos Isada, M.D., "Spinal Tuberculosis Deserves a Place on the Radar Screen," *Cleveland Clinic Journal of Medicine* 71, no. 7 (July 2004): 537–49. Nonetheless, the progression of the disease would seem to be too slow for spinal TB to be the source of his problem.

27. On pilonidal cysts, see http://www.mayoclinic.com/health/pilonidal-cyst/DS00747/DSECTION=1 (accessed July 19, 2007). Thanks to Dr. Ralph Bransky.

28. CK to JH, 12 Nov. 1888; CK to JH, n.d. Dec. 1888; Hay Collection, Brown. On the Arlington Hotel, see Ann L. Greene, "The Arlington Hotel: An Arkansas Institution, 1875–1945," *The Record* (Garland County Historical Society, 1996): 1–22 (citation courtesy of Wendy Richter).

29. HA to JH, 1 June 1889, *Letters of Henry Adams*, 3:177–78; CK to JH, 2 Oct. 1889, Hay Collection, Brown; JH to HA, 21 Sept. 1889, *Letters of John Hay*, 2:176; HA to Lucy Baxter, 10 Oct. 1889, *Letters of Henry Adams*, 3:202; HA to Sir Robert Cunliffe, 20 Oct. 1889, *Letters of Henry Adams*, 3:204; JH to HA, 22 Oct. 1889, *Letters of John Hay*, 2:180–81.

30. JH to Sir John Clark, 14 May 1887, *Letters of John Hay*, 2:113.

31. CK to JH, 2 Oct. 1889, Hay Collection, Brown.

32. I have been unable to locate a copy of Leroy's birth certificate. His date of birth is roughly affirmed by the confirmed date of birth for the Todds' second child in January 1891. Ada refers to Leroy in "Mammy Bares Life," 3–4.

33. CK to HA, 25 Sept. 1889, cited in Wilkins, *King*, 366.

34. JTG to S. F. Emmons, receipt dated 10 Feb. 1902.

35. CK to JH, 2 Mar. 1890, Hay Collection, Brown.

36. On George S. Howland's life and career as a painter, see *Quarter Centenary Record of the Class of 1888: Sheffield Scientific School, Yale University*, comp. Percey F. Smith (New Haven, CT: Printed for the class, 1915), 114; Edward S. Moore, comp., *Forty-Year Book of the Class of 1888: Sheffield Scientific School, Yale University* (New Haven, CT: Printed for the class, 1929), 82–87; Edward F. R. Wood Jr., *Old Mattapoisett: A Summer Portrait* (Mattapoisett, MA: Quadequina Publishers, 1995), 156–59; "George Howland Dies at French Resort," *New York Times*, Sept. 16, 1928, 37. Howland moved to France in the mid-1890s and remained there until his death in 1928. Citations courtesy of Neilson Abeel.

37. CK to JH, 2 Mar. [1890], Hay Collection, Brown.

38. JTG to S. F. Emmons, receipt dated 10 Feb. 1902.

39. JH to William Dean Howells, 30 Jan. 1890, in *John Hay–Howells Letters: The Correspondence of John Milton Hay and William Dean Howells, 1861–1905*, ed. George Monteiro and Brenda Murphy (Boston: Twayne Publishers, 1980), 97.

40. Michael Burlingame, ed., *At Lincoln's Side: John Hay's Civil War Correspondence and Selected Writings* (Carbondale and Edwardsville: Southern Illinois University Press, 2000), 23, 127.

41. On Hay and race, see Kenton J. Clymer, *John Hay: The Gentleman as Diplomat* (Ann Arbor: University of Michigan Press, 1975), 65–91.

42. See O'Toole, *Five of Hearts*, 217–20.

43. CK to JH, 16 Oct. 1890, Hay Collection, Brown.

44. JH to HA, 30 Dec. 1890, *Letters of John Hay*, 2:208.

45. Ibid.

46. For Alexander Lancaster's birth date, see 1900 U.S. Federal Census, Bronx Borough, New York County, NY, SD 1, ED 1057, sheet 1, http://content.ancestrylibrary.com/iexec/default.aspx?htx=View&r=5542&dbid=7602&iid=NYT623_1128-0158&fn=Alexander&ln=Lancaster&st=r&ssrc=&pid=45366684 (accessed Aug. 15, 2007).

47. Wilkins, *King,* 405.

48. Raymond, "Biographical Notice," in Hague, *Memoirs,* 347.

49. Ibid.

50. Wilkins, *King,* 382–83.

51. Raymond, "Biographical Notice," in Hague, *Memoirs,* 349.

52. CK to JH, Dec. 1890, Hay Collection, Brown.

53. *Official Register of the Officers and Cadets of the U.S. Military Academy, West Point, N.Y.* (June 1887), 4; "Indian Wars Campaigns That the 4th U.S. Artillery Participated in, 1870–1881," http://www .batteryb.com/officersofthe4thartillery/battles-indians.html (accessed Aug. 24, 2004); *Newport, Rhode Island, 1890* (Newport: Sampson, Murdock, 1890).

54. "Newport Improvements," *New York Times,* Jan. 11, 1891, 14.

55. FKH to Clara Hay, 6 July 1890, cited in O'Toole, *Five of Hearts,* 259.

56. CK to JH [Jan. 1891], Hay Collection, Brown.

57. "Down Fell Pole and Wire: Destructive Work of Saturday Night's Big Storm," *New York Times,* Jan. 26, 1891, 1.

58. Burrows and Wallace, *Gotham,* 1066–68.

59. Certificate of Birth, Brooklyn. 920 for _____ Todd, 24 Jan. 1891, New York City Department of Records and Information Services, Municipal Archives. On P. E. Kidd, see 1900 U.S. Federal Census, Borough of Brooklyn, Kings County, NY, SD 2, ED 120, sheet 1, http:// content.ancestrylibrary.com/Browse/view.aspx?dbid=7602&path=New+York.Kings.Brooklyn+ Ward+9.120.1&fn=P%20Edwin&ln=Kidd&st=r&pid=48483451&rc=&zp=50 (accessed Aug. 15, 2007).

60. Wm. M. Lively, M.D., "Medical Union Needed," *New York Age,* Feb. 16, 1889, 4.

61. JH to HA, 20 Jan. 1891, *Letters of John Hay,* 2:213. King was in Newport later in February, along with the other "Summer residents" who gathered then to help make arrangements for the summer season. "Getting Ready for Summer: Newport Putting Itself in Shape for the Coming Season," *New York Times,* Mar. 1, 1891, 17.

62. As discussed in chapter 3, it is difficult to ascertain which Ada Copeland in the 1870 Georgia census might actually be the young Ada Todd, and no likely candidates appear in the 1880 census. Nonetheless, even if Ada appears in these records, we might imagine that the census agents obtained their information about her from someone else living in the household. Ada likely spoke to the federal census taker who called on her Hudson Avenue apartment in 1890, but that information disappeared in the fire that destroyed most of the 1890 census records. And if she spoke to an official record keeper on the occasion of Leroy's birth, those records cannot be found. Hence her daughter's birth certificate becomes the earliest account of Ada's own life, in her own words.

63. Certificate of Birth, Brooklyn. 920 for _____ Todd, 24 Jan. 1891.

64. JH to HA, 6 Jan. 1892, *Letters of John Hay,* 2:234; CK to JH, May 1891, Hay Collection, Brown.

65. "Dinner to General Greene," *New York Times,* May 6, 1891, 5; "Cottagers at Newport," *New York Times,* June 21, 1891, 13.

66. CK to JH, Dec. 1890, Hay Collection, Brown.

67. Ibid., [n.d. 1891].

68. Ibid.

69. I infer the timing of the family's move from Certificate of Birth, Brooklyn. 998, for Ada Todd, who was born at 72 Skillman Street on Jan. 31, 1892 (New York City Department of Records and Information Services, Municipal Archives). Ada's older sister, Grace, was born fifty-three weeks earlier at the Hudson Avenue house. On the geography of Brooklyn's black community, see Scheiner, *Negro Mecca,* 23–24.

70. Scheiner, *Negro Mecca,* 34.

71. CK to JH, May 1891, Hay Collection, Brown. The loan is dated Apr. 20, 1891, in JTG to S. F. Emmons, receipt dated 10 Feb. 1902.

72. JH to HA, 4 June 1891, *Letters of John Hay*, 2:221.

73. CK to Mrs. Hay [July 1891], reel 8, Hay Collection, Mss. Div., LC.

74. See the street maps, including 72 Skillman Street, in [Sanborn Map Company Insurance Maps of New York], Atlas 69, vol. 3, 1887, sheet 64, and Atlas 70, vol. 3, 1904, sheet 55, Map Division, New York Public Library.

75. "72 Skillman Street," in "Brooklyn, New York Directories, 1888–1890," http://search.ancestry library.com/cgi-bin/sse.dll?rank=0&f0=&f4=&f5=&gskw=72+skillman&prox=1& db=1890brookny&ti=5542&ti.si=0&gl=&gss=mp-1890brookny&gst=&so=3 (accessed Feb. 2, 2005).

76. Johnson, *Along This Way*, 48.

77. Congrès Géologique International, *Compte rendu de la 5me session, Washington, 1891* (Washington: Imprimerie du Gouvernement, 1893). Thanks to Clifford M. Nelson for bringing to my attention this published volume, which includes lists of the conference attendees and accounts of the proceedings.

78. CK to JH, 8 Sept. [1891], Hay Collection, Brown. It is not entirely clear who "Augusta" might have been. An Augusta Riley appears in the Newport federal census records for 1880 and 1900 (the 1890 records are missing), recorded as "black" and designated first as a laundress and later as a cook. One record describes her as Maryland born, the other as from Virginia. See 1880 U.S. Federal Census, Newport, RI, SD 121, ED 94, http://content.ancestrylibrary.com/iexec/ ?htx=View&r=5542&dbid=6742&iid=RIT9_1210-0415&fn=Augusta&ln=Riley&st=r& ssrc=&pid=16507663, and 1900 U.S. Federal Census, Newport, RI, Ward 4, ED 221, sheet 8, http://content.ancestrylibrary.com/Browse/view.aspx?dbid=7602&path=Rhode+Island .Newport.Newport+Ward+4.221.16&fn=Augusta&ln=Riley&st=r&pid=69137131&rc= &zp=50 (both accessed July 15, 2007).

79. John Duffy, *A History of Public Health in New York City, 1866–1966* (New York: Russell Sage Foundation, 1974), 212. On the efforts of the New York Health Department during the early 1890s to assure the safety of the milk supply, see ibid., 132–36.

80. Sacks, "'We Cry,'" 233.

81. JH to HA, 6 Jan. 1892, *Letters of John Hay*, 2:234.

82. Certificate of Birth, Brooklyn. 998, for Ada Todd, Feb. 1, 1892 (filing date), New York City Department of Records and Information Services, Municipal Archives.

83. CK to JH, Jan. 1892, Hay Collection, Brown.

84. Ibid., 25 Jan. 1892; n.d. Feb. 1892; 9 Feb. 1892.

85. *New York Freeman*, Sept. 11, 1886, cited in Scheiner, *Negro Mecca*, 163.

86. CK to William Brewer, 15 May [1892], HM 27833, HEH.

87. William H. Brewer, "Heredity: Race Crossing," speech delivered Nov. 1, 1879, to the Social Science Club, Brewer Papers, Yale.

88. Brewer's response to King cannot be found, and no references to King's letter can be located in the Brewer Papers.

89. CK to JH, 28 May 1892, Hay Collection, Brown.

90. Ibid., 10 July 1892.

91. Ibid., 30 July 1892.

92. Ibid., 14 Oct. 1892.

93. Although none of the actual letters are known to survive, some of them were read out loud in court when Ada King pressed her claims for King's estate in 1933. Both court reporters and newspaper reporters avidly transcribed the words. See below, chapter 10.

94. "White Scientist's Love Letters to Colored Wife Are Bared in Court," *Pittsburgh Courier*, Dec. 2, 1933, sec. 1, 5.

95. "Scientist's Letters Reveal His Love for Colored Wife," *New York Daily News*, Nov. 22, 1933, 3.

96. The letter King wrote from his deathbed instructing Ada in how to address his letters (see Defendant's Exhibit C, Plaintiff's Trial Memorandum, 171, in *King v. Peabody et al.*, file no.

26821=1931; Records of the Supreme Court of the State of New York, New York County Clerk's Office) suggests that she had heretofore been writing to him under his alias.

97. JH to HA, 25 Nov. 1892, *Letters of John Hay*, 2:249. Evidence for his visit with Ada comes from the estimated date of conception for their son Sidney, who was born on July 19, 1893.

98. Adams, *Education*, 321, 325.

99. Ibid., 328.

100. HA to JH, 5 Nov. 1893, *Letters of Henry Adams*, 4:138.

101. R. Hal Williams, *Years of Decision: American Politics in the 1890s* (New York: John Wiley & Sons, 1978), 76–77.

102. Junius Henri Browne, "The Bread and Butter Question," *Harper's Monthly* 88 (Dec. 1893): 278, cited in Dunlop, *Gilded City*, 134.

103. *Chicago Daily Tribune*, Mar. 15, 1893, 4; "Dined by Whitelaw Reid," *New York Times*, June 2, 1893, 5; "A Newport Society Feast," *Washington Post*, Aug. 18, 1893, 5.

104. Wilkins, *King*, 353, 386–87.

105. Certificate of Birth, Brooklyn. 8698, 21 July 1893 (filing date) New York City Department of Records and Information Services, Municipal Archives. The 1880 U.S. Federal Census for Brooklyn, King's County, NY, SD 2, ED 193, p. 24, notes that Samuel Stiles was then working at the Brooklyn Homeopathic Hospital. By 1890, reported the *Brooklyn, New York Directory for 1890–91* (Brooklyn: Lain, 1890), he was in practice at 51 Greene Avenue, with that rare new commodity...a telephone. For more on Stiles, who was an ardent genealogist, see "Samuel Edward Stiles, M.D.," *New York Genealogical and Biographical Record* 33, no. 1 (Jan. 1902): 5.

106. Sidney's middle initial is noted on his death certificate. See New York State Department of Health Certificate of Death, 42437, for Sidney C. King (10 July 1942), New York State Department of Health, Vital Records Section, Albany.

107. "A Newport Society Feast"; "His Mind Unbalanced: Clarence King Taken to the Bloomingdale Insane Asylum," *New York Daily Tribune*, 4 Nov. 1893, 7.

108. CK to S. F. Emmons, 23 Oct. 1893, box 11, S. F. Emmons Papers, LC.

109. Defendant's Exhibit L, Plaintiff's Trial Memorandum, 162. This letter is undated. My placing of it here is conjectural, based on King's diminishing economic prospects during the depression of 1893.

110. CK to S. F. Emmons, 23 Oct. 1893, box 11, S. F. Emmons Papers, LC.

111. CK to JH, [1893], Hay Collection, Brown.

CHAPTER 7: BREAKDOWNS

1. *Chicago Tribune*, Nov. 4, 1893, 3. See also *Washington Post*, Nov. 5, 1893, 4.

2. The comment on the Menagerie's popularity comes from Mabel Parsons; ed., *Memories of Samuel Parsons: Landscape Architect of Public Parks, New York* (New York: G. P. Putnam's Sons, 1926), 67. On the animals, see *Rand McNally Guide* (1895), 64–65, and on the animal-rights issue, see Dunlop, *Gilded City*, 251–52. On the Irish names, see "No More Offensive Names," *New York Times*, Apr. 21, 1893, 9. For the weather report, see "Hudnut's Weather Report," *New York Times*, Oct. 30, 1893, 2.

3. This account of King's arrest is drawn largely from "Arrested in Central Park: A Man Who Said He Was Clarence King and Lived at the Union League," *New York Daily Tribune*, Oct. 31, 1893, 4. On Parsons, see *Memories of Samuel Parsons* and Charles A. Birnbaum and Lisa E. Crowder, eds., *Pioneers of American Landscape Design* (Washington, DC: National Park Service, 1993), 93–96.

4. "His Mind Unbalanced," 7.

5. Ibid.; "Registers of Admission, Bloomingdale Asylum, NYH: 1891–1924," vol. 1, "1891–1896," 51, transcription courtesy of James L. Gehrlich, Head of Archives, Medical Center Archives, New York–Presbyterian/Weill Cornell. See also "C. W. Gould Is Dead in California Home," *New York Times*, Mar. 20, 1931, 25. Gould was a founder of Gould and Wilkie, the New York law firm that would later handle King's estate.

6. James L. Gehrlich, e-mail communication with author, June 22, 2006.

7. "Is Clarence King Insane?" *New York Sun*, Nov. 3, 1893, 1.

8. "His Mind Unbalanced," 7; La Farge to HA, 7 Nov. [1893], Hay Collection, Brown, cited in Wilkins, *King*, 388.

9. Emmons, "Clarence King—Geologist," in Hague, *Memoirs*, 293.

10. "His Mind Unbalanced," 7. Lincoln dabbled in western mining investments and may have had a personal as well as professional connection to King. See *Hinchman v. Lincoln*, 124 U.S. 38 (1888).

11. "People in General," *Washington Post*, Nov. 24, 1893, 4.

12. Gail Satz, *Anatomy of a Secret Life: The Psychology of Living a Lie* (New York: Morgan Road Books, 2006), 2.

13. Charles W. Gould, *America, a Family Matter* (New York: C. Scribner's Sons, 1922).

14. Williamson, *New People*, 102; Nella Larsen, *Quicksand and Passing*, ed. Deborah McDowell (New Brunswick, NJ: Rutgers University Press, 1986), 157.

15. "His Mind Unbalanced," 7.

16. "Clarence King Insane," *Washington Post*, Nov. 5, 1893, 4; article reprinted from the *New York Herald*.

17. HA to JH, 5 Nov. 1893, and HA to Charles Milnes Gaskell, 26 Nov. 1893, in *Letters of Henry Adams*, 4:137–140.

18. Adams, "King," in Hague, *Memoirs*, 164.

19. Adams, *Education*, 338.

20. Moses King, *King's Handbook of New York City* (Boston: Moses King, 1892), 426–28; CK to HA, 31 Dec. 1893, Adams Papers, MHS.

21. HA to JH, 15 Dec. 1893, *Letters of Henry Adams*, 4:145.

22. On Gardiner, see Moore, *King of the 40th Parallel*, passim, which focuses almost as much on Gardiner as on King.

23. CK to JH, 3 Feb. 1894, in Harold Dean Cater, comp., *Henry Adams and His Friends: A Collection of His Unpublished Letters* (Boston: Houghton Mifflin, 1947), 305–6n.

24. J. D. Hague to JH, 24 Nov. 1893, "Letter Book 24 Nov. 1893–14 Dec. 1895," L17, James D. Hague Papers, HEH.

25. Bronson, *Reminiscences*, 329.

26. S. Weir Mitchell, *Nurse and Patient, and Camp Cure* (Philadelphia: J. B. Lippincott, 1877), 41; Edward M. Brown, "An American Treatment for the 'American Nervousness': George Miller Beard and General Electrization," paper presented to the American Association of the History of Medicine, Boston, 1980, http://bms.brown.edu/HistoryofPsychiatry/Beard.html (accessed Aug. 17, 2007).

27. Mitchell, *Nurse and Patient, and Camp Cure*, 45, 54.

28. Ibid., 45, 54, 55. On Mitchell and the rest cure, see also Barbara Will, "The Nervous Origins of the American Western," *American Literature* 70, no. 2 (June 1998): 293–316.

29. For an overview of the appeal of the West to elite urban easterners in the late nineteenth century, see G. Edward White, *The Eastern Establishment and the Western Experience: The West of Frederic Remington, Theodore Roosevelt, and Owen Wister* (New Haven, CT: Yale University Press, 1968).

30. Mitchell, *Nurse and Patient, and Camp Cure*, 56, 57.

31. Hague, "Editorial Note," in Hague, *Memoirs*, 317n.

32. CK to JH, [n.d. 1893], Hay Collection, Brown.

33. David M. Rein, *S. Weir Mitchell as a Psychiatric Novelist* (New York: International Universities Press, 1952), 129–31.

34. J. D. Hague to JH, 24 Nov. 1893; Hague to E. B. Bronson, 4 Dec. 1893; Hague to Bronson, 11 Dec. 1893, in "Letter Book," L17, Hague Papers, HEH; CK to JH, 3 Feb. 1894, in Cater, *Henry Adams and His Friends*, 305–6n; CK to JH, 16 May 1894, Hay Collection, Brown.

35. Frederick Jackson Turner, "The Significance of the Frontier in American History," *Annual*

Report of the American Historical Association for the Year 1893 (Washington, DC: GPO, 1894): 199, 200, 226–27.

36. Ibid., 227.

37. See, for example, Henry Nash Smith, *Virgin Land: The American West as Symbol and Myth* (Cambridge, MA: Harvard University Press, 1950).

38. King, "Biographers of Lincoln," 862.

39. "Society News from Newport," *New York Times*, Dec. 24, 1893, 13.

40. Harry Hazel and S. L. Lewis, *The Divorce Mill: Realistic Sketches of the South Dakota Divorce Colony* (New York: Mascot, 1895), 10. The ninety-day residency rule changed to a six-month requirement in 1893.

41. CK to HA, 31 Dec. 1893, Adams Papers, MHS.

42. CK to Becker, 31 Dec. 1893, box 3, Merrill Collection, LC. See also ibid., Sunday, [n.d.].

43. Ibid., Sunday, [Jan. 1894], box 2. Thanks to Clifford M. Nelson of the USGS, for first alerting me to this document. See also Passport Application for Native Citizen, No. 6632, submitted by King on Jan. 16, 1899, accessed on Ancestry.com June 20, 2008.

44. "Col. Waring's Messenger Promoted," *New York Times*, June 29, 1895, 16; "Col. Waring Returns to Town," *New York Times*, Aug. 21, 1895, 12.

45. Wilkins, *King*, 207, 218.

46. "Registers of Discharge, Bloomingdale Asylum, NYH: 1891–1933," vol. 1, "1891–1921," 12, transcription courtesy of James L. Gehrlich. The medical records relating to King's case do not survive, most likely a casualty of the disorder surrounding the Bloomingdale Asylum's move from Morningside Heights to White Plains just a few months after King's discharge. James Gehrlich, e-mail communication to author, June 19, 2006.

47. CK to JH, 3 Feb. 1894, in Cater, *Henry Adams and His Friends*, 305–6n.

48. CK to JH, [March?] 1888, Hay Collection, Brown.

49. King, "Draft of novel," E1, King Papers, HEH.

50. HA to JH, 27 Feb. 1894, in Cater, *Henry Adams and His Friends*, 309–11.

51. Adams, "King," in Hague, *Memoirs*, 167; HA to Elizabeth Cameron, 1 Mar. 1894, *Letters of Henry Adams*, 4:170.

52. Adams, "King," in Hague, *Memoirs*, 168.

53. HA to Elizabeth Cameron, 16 Feb. 1894; HA to Mabel Hooper, 22 Feb. 1894, in *Letters of Henry Adams*, 4:162–64.

54. Adams, "King," in Hague, *Memoirs*, 172.

55. Adams, "King," in Hague, *Memoirs*, 173; King, "Shall Cuba Be Free?" *Forum* 20 (Sept. 1895): 65. On King's Cuba views, see also his essay "Fire and Sword in Cuba," *Forum* 22 (Sept. 1896): 31–52.

56. Adams, "King," in Hague, *Memoirs*, 172–73.

57. Wilkins, *King*, 395; HA to JH, 11 Apr. 1894, *Letters of Henry Adams*, 4:180.

58. HA to Abram S. Hewitt, 25 Apr. 1894, *Letters of Henry Adams*, 4:182.

59. HA to Abram S. Hewitt, 27 Apr. 1894, in Allan Nevins, *Abram S. Hewitt: With Some Account of Peter Cooper* (New York: Harper & Brothers, 1935), 549.

60. CK to HA, 11 May 1894, Adams Papers, MHS.

61. Ibid.

62. CK to JH, 16 May 1894, Hay Collection, Brown.

63. Ibid.

64. HA to Sir Robert Cunliffe, 21 June 1894, *Letters of Henry Adams*, 4:195; CK to HA, 12 June 1894, Adams Papers, MHS.

65. "Two Shots, Close Range: Murder at Park Avenue and Skillman Street," *Brooklyn Daily Eagle*, May 31, 1894, 1.

66. JH to Clara Stone Hay, 28 July 1894, *Letters of John Hay*, 2:308; HA to Elizabeth Cameron, 29 July 1894, *Letters of Henry Adams*, 4:206.

67. CK to HA, 22 July 1894, Adams Papers, MHS.

68. CK to JH, 30 Aug. 1894, Hay Collection, Brown.
69. HA to Elizabeth Cameron, 25 Sept. 1894, *Letters of Henry Adams*, 4:211; HA to JH, 26 Sept. 1894, ibid., 214.
70. JH to HA, 10 Oct. 1894, *Letters of John Hay*, 2:336; HA to Elizabeth Cameron, 2 Oct. 1894, *Letters of Henry Adams*, 4:218.
71. CK to HA, 21 Nov. 1894; CK to HA, 26 Nov. 1894, Adams Papers, MHS.
72. CK to HA, 29 Dec. 1894, Adams Papers, MHS. King writes about his plan to spend Christmas in Newport in a letter to S. F. Emmons, [Dec. 1894], Clarence King Papers, APS.
73. "To Release William H. King," *New York Times*, Aug. 30, 1893, 2. "An Unsolved Mystery," *National Police Gazette*, Jan. 26, 1895, 6; "William H. King Is Dead," *New York Times*, Mar. 7, 1897, 3; "Says She Is King's Child," *New York Times*, Dec. 2, 1894, 1; "Sensations in the King Case," *Chicago Daily Tribune*, Dec. 30, 1894, 7.
74. "Says She Is King's Child," 1.
75. "Fight for the King Fortune," *New York Times*, July 10, 1898, 10.
76. JH to HA, 14 June 1895, *Letters of John Hay*, 2:355.
77. Ibid., 3 Sept. 1895, 361.
78. CK to HA, 13 Nov. 1895, Adams Papers, MHS.
79. HA to JH, 14 Nov. 1895, in Cater, *Henry Adams and His Friends*, 351.
80. CK to HA, 28 Nov. 1895, Adams Papers, MHS.
81. CK to JH, 14 Nov. 1895, Hay Collection, Brown.
82. CK to HA, 28 Nov. 1895, Adams Papers, MHS.
83. "London Men Are on the Ground," *Chicago Daily Tribune*, Dec. 20, 1895, 5.
84. "Scientist's Letters Reveal His Love for Colored Wife," 8.
85. "London Men Are on the Ground," 5; HA to Sir Robert Cunliffe, 17 Feb. 1896, *Letters of Henry Adams*, 4:373; HA to Anne Palmer Fell, 22 Dec. 1896, *Letters of Henry Adams*, 4:441.
86. HA to Charles Milnes Gaskell, 4 Jan. 1897, *Letters of Henry Adams*, 4:446.
87. Adams, "King," in Hague, *Memoirs*, 184–85. King's letter, included in the Adams Papers, MHS, is undated.
88. " 'Bloods' Hid Scion's Love for Negress," *New York Daily Mirror*, Nov. 22, 1933, 9.
89. Darby Richardson, ed., *Illustrated Flushing and Vicinity* (New York: Business Men's Association of Flushing, 1917), 16, 25; George Von Skal, *Illustrated History of the Borough of Queens, New York City* (New York: F. T. Smiley, 1908), 23, 63, 74–75; *Atlas of the Borough of Queens: City of New York*, vol. 3 (Brooklyn Borough: E. Belcher Hyde, 1904), plate 5. A photograph of the mansion at 42 North Prince Street is included in "Photographic Views of New York City, 1870s–1970s" ("Queens: Prince Street–35th Avenue," digital image ID 727693F), in the New York Public Library Digital Gallery, http://digitalgallery.nypl.org/nypldigital/dgkeysearchdetail.cfm?trg=1&strucID=417509&imageID=727693F&word=prince%20street%20queens&s=1&notword=&d=&c=&f=&lWord=&lField=&sScope=&sLevel=&sLabel=&total=26&num=12&imgs=12&pNum=&pos=14# (accessed Aug. 19, 2007). The Todd family is listed as living at the Prince Street residence in *Trow's Business and Residential Directory of the Borough of Queens City of New York* (New York: Trow Directory, Printing & Bookbinding, 1898). But Wallace [Todd] King's World War I draft registration and military records note that he was born in Flushing on April 26, 1897. Thus the family likely moved to Prince Street sometime before that date. See World War I Military Service Record for Wallace A. King (U.S. Army serial no. 4 135 642), New York State Archives, and World War I draft registration card for Wallace Archer King (Local Board Division 185, City and State of New York, registration no. 60), http://content.ancestrylibrary.com/iexec/default.aspx?htx=View&r=5542&dbid=6482&iid=NY-1818488-2698&fn=Wallace+Archer&ln=King&st=r&ssrc=&pid=1644001 (accessed May 4, 2004). On the number of rooms in the house, see "Widow Tells of Ceremony and Children," 2. On the lot size, see "In the Real Estate Field," *New York Times*, Aug. 17, 1898, 10.
90. *Trow's Business and Residential Directory of Queens* (1898), 1:60.

91. Description of block compiled from *Trow's Business and Residential Directory of Queens* (1898) and the 1900 U.S. Federal Census. The James Todd on South Prince Street is listed in *Trow's*, 60. On the racial breakdown of Queens in 1900, see *Census Reports*, vol. 1, *Twelfth Census of the United States, Taken in the Year 1900: Population, Part 1* (Washington, DC: United States Census Office, 1901), 631. On a music teacher for the Todd children, see "Negro Woman Sues as Widow of Millionaire," *New York American*, Nov. 21, 1933, 2.

92. For Wallace's birth date, see his World War I draft registration card (n. 89 above). On the weather, see "The Weather," *New York Times*, Apr. 27, 1897, 1.

93. "All Honor to Grant," *New York Times*, Apr. 27, 1897, 1; National Park Service Web site for General Grant National Memorial, http://www.nps.gov/gegr/ (accessed Aug. 8, 2007).

94. Eleanor and Marian Hague, as cited in Wilkins, *King*, 384.

95. "Joseph Meets Old Foes," *New York Times*, Apr. 27, 1897, 1.

96. *Arizona Weekly Journal*, May 12, 1897, 3, and July 28, 1897, 3.

97. Wilkins, *King*, 403.

98. "Clarence King's Views: The Mining Engineer Preparing an Expedition to the New Region," *New York Times*, Aug. 7, 1897, 3; "Opening of a Mining Era: Sanguine Views of Clarence King, a Former Chief of the Geological Survey," *Chicago Daily Tribune*, Sept. 7, 1897, 3.

99. CK to JH, Dec. 1897, Hay Collection, Brown.

100. JH to HA, 27 Dec. 1897, *Letters of John Hay*, 3:106.

101. Wilkins, *King*, 404–5; Alexander R. Becker to S. F. Emmons, 23 June 1902, box 12, S. F. Emmons Papers, LC; "The President Dines with Mr. Hay," *New York Times*, Jan. 14, 1900, 13.

102. Letter from Butte quoted in " 'Bloods' Hid Scion's Love," 3, 9.

103. Alexander R. Becker to S. F. Emmons, 23 June 1902, box 12, S. F. Emmons Papers, LC.

104. Ibid.

105. See the entries for Phoebe Martin and Clarine Eldridge in 1900 U.S. Federal Census, Borough of Queens, Queens County, NY, SD 2, ED 665, sheet 4, http://content.ancestrylibrary .com/iexec/?htx=View&r=5542&dbid=7602&iid=NYT623_1149-0204&fn=Ada&ln=Todd& st=r&ssrc=&pid=56465284 (accessed Aug. 18, 2007). "Phebe Martin," the widow of Jackson T. Martin, is noted as residing at 149 West Twenty-fourth Street in the 1890 *Trow's City Directory for New York*, Ancestry.com (accessed Dec. 3, 2004).

106. "Widow Tells of Ceremony and Children," 1–2; "Negro Woman Sues," 2.

107. Roi Ottley and William J. Weatherby, eds., *The Negro in New York: An Informal Social History* (New York: New York Public Library and Oceana Publications, 1967), 134.

108. "Mammy Bares Life," 3–4.

109. "Widow Tells of Ceremony and Children," 2.

110. " 'Bloods' Hid Scion's Love," 9.

111. Plaintiff's Trial Memorandum, 163.

112. "Facts from Flushing," *New York Age*, Jan. 4, 1900, 3.

113. Ottley and Weatherby, *Negro in New York*, 134–35.

114. "Facts from Flushing," 3.

CHAPTER 8: ENDINGS

1. Brown recorded the data for his own household a few days after he called on the Todds. See Twelfth Census of the United States, New York, Queens, SD 2, ED 665, sheet 10B, http:// content.ancestrylibrary.com/Browse/View.aspx?dbid=7602&path=New+York.Queens .Queens+Ward+3.665.20 (accessed Aug. 1, 2007). All forty-four of the census sheets he filled out for his enumeration district, number 665, are accessible at http://content.ancestrylibrary .com/Browse/view.aspx?dbid=7602&iid=NYT623_1149-0197. For details on the census-taking process, see "Census Locally Important," *Brooklyn Daily Eagle*, Mar. 8, 1900, 13; "Census Enumerators Making the Rounds," *Brooklyn Daily Eagle*, June 1, 1900, 1; "Polite Census Takers,"

New York Tribune, June 8, 1900, 6; "Police to Aid Census Takers," *New York Tribune,* May 31, 1900, 7.

2. The school year would not end until June 29, 1900. "Queens Borough Schools," *Brooklyn Daily Eagle,* May 16, 1900, 13.

3. "No School Exclusion for Negro Children," *Brooklyn Daily Eagle,* Mar. 30, 1900, 3; "Wallace Will Win His Case: Defeated in the Courts He Asks Legislature to Abolish Colored Schools," *Brooklyn Daily Eagle,* Apr. 2, 1900, 13; "Negro Teachers for Whites: First Effect of the Law Will Be Felt in the Opening of the Schools," *Brooklyn Daily Eagle,* Sept. 7, 1900, 8.

4. The Todd household is recorded on the 1900 U.S. Federal Census, Borough of Queens, Queens County, NY, SD 2, ED 665, sheet 4B, http://content.ancestrylibrary.com/Browse/View.aspx ?dbid=7602&path=New+York.Queens.Queens+Ward+3.665.8 (accessed Aug. 1, 2007).

5. Martha Hodes, "Fractions and Fictions in the United States Census of 1890," in *Haunted by Empire: Geographies of Intimacy in North American History,* ed. Ann Laura Stoler (Durham, NC, and London: Duke University Press, 2006), 240–70; David Theo Goldberg, *Racial Subjects: Writing on Race in America* (New York: Routledge, 1997), 36–41.

6. Henry Gannett, "The Average American," *Everybody's Magazine* 5, no. 25 (Sept. 1901): 318 (citation courtesy of Jean-Christophe Agnew); N. H. Darnton, "Memoir of Henry Gannett," *Annals of the Association of American Geographers* 7 (1917): 68–70.

7. "Twelve Numerators Weary of the Census," *Brooklyn Daily Eagle,* June 2, 1900, 6.

8. See the entry for James Todd, 1900 U.S. Federal Census.

9. Bronson, *Reminiscences,* 326; CK to George F. Becker, 31 Dec. [1893], cited in Wilkins, *King,* 169.

10. CK to HA, 29 Apr. 1895, Adams Papers, MHS.

11. A search of the 1850 and 1860 census records accessible through Ancestry.com reveals just two black West Indians living in Newport in 1850, five in 1860.

12. Wilkins, *King,* 6.

13. On the changing legal and social perceptions of mixed-race Americans, see Williamson, *New People.*

14. Mangum, *Legal Status of the Negro,* 2–13. There is a large body of writing about *Plessy v. Ferguson.* For a useful introduction, see *Plessy v. Ferguson: A Brief History with Documents,* ed. and with an introduction by Brook Thomas (Boston: Bedford Books, 1997).

15. Cited in Martha Hodes, "The Mercurial Nature and Abiding Power of Race: A Transnational Love Story," *American Historical Review* (Feb. 2003): 106.

16. Hodes's wonderful essay "The Mercurial Nature and Abiding Power of Race" offers an illuminating discussion of the ways in which race and complexion could be understood differently in late-nineteenth-century Jamaica and Massachusetts as interpreted through the "lived experience" of one family. See also her book *The Sea Captain's Wife: A True Story of Love, Race and War in the Nineteenth Century* (New York: W. W. Norton, 2006).

17. "Mulattoes Not Negroes," *Brooklyn Daily Eagle,* Dec. 5, 1902, 18.

18. *The Statistics of the Population of the United States Embracing the Tables of Race, Nationality, Sex Selected Ages, and Occupations…from the Original Returns of the Ninth Census* (Washington, DC: GPO, 1872), 391.

19. Sacks, "'We Cry,'" 40.

20. *Twelfth Census of the United States: Population, Part I,* 803. This figure excludes immigrants from Cuba and Puerto Rico.

21. Ottley and Weatherby, *Negro in New York,* 192; Sacks, "'We Cry,'" 40–42, 55–56; Johnson, *Along This Way,* 65.

22. Ovington, *Half a Man,* 212.

23. Ottley and Weatherby, *Negro in New York,* 192.

24. Davis R. Dewey, *Employees and Wages* [Special Report of the Twelfth Census of the United States, 1900] (Washington, DC: United States Census Office, 1903), 672–73; David Brody,

Steelworkers in America: The Nonunion Era (Cambridge, MA: Harvard University Press, 1960), 46.

25. "'Bloods' Hid Scion's Love," 9.

26. DuBois, *Philadelphia Negro,* 367.

27. "'Bloods' Hid Scion's Love," 9.

28. "Justice Stays Ruling in King Trust Estate," *New York American,* Nov. 22, 1933, 3.

29. "'Bloods' Hid Scion's Love," 9.

30. Ibid.

31. Ibid.

32. Johnson, *Black Manhattan,* 127–29.

33. Ibid., 426; Sacks, "'We Cry,'" 64–65.

34. "Race Riot on West Side," *New York Times,* Aug. 16, 1900, 1; "Police in Control in Riotous District," *New York Times,* Aug. 17, 1900, 2.

35. Sacks, "'We Cry,'" 69; "Negro Aliens Complain," *New York Times,* Aug. 25, 1900, 1.

36. "Rias Body, Ex-Slave," WPA interview, Apr. 9, 1946, "Born in Slavery: Slave Narratives from the Federal Writers' Project, 1936–1938," Library of Congress American Memory Web site.

37. JH to Sir John Clark, 18 Sept. 1900, *Letters of John Hay,* 3:191.

38. Wilkins, *King,* 407–8; King to S. F. Emmons, 28 Dec. 1900, box 12, S.F. Emmons Papers, LC; Henry M. Adkinson to J. D. Hague, 22 Aug. 1904, A1, King Papers, HEH.

39. HA to Elizabeth Cameron, 3 Mar. 1901, *Letters of Henry Adams,* 5:213; ibid., 22 Apr. 1901, 224; Wilkins, *King,* 408–9; JH to HA, 7 May 1901, *Letters of John Hay,* 3:207; Adams, *Education,* 395; S. F. Emmons, Diary, 20 Apr. 1901, box 4, S. F. Emmons Papers, LC.

40. "Mammy Bares Life," 3–4.

41. "Negro Woman Sues," 2.

42. Plaintiff's Trial Memorandum, 169. All legal citations in this chapter are to *King v. Peabody et al.* unless otherwise noted.

43. Ibid.; "Negro Woman Sues." Research has failed to locate Logan School: Andrew Rodger, Library and Archives Canada, e-mail correspondence to author Sept. 20, 2004. On King and the Canadian mining interests of the War Eagle Consolidated Company, see "Shareholders Re-elect the Old Management to Office," *Toronto Globe,* Feb. 22, 1900, 7; citation courtesy of Andrew Rodger.

44. See Robin W. Winks, *The Blacks in Canada: A History,* 2nd ed. (Montreal and Kingston: McGill–Queen's University Press, 1997), esp. 288–320, 331–32, 362–76, 484–96. Ada Todd and her children lived in Toronto for less than a year, and I have been unable to find a trace of them in city records.

45. JH to HA, 9 Aug. 1901, *Letters of John Hay,* 3:222–23; Hay quotes from King's letter. See also Wilkins, *King,* 409.

46. JH to HA, 9 Aug. 1901, *Letters of John Hay,* 3:223; JH to CK, 6 Aug. 1901, ibid., 221.

47. CK to JH, 22 Aug. [1901], reprinted in Tyler Dennett, *John Hay,* 161–62.

48. Ibid.

49. Ibid.

50. Adams, *Education,* 346–47.

51. CK to JH, 22 Aug. 1901, in Dennett, *John Hay,* 161–62.

52. Ibid.

53. Hay, "Clarence King," in Hague, *Memoirs,* 126.

54. Bronson, *Reminiscences,* 328.

55. CK to JH, 30 Nov. 1885, Hay Collection, Brown.

56. Ibid., 28 July 1887.

57. Ibid., 4 July 1886.

58. JH to HA, 25 Aug. 1887, *Letters of John Hay,* 2:131.

59. CK to JH, 12 Aug. [1888], Hay Collection, Brown.

60. [H. Lay ?] to James D. Hague, 18 Dec. 1903, box 2, A3, King Papers, HEH.

61. Hay, "Clarence King," in Hague, *Memoirs*, 126–27.

62. Emmons, "Clarence King—Geologist," in Hague, *Memoirs*, 291.

63. Raymond, "Biographical Notice," in Hague, *Memoirs*, 355.

64. Emmons, "Clarence King—Geologist," in Hague, *Memoirs*, 291.

65. Raymond, "Biographical Notice," in Hague, *Memoirs*, 354–55.

66. Owen Wister, *The Virginian: A Horseman of the Plains* (New York: Macmillan, 1904), 502.

67. Wilkins, *King*, 365, 385–86, 397–98.

68. George Wharton James, "Clarence King," 34.

69. Emmons, Diary, 15–21 Oct. 1901, box 4, S.F. Emmons Papers, LC.

70. Defendant's Exhibit C, Plaintiff's Trial Memorandum, 171.

71. Ada apparently turned the letter, or a copy of it, over to James T. Gardiner and his associates after her husband's death. See Plaintiff's Trial Memorandum, 165.

72. See Defendant's Exhibit N, Plaintiff's Trial Memorandum, 166.

73. Ibid., 167.

74. Plaintiff's Trial Memorandum, 165.

75. Ibid., 166.

76. JH to HA, 21 Oct. 1901, *Letters of John Hay*, 3:241–42.

77. HA to JH, 2 Nov. 1901, *Letters of Henry Adams*, 5:308; S. F. Emmons to J. D. Hague, rc'd 18 Dec. 1901, box 1, King Papers, HEH.

78. Charles Walcott to S. F. Emmons, 3 Oct. 1901, box 12, S. F. Emmons Papers, LC.; Arthur T. Hadley to Charles Walcott, 25 Sept. 1901, ibid.

79. In the James D. Hague Papers (box 12, M16) at the Huntington Library is a telegram from King to Hague dated 2 Oct. 1901, which is clipped to an undated note to Hague that conveys these directions for Gardiner. That the letter was written at about the same time as the telegram seems likely but is not certain.

80. Plaintiff's Trial Memorandum, 110.

81. JH to S. F. Emmons, 15 Dec. 1901, box 12, S. F. Emmons Papers, LC.

82. FKH to Charles Webb Howard, 17 Jan. 1902, cited in Wilkins, *King*, 410.

83. Emmons, "Clarence King—Geologist," in Hague, *Memoirs*, 294.

84. G. W. Middleton to S. F. Emmons, 5 Apr. 1902, box 12, S. F. Emmons Papers, LC.

85. Wilkins, *King*, 410.

86. See notes on the weather, *Toronto Globe*, Dec. 23–25, 1901, 1.

87. Bronson, *Reminiscences*, 358.

88. James T. Gardiner to James D. Hague [telegram], 24 Dec. 1901, Hague Papers, HEH; "Standard Certificate of Death" [for Clarance [*sic*] King, d. Dec. 24, 1901], http://genealogy.az.gov/azdeath/006/10060764.pdf (accessed Aug. 18, 2007).

89. "E. C. Stedman's Tribute," *New York Tribune*, Dec. 27, 1901, 7.

90. Wilkins, *King*, 411; King Certificate of Death; Arizona State Board of Health, "Certificate of Death for Robert Wallace Craig," filed 13 July 1933 (state file no. 152V, registration no. 900).

91. [King], "Style and the Monument," 443–44.

92. "Riot in New York," *Toronto Globe*, Dec. 26, 1901, 1.

93. J. D. Hague to James T. Gardiner, 6 Jan. 1902, Letter Book L-27, Hague Papers, HEH; Gardiner to Hague [telegram], 24 Dec. 1901, Hague Papers, HEH.

94. In August 1912 Townsley, now a colonel, was appointed superintendent of the United States Military Academy at West Point. See "Army Orders," *Washington Post*, Aug. 21, 1912, 6; "Will Rule at West Point," *Washington Post*, Aug. 21, 1912, 6. After four years at West Point, he was promoted to brigadier general in 1916 and shortly thereafter assumed command of the army in the Canal Zone in Panama. He died in 1926. See "Promotions in Army," *Washington Post*, July 4, 1916; "Army Orders," *Washington Post*, Sept. 7, 1917, 6; "General Townsley Rests at West Point," *New York Times*, Jan. 1, 1927, 4.

95. "Death of Clarence King," *New York Times*, Dec. 25, 1901, 7.
96. "In Memory of Clarence King," *Washington Post*, Dec. 31, 1901, 2.
97. See King's comments on the draft of the biographical entry about him that Hague had prepared for *Appletons'*, box 1, A1, King Papers, HEH.
98. FKH to J. D. Hague, 27 July [1904?], box 2, A3, King Papers, HEH.
99. Brownell, "King at the Century," in Hague, *Memoirs*, 219; *American Heritage Dictionary*, s.v. "Paradox."
100. Adams, "King," in Hague, *Memoirs*, 167.
101. "Weather," *New York Times*, Jan. 2, 1902, 9.
102. Howells, "Meetings with King," in Hague, *Memoirs*, 153.
103. J. D. Hague, Letter Book L27, 527, Hague Papers, HEH. Hague's notes indicate two other pallbearers, identified only as Olyphant and Gould.
104. Poet Edmund Clarence Stedman as quoted in [JTG], "Clarence King's Boyhood," King Papers, HEH.
105. "Funeral of Clarence King," *New York Times*, Jan. 2, 1902, 7; Emmons, Diary, 1, 2 Jan. 1902, box 4, S. F. Emmons Papers, LC; Wilkins, *King*, 411. On King's gravesite, see Robert Wilson, "Looking for Newport's Own," *Preservation* (Jan./Feb. 2006): 18–19, 61.

CHAPTER 9: ON HER OWN

1. *New York Herald*, Mar. 19, 1902, 1; "Weather," *New York Times*, Mar. 17, 1902, 1.
2. Memorandum for Defendants, *King v. Peabody et al.* (file no. 26821-1931; Records of the Supreme Court of the State of New York, New York County Clerk's Office), 35. All legal citations in this chapter are to *King v. Peabody et al.* unless otherwise noted.
3. "Slot Machine Room Raided," *New York Times*, Dec. 4, 1900, 3; "Notes of the Campaign," *New York Times*, Oct. 8, 1900, 2; "Yesterday's Fires," *New York Times*, Nov. 24, 1897, 3; 1900 U.S. Federal Census, Manhattan, New York County, NY, SD 1, ED 684, sheet 14.
4. 1900 U.S. Federal Census, Manhattan, New York County, NY, SD 1, ED 684, sheet 14. The "Mannel Coopland" listed in the Manhattan census of 1880 would seem to be the same man as the "Emanuel Copeland" listed in the 1900 census, sharing the same birthplace and approximate date of birth. See 1880 U.S. Federal Census, New York City, New York, SD 1, ED 570, 25. For the Virginia-born black Copelands residing in Harris County, Georgia, in 1870, see the summary of census data, http://search.ancestrylibrary.com/cgi-bin/sse.dll?rank=0&gsfn=&gsln=copeland&sx=&f5=GA&f4=&f7=&f21=virginia&rg_81004011__date=&rs_81004011__date=0&f15=Colored&f28=&gskw=&prox=1&db=1870usfedcen&ti=5542&ti.si=0&gl=&gss=IMAGE&gst=&so=3 (accessed Oct. 10, 2006).
5. "Negro Woman Sues," 2.
6. Value is from CPI-based conversion calculated on www.measuringworth.com.
7. Defendants' memorandum, 34–35; Plaintiff's Trial Memorandum, 33, passim.
8. "Howard Dutcher Sues for Divorce," *New York Times*, Jan. 9, 1909, 5; "Mexican Coal & Coke Company" [advertisement], *New York Times*, Feb. 24, 1902.
9. "Howard Dutcher Sues," 5.
10. "Widow Tells of Ceremony and Children," 1–2.
11. Plaintiff's Trial Memorandum Relating to the Existence of the Trust, 5, 7.
12. Ibid., 5; Memorandum for Defendants, 54–55. For the legal transactions surrounding this piece of property, see Queens County Register, Jamaica, Queens, Deeds, Queens County, Liber 1307, 449 (Lena York to Howard Dutcher, 13 July 1903), and Deeds, Queens County, Liber 1313, 227 (Howard Dutcher to James T. Gardiner, 11 Sept. 1903). The house still stands and has been renumbered as 137-55 Kalmia Avenue.
13. Plaintiff's Trial Memorandum, 7.
14. *Atlas of the Borough of Queens, City of New York* (Brooklyn: E. Belcher Hyde, 1904), 6.

15. Description of house interior from Patricia Chacon, personal communication with author, Wilmington, NC, June 20, 2006.

16. Harry Herbert Crosby relates this story in his 1953 Stanford University Ph.D. dissertation, "So Deep a Trail: A Biography of Clarence King" (p. 359), citing a personal communication from Mrs. C. S. Fayerweather, 21 Oct. 1951. Dr. Crosby reports that he no longer has a copy of this document. The story about the Gardiner servants may be apocryphal. Surviving census records list only white servants in the Gardiner household: housekeepers from Virginia and Canada, and a nursemaid from Switzerland. Since the story first surfaced some twenty years after King's secret life became public knowledge, its particulars may be burnished by the imperfections of memory and the human desire to be party to the drama of the past. Information on the Gardiner family's white servants comes from the 1900 U.S. Federal Census, where the family appears under "Gardner" in the Manhattan census, SD 1, ED 689 (accessed on Ancestry.com, Apr. 20, 2004).

17. Adams, "King," in Hague, *Memoirs*, 160.

18. S. F. Emmons, Diary, 26–30 Dec. 1901, box 4, S. F. Emmons Papers, LC.

19. R. W. Raymond to J. D. Hague, 17 Jan. 1902, A3, King Papers, HEH.

20. James D. Hague, "Preface," in Hague, *Memoirs*, iii–iv.

21. HA to J. D. Hague, 14 Oct. 1903, Biographical Papers, A2, King Papers, HEH. The handwritten draft of Adams's essay can be found here as well.

22. The original draft of Hay's essay is in A2, King Papers, HEH.

23. Stedman, "Frolic," in Hague, *Memoirs*, 208.

24. Hay, "Clarence King," in Hague, *Memoirs*, 128.

25. S. F. Emmons, "Clarence King," *American Journal of Science* (Mar. 1902): 224–37.

26. HA to Frank Emmons, 17 Mar. [1904], box 12, S.F. Emmons Papers, LC.

27. Hague, *Memoirs*, 37.

28. Copies of the sales solicitations can be found in A2, folder A3, King Papers, HEH.

29. FKH to D. C. Gilman, 27 Oct. 1903, A2, King Papers, HEH.

30. FKH to King Memorial Committee, 16 May 1904, A2, King Papers, HEH.

31. "A Brilliant American," *New York Tribune*, May 12, 1904, 8.

32. "A Memorial Volume," *New York Times Book Review*, June 25, 1904, 443.

33. J. D Hague to Mrs. Howland, 18 Jan. 1902, 28 Jan. 1902, 8 Apr. 1902, 21 Apr. 1902, Letter Book L27, Hague Papers, HEH; Charles Scribner's Sons display ad, *New York Tribune*, Nov. 12, 1902, 3.

34. "A Mountaineering Classic: King's Fine Chronicle of the Exploration of the Sierra Nevada Reprinted after Thirty Years," *Brooklyn Daily Eagle*, Dec. 5, 1902, 14.

35. JTG to JH, 27 June 1904, reel 19, Hay Collection, LC. One can only wonder what King wrote to his mother over the years. The correspondence is not known to survive.

36. "State Courts," *New York Times*, Mar. 13, 1902, 11; Plaintiffs' Trial Memorandum, 16.

37. FKH to JH, 5 Apr. 1902, quoted in O'Toole, *Five of Hearts*, 365.

38. On the auction see "Monet's Paintings Bring Good Prices," *New York Herald*, Mar. 14, 1903, and *Catalogue of Valuable Paintings and Water Colors to Be Sold at Unrestricted Public Sale by Order of the Executors and Trustee of the Estates of the Late Clarence King, William H. Fuller and Theodore G. Weil, the Trustees of H. Victor Newcomb* (New York: Press of J. J. Little, 1903).

39. The print still hangs in the home of Ada's great-granddaughter, Patricia Chacon.

40. S. F. Emmons paid $100 for a Gustave Doré watercolor of a French landscape: see *Catalogue*, lot 30; Hague to JTG, 5 Mar. 1902, box 1, King Papers, HEH. See also "The King and Fuller Sale," *New York Times*, Mar. 12, 1903, 2.

41. The copy of *Catalogue* that has been microfilmed as a part of the Archives of American Art collection is annotated to include the sales prices of the various lots. The total of $34,905 for King's paintings is substantially below the figures later cited by Ada King and the Gardiner estate in *King v. Peabody et al.* Those figures likely include the additional sums realized for the sale of his books, textiles, and other collectibles.

42. Plaintiff's Bill of Particulars, Dec. 8, 1931.

43. Plaintiff's Trial Memorandum, 172, 181–82.

44. Ibid., 94.

45. Testimony of William G. Winne, Memorandum for Defendants, 10, 16; Plaintiff's Trial Memorandum, 17.

46. Winne Deposition (19 Nov. 1931), 2.

47. Ibid.

48. W. E. Burghardt DuBois, "The Black North: A Sociological Study," *New York Times*, Nov. 17, 1901, 10; J. Clay Smith Jr., *Emancipation: The Making of the Black Lawyer, 1844–1944* (Philadelphia: University of Pennsylvania Press, 1993), 624 (app. 2).

49. "Afro-American as a Race Name," *New York Times*, Feb. 25, 1893, 6.

50. On Waring, see A. Briscoe Koger, *The Negro Lawyer in Maryland* (Baltimore: A. B. Koger, 1948), 7; "Black Baltimore 1870–1920, Everett J. Waring: Personal Life," Maryland State Archives, http://www.mdarchives.state.md.us/msa/stagser/s1259/121/6050/html/17454000 .html (accessed Oct. 10, 2005); and Smith, *Emancipation,* 143–44. Before graduating from law school, Waring had a brief career as an educator, a newspaper editor, and a federal examiner of pensions.

51. Smith, *Emancipation,* 145; "Black Baltimore"; Richard R. Wright Jr., *The Philadelphia Colored Business Directory, 1913* (Philadelphia: Philadelphia Negro Business League, 1914), 87, citation courtesy of Randall Burkett. On *Jones v. United States*, see *Jones v. U.S.*, 137 U.S. 202 (1890).

52. Winne Deposition (19 Nov. 1931), 2. Whatever compelled Waring to drop the case, he was not the sort to give in easily or cave to intimidation. As one brief account of his career noted, he "defended or assisted in defending nineteen first degree murder cases, and not a single hanging resulted"; see Wright, *Philadelphia Colored Business Directory,* 87. The determination of Bridgham's race comes from his record in the 1910 U.S. Federal Census, Manhattan, New York County, NY, SD 1, ED 1299, sheet 1B, Ancestry.com (accessed Aug. 18, 2007).

53. See the Legal Aid Society home page: http://www.legal-aid.org/DocumentIndex.htm ?docid=98&catid=13 (accessed Feb. 27, 2005).

54. Winne Deposition (19 Nov. 1931), 2.

55. On J. Douglas Wetmore's family, see 1880 U.S. Federal Census, Jacksonville, Duval County, FL, SD 18, ED 34, 17; George W. Wetmore, record no. 7377, Freedmen's Bank Records, Ancestry.com (accessed July 28, 2005).

56. Johnson, *Along This Way,* 76. On Johnson's use of "D." as the inspiration for the protagonist of *The Autobiography of an Ex-Colored Man,* see Joseph K. Skerrett Jr., "Irony and Symbolic Action in James Weldon Johnson's *The Autobiography of an Ex-Colored Man," American Quarterly* (Winter 1980): 540–58. On "D." as J. Douglas Wetmore, see Eugene Levy, *James Weldon Johnson: Black Leader, Black Voice* (Chicago: University of Chicago Press, 1973), 16n23, 63n29. Wetmore's father, George, the son of an Englishman, described himself as "very light" and worked as a hostler and later as a policeman in Jacksonville.

57. Wetmore to Booker T. Washington, 23 Sept. 1904, cited in Levy, *James Weldon Johnson,* 62n28.

58. See Shira Levine, " 'To Maintain Our Self-Respect': The Jacksonville Challenge to Segregated Street Cars and the Meaning of Equality, 1900–1906," *Michigan Journal of History* (Winter 2005), http://www.umich.edu/-historyj/papers/winter2005/levine.htm. Wetmore wrote to W. E. B. DuBois shortly after the publication of DuBois's *The Souls of Black Folk* in 1903, addressing the author as his fellow black man and asserting that not since Frederick Douglass had their people had such a voice. See David Levering Lewis, *W. E. B. DuBois: Biography of a Race, 1868–1919* (New York: Henry Holt, 1993), 292.

59. On Wetmore's involvement with *Florida v. Patterson,* see Levine, " 'To Maintain Our Self-Respect.' "

60. "Wetmore Here for Good," *New York Age,* Apr. 26, 1906, 1.

61. Johnson, *Along This Way,* 222; "Wetmore Here for Good," 1.

62. For more on the Afro-American Council, see Shawn Leigh Alexander, "'We Know Our Rights and Have the Courage to Defend Them': The Spirit of Agitation in the Age of Accommodation, 1883–1909" (Ph.D. diss., University of Massachusetts, 2004).

63. "Negroes Ask Roosevelt to Act in Race Riot," *New York Times*, Oct. 11, 1906, 4.

64. For weeks, local residents of the deeply segregated town had provoked the soldiers, and on a hot mid-August night in 1906 a handful of soldiers allegedly went on a nighttime shooting spree through the town. When the troops refused to identify their guilty comrades, Roosevelt dismissed "without honor" all 167 of the black troops stationed at Fort Brown on the night of the shooting, including six who had received the Medal of Honor. Wetmore argued that Roosevelt had no right to punish the black soldiers without a formal court-martial or trial. See "Negro Soldiers to Sue on Roosevelt's Order," *New York Times*, Nov. 17, 1906, 6; "Col. Bacon Challenges Dismissal of Troops," *New York Times*, Jan. 3, 1907, 3; Gerald Astor, *The Right to Fight: A History of African Americans in the Military* (Novato, CA: Presidio Press, 1998), 79–89.

    Subsequent investigations cast doubt on the soldiers' involvement in the nighttime shootings; in 1972 President Richard Nixon directed the army to redress the wrongs by granting retrospective honorable discharges to the men involved and a token payment to the one surviving soldier.

65. Wetmore's letter to the editor of the *Evening Post* is reprinted in *New York Age*, Nov. 15, 1906, 5.

66. See, for example, the ads that ran in the *New York Age* beginning on May 23, 1907, 5.

67. In 1904 Perry represented the heirs of George T. Downing, a "mulatto" resident of Newport, in a bizarre lawsuit against some of New York's most formidable public figures. Perry charged that the Adirondack land upon which the Morgans and Vanderbilts had built their summer camps actually belonged to the Downing heirs, who had inherited property deeds given to a group of black beneficiaries in the 1840s by the abolitionist Gerrit Smith. When the state of New York passed a law in 1846 that required all "men of color" to possess $250 in real estate in order to vote, Smith redistributed his own property to enfranchise a group of black New Yorkers. "Negro's Heirs Claim Vast Game Preserves," *New York Times*, Nov. 18, 1904, 6; "Tale of Gerrit Smith behind Adirondack Suit: Downing Heirs' Story Runs Back to Eccentric Philanthropist," *New York Times*, Nov. 19, 1904, 11; "The Rev. Rufus L. Perry Dead," *New York Times*, June 20, 1895, 16. The New York State law regarding property qualifications for enfranchisement was repealed in 1868. See Franklin Johnson, *The Development of State Legislation Concerning the Free Negro* (1919; repr., Westport, CT: Greenwood Press, 1979), 148–49.

68. *Benevolent and Protective Order of Elks v. Improved Benevolent and Protective Order of Elks* (60 Misc. 223, 111 N.Y.S. 1067).

69. Plaintiff's Trial Memorandum, 181.

70. Winne Deposition (19 Nov. 1931), 2.

71. Johnson, *Along This Way*, 241.

72. On Wetmore's real estate career, see "The Real Estate Field," *New York Times*, Feb. 21, 1914, 16; "Hotel Langwell Sold to Investors," *New York Times*, Feb. 24, 1923, 19; "Latest Dealings in Realty Field," *New York Times*, Mar. 11, 1923, RE15; "Big Loft in Trade," *New York Times*, June 10, 1924, 35.

73. Johnson, *Along This Way*, 390.

74. Ibid., 252.

75. " 'Doug' Wetmore, Prominent Lawyer, Commits Suicide by Shooting Self with Revolver at His Summer House," *New York Age*, Aug. 2, 1930, 1.

76. 1930 U.S. Federal Census, New York City, New York County, NY, SD 22, ED 31–491, sheet 34B, http://content.ancestrylibrary.com/Browse/print_u.aspx?dbid=6224&iid=NYT626_1559 -1038 (accessed Aug. 19, 2007).

77. James Weldon Johnson, *The Autobiography of an Ex-Colored Man* (1912; repr., Dover thrift ed., New York: Dover, 1995), 90.

78. Ibid., 99–100. Johnson published his book anonymously in 1912. Ada probably did not read it, and neither she nor anyone else would associate the book's protagonist with Wetmore; scholars

working with Johnson's papers would not discover that connection until more than half a century later.

79. I have been unsuccessful in locating any official name change notices for Ada Todd and her children in the New York records.

80. *Trow's Business Directory of the Borough of Queens, City of New York, 1904* (New York: Trow Directory, Printing & Bookbinding, 1904), 42; *Trow's Business Directory of the Borough of Queens, City of New York, 1906–7* (New York: Trow Directory, Printing & Bookbinding, 1906), 20.

81. *Trow's Business Directory of the Borough of Queens, City of New York, 1908–9* (New York: Trow Directory, Printing & Bookbinding, 1908), 12.

82. See the entry for Todd Household, 1910 U.S. Federal Census, Queens, NY, 34th Ward, SD 2, ED 1290, sheets 8A and 8B, http://content.ancestrylibrary.com/Browse/view.aspx?dbid=7884 &path=New+York.Queens.Queens+Ward+3.1290.15 (accessed Aug. 19, 2007).

83. Martha Hodes, "Fractions and Fictions," in Stoler, *Haunted by Empire*, 264; Goldberg, *Racial Subjects*, 37.

84. Todd Household, 1910 census.

85. Virgil H. Hite and Ada N. King, Certificate and Record of Marriage, 17 Mar. 1913, certificate no. 6793, New York City Department of Records and Information Services, Municipal Archives; World War I draft registration card, Virgil Hite, Miller County, AR, 5 June 1917, http://content.ancestrylibrary.com/iexec/?htx=View&r=5542&dbid=6482&iid=AR-1530561-0258&fn=Virgil&ln=Hite&st=r&ssrc=&pid=23882999 (accessed Aug. 18, 2007); see the entry for Virgil Hite, 1910 U.S. Federal Census, Murfreesboro Town, Thompson Township, Pike County, AR, SD 4, ED 96, sheet 1A, http://content.ancestrylibrary.com/iexec/?htx=View&r=5542& dbid=7884&iid=ART624_60-1317&fn=Virgil+A&ln=Hite&st=r&ssrc=&pid=191642392 (accessed Aug. 19, 2007); see the entry for 942 Third Ave., 1910 U.S. Federal Census, New York, NY, 19th Ward, SD 1, ED 1136, sheets 1A and B, http://content.ancestrylibrary.com/ Browse/view.aspx?dbid=7884&path=New+York.New+York.Manhattan+Ward+19.1136.1 (accessed Aug. 19, 2007); see the entry for 942 Third Ave., 1900 U.S. Federal Census, Manhattan, New York County, NY, SD 1, ED 654, sheet 14A, http://content.ancestrylibrary .com/Browse/view.aspx?dbid=7602&path=New+York.New+York.Manhattan.654.34 (accessed Aug. 19, 2007).

86. James A. Burns and Grace M. King, Certificate and Record of Marriage, 3 Sept. 1913, certificate no. 21886, New York City Department of Records and Information Services, Municipal Archives.

87. Information courtesy of Grace's granddaughter, Patricia Chacon, personal communication with author, Wilmington, NC, June 20, 2006.

88. Ada Hite said in 1929 that her husband was also a soldier stationed at Fort Totten when she married him in 1913. Either Hite misrepresented his profession and his address on his marriage certificate, or he joined the military soon thereafter. See "Man Shot in Car Mystifies Police," *New York Evening Post,* Nov. 14, 1929, 4; "Widow Keeps Hope Burning," *Amsterdam News,* Nov. 29, 1933, 1, 3.

89. "Bills Against Intermarriage Being Introduced in Various Legislatures," *New York Age,* Jan. 23, 1913, 1.

90. This information on Clarence Burns comes from his application for a Social Security number on Nov. 25, 1936. He identifies his father as James Burns and his mother as Mildred Bergan. He gives his date of birth as June 8, 1910, and identifies his "color" as "white." See "U. S. Social Security Act, Application for Account Number," 056-10-1871.

91. Grace Burns, Certificate of Birth, State of NY, no. 5134, filed July 21, 1915.

92. State of New York, Department of Health of the City of New York, Bureau of Records, Standard Certificate of Death for Grace Margaret Burns, record no. 113, 5 Jan. 1916, and Standard Certificate of Death for Grace Margaret Burns, record no. 156, 7 Jan. 1916, New York City Department of Records and Information Services, Municipal Archives. Grace King Burns is buried in plot 532-R in Flushing Cemetery.

93. Information on James Burns's profession comes from his granddaughter, Patricia Chacon, personal communication with author, June 20, 2006. On the makeup of Ada's household in 1910 (Todd) and 1920 (King, where Clarence and Thelma Burns are listed as her grandchildren and members of her household), see the U.S. federal census records for Queens. The census records for 1920 and 1930 variously list the children's father as born in Michigan and Tennessee.

94. "Man Shot in Auto Dies," *New York Times*, Nov. 15, 1929, 22; "Man Shot in Car Mystifies Police," *New York Evening Post*, Nov. 14, 1929, 4 (these accounts of a shooting to which the younger Ada King was a witness make reference to her early marriage and divorce). Ada is back living with her mother and using her maiden name by 1920; see Ada King, 1920 U.S. Federal Census, Flushing, Queens, NY, SD 4, ED 216, sheet 1B, http://content.ancestrylibrary.com/Browse/view.aspx?dbid=6061&path=New+York.Queens.Queens+Assembly+District+4.216.2&fn=Ada&ln=King&st=r&pid=48685357&rc=&zp=50 (accessed Aug. 18, 2007).

95. Patricia Chacon, personal communication with author, June 20, 2006.

96. World War I draft registration card, Virgil Hite.

97. Quoted in Gerald Astor, *The Right to Fight: A History of African Americans in the Military* (Novato, CA: Presidio, 1998), 110.

98. For Sidney King's military records, see Sidney C. King Military Service Record, New York State Archives, and World War I draft registration card, Sidney King, http://content.ancestrylibrary.com/Browse/view.aspx?dbid=6482&path=New+York.Queens+City.185.K.215&rc=&zp=100 (accessed Aug. 19, 2007). For James Weldon Johnson's view of the Fifteenth Regiment, see Johnson, *Black Manhattan*, 231–38. On the terms of Sidney King's discharge, see *Regulations for the Army of the United States 1913* (New York: Military Publishing, [1918]), 37–38. On the Fifteenth Regiment, see also Emmett J. Scott, *Scott's Official History of the Negro in the World War* (n.p., 1919), 197–213. Also accessible on Ancestry.com is a copy of the blank form introduced for World War I draft registrations on June 5, 1917, which includes the directions to the draft board registrars about race.

99. World War I draft registration card, Wallace Archer King, http://content.ancestrylibrary.com/Browse/view.aspx?dbid=6482&path=New+York.Queens+City.185.K.216&rc=&zp=100 (accessed Aug. 9, 2007).

100. Astor, *The Right to Fight*, 110.

101. Wallace A. King, Abstract of World War I Military Service, New York State Archives.

102. W. E. B. DuBois, "Our Special Grievances" and "The Reward" [editorials], *The Crisis* 16 (Sept. 1918), 217, cited in Ulysses Lee, *The Employment of Negro Troops* (Washington, DC: Office of the Chief of Military History, United States Army, 1966), 4–5.

103. "Will Rule at West Point," *Washington Post*, Aug. 21, 1912, 6; "Promotions in Army," *Washington Post*, July 4, 1916, [1]; "Army Orders," *Washington Post*, Sept. 7, 1917, 6.

104. Ida Clyde Clarke, *American Women and the World War* (New York: D. Appleton, 1918), chap. 30, http://www.lib.byu.edu/~rdh/wwi/comment/Clarke/Clarke30.htm (accessed Aug. 19, 2007).

105. King family, 1920 U.S. Federal Census.

106. Complaint, *King v. Peabody et al.*; Sidney King, Incompetent, case 12586-1921, Kings County Clerk's Office; New York State Department of Health Certificate of Death, 42437, for Sidney C. King (d. 10 July 1942), New York State Department of Health, Vital Records Section, Albany. The death certificate notes that he had suffered from "dementia praecox," another term for schizophrenia, since approximately 1918. For his profession as a laborer, see the 1920 census records. For the designation of mental patients as "inmates," see 1930 U.S. Federal Census, Kings Park State Hospital, Smith Town, Village of Kings Park, Suffolk County, NY, ED 109, SD 36, sheet 14A http://content.ancestrylibrary.com/iexec/?htx=View&r=5542&dbid=6224&iid=NYT626_1652-0112&fn=Sydney&ln=King&st=r&ssrc=&pid=46459090 (accessed Aug. 19, 2007).

107. "Queens Contractor Shot," *New York Times*, Nov. 14, 1929, 34; "Man, Shot in Auto, Dies," *New York Times*, Nov. 15, 1929, 22; "Sought in Queens Killing," *New York Times*, Nov. 16, 1929, 10; "Woman Held in Queens Murder," *New York Times*, Nov. 17, 1929, 20; "Man Shot in Car

Mystifies Police," *New York Evening Post,* Nov. 14, 1929, 4; "In Mystery Shooting" [photo], *New York Daily News,* Nov. 15, 1929, front page, pink ed.

108. "Widow Keeps Hope Burning," *Amsterdam News,* Nov. 29, 1933, 1–2.

109. See the entry for the King family, 1930 U.S. Federal Census, Flushing, Queens, NY, SD 34, ED 40–1090, sheet 2A, http://content.ancestrylibrary.com/Browse/view.aspx?dbid=6224& path=New+York.Queens.Queens+(Districts+1001-1250).1095.3 (accessed Aug. 9, 2007).

110. Ibid.; Goldberg, *Racial Subjects,* 35–36.

111. Kings Park State Hospital, 1930 U.S. Federal Census.

112. Patricia Chacon, personal communication with author, June 20, 2006, and e-mail communication to author, June 27, 2006.

113. Patricia Chacon, personal communication with author, June 20, 2006, and phone call to author, Sept. 21, 2005.

114. "National Affairs," *Time,* Apr. 6, 1925, http://time-proxy.yaga.com/time/archive/printout/ 0,23657,720125,00.html; Napoleon Hill, *The Law of Success in Sixteen Lessons* (Meriden, CT: Ralston University Press, 1928), 64.

115. "M. W. Littleton Sr. Lawyer, Dies at 62," *New York Times,* Dec. 20, 1934, 1, 23.

116. "Many Candidates Admitted to Bar," *New York Times,* Apr. 13, 1924, E22; "Raid Nassau Speakeasies," *New York Times,* Sept. 14, 1929, 37. The only reference to Littleton serving as Ada King's attorney is in Wynne Response, *King v. Peabody et al.*

117. Plaintiff's Trial Memorandum, Brief No. 2, 24.

CHAPTER 10: THE TRIAL

1. "The Weather," *New York Times,* Nov. 21, 1933, 41.

2. "Negro Woman Sues," 2; "White Scientist's Love Letters," sec. 1, 5.

3. "Widow Tells of Ceremony and Children," 1–2.

4. "Old Negress Suing Estate, Reveals Love," *New York Daily Mirror,* Nov. 21, 1933, 3, 8.

5. " 'Bloods' Hid Scion's Love," 3.

6. "Widow Keeps Hope Burning," 1.

7. "Colored Woman Sues as Widow of Society Man," *New York Daily News,* Nov. 20, 1933, Manhattan ed., 3; "Mammy Bares Life," 3; "Old Negress," 3.

8. " 'Bloods' Hid Scion's Love," 3.

9. "Widow Tells of Ceremony and Children," 1–2; "New York Woman in Court Fight to Recover $80,000," *Chicago Defender,* Nov. 25, 1933, national ed., 1.

10. "Court Hears Suit for $80,000 against White Man's Estate," *New York Age,* Nov. 25, 1933, 1.

11. "New Capitol Bronzes," *Washington Post,* May 3, 1908, R2.

12. Robert Dudley French, *The Memorial Quadrangle: A Book about Yale* (New Haven, CT: Yale University Press, 1929), 389. Thanks to Adam Sandweiss Horowitz and to Judith Schiff, chief research archivist, Manuscripts and Archives, Yale University Library.

13. "Court Hears Suit for $80,000," 1; "Widow Tells of Ceremony and Children," 1; "Colored Woman Sues," 3.

14. Otto D. Tolischus, "Marriage Rate Up, Delighting Nazis," *New York Times,* Nov. 20, 1933, 7.

15. "Roosevelt Is Asked to Intervene to Protect Scottsboro Negroes," *New York Times,* Nov. 20, 1933, 1.

16. "Court Hears Suit for $80,000," 1.

17. The long and complicated paper trail for the proceedings is found in *Ada King et al. v. George Foster Peabody et al.* (file no. 26821-1931, Records of the Supreme Court of the State of New York, New York County Clerk's Office). All legal citations in this chapter are to *King v. Peabody et al.* unless otherwise noted.

18. See entry for Morris Bell, 1930 U.S. Federal Census, Bronx, NY, SD 25, ED 3–224, sheet 7A, http://content.ancestrylibrary.com/iexec/?htx= View&r=5542&dbid=6224&iid=NYT 626_1470-0270&fn=Morris&ln=Bell&st=r&ssrc=&pid=31248902 (accessed Aug. 9, 2007).

19. "Plaintiff's Complaint" (19 Nov. 1931).

20. Ibid., 3.

21. William G. Winne, Amended Answer to Complaint (19 Nov. 1931).

22. The heirs named in the complaint were Florence Gardiner Hall, Margaret D. Fayerweather, Doane Gardiner, Elizabeth G. Gardiner, Anne G. Pier, Benjamin W. Frazier, and the Philadelphia Trust Company (executors of the will of Mary S. Frazier). Neither Florence Gardiner Hall nor Doane Gardiner employed Henry W. Jessup as counsel. William Pier, Gardiner's grandson, recalled for King biographer James Gregory Moore his mother's "irritation" with Ada King's lawsuit. James Gregory Moore, e-mail communication to author, May 30, 2006.

23. See the entry for Henry W. Jessup, 1930 U.S. Federal Census, New York, NY, SD 22, ED 31–54a, sheet 21B, http://content.ancestrylibrary.com/iexec/?htx=View&r=5542&dbid=6224&iid=NYT626_1566-0616&fn=Henry+W&ln=Jessup&cst=r&ssrc=&pid=42626296 (accessed Aug. 19, 2007); Henry Harris Jessup Papers, http://history.pcusa.org/finding/phs%20183.xml (accessed Aug. 19, 2007). Jessup's many publications include three novels (several of which hinge on legal themes) and at least six nonfiction titles, including *Professional Ideals of the Lawyer, Law for Wives and Daughters, The Bill of Rights and Its Destruction*, and *History of the Fifth Avenue Presbyterian Church*. See also "Club Members Pay Tribute to Hallman," *New York Times*, Mar. 20, 1934, 24, and "H. W. Jessup Dead; Noted as Lawyer," *New York Times*, Dec. 10, 1934, 21.

24. Morris Bell, 1930 U.S. Federal Census. On Bell's work agreement with the Kings, see Morris Pottish Deposition to the Court, 8 Feb. 1934.

25. "John S. Melcher: Lawyer Headed Society to Aid Ruptured and Crippled," *New York Times*, July 29, 1945, 39; "Miss Gardiner Married," *New York Times*, Aug. 25, 1901, 3.

26. "Seth S. Terry Dead; Long Lawyer Here," *New York Times*, Dec. 19, 1932, 15.

27. "Secret 'Union' of Pair Unearthed by Struggle in Court," *Amsterdam News*, Dec. 30, 1932, 1.

28. David O'Donald Cullen, "George Foster Peabody," *American National Biography Online*, http://www.anb.org/articles/15/15-00539.html (accessed Aug. 19, 2007); Louise Ware, "George Foster Peabody," *Dictionary of American Biography* (New York: Charles Scribner's Sons, 1958), 23:520–21; "Roosevelt Drives Own Car at Warm Springs; Takes Two Trips as He Begins His Holiday," *New York Times*, Nov. 20, 1933, 2.

29. Winne, Amended Answer to Complaint.

30. Bell filed a petition for financial redress by requesting a lien on Ada King's house on 30 Jan. 1934. See Morris Pottish Deposition to the Court, 8 Feb. 1934: "Both Mr. Bell and I advised against bringing this action for just that reason that the result of the action might probably be the very result which has been attained. It was only under constant and determined pressure from the plaintiffs and against the advice of Mr. Bell that this action was commenced."

31. See the entry for Herman Schwartz, 1930 U.S. Federal Census, Brooklyn, NY, ED 24–765, SD 30, sheet 10A, http://content.ancestrylibrary.com/Browse/view.aspx?dbid=6224&path=New+York.Kings.Brooklyn+(Districts+751-1000).765.19 (accessed Aug. 18, 2007).

32. William G. Winne, Response to Affidavit of Herman N. Schwartz (18 Nov. 1931), 6.

33. Winne, Amended Answer to Complaint, 2–4.

34. Ibid., passim.

35. Schwartz to Jessup, 9 Dec. 1931, Reply to Answer of the Defendants.

36. Winne Response to Bill of Particulars, 5 Dec. 1931.

37. Herman N. Schwartz Affidavit, 21 Dec. 1931, 3.

38. Jessup to Schwartz, 9 Dec. 1931, Response to Request for a Bill of Particulars, 11 Dec. 1931.

39. Schwartz to Jessup, 9 Dec. 1931, Reply to the Defendants.

40. Deposition of Henry W. Jessup, 11 Jan. 1932, 1–3.

41. Motion on Behalf of the Defendants for Judgment on the Pleadings, 7.

42. Ibid., 8–9.

43. Memorandum in Opposition to Defendants' Motion for Judgment on the Pleadings, 6, 9.

44. Ibid., 7.

45. "Millionaire's 'Love Wife' Sues for Share in Huge Fortune," *Chicago Defender,* Jan. 2, 1932, national ed., 1.

46. J. Dore, Judgment on the Pleadings, 1 Mar. 1932, Supreme Court, New York County, Special Term, Part 3.

47. "Court Grants 1st Round to Scion's Colored Love," *New York Daily News,* Mar. 28, 1932, 8.

48. "New York Woman May Share in $80,000 Trust Fund," *Chicago Defender,* Apr. 9, 1932, national ed., 1.

49. "Secret 'Union,'" 1–2.

50. Kenny A. Franks and Paul F. Lambert, *Early Louisiana and Arkansas Oil: A Photographic History, 1901–1946* (College Station: Texas A&M University Press, 1982).

51. "Secret 'Union,' " 1–2; "Sues for Share of White Man's Estate," *New York Age,* Jan. 2, 1932, 1, 3.

52. "Secret 'Union,' " 1–2; "Negress Asks $200 a Week," *New York Times,* Mar. 15, 1928, 13; "Carleton Curtis Wins Suit," *New York Times,* Mar. 20, 1928, 35; "Stage All Set for Sensational Separation Suit," *Amsterdam News,* Mar. 14, 1928, 1. Despite this publicity, the King trial never received the notoriety of the Curtis trial or the sensational Rhinelander trial of 1925 (in which a wealthy white New Yorker sought to annul his recent marriage to a working-class woman whom he accused of concealing her "colored" identity) largely because King was no longer alive and in the public eye. On the Rhinelander trial, see Earl Lewis and Heidi Ardizzone, *Love on Trial: An American Scandal in Black and White* (New York: W. W. Norton, 2002).

53. Memorandum on Motion to Compel Service of Bill of Particulars, 2, 4.

54. Brief in Opposition to Motion to Compel Defendants to Serve a Bill of Particulars, 2.

55. *New York Daily News,* Nov. 21, 1933, cover, 3.

56. "New York Woman in Court Fight," 1.

57. "Justice Bernard L. Shientag Dies of Heart Attack in His Home Here," *New York Times,* May 24, 1952, 1.

58. Harris J. Griston, *Shaking the Dust from Shakespeare* (New York: Cosmopolis, 1924); "Harris J. Griston, Lawyer, Architect," *New York Times,* Oct. 3, 1952, 23. Griston argued in his Shakespeare text that the prototype for Shakespeare's Shylock was not a Jew but a figure from a medieval story who was a rich slave.

59. On the history of the firm, see www.emmettmarvin.com. Its name appears on the Defendants Trial Memorandum prepared in late 1933 and on the subsequent appeal documents.

60. "Mammy Bares Life," 3; "Payne Whitney Dies Suddenly at Home," *New York Times,* May 26, 1927, 1, 25; William G. Winne Testimony (21 Nov. 1933), 11–12, Memorandum for Defendants.

61. Memorandum for Defendants, 7.

62. William G. Winne Testimony (21 Nov. 1933), passim.

63. Plaintiff's Trial Memorandum, 116.

64. Ibid., 117–18.

65. Ibid., 118.

66. Although a newspaper account reported that Ada King identified twenty letters as King's, the trial memoranda refer to only about seven letters. See "Justice Stays Ruling in King Trust Estate," *New York American,* Nov. 22, 1933, 3. Characterization of the old letters comes from "Scientist's Letters Reveal His Love for Colored Wife," 3.

67. Plaintiff's Trial Memorandum, 169–72. The letters introduced at the trial no longer exist, and their content is known only through newspaper accounts and various legal summaries written in conjunction with the trial.

68. See, for example, "Negro Claiming Fund as Wife of King, Geologist," *New York Herald Tribune,* Nov. 22, 1933, 7.

69. "Mammy Bares Life," 4.

70. Plaintiff's Trial Memorandum, 179. "She testified . . . that she and Ada King had been in Gardiner's office on a number of occasions, between 1903 and 1911."

71. "Widow Tells of Ceremony and Children," 1–2.

72. Plaintiff's Trial Memorandum, 182–83.

73. " 'Bloods' Hid Scion's Love," 3.

74. "Negro Claiming Fund as Wife of King," 7.

75. Ada King's testimony is reconstructed through news accounts. See "Negro Woman Sues," 2; "Negro Claiming Fund as Wife of King," 7; "Mammy Bares Life," 3–4; "Widow Tells of Ceremony and Children," 1, 2.

76. Memorandum for Defendants, 36–37.

77. Plaintiff's Trial Memorandum, 185–87.

78. Memorandum for Defendants, passim.

79. Hon. Bernard L. Shientag, Judgment (Jan. 1934); Scheintag, Opinion (22 Jan. 1934).

80. "Claim on King Art Fails," *New York Times*, Jan. 24, 1934, 14.

81. "Negro Woman Loses Suit for Clarence King Trust," *New York Herald Tribune*, Jan. 24, 1934, 16.

82. Petition of Morris B. Bell (30 Jan. 1934).

83. See Order to Dismiss Appeal, *King v. Peabody et al.*, 25 Sept. 1934, Appellate Division of the Supreme Court, First Judicial Department, State of New York.

84. "Widow Keeps Hope Burning," 2.

85. Patricia Chacon, interview with author, Wilmington, NC, June 19, 2006.

86. King, *Mountaineering*, 11–20.

87. King, "The Helmet of Mambrino," with an introduction by Francis P. Farquhar (San Francisco: Book Club of California, 1938), x.

88. Dennett, *John Hay*, 157.

89. Bernard DeVoto, *The Year of Decision: 1846* (Boston: Little, Brown, 1943), 348.

90. Stegner, *Beyond the Hundredth Meridian*, 344–45.

91. Crosby, "So Deep a Trail," v, 467, 355, 357.

92. HA to S. F. Emmons, 17 Mar. [190?], cited in Wilkins, *King*, vii.

93. Wilkins, *King*, 317, 320, 322.

94. Louise Hall Tharp, "Great Men Called Him Their Ideal," *New York Times*, Aug. 3, 1958, book review, 1.

95. "Thurman Wilkins," *Contemporary Authors Online* (2006).

96. Wilkins, *King*, 412–413.

97. Wallace A. King, U.S. World War II Army Enlistment Records, 1938–1946 Record, accessed on Ancestry.com; Wallace A. King, NA Form 13164, obtained from the National Archives under the Freedom of Information Act. King's army enlistment record notes his occupation as a musician and states that he was sixty-three inches tall and weighed 141 pounds. On Wilkins, see "Thurman Wilkins," *Contemporary Authors Online*.

98. Wallace King's high school attendance is recorded on his World War II enlistment form.

99. Patricia Chacon, interview with author, June 19, 2006; Ada McDonald, Certificate of Death, City of New York, 156-81-409001, New York City Department of Health and Mental Hygiene.

100. Sidney C. King, New York State Department of Health Certificate of Death, 42437.

101. Estate of Ada King, Surrogates Court, Queens County, index no. 3507-1966.

102. Patricia Chacon, interview with author, June 19, 2006.

103. Ibid. Chacon is the source for the subsequent descriptions of the King household.

104. Martin Luther King Jr., "I Have a Dream" (speech, Aug. 28, 1963), "Martin Luther King, Jr. Papers Projects Speeches: Address at March on Washington," http://www.stanford.edu/group/King/publications/speeches/address_at_march_on_washington.pdf.

105. Ibid.

106. Ada King, Certificate of Death, City of New York, 156-64-404943, New York City Department of Health and Mental Hygiene.

107. Wallace A. King, Certificate of Death, City of New York, 156-81-413685, New York City Department of Health and Mental Hygiene; Ada McDonald, Certificate of Death, City of New York, 156-81-409001, New York City Department of Health and Mental Hygiene.

EPILOGUE: SECRETS

1. Harris Co., GA, DV M:205, 19 Feb. 1883/24 Feb. 1883, Harris County Courthouse, Hamilton, GA; citation courtesy of Lea Dowd.

2. I attended the Copeland Family Homecoming in Pine Mountain Valley, GA, on Aug. 7, 2005. None of the approximately 120 gathered family members knew of Ada or had heard stories about a family member who had gone north to New York in the 1880s.

3. The important exception is Patricia O'Toole, who uncovered new evidence about King's secret marriage—including Ada's maiden name—while doing research for her group biography, *The Five of Hearts*. The marriage, though, was not the focus of her book, and she devotes only about eleven pages to a discussion of the relationship between Clarence King and Ada Copeland. More recently, there have been two new biographies of King. Robert Wilson's *The Explorer King: Adventure, Science, and the Great Diamond Hoax—Clarence King in the Old West* (New York: Scribner, 2006) relies largely on secondary sources to narrate King's western survey work up through his involvement in the diamond hoax of 1872, with only a passing reference to his later professional career and barely a mention of his private life. James Gregory Moore's *King of the 40th Parallel: Discovery in the American West* (Stanford, CA: Stanford University Press, 2006) provides a lively account of King's western survey work that, as befits a book written by a former geologist for the United States Geological Survey, conveys a vivid sense of how King worked in the field. Focusing on King's career as an explorer, the author gives scant attention to King's life after his departure from the USGS in 1881 and mentions Ada only in passing. Aaron Sachs, in *The Humboldt Current: Nineteenth-Century Exploration and the Roots of American Environmentalism* (New York: Viking, 2006), speculates briefly about the precise nature of King's relationship to Ada, seeing it as "a characteristic attempt to seek connection in a way that was guaranteed to fail" (261). Zeese Papanikolas, in *American Silences* (Lincoln: University of Nebraska Press, 2007), reimagines the lives of a broad range of American cultural figures from Henry Adams to Jackson Pollock, and likewise gives fleeting attention to Ada King. But alone among these writers, he imagines her as central to King's life, speculating that with his marriage "King's life was cut in two" (47).

Index